BUSINESS COMMUNICATION

ABOUT THE AUTHORS

Roy W. Poe is an educational consultant and former president of the McGraw-Hill Continuing Education Center in Washington, D.C. He was awarded the bachelor of science and master of science degrees by Oklahoma State University and has completed postgraduate courses at the University of California at Berkeley. In 1966 he was awarded an honorary doctorate of commercial science by Fort Lauderdale University. He has taught in high schools, business colleges, community colleges, and universities and has acted as correspondence consultant to leading companies. He has served as associate dean of Golden Gate University, supervisor of training for the Veterans Administration, and president of The Gregg College. Later, he was editorial director of the Gregg Division and vice president and editorial director of the McGraw-Hill Book Company. Recently, he served as educational consultant to M-W Education Corporation (a subsidiary of Montgomery Ward) and to various publishers. He is coauthor of three other textbooks in business and is currently writing another.

Rosemary T. Fruehling is vocational education professions development consultant of the State Department of Education in St. Paul, Minnesota. An internationally known lecturer in the field of business and office education, she is currently a candidate for the doctor of philosophy degree at the University of Minnesota, where she received her bachelor of science and master of arts degrees. She has served as adjunct professor of vocational education at the University of Minnesota and as associate professor in the Secretarial Science Department of the County College of Morris in Dover, New Jersey. Prior to that, she taught in high schools for ten years. She has conducted graduate school classes and teacher-training seminars in all fifty states. In 1966 Professor Fruehling was named executive director for the Minnesota Office Education Association, and in 1971 she received the Outstanding Educator in America Award. She has served as a commissioner for the New Jersey Broadcasting Authority and has worked as a consultant in business, education, and government. A frequent contributor to professional journals, she has also coauthored several textbooks on psychology, human relations, and motivation and on business correspondence. She is presently completing a nationally funded research project entitled *Life History Correlates of Vocational Needs and Values.*

BUSINESS COMMUNICATION
A PROBLEM-SOLVING APPROACH
SECOND EDITION

ROY W. POE
ROSEMARY T. FRUEHLING

GREGG DIVISION | **McGraw-Hill Book Company**

New York   St. Louis   Dallas   San Francisco   Auckland
Bogotá   Düsseldorf   Johannesburg   London   Madrid   Mexico
Montreal   New Delhi   Panama   Paris   São Paulo
Singapore   Sydney   Tokyo   Toronto

Sponsoring Editor: Joseph Tinervia
Senior Editing Manager: Elizabeth Huffman
Editing Supervisor: Gloria Schlein
Production Manager: Gary Whitcraft
Design Supervisor: Edwin Fisher
Designer: William Frost

Library of Congress Cataloging in Publication Data

Poe, Roy W   Date
    Business communication.

    1.   Commercial correspondence.   I.   Fruehling,
Rosemary T., joint author.   II.   Title.
HF5721.P6   1978   651.7′5   77-21681
ISBN 0-07-050362-1

BUSINESS COMMUNICATION: A Problem-Solving Approach
Second Edition

 2 3 4 5 6 7 8 9 0   DODO   7 8 7 6 5 4 3 2 1 0 9 8

PREFACE

Teachers—and their students—responded magnificently to the first edition of *Business Communication: A Problem-Solving Approach* and strengthened the authors' conviction that the time had indeed come for a new approach to the subject. The new approach taken in the first edition is therefore retained and enhanced in this edition.

This new approach to business writing embraces seven major concepts:

1. *Business communications are highly individualistic and cannot be written to formula.* There is no magic formula for writing a good letter or report; individual writers approach a communication situation differently (and each produces a unique letter or report), depending on how they feel about their job and the matter to be communicated, their relationship to each reader, and the attitudes and policies of the organization they represent.

2. *To produce effective communications, students should be involved as deeply as possible in each writing situation.* It is extremely important that students really care about the results of their communications. But this is very difficult to bring about when assignments are presented as abstract situations in which students feel only a bystander role. To implement this involvement concept, the authors ask students to imagine themselves in various positions—assistant office services manager, assistant manager, assistant personnel manager, and so on—thus approaching each communication problem as a participant rather than as an onlooker. Each case is constructed around a role-playing situation—even the writing projects at the end of each case are similarly designed.

3. *Examples of letters and reports are most effective when related to situations with which students are familiar.* In the typical textbook, students are shown primarily "good" examples of communications—and always in situations unrelated to the students' experience. In *Business Communication: A Problem-Solving Approach,* students have a direct involvement in the case problems, and the examples are possible solutions to these problems; the examples offer one or more "wrong" solutions, with analyses, and one or more recommended solutions, again with analyses. This device, the authors believe, is much superior to narrative presentation of "rules" followed by an abstract illustration of the rules.

4. *Most of the challenging communication situations faced by the writer on the job are those that require choosing between alternatives—which may be only unpleasant alternatives.* Many students have been taught that every communication must be friendly, tactful, positive, and goodwill-engendering. Although this is true for many letters and reports, as a generalization it is idealistic. Writers face many problems that arise out of human error, misunderstandings, and carelessness, and students should be prepared to deal with them. Thus numerous situations are given in which the student, as a writer-entrepreneur, must say no, apologize for the mistakes of fellow employees, reprimand recalcitrant customers and suppliers, and take the hard line when there is no other recourse.

v

5. *Business communications defy discrete "typing" or classification.* In the typical business organization, letter "types"—adjustment, claim, credit, collection, inquiry, response, and so on—are virtually unknown. Thus the authors avoid rigid classifications, preferring to group letters according to job responsibilities of typical business employees rather than according to letter "types."

6. *Since the typical employee writes many interoffice memorandums, they should be introduced early in the course, and students should be given frequent opportunity to use this form of communication.* Memos are in reality letters, and the general principles of writing effective letters that are to go outside the organization also apply to effective letters sent to fellow employees. Therefore, students are exposed early to this very important communication medium and continue to deal with it throughout the course.

7. *There should be a culminating project, which embraces all the principles covered throughout the course, to provide students with an experience that simulates a real-life job situation.* In the Communications Project at the end of *Business Communication: A Problem-Solving Approach,* the student acts as sales manager of the regional office of a book publishing firm and faces 33 situations that demand not only writing skill but the exercise of judgment and selection of alternatives.

The concepts just presented have been retained in the Second Edition. In addition, considerable new material has been added and other changes made.

SOME FEATURES OF THE SECOND EDITION

Following are some of the major features of the Second Edition.

• **Reading Before Writing.** Because few students have been exposed to typical communications that flow in and out of a business office, a new introductory section provides many examples of effective letters and memorandums that illustrate some of the most important uses of communications. By reading and analyzing successful letters and memos at the outset, students will be better prepared to understand the principles of business writing that follow.

• **Human Relations in Communication.** Good writing is largely the application of effective human relations and sound management principles to communication situations. In the Second Edition the qualities that are common to good writers and good managers are stressed.

• **Word Usage.** Greater attention is given to word usage in communications, with emphasis on avoiding "businessese" and "federalese," clichés, euphemisms, slang, exaggeration, jargon, and other faults that can destroy effectiveness.

• **Craftsmanship.** The treatment of sentences in business communications has been greatly expanded, with emphasis on sentence length, the flow of ideas between sentences, and such faults as fragments, run-ons, imbalance, omission of words, and dangling modifiers.

- **Planning for Writing.** The discussion of planning for writing has also been expanded, and new emphasis is given to the importance of visualizing the reader and taking into account his or her preparedness, interests, and prejudices.

- **Communicating With Customers.** Winning and keeping customers and solving their problems are topics of great importance in the business communication program, and they have been expanded in this edition.

THE WORKBOOK

A new workbook is available which is carefully integrated, unit by unit and case by case, with the textbook and provides supplementary practice in writing letters, memorandums, and reports. The workbook emphasizes analyzing communications, editing and revising weak communications, and restructuring and simplifying garbled and incoherent messages. In many instances, letterheads and interoffice memorandum forms are provided. A special feature of the workbook is an English Usage Drill for each of the cases in the textbook. These drills provide practice in dealing with problems in punctuation, capitalization, sentence structure, possessives, word usage, spelling, grammar, and so on.

TAPES FOR INSTRUCTORS AND STUDENTS

A set of tapes is available for classroom use by the instructor or for individual use by students. Together, the twelve lectures provide students with an excellent general introduction to on-the-job business writing. The tapes discuss the need for writing letters, memos, and reports and thus help students understand why business messages are so important. In addition, the tapes focus on the ways in which letters, memos, and reports are used to accomplish specific purposes, and they offer students helpful suggestions for planning effective messages.

INSTRUCTOR'S MANUAL AND KEY

The *Instructor's Manual and Key* contains teaching suggestions and the key to both the textbook and the workbook. It also includes supplementary illustrations and problems for certain topics.

Roy W. Poe
Rosemary T. Fruehling

CONTENTS

PART 1

BACKGROUND FOR BUSINESS WRITING

UNIT 1

THE SETTING FOR BUSINESS WRITING

Most of the writing you do in a business office will be in the form of either a letter or a memorandum. When you write to someone outside the firm, you will nearly always use a letter. And when you write to someone inside the organization, you will generally use a memorandum—which is why a memorandum is sometimes called an "internal letter."

The memorandum form is designed to save time and cut stationery costs when you are writing to members of your own office "family." Letters are sent to people you might think of as "guests" (customers and others you would like to make a good impression on). The stationery, letterhead, and style for a letter are selected to create a favorable company image. But whether you are writing an interoffice memorandum or a letter, you will want to use the appropriate tone and be able to express your message clearly and grammatically. In other words, you don't ordinarily wear one "writing hat" for a memo and another for a letter.

WHY *WRITTEN* COMMUNICATIONS?

Why put things in writing? One obvious reason is that it is more convenient and less costly than face-to-face communications, particularly where distance is involved. But often there is simply no substitute for a written communication—for example, describing a firm's unique product or service to a customer, reporting the results of an organization's study of employee turnover, or announcing an important change in company policy. And written communications provide valuable records for an organization without which it simply could not function.

Some of the most important uses of written communications are to:

1. Confirm agreements and actions.
2. Motivate sales.
3. Build goodwill and effective public relations (PR).
4. Enhance internal human relationships.
5. Keep people informed.

Confirming Agreements and Actions. Every business day people discuss issues and make agreements which, if they are really important, should be confirmed in writing. A written confirmation clarifies an issue or agreement, pinpoints responsibilities, and prevents misunderstanding. It also provides a valuable record for future reference.

Following are examples of typical confirmation letters and memorandums.

Society for Scientific Management
Burdine Building
849 Peachtree, N.E.
Atlanta, Georgia 30308

August 14, 19—

Mr. Philip G. Oliver, President
Oliver Associates
201 Massachusetts Avenue, N.W.
Washington, DC 20001

Dear Mr. Oliver:

It was good to talk with you yesterday and to learn that you can be with us at our October 15 meeting. The topic you suggested, "Motivation Through Employee Participation," seems just right; it ties in beautifully with this year's theme of personnel development.

Our meeting, which is held in the Green Room of the Ambassador Plaza Hotel (98 Forsyth, N.W.), starts off with a social hour at 5:30. Dinner begins at 6:30, followed by your talk at 7:30. We hope you will plan to speak for about 30 minutes and then to answer questions for another half hour.

If you would like to be picked up at the airport, please tell me when you expect to arrive and I'll be there. I have made a reservation for you at the Ambassador Plaza.

Sincerely yours,

Kati Farnsworth

Kati Farnsworth
Program Chairman

Analysis. Notice these things about the letter from Kati Farnsworth:

1. The friendly tone. Mr. Oliver is made to feel that he will have a warm reception when he comes to Atlanta. This is always important to a visitor, especially a guest speaker.
2. The confirmation of details concerning the speech. Unless these details are put in writing, the speaker might forget the title of the speech or the length of time he is to talk. Notice, too, the reminder that he will be expected to answer questions from the audience.
3. The reminder about the time and place of the meeting. Mr. Oliver will have a record that he can refer to later; such details as these are especially easy to forget.

4. The offer to supply transportation from the airport to the hotel. Whether Mr. Oliver accepts the offer or not, it is a courteous gesture that he will appreciate.
5. The confirmation of the hotel reservation. If this is not mentioned, Mr. Oliver is likely to be uneasy: "Let's see, did Miss Farnsworth say she would make my hotel reservation, or was I to do it?"

Memorandum Confirming a Decision

HILL & SCHUSTER
Interoffice Memorandum

TO: R. K. Genuario   **FROM:**   Margaret F. Quinlan *mFQ*
SUBJECT: Advertising Budget **DATE:**   November 14, 19—

This is a confirmation of our discussion yesterday in which we decided to trim our advertising budget for next year from $80,000 to $60,000 and to allocate the expenditures as follows:

Direct mail	$20,000
Trade papers	15,000
Point-of-purchase displays	11,000
Exhibits	8,000
Miscellaneous (premiums, etc.)	6,000
	$60,000

Are we together on this? Obviously, we will have to study our allocations during the year and be prepared to make some changes. We can't, however, exceed the $60,000 maximum.

Analysis. As you can see, Mrs. Margaret F. Quinlan has met with a subordinate, R. K. Genuario, to discuss a reduction in the advertising budget for the coming year (probably the result of a companywide campaign to reduce expenses). During such discussions, opinions are exchanged and figures are put down, revised, and put down again. Unless such agreements are followed up with a written communication, the people present may walk away from the meeting with different ideas about what was agreed upon.

Observe these things:

1. The purpose of the memorandum is clearly stated—"a confirmation of our discussion ... to trim our advertising budget ...."
2. Specific data is included; it has been itemized in the memorandum for easy reading and reference and leaves no doubt about what was decided at the meeting.
3. In the final paragraph, Mrs. Quinlan invites Genuario to respond if his figures don't agree with hers. If he doesn't disagree, then he will be held responsible for the figures recorded.

Memorandum
KHARMANN INC.

TO: Kathleen Gilbert **FROM:** S. K. Chang

SUBJECT: Approval of Promotion **DATE:** November 4, 19—

Dear Kathleen:

I am pleased to tell you my recommendation that you be appointed to the new position of publicity director, effective December 1, has been approved by the Executive Committee. Your new salary will be $18,000 a year.

It will be best, I think, to keep this information confidential until we can get out a general announcement, which I expect to do sometime next week. In the meantime, would you try your hand at a description of the job as you see it? I will be thinking about it, too, and in a week or so we'll get together to compare notes.

I don't need to tell you how happy I am about your promotion. I have felt for a long time that we need a publicity director, and you are the person I always had in mind for the job.

Sincerely,

S. K. Chang

Analysis. This is a typical interoffice letter confirming an action that has been taken. Before Mr. Chang asked for Executive Committee approval, he spoke to Miss Gilbert to find out about her interest in the position of publicity director.

This confirmation could easily have been given orally instead of in writing; indeed, the good news probably was first transmitted orally. However, a written communication will be much more meaningful to Miss Gilbert. Too, it gives Mr. Chang an opportunity to:

1. Confirm the effective date and the salary, so that no question will arise later about these points.
2. Caution Miss Gilbert about keeping the news confidential for now.
3. Mention the need for a job description, which might or might not have been discussed previously.
4. Offer personal congratulations.

Motivating Sales. Letters are often used to promote the sale of products and services. In fact, in terms of dollars spent by American business, direct-mail promotion ranks in the top three advertising media. Although direct mail can be fairly expensive, it offers an advantage almost no other medium can match: selectivity. That is, a promotion manager can decide specifically who should see promotion material—hardware dealers or doctors or engineers, for example. This high selectivity is not possible with newspapers, radio, television, and similar media.

A Sales Promotion Letter

A Fedders-Logan Publication

MONTHLY 435 South Ironwood Drive • South Bend, Indiana 46675

Dear Fellow Golfer:

Bobby Jones . . . Walter Hagen . . . Gene Sarazen . . . Ben Hogan . . .
Sam Snead . . . Patty Berg . . . Arnold Palmer . . . Jack Nicklaus . . .
Byron Nelson . . .

Pardon me for name dropping, but I have exciting news about these and
other all-time golf greats that I want to share with you. You know, of
course, that each of these players blazed the pro circuit in a different
era, leaving an indelible imprint on golfing history. But did you also
know that they were also prolific writers on the subject and that their
books have become classics?

Golf Monthly plans to reissue these books, some of which have been out
of print for several years. The first will be Bobby Jones on Golf. When
Jones was competing all over the world, he wrote a syndicated newspaper
column in which he told how the game should be played. And not surprisingly, Jones's thoughts on golf are as pertinent and valuable today
as when they were first written.

This special edition of Bobby Jones on Golf (246 pages) is profusely
illustrated by America's leading golf artist, Eklund Nilssen, and is handsomely bound in a rich-looking, leather-like cover. From Jones's own words,
you will learn how to get the "feel" of the club, place the feet, address
the ball, use the body, and develop a natural, fluid swing. He offers
graphic pointers on using long irons, chipping, playing out of traps,
putting, and every other important stroke in golf.

Bobby Jones on Golf will be followed by equally instructive books by
Hagen, Sarazen, Hogan, Snead, Berg, Palmer, Nicklaus, Nelson, and several
others, including some of the young new pros who are making headlines today and pro teachers like Bob Toski.

Use the enclosed postage-free card to order your copy of Bobby Jones
on Golf. The price is only $7.95 (plus 60 cents for shipping and handling).
We'll accept your personal check now, or we can bill you later.

Special bonus! If your order reaches us before May 15, we'll in-
clude--absolutely free--a beautifully illustrated, 24-page booklet, Back
to Fundamentals. It could lower your handicap by ten strokes!

Sincerely yours,

Brad Harriman

Brad Harriman

Analysis. Sales and sales promotion letters often take a quite different form from the typical business letter. For example, large display type and artwork are very common. Some writers attach gimmicky objects such as a coin, swatch of cloth, tape measure, or pencil to the letterhead in order to attract attention.

Notice the attention-getting opening—a *must* for any sales letter. Notice, too, how this sales promotion letter follows the typical pattern for sales-letter writing. The letter:

1. Attracts the reader's attention.
2. Builds the reader's interest.
3. Creates desire for the product or service.
4. Encourages the reader to take positive action, such as placing an order, filling out a coupon, or telephoning.

Building Goodwill and Effective Public Relations. Letters can be used to promote goodwill and build effective public relations for an organization. The term *goodwill* has special application to customers. Through their letters, business people want to make the customer feel happy about being a customer. And they want to motivate the customer not only to remain loyal but also to increase his or her patronage. Public relations letters, on the other hand, are designed to create a favorable image of the firm in the eyes of the general public.

It is true that almost every letter we write to someone outside the firm gives us an opportunity to build goodwill or create a favorable impression. There are, however, some letters that have no other purpose than to establish or strengthen friendly relationships.

Letter Expressing Appreciation for Support

kennel-treat Inc.

2408 North Louise
Sioux Falls, South Dakota 57107

December 18, 19—

Mr. A. R. Allen, President
Allen Distributing Company
2525 West 26 Street
Sioux Falls, South Dakota 57105

Dear Al:

As the year closes, I want to express my appreciation for your support of Kennel-Treat products. You know how tough it is for a new enterprise to get a foothold in a highly competitive market, and there were times during the year when even *our* faith wavered a bit. Thank goodness, yours didn't. And because of you and a few other loyal supporters, we are winding up the year in good shape, and we're happy to say that the future looks promising.

I hope that we can show our appreciation to you by giving you even better products, faster service, and "pencil-sharpened" prices during the coming year. We're all dedicated to that goal.

Cordially yours,

Bob Barbot

Robert T. Barbot
President

RTB:cn

Analysis.   Mr. Barbot, the owner of a newly established firm, has obviously had to scramble to keep his business solvent during its first year of operation. The support of Allen Distributing helped Kennel-Treat to continue operating. Such a thank-you letter, then, is very appropriate.

As you read the letter, observe its personal flavor; the tone is conversational—not unlike the language you would use in speaking to a personal friend. This is important. Business associates do become personal friends; and then, the "language of business" is the language of friendship.

Letter Expressing Appreciation for Patience

Peninsula Engineering Company

2422 El Camino Real, Palo Alto, California 94306

March 16, 19—

Mr. Leon G. Monroe, Plant Manager
Nu-Way Electronics Inc.
3124 West Coast Highway
Newport Beach, California 92660

Dear Mr. Monroe:

I want to thank you sincerely for your patience with us during the past couple of months. I realize that you had a lot of complaints from your customers because we couldn't deliver the parts you ordered, but I also know that you understand there was very little we could do about it. We couldn't get them either.

It looks as though the labor problems of our major supplier have at last been straightened out. Although there may be a few gaps until production catches up with the backlog, I'll certainly try to see that you get the highest priority.

My guess is that you are having an excellent first quarter. I certainly hope so, and that the second quarter will be even better.

Yours very sincerely,

C. T. Austad

C. T. Austad, Manager
Customer Services

CTA/fl

Analysis. Sometimes, for reasons beyond the supplier's control, a customer's request for a product or service cannot be filled. A letter such as the one Mr. Austad sent to Mr. Monroe is simply an acknowledgment that Nu-Way Electronics was inconvenienced. Even though Mr. Monroe was aware of the strike and didn't blame Peninsula Engineering Company for the problem, he will feel better about things knowing that somebody cared enough to apologize. Mr. Austad's good news about the end of the strike and his promise of "the highest possible priority" in shipping the parts will help further to patch things up. This letter and the preceding one, then, are examples of *not* taking a customer for granted.

Letters of apology are even more important when it is the supplier who is at fault, as a result of poor planning, a misunderstanding, or human error. It is hard to estimate how many customers are lost because of an unfortunate experience or two with a supplier (usually they don't tell anybody about their dissatisfaction—they just quietly fade away as customers). But one thing is certain: a great many of them could have been saved if the supplier had written an "I'm sorry" letter that included a promise to try to do better next time.

A Public Relations Letter

Placement Services Unlimited

Armitage Building • Bristol, Tennessee 37620

August 14, 19—

Dear Ms. O'Rourke:

It was a real pleasure to read in Banking News and in the local papers that you have been elected president of the Women in Banking Association at that organization's annual convention in Washington.

You do honor not only to Bristol but also to the entire profession of banking, and I congratulate you on this recognition of your ability.

We at Placement Services Unlimited are happy to be associated with you and the other fine people at American National, and we hope that we can continue to be of service to you.

Cordially yours,

Chuck

C. K. Milford

Ms. Patricia O'Rourke
First Vice President
American National Bank
Bristol, Tennessee 37620

Analysis. Congratulatory letters such as the one to Ms. O'Rourke often have the hidden motive of promoting one's firm (note that American National Bank, Ms. O'Rourke's employer, is a client of Placement Services Unlimited). But such a gesture, regardless of the writer's motive, is an effective way to establish or maintain good business relationships. When Ms. O'Rourke receives the letter from C. K. Milford, she will no doubt be pleased to have the letter and read the commendatory comments.

Some executives feel so strongly about the importance of such letters that they search for opportunities to write them. They read the local papers, trade journals, and other periodicals to keep abreast of events in which customers, potential customers, and influential people are prominent—promotions, elections to office, honors, and so forth.

Another Public Relations Letter

---

faranfino's
Norwood, Minnesota 55368

April 27, 19—

Dear Fellow Norwoodian:

Building a new store can be a messy business—as you have undoubtedly noticed from the dust clouds we stir up, the rerouting of traffic on Mulburry Road, and the noise and general confusion we create lately.

Although things are still unsettled, we are doing everything we possibly can to eliminate inconvenience and discomfort for our friends. The good news is that we expect to finish the "dirty" work by June 1 and then get back to normal.

Thank you for your patience. Although we regret all the inconvenience to our good neighbors, we think you will be proud of this new Farantino's—a full acre of shopping pleasure—which is scheduled to open on December 1 of this year.

Sincerely yours,

Ralph Farantino III

Ralph Farantino III
President

RF/my

Analysis. Business firms are increasingly aware of the importance of being good citizens in the community in which they are located. Management encourages employees to be active in local affairs and provides financial and human resources for community development.

The letter from Farantino's is an example of the modern business owner's motto: "Good citizenship is good business." Ralph Farantino III apologizes for inconveniences, and many people will consider this a thoughtful gesture. But you can see that he has also dropped the gentle hint that the store will be ready to welcome customers on December 1 with "a full acre of shopping pleasure." Public relations letters, then, have sales value as well as general goodwill value.

Enhancing Internal Relationships. Many communications are written simply to enhance human relationships within an organization. Although not absolutely necessary, such communications lift the spirits, build morale, and give new meaning to work. Here are two examples.

Memorandum Expressing Appreciation

OFFICE LETTER

Glasser Steel Inc.

TO: Fran Lawrence   **FROM:**   J. T. Sykes

SUBJECT: **DATE:**   March 7, 19—

Dear Fran:

I greatly appreciate the way you managed the Open House yesterday. It was elegantly done; and arranging the tour so that our 57 guests saw everything they came to see—with no bottlenecks or delays—took a lot of planning and synchronizing.

It was an enormously successful affair, Fran, judging by what I saw and heard, and I am grateful to you for putting it over so well. Good show!

Sincerely,

JTS

cc Miss C. D. Krantz

Analysis.   Everyone is happy to receive a warm, personal communication such as this one. No matter how highly we are praised by word of mouth for a job well done, we feel much better about it when it is put in writing. The achievement seems so much more important when it is on record.

Note that a carbon of the memo was sent to C. D. Krantz—Fran Lawrence's immediate supervisor. This is a very effective device for enhancing good human relationships.

Letter Offering Congratulations

Buckman and Marco, Incorporated

Empire Life Building
435 South Ironwood Drive
South Bend, Indiana 46615

July 15, 19—

Dear Mrs. Boyer:

The announcement of your promotion to the position of assistant vice president and controller of Buckman and Marco arrived on my desk this morning—and what good news it is!

Surely no one in the organization could bring to this position a broader background in terms of education, experience, and job performance, and I predict that you will quickly prove to be precisely the right choice for this big responsibility.

I look forward to working with you. Certainly I—and all the people in Customer Services—stand ready to help you in every way possible.

Sincerely yours,

Charles F. Larned

Charles F. Larned
Vice President, Customer Services

Mrs. Aileen F. Boyer
Assistant Vice President and
    Controller
Buckman and Marco, Incorporated

Analysis.   In the typical organization, when an employee is promoted to a higher position, she or he will receive a number of congratulatory messages similar to the one sent to Mrs. Boyer. There is no better way to build good relationships among people in the same organization. Indeed, the satisfaction of a promotion or other honor may come largely from congratulatory letters and memorandums from friends and associates. In this case, Mr. Larned chose to use a letterhead instead of a memorandum form. Either is all right; however, a letterhead message is more personal.

Keeping People Informed.   When a business is small, communication among employees is usually a simple matter. Group meetings, to which all the employees involved are invited, are held at a moment's notice; and everybody's door is open to anyone who wants to talk. But as the number of people in an organization increases, it becomes harder to get everybody together, so important information must often be shared by means of written communications. Here are three examples of when information-sharing communications can be used:

1. To announce personnel changes, such as promotions, reorganizations, and retirements.
2. To state changes in company policy and procedures—employee benefits, customer/dealer relationships, employee compensation, etc.
3. To report the results of studies and analyses—for example, efficient use of equipment, forms design and control, and departmental profit ratios.

Following are typical communications written to keep people informed.

EXECUTIVE MEMORANDUM 33
Kimbrough Inc.

TO: Staff   **FROM:** Bruce A. Kimbrough
SUBJECT: New Position   **DATE:** February 16, 19—

It is a matter of great pride to us that our rate of growth over the past five years is unmatched in the publishing industry. And as our business gets larger, our relationships with our various "publics"—our employees, suppliers, customers, stockholders, the financial community, and the general public—become increasingly important. We are convinced that we can no longer allow communications with these groups to be a hit-or-miss affair.

Therefore, effective March 1, we are establishing the new position of Director of Public Relations, and Ms. Sophie Margulies is appointed to that position. Ms. Margulies is eminently qualified to head up this new department. She comes to us from Baker-Walden Inc., where she was Director of Public Affairs and Publicity for the past three years, achieving national prominence in that role. Prior to that she ran her own public relations consulting firm in Dayton. Ms. Margulies is a graduate of the School of Journalism at the University of Missouri; she is the author of numerous articles on public relations and has spoken widely on the subject. In her new position she will report to F. L. DeBenning, Executive Vice President.

I know you join me in welcoming Sophie Margulies to the Kimbrough family and in wishing her every success in this new endeavor.

Bruce A. Kimbrough

Analysis.   In this executive memorandum, the company president, Bruce A. Kimbrough, keeps employees up to date by announcing the creation of a new position. Without such an announcement, it would take a long time for most employees to learn about the new position and Ms. Margulies' appointment to it. This not only might be embarrassing to her but also might handicap her in doing her job. Observe how the memorandum is organized. It includes:

1. Background information on the need for a director of public relations.
2. An announcement of the appointment of Sophie Margulies and the date her appointment takes effect.
3. A description of Ms. Margulies' qualifications.
4. The name of the executive to whom Ms. Margulies will report.
5. An invitation to employees to welcome Ms. Margulies to the organization.

Century Manufacturing Company
Interoffice Memo

TO: All Department Managers   **FROM:**   A. R. Blyden,
                                                Personnel Director

SUBJECT: Payroll Reviews   **DATE:**   November 16, 19—

As you know, we have made it a practice to review all salaries twice a year—March 15 and September 15. In recent months, however, it has become more and more obvious that reviews should be made on a quarterly basis; and effective in January, payroll review sheets will be distributed four times a year—March 15, June 15, September 15, and December 15.

The policy that a recommended merit increase must be at least 5 percent will remain in effect. However, the maximum of 7 percent will no longer apply when the new system takes effect; instead, 10 percent merit increases will be permitted. As in the past, the ceiling for promotion increases will be 15 percent.

Complete details on these new policies will be issued later this month. In the meantime, I see no reason why you cannot share the information in this memorandum with employees.

ARB

Analysis.   This memo announcing a change in company policy about salary reviews is an example of the importance of written communications in a business organization. The information in the memorandum is very specific, and the managers to whom it is addressed should have no difficulty understanding the new policy and explaining it to employees. You can imagine the confusion that might result if such a policy change were transmitted by telephone or in person-to-person conversations. Everyone could come away with a different set of facts, and then there would be chaos.

YOUR RESPONSIBILITY FOR WRITTEN COMMUNICATIONS

Written communications make those who prepare them highly visible in an organization, and it is baffling to management why so many educated people fall short in their ability to express themselves clearly and persuasively. Perhaps one big reason there is a scarcity of good writers is that people don't expect to do much writing, and they give it little thought until they are faced with the responsibility. Engineering students who thought their jobs would require them only to build bridges or design machinery or do technical research often discover too late that nearly everything they do involves a written report. Accounting majors are likely to visualize themselves essentially as consultants to top management on financial matters, only to learn on the job that their recommendations take the form of memorandums, reports, and letters. Secretaries who expect to record in shorthand the words of highly articulate executives frequently discover that their bosses don't like to write and expect somebody else to do it for them or at least polish up their rough drafts. Those who aspire to jobs as buyers, personnel recruiters, department managers, purchasing agents, or office supervisors are often shocked to find out that these jobs can frequently require an endless stream of written communications.

You can be pretty certain, then, that if you wind up in any kind of supervisory or management job, you are going to do a good deal of writing. Although it is possible that your communications will take only a small fraction of your time, it is also possible that they could turn out to be your principal activity. Rank in the organization usually has little to do with one's output of written communications: a sales correspondent or an insurance adjuster may write five times as many letters as the company president. But even if the first job you have involves very little writing, the next one up the ladder may call for heavy writing responsibilities. For example, a promotion from sales representative to district sales manager or from accountant to manager of accounting services can immediately change one's duties from basically oral communications to basically written ones.

Given the importance of written communications in business, it is little wonder that management is quick to notice those who are skillful writers and to penalize those who are clumsy in expressing themselves. Both letters and reports become permanent evidence of an employee's ability to communicate; copies often find their way to top management, even when we least expect it. Written communications put us on record—they cannot be erased or, like oral conversations, quickly forgotten. Reports and memos written to people in the same company represent primarily the person who writes them; letters and reports that go to people outside the company represent primarily the organization for whom the writer works. In both cases, your written communications are important enough to have an enormous effect on your career.

Projects

(A) There are 12 employees in the personnel department of Whitmore Inc. The director of personnel, David Kawamura, and the assistant director, Freda Kapp, recently met to plan a major reorganization of the department. The new organization is to take effect on the first of the coming month. Is it important that the changes be described in writing? If so, what essential details should be covered in the announcement? Who in the company should receive it?

(B) Susan Welker, traffic manager for Florida Van Lines, has resigned to accept a similar position with a larger firm in another city. Ms. Welker is being replaced by Byron Janssen. If you were writing an announcement to employees about this personnel change, which event would you feature—Ms. Welker's resignation or Mr. Janssen's appointment?

(C) Contemporary Sound Inc., manufacturers of audio equipment, sell their products only through authorized dealers (retail stores, for example). Recently an individual wrote to the company, placing an order for two tape decks that he saw advertised in *Audio Systems Dealer,* a trade journal. In terms of goodwill-building, what do you think of the response given in the letter below?

Dear Sir:

We are unable to fill your order for Contemporary Sound tape decks about which you inquired in your letter of March 14. This equipment is sold only through authorized dealers.

Very truly yours,

D Following are the opening paragraphs from nine different communications. Identify the purpose of each letter or memorandum, referring to the five uses of written communications discussed in this unit. (Some may have more than one purpose.)

1. *Letter from a publishing house to a bookstore manager:* The 15 copies of *Winning at Tennis* arrived this morning, and we are happy to credit your account for $93.75.
2. *Letter to a critic who has lambasted a company for its "tasteless advertising" on television:* I appreciate this opportunity to tell you what we are doing about the television advertisements that you find objectionable.
3. *Letter to a dealer who is a prospect for the firm's new line of chain saws:* You will want to know that on all orders for Little Giant chain saws placed in January we are offering an additional trade discount of 12½ percent.
4. *Memo from accounts receivable supervisor to the department manager:* Here are the details concerning the Kimball account, on which you asked for a status report in your memo of September 9.
5. *Memo from the executive vice president of Eagle Mills to the staff:* I am delighted to tell you that the Eagle Mills annual report was given the Award of Excellence by *Financial Journal.* This is a great honor, and special commendation is due John Zlombicki and his staff.
6. *Memo from marketing director to district sales managers:* Some of you have long felt that our policy in accepting unsold merchandise from customers is much too tough compared with that of our major competitors. I am glad to announce that a new policy, which goes into effect May 1, will bring us into line.
7. *Memo from the president to major executives:* This will bring you up to date on our negotiations with Casey-Robbins for an exclusive distributorship of the Weyland line of electronic calculators.
8. *Memo from director of the executive committee to the personnel relations manager:* Dear Joe: This is a confirmation of our agreement at yesterday's EC meeting to undertake a thorough analysis of our employee benefits program to see how it compares with industrywide programs.
9. *Letter answering an inquiry about local outlets for a firm's products:* Dear Mrs. Isaacs: Here is a list of retail stores in Osage County that handle the Grass Grabber mower.

E Often in corresponding with customers a business writer must say no. In doing so, however, he or she tries to be friendly and tactful. Mission: To get customers to accept the no and *remain* customers.

Compare the two "no" letters below. Which one is more likely to keep the customer's friendship? Why?

Dear Madam:

Sorry but we cannot permit you to return for credit the draperies you purchased, since we are not able to dispose of them. It is too bad that these drapes do not fit the windows you bought them for, but since they were sold to you well under the regular price and on an "all sales final" basis, there is little we can do about it.

Trusting you will appreciate our position in this matter, we are,

Very truly yours,

Dear Mrs. Kirkendall:

I appreciate your request to return for refund the draperies you recently purchased from Avery's.

You will remember, Mrs. Kirkendall, that these drapes were offered at a greatly reduced price (actually, 40 percent off) and that for this special sale all merchandise was advertised "Not returnable." As much as I would like to make an exception in your case, I'm afraid I cannot since this was a closeout on the Beekman line, and we do not plan to restock it.

I know you will understand our position, Mrs. Kirkendall. Incidentally, our interior design consultant tells me that many people purchased these drapery materials for use as upholstery coverings and bedspreads.

Sincerely yours,

UNIT 2

HUMAN RELATIONS IN COMMUNICATION

If you can think clearly and compose reasonably intelligent sentences, you can become a top-notch business writer. This could be enormously important to you in your business career; those who can write clearly and persuasively become highly visible in any organization—there is probably no better medium than the written word for demonstrating your job competence.

In this course, we'll provide you with the fundamentals of effective business writing, show you dozens of examples of good and bad writing, and give you many opportunities to write letters, memorandums, and reports in typical business situations.

But there is one thing you must provide: a "success" attitude. By that we mean you have to care enough about the results you get from your communications to make sure that they cannot (or will very rarely) fail. Expert business writers genuinely care about getting and keeping as many good customers as possible. They are very concerned about what their suppliers, customers, and the public at large think about the company, so they do all they can to present a favorable company image. They believe that they can do their job best when they work hard to create and maintain effective human relationships both inside and outside the company. And they experience enormous satisfaction from contributing their share.

What we're saying is that you can't be a really effective writer if the people you're working for and the things you're writing about aren't very important to you. People who write well are generally those whose enthusiasm for their employer and the people they work with shows through in all their communications. Indeed, most of the traits possessed by good executives, managers, and supervisors are also those possessed by good writers.

1. They have a high "people IQ"; that is, they are sensitive to the feelings and needs of the people they deal with.
2. They are basically reasonable people, willing to make allowances for human frailties.
3. They have an open mind, avoiding petty biases and stereotyping of people.
4. They are imaginative and constantly look for better ways of saying and doing things.
5. They are patient, but they are tough when they have to be.

WHAT IS GOOD BUSINESS WRITING?

What is good business writing? Simply put, business writing is "good" when it achieves the purpose the author intended. The purpose may be to collect money from a slow-paying customer, to convince a prospective buyer that he or she ought to become a regular customer, to sell an idea to top management, to clarify a company policy or procedure, to win back a customer who has strayed, to patch things up with an angry client, and so on. When the reader reacts in the manner the writer intended, then the communication has done its job.

There really is no other measure of the effectiveness of a communication than the reader's reaction to it. The words, sentences, and paragraphs may please the writer immensely—indeed, the message may be perfectly constructed—but if the reader does not respond to it as the author intended, it is a failure.

Because the only qualified judge of a communication is the reader, there is no magic formula that will always guarantee an effective letter, memorandum, or report. If there were, all we would have to do is memorize it, and then we could be sure of producing sales letters that consistently pull in swarms of new customers, collection letters that invariably bring in money, and memos and reports that never fail to gain applause from the boss. But people are different and situations vary. If you are writing to an old and loyal customer about an amount he owes but has simply overlooked paying, your letter will have quite a different flavor from one you would write to a new customer who has ignored several strong reminders. Thus each situation calls for a different approach.

To compound the problem of producing effective communications, two readers in very nearly identical situations may react quite differently to the same message. While one customer may be offended by the statement in a collection letter, "No doubt you want to maintain your good credit reputation," another may find it a perfectly reasonable admonition. And unfortunately, when you place a communication in the mail, you usually won't know how your reader will respond to it.

All this may suggest that trying to become a good business writer is a waste of time since the recipients of communications are so unpredictable. Not so! Indeed, recognizing the unpredictability of readers is the first step in building writing skill. Every person is different from every other person, and every situation is different. So you have to think hard about who your reader is and the circumstances that brought about the need for a letter or memorandum. Then it will be easier to decide what to say and how to say it to reach that particular person.

Although there are no foolproof formulas for writing, what we do know about human beings allows us to build a general framework for effective communications. We know that people respond most favorably to communications that:

- Are direct, simple, and personal.
- Are positive, friendly, and courteous.
- Show the writer's eagerness to be helpful.
- Are clear and easy to understand.
- Are honest and believable.
- Show respect for the reader's intelligence and integrity.

You won't always be able to achieve every one of these objectives. For example, if you have to tell a customer that he is being sued because he won't pay what he owes, or respond to someone who consistently challenges your honesty, or answer a critic who makes an accusation that is libelous, you will have a hard time being positive, friendly, and courteous. Indeed, in some instances you may have to challenge a person's integrity. But remember that these situations are rare, and in a great majority of cases you can produce communications that satisfy the criteria listed above.

WRITING STYLE

We said that most people prefer to read communications that are direct, simple, and personal. Why, then, do you suppose so many writers—warm, friendly, and outgoing in their personal relationships—assume an entirely different character when they write? The most likely answer is that words on paper frighten them because they are so permanent, and these people probably feel they must put their intelligence, importance, and scholarship on record for posterity. Of course, this attitude is ridiculous.

For example, a chief accountant, concerned that the company is sloppy in its procedures for receiving and paying out cash, wrote a memorandum to various department heads. The memorandum contained this statement:

It is a fundamental truism of effective cash control that responsibility for receiving and disbursing funds be divided among personnel.

The accountant's sentence is an example of what can be called "businessese" (or in government offices, "federalese"), meaning pompous, stilted writing that causes readers to squirm, blink, and make a second try at understanding it. What the accountant really meant is:

The main thing we have to remember about cash control is that the person who receives cash should not be the same one who pays out cash.

Because they see so much businessese in communications, newcomers to the business world may get the idea there is a language that is unique to business. This is not so; there is no such thing as a "business style." There is only a personal style that is adapted to business situations. The best writers are those who don't put on airs or beat around the bush; they bend over backwards to humanize their writing so that it is not only easy to understand but also interesting to read.

Let's look at some more examples of businessese and then see how each could have been written.

1. A personnel supervisor writes about the importance of providing each employee with a description of his or her job.

Businessese: Individuals who know their responsibilities are in a position to concentrate their efforts on the requirements of their job rather than trying to ascertain what their job is.

Direct, Simple, Personal: When people know exactly what their job duties are, they won't waste time trying to decide what they should be doing.

2. An office services manager discusses the efficient use of office machines.

Businessese: High-level volume and quality of work are not obtainable unless operators are properly trained and the machines used are in suitable condition for work.

Direct, Simple, Personal: You can't expect a big volume of high-quality work if you don't have trained operators and machines that are in good condition.

3. The attorney for a business firm writes about a contract that is to be signed.

Businessese: The contract appended herewith should be executed in triplicate.

Direct, Simple, Personal: Please sign all three copies of the enclosed contract.

One of the drawbacks you may have noticed about the businessese examples is the use of big words and clumsy phrases. (We'll talk about those later.) But also notice that businessese writing is usually passive and impersonal. By passive we mean that *people* don't make things happen—they simply happen: for example, *These duties have been performed, This decision was reached, Their accounts were examined, All the advertisements have been placed,* and *Four letters were written.* Using active-voice verbs, these examples would be people-activated: *We performed these duties, They reached this decision, She examined their accounts, He placed all the advertisements,* and *I wrote four letters.* Here are more examples of what we mean:

Passive	People-Activated
During the November meeting of the Executive Committee, the decision was reached to eliminate trading stamps.	At its November meeting, the Executive Committee decided to eliminate trading stamps.
In the third quarter, full-page ads were placed in 120 small-town weeklies.	We placed full-page ads in 120 small-town weeklies in the third quarter.
Recognizing that a problem exists is the first step in solving it.	When you recognize that a problem exists, you have taken the first step toward solving it.
When the tabulations were completed, they revealed some shocking information.	We were shocked when we saw the final tabulations.

You can see that by getting people into the act you avoid the deadly businessese and federalese that most readers abhor.

However, there are exceptions. You will purposely avoid personal references when they are likely to offend.

Offensive	Better
You are prohibited from smoking in the stockroom.	Smoking in the stockroom is prohibited.
You should not have deducted the 5 percent discount.	The 5 percent discount should not have been deducted.
We don't think you are entitled to a refund.	In this instance, a refund does not seem to be justified.

In most of your writing, however, you should strive for a people-activated style. Using *I, you, we, they, our,* and other pronouns will help to make your communications lively, interesting, and easy to understand.

CONVERSATIONAL ENGLISH

Although a communication that appears on a company letterhead represents the company, it is the writer who gives the communication its personality. Most executives will encourage you to write in a conversational tone, but at the same time, you will generally have considerable freedom to develop your own personal style. In the examples that follow, you will see what a difference a conversational approach can make. Suppose, for example, you have received your first order from Ms. Beth Phelan whom your company has been trying for months to woo away from a competitor. Are you likely to respond like this?

> Dear Madam:
>
> This will acknowledge receipt of your order, which will receive prompt attention.

Not if you want Ms. Phelan to feel like a welcome and valued customer! This response contains no evidence that she is anything at all special, even though a lot of people probably worked hard to win her business. This is typical of impersonal, to-whom-it-may-concern letters that we see too often in business. If you want to express what you and your colleagues in the company really feel, you will probably say something like this:

> Dear Ms. Phelan:
>
> All of us at Arkins were delighted to have your first order. Thank you! The Tot Trikes left here this morning by Premier Motor Freight, so you should have them by Thursday.

Let's look at another example.

Case Example: The customer service correspondent for the Timely Publishing Company received a mild note of complaint, along with a check, from Professor Ogilvie, who had ordered a Timely book, *Introduction to Psychology,* and received a bill for $6.75. On the inside of the book jacket, however, Professor Ogilvie found the price of $6.25. When he sent his check for $6.75, he asked for an explanation. The fact is that prices of books often increase after they are published, and it is not always possible to indicate the change on the flap of the book jacket.

What do you think of this response?

> Dear Sir:
>
> This will acknowledge receipt of your inquiry of August 20 about the list price of McKeown's Introduction to Psychology, which is indicated on the jacket of the book as $6.25 but which was invoiced to you at $6.75.
>
> With regard to this matter, allow us to advise you that it is common practice in the publishing industry to change prices from time to time after a book is first printed because of increases in manufacturing and marketing costs. In the event a price is changed, however, every endeavor is made to remove the original price from the jacket before the book is shipped; but books are often shipped prepackaged from the printing plant, and we are prevented from taking the original price out of the jacket. Thus there will often be a discrepancy between the price printed on the jacket and the price indicated on the invoice.
>
> Trusting this explanation will be satisfactory, I am
>
> Very truly yours,

The trouble with this letter is that it doesn't acknowledge the fact that Professor Ogilvie is a living, breathing human being (and a customer besides). It might as well have been addressed To Whom It May Concern. Let's personalize it.

Dear Professor Ogilvie:

It is easy to see why you were confused by the price of McKeown's Introduction to Psychology, which is shown as $6.25 on the jacket and $6.75 on the invoice. Let me explain.

After a book is published, we may have to change the price two or three times because of increases in our manufacturing and marketing costs. When we change a price, we make it a practice to snip off the old price. Lately, however, more and more of our books are being shipped directly from the printing plant to the customer, and the printer doesn't provide this "snipping" service.

Thank you for giving me an opportunity to clear up this matter, Professor Ogilvie. I hope you will find Dr. McKeown's book ideally suited to your evening classes at Russell Sage. It is fast becoming the most respected introductory text in the field.

Sincerely yours,

Don't you think Professor Ogilvie will feel better about the second letter than the first? The reason, of course, is that it is a personal letter *intended for him.*

Write As You Talk?   Although striving for a personal, conversational tone in your communications is a good idea, you should not try to write exactly as you talk. When you talk, you have the advantage of gestures, facial expressions, and voice to help you convey your message; but when you write, you have only words on paper. Therefore, you have to be a little more careful. For example, a purchasing manager can say to one of his vendors in the office or on the street, "Hey, Murray, why is it taking you fellows forever to get those parts to us? You're killing us!" and, with a smile and a handshake, make the remark sound like a good-natured rib. In writing, however, the tone is a little more guarded:

We've got a lot of customers who can't understand why we don't have the parts they need. Would you see what you can do to speed things along?

A salesperson can say to a customer who comes into the store to exchange what she thinks is a defective record player: "No wonder you're getting distortion on your 33⅓ LPs. You've got the needle set on 78." If this little lecture puts the customer on the defensive, the salesperson can quickly recover with, "I didn't mean you personally, of course." But the *writer* can't count on getting a second chance; therefore, he or she would probably be more cautious in an explanation:

The only thing I can find wrong with the sound of your record player, Mrs. Folsom, is that the needle has been accidentally set on 78 rather than on 33⅓. A lot of people forget to check the setting when they change to a different record speed.

As you write, then, think about what you would say if you were facing your reader, then edit out those expressions that sound better when spoken than they look on paper.

PERSONALIZING MEMORANDUMS

People who write memorandums are even more inclined to produce stilted, pompous communications than those who write letters. Perhaps this is because memos are written primarily to transact business rather than to make friends and win customers. Yet there is generally no reason why the style of the two communications should differ. Let's look at an example.

Case Example: M. V. Holcomb, director of marketing at the Cranston Rubber Company, prepared a memo to the president concerning sales performance.

TO:	J. W. Holmes Jr.	**FROM:**	M. V. Holcomb
SUBJECT:	Sales Performance	**DATE:**	January 12, 19—

Per person sales performance was substantially improved during the past year. Volume is significantly higher (40 percent) with fewer representatives, leading to the conclusion that the caliber of sales personnel is superior to that in any previous period in Cranston history. This can no doubt be attributed to improved training and supervision.

MVH

Do you think this is the way M. V. Holcomb would talk to Mr. Holmes if they were sitting down together? Probably not; it's a very stiff, impersonal memorandum. Mr. Holcomb could have made his memorandum much more human if he had written something like this:

I am glad to report that we have the best sales force we have ever had. Although we have 20 fewer representatives this year than last, our volume is up nearly 40 percent; so you can see that individual performance is much better. The reason? I think it's simply better training and supervision.

INDIVIDUALITY IN COMMUNICATIONS

When we speak of humanizing your communications, we are not suggesting that every writer should strive for the same style. Although most communications have more impact on readers when they are conversational in tone, we must recognize that people carry on conversations in different ways. Some people are naturally gregarious, and their writing style reflects their outgoing, social attitude. Others are inclined to be a little more reserved, and a chatty, garrulous writing style does not come naturally to them. For example, in congratulating a fellow employee on the way a workshop was conducted, one writer might say this:

You did a beautiful job, Roger, in running the workshop on employee safety. I was really happy to be a part of it.

Another writer might put it this way:

The workshop you recently conducted on employee safety was very profitable. It was a pleasure for me to participate in it.

Which is better? The only answer to that question is, It all depends. If the more formal style suits your personality better, certainly there is nothing wrong with it—you can be sure it won't offend anyone. We prefer the more casual, informal style for most communications—and probably the majority of readers will too—but it may not work for all writers or, indeed, in all situations.

THE WRITER-READER RELATIONSHIP

Often your relationship with your reader will largely determine the style of your writing. If you are a personal friend of the addressee, your communications with her or him are quite likely to be warm and casual. But if your reader is only a name to you, the tone of your message will be slightly more reserved.

Case Example: Here are letters written by two different people to the same person about an appointment. In the first example the writer is a longtime friend of the addressee, Alberto Mucelli; in the second example the writer has never met Mr. Mucelli.

Dear Moose:

Can you spare me a half hour or so Tuesday morning, May 9, around ten o'clock? I'm making a quick trip to Richmond that day to go over some stuff with our new controller there (JR will be along).

I'd like to drop in to see you about my plans for the October CAA Seminar in Absecon. I need to get your advice about the theme of the workshop and check off my ideas about speakers and panelists. I think I've got a great keynoter lined up.

Don't count on my staying past eleven—I've got to be at our plant by noon for a special retirement luncheon for Fred Lowe.

How's Muriel?

Cordially,

Dear Mr. Mucelli:

I expect to be in Richmond Tuesday, May 9, on company business. Could I see you at your office about ten o'clock on that day? I want to go over with you the plans I have made for the October Seminar of the Cost Accounting Association at Absecon, New Jersey.

I won't need more than a half hour, I believe. I know your time is limited, and my own schedule is tight too.

Sincerely yours,

Formulas.   Do you see now why it is not possible to write according to a fixed formula? You know by now that what you say, how you say it, and the sequence in which you deliver your ideas, all depend on who the reader is and your relationship with each other.

One so-called "formula" suggests this sequence:

1. Get to the purpose of your communication immediately, and make that first paragraph short and pithy.
2. Move on quickly in the second paragraph to the details you want to emphasize.
3. Close with an action statement—that is, tell what you expect your reader to do.

It is true that such a formula will work fine in certain situations. But in others it will produce a very poor letter indeed. Suppose you are writing to a former classmate and fellow accountant whom you saw, along with her husband, at a recent convention. Your main purpose is to remind her that she promised to send you an organization chart of the accounting department in her company. If you follow the formula shown, you won't waste any time getting down to business:

Dear Norma:

Please send me the organization chart of your accounting department, which you referred to at the Syracuse DPA meeting.

But let's look at that reader again. We said she is a former classmate and fellow accountant. Under these circumstances would you be likely to show such abruptness in your opening? Of course not. You would be more likely to write a letter like this one:

Dear Norma:

It was great seeing you and Al in Syracuse last week. You look very fit in spite of the apparently "soft" life you have at Lake Placid. If that outfit of yours needs another accountant, remember me!

I wonder if you remember that you promised to send me the organization chart of your accounting setup at Baggett and Knowland. I'm trying to reorganize our department, and I think your plan may be just right for us.

Best regards to Al. I thought the DPA convention was especially good this year, didn't you?

Sincerely,

Remember that you must have a complete picture of your reader before you decide on the contents of your letter or the sequence in which you will present your points. For example, suppose that your former classmate Norma had lost her luggage, or had her hotel room broken into, or had been elected vice president of the DPA. The "formula" would not work in any of these cases either. Instead, you would have to try to look into Norma's mind to determine the best approach. Thus you might start off your letter with congratulations (if Norma was elected vice president), or a question (Did the missing luggage turn up?), or a reference to the break-in.

The Effect of Rank on Tone.   Frequently, though not always, communications to top executives in your company are a little more formal in tone than those addressed to your associates.

Case Example: Suppose your immediate boss has asked you to prepare a report on the loss of valuable contracts from the company's files. If the report is to be addressed to the company president, with whom you have had little association, it might look something like this:

TO:	Barry R. Jacobs	**FROM:**	Your Name
SUBJECT:	Loss of Company Contracts	**DATE:**	February 11, 19—

Various methods have been tried to control losses of contracts from the company's open files, but the situation remains serious.

After extensive study, I have reached the conclusion that the problem will be solved only when a central control, such as the library, is established for these files and employees are required to check out contracts and are made responsible for their safe return.

If that same report were being addressed to your immediate supervisor, with whom you are on a first-name basis, it might be worded as follows:

TO:	Eileen T. Corbett	**FROM:**	Your Name
SUBJECT:	Loss of Company Contracts	**DATE:**	February 11, 19—

I've tried several different ways of solving the mystery of lost contracts, and nothing seems to work. Nearly every month a contract gets away from us and is apparently lost.

It seems to me, Eileen, that the only way we'll get on top of this thing is to put these files under central control (the library?) and check them out to people who want them.

We don't mean to imply that all communications to VIPs in the company are formal and impersonal—some executives like every employee to call them by their first name. But until you know what is expected of you, it is probably best to keep your guard up slightly.

The same advice applies to influential people outside the company— an important stockholder, for example. Just be sure of your ground before you get too conversational or chummy.

Subject Matter and Tone.   Finally, the subject matter of a communication can have a decided bearing on tone and style. For example, a personnel director's memorandum to employees announcing a new retirement program will be more reserved in tone than an invitation to sign up for the Travel Club's "Caribbean Cruise"; a letter turning down a request for credit is likely to be more sober than one welcoming a new charge customer; and the treasurer's report on slipping company profits isn't likely to be as casual as one on the company's dynamic growth.

Projects

  Rewrite the following statements, giving them a more personal flavor.

1. Carlton's display rooms are open to the general public Wednesday afternoons from 3 until 5:30.
2. Unfortunately, requests for copies of our contract forms must be denied.
3. Customers are advised to place their orders early because these Hogan irons are in short supply and great demand.
4. Your letter stating that you received 12 Big Tom Lawn Mowers instead of 12 Big Tom Lawn Sweepers has been referred to the writer. This error is regrettable.
5. The beneficiary form X-388 is being returned because it has not been signed.
6. Should further copies of the brochure be required, requests should be addressed to our Publications Office, specifying requirements.
7. In acknowledgment of your letter of April 12, a catalog was mailed today.
8. The suggestion of a "Car Pool Campaign" appears to be very timely, and the writer pledges full support.
9. Subject report was received and read carefully.
10. In order to minimize costs, clerical productivity must be maintained at the highest possible level commensurate with equitable employment practices.
11. It is recommended that employees who are in disagreement with company policy concerning automobile leasing communicate with the assistant marketing director or the undersigned for clarification of the company's position.
12. Recreational facilities at Wilderness Lodge are free to guests.

  Personalize the following letter from a manufacturer to a dealer.

Dear Sir:

Enclosed please find ten copies of a new price schedule, which will take effect November 16.

Particular attention should be given to the new discount policy (page 4). Although there is an increase in the list price of several items, the more generous discounts offered actually mean a reduction in net prices on all merchandise.

Your next order is eagerly anticipated and will be given prompt attention.

Very truly yours,

C Personalize the following memorandum:

TO: L. K. Brinkmeyer   **FROM:** C. R. Marx

SUBJECT: Request for New Typewriter   **DATE:** October 12, 19—

Permission is desired by the writer to purchase an additional electric typewriter for use in this department. A new typist was recently hired and is forced to share a machine with another party.

It will be recalled that this department is considerably behind in its production, and it does not appear likely that this situation will be remedied until all workers are fully equipped.

Investigation reveals that a new Carter Electric which meets the requirements of this department can be purchased for $530. A purchase order is attached for your signature.

CRM

D Edit the following conversation so that it is suitable for a written communication:

Look, Mr. Nesbitt, you'd be crazy not to take advantage of the special price on these cars. I've got them marked down to the point where I'm not going to make a dime on them—in fact, I'm going to lose money—but I've got to get rid of them so that I'll have room for the new models. Five days—that's all the time I can give you to make up your mind.

E The following letter was written by a special sales representative to an individual with whom he is well acquainted (a longtime customer). Rewrite it so that it would be suitable for a potential customer who is not known to the writer.

Dear Paula:

Thanks for stopping by our exhibit at the Tulsa Business Show last month. I was very pleased to see your name among those who signed up for a demonstration of the Tutor-Trainer.

I will be in Topeka the week of April 11, and any day that week that is convenient for you would suit me fine. Just tell me where and when. I need to know right away, though, because I've got several other people to see while I'm in town. By the way, the demonstration shouldn't take more than an hour. Bring your friends!

I look forward to seeing you again. What did you think of our exhibit—quite an extravaganza, eh?

Yours,

F Rewrite the following sentences in active voice.

1. The speaker's presentation was enjoyed by the entire audience.

2. The display signs will be shipped by August 19.
3. Every complaint received by the company should be looked upon by employees as an opportunity to make a friend.
4. A business reply envelope is enclosed for your convenience.
5. Your support of our new line of video recorders is much appreciated.
6. Interest is paid from the date of deposit.
7. Submission of advertising copy is required two months prior to publication date of the magazine.
8. Caution is advised when entering or leaving the construction area.
9. Early registration for the convention is recommended.
10. A total of 412 responses were received from the *Fleet Owner* advertisement.

(G) The following special announcement was issued to passengers on Skymaster Airlines recently. Rewrite it, correcting any errors you find and making the message more personal.

To Our Passengers:

Effective August 1, the price of alcoholic beverages will be increased to $1.50 a drink. Regretfully, Skymaster has found it necessary to make this adjustment due to substantial increases we have experienced in our costs. Light refreshments are still being served complimentary. It is appreciated that you chose Skymaster Airlines, and every effort will be made to make your flight enjoyable.

SKYMASTER AIRLINES

UNIT 3

GETTING RESULTS FROM YOUR COMMUNICATIONS

Business communications that achieve the results the writer wants are not only direct, simple, and personal; they are also reader-directed, positive, friendly, courteous, and helpful.

THE "YOU" EMPHASIS IN COMMUNICATIONS

The "you" emphasis in business communications means looking at things from the reader's point of view and phrasing your message so that it is clear you are thinking of him or her instead of yourself. In the following examples, note how the "you" emphasis sentences are more reader-directed than the "we" or "I" emphasis sentences.

"You" Emphasis	"We" or "I" Emphasis
You will be delighted with the authentic styling of Montclair Colonial cabinets. Indeed, you might find it hard to distinguish between these copies and the originals that were made during the time of the American Revolution.	We have styled the Montclair Colonial cabinets so expertly that we defy the average person to distinguish between them and the originals that were made during the time of the American Revolution.
You will quickly see that you have been given credit for the difference between the higher-priced Champion and the Regent you received.	When we realized our error, we immediately made an adjustment for the difference in cost between the Champion and the Regent we sent you.
Your suggestions for promotion tie-ins are very appropriate. Do you think the following plan, based on your ideas, would serve your needs better?	We received your valuable suggestions for promotion tie-ins, and based on them, we designed a new plan which we think will do a better job.
Your success in reaching the rural market encourages us to ask for your opinion concerning . . .	We haven't had much success in reaching the rural market, and we would like to find out from our successful dealers what we might do to . . .

Unfortunately, some people think of the "you" emphasis as merely inserting the pronouns *you* and *your* wherever they can and avoiding the pronouns *I* and *we*. Let's look at an example that proves the fallacy of this kind of thinking.

You failed to supply complete information in your order; therefore, you cannot expect to have your lathes when you want them.

The example contains five *you's,* but the tone does not convey the "you" emphasis at all. The writer has said that the reader is to blame for the problem and is going to suffer the consequences. Indeed, more of a "you" emphasis could be displayed without even using the pronoun *you.*

Unfortunately, the information given me was not complete, and I wasn't able to make shipment immediately.

But the "you" emphasis means putting yourself in your reader's place, trying to imagine yourself to be him or her. Here is the way a "you" writer would handle the problem of the delay in shipping the lathes.

I'm sorry the lathes could not be shipped to you at once, but since I wanted to make sure you receive exactly what you want, I held up the order until I could get more precise information.

Does the use of *I* four times destroy the "you" emphasis? We don't think so. The reader learns that somebody is looking after his or her interests and is going to do everything possible to solve the problem. That's what the "you" emphasis is all about.

POSITIVENESS

Imagine a salesperson approaching a customer and saying, "You don't want to buy a set of these encyclopedias, do you?" In putting the question negatively, the salesperson makes it easy for the prospect to say no and has probably lost the opportunity to make the sale. The positive salesperson is likely to say, "Would you like to see your children develop a real thirst for knowledge?" or "Would you like to be the proud owner of these 30 handsome volumes?" and certainly has improved the chances of making a sale by using a positive approach.

Becoming adept in the art of persuasion, so important in all human relationships, requires positiveness—stressing the favorable and playing down the unfavorable. This is not to say that one should never be negative; sometimes a lusty no is the only appropriate response. Nor does being positive mean ignoring the truth in order to win acceptance. If you receive an order for merchandise that you do not carry and you can offer no reasonable substitute, you would be wasting both your time and your reader's by pretending. On the other hand, if you do carry the article but are temporarily out of stock, you can accentuate the positive.

Case Example 1: The Exact Time Watch Company has received an order from Dawson's Drugstore for six Dolly Madison clocks. Unfortunately, this particular model has been sold out, and a new shipment is not due for about ten days. A sales correspondent for Exact Time Watch Company, distressed that she could not fill the order immediately, wrote this letter:

> Dear Miss Tobias:
>
> I am very sorry that we are out of stock on Dolly Madison clocks—we simply have not been able to keep up with the orders. I know it will disappoint you that we do not expect a new shipment from the factory for another ten days. Can you wait that long?
>
> Very truly yours,

The situation is not quite as serious as the sales correspondent believes. What might she have said?

> Dear Miss Tobias:
>
> Thank you for your order for six Dolly Madison clocks. This model has been so popular this Christmas season that the factory is a little behind in filling orders.
>
> We do expect a new shipment about November 14. In order to save you time, I am asking that the six clocks be sent directly to you from the plant in Williamsburg. This means that you will have yours by the time we get ours.
>
> Sincerely yours,

Note how the sales correspondent has turned a negative situation into a positive one.

Case Example 2: Assume that you are assistant to the sales manager of Peerless Hardware Corporation. One of your slow-paying customers, Riverdale Hardware

Store, has been placed on a cash-only basis by the credit manager because of the difficulty your company has had collecting from this customer. Riverdale is not to receive shipments unless each order is accompanied by a check.

Today you receive a $76.60 order from Howard Malden, owner of Riverdale Hardware. In his letter, Mr. Malden refers to the "enclosed check," but it is *not* enclosed. How would you respond to this order? Like this?

> Dear Sir:
>
> The check in the amount of $76.60, which you indicated you were sending with your order for two Peerless metal miter boxes, was not among the contents of the envelope.
>
> According to policy concerning your account, shipment of any order cannot be made unless it is accompanied by payment.
>
> Please advise.
>
> > Yours sincerely,

If you suspect that Mr. Malden, by not enclosing his check, is trying to pull something, you might be tempted to write a letter like the one shown. But let's give him the benefit of the doubt. His business is as good as anybody else's when he pays cash, and your mission is to turn him down for credit but retain him as a cash customer. With that idea in mind, you might write a more positive letter like this:

> Dear Mr. Malden:
>
> It was a pleasure to receive your order for two Peerless metal miter boxes. Thank you.
>
> Your check for $76.60, which I'm sure you intended to enclose with your order, did not arrive. No doubt you have already discovered this oversight and have placed your check in the mail. In the meantime, I shall see that the two miter boxes are ready for shipment as soon as payment is received.
>
> We appreciate very much your continued support of the Peerless line.
>
> > Sincerely yours,

In the second letter, you assumed that the customer simply forgot—some people do forget—even though you might have suspected otherwise. Mr. Malden can hardly take offense at this letter; indeed, the chances are good that he will come back with a check. The effective business writer keeps a positive outlook until he knows there is no hope left.

GIVING SATISFACTION TO YOUR READER

Sometimes, through oversight or lethargy, we fail to give people the precise information they ask for. Good human relations requires that we take pains to understand exactly what information is wanted and that we do everything we can to provide it. Not to do so is an insult to the people we communicate with.

Case Example: The Modern Press prints many books in binder form, such as cookbooks, how-to books, laboratory manuals, and the like. After a book has been in print a few years, the publisher may decide to issue a new edition and let the old edition go out of print. The new edition may be of a different size and format, bearing little resemblance to its predecessor.

Such a situation is the subject of the exchange of letters that follows. A lady in Salt Lake City purchased the first edition of a loose-leaf cookbook. After she had used it for six or seven years, the cover began to fall apart, so she wrote the publisher the following letter:

Gentlemen:

I purchased the first edition of the Martha Johnson Picture Cookbook at a local bookstore about seven years ago, and I have enjoyed using it very much. Now the cover is falling apart (I suppose you would call it the binder), and I would like to have a new one for it.

Could I purchase a new five-ring binder from you? Please let me know how to go about it and what the price would be.

Sincerely,

Here is the response she received:

Dear Mrs. Hamm:

Thank you for your letter of November 2, concerning your Martha Johnson Picture Cookbook.

It is company policy to replace all defective books. However, the first edition is out of print and is no longer available. It has been replaced with a newer edition in a six-ring binder.

Therefore, I cannot send you a cover for your book.

I am sorry that I cannot help you. I know how difficult it must be to use a book in this condition.

Sincerely yours,

The general tone of the letter to Mrs. Hamm is good. The first paragraph expresses appreciation for the letter, and the last paragraph offers an apology that seems to indicate that the writer is sympathetic with the customer's problem.

Unfortunately, the writer misses the point in the second and third paragraphs. In the first place, the term *company policy* is irritating to most people; it induces visions of a big rule book the organization has prepared to hide behind when a "no" answer must be given. In the second place, the fact that the first edition is out of print and no longer available has little to do with the availability of a cover. After all, the contents may be out of print but extra covers might be available—not likely, but possible. Thus the customer's request was never really answered. All the publisher's correspondent had to do was say something like this:

> I wish we had a cover available to fit your edition of the Martha Johnson Picture Cookbook. Just to make sure I checked with the bindery as well as with our warehouse, but there isn't a single one left.

In responding to communications from customers and others, some correspondents fail to deal with the question or request squarely and thus give no satisfaction to the person making the inquiry. Of course, it is not always possible to grant a request—thousands of requests that must be turned down are received by business firms every day. But actually saying no and avoiding the request entirely (as was done in the response to Mrs. Hamm) are two different things.

The fact that the letter to Mrs. Hamm was unsatisfactory is evidenced by the following letter she fired back to the publishing house—this time addressed to the president—along with the letter that she had received.

> Dear Mr. Marshall:
>
> Isn't this the height of something? The more I think of it, the angrier I become.
>
> In my letter, I asked whether I could buy a five-ring cover to replace my very worn one. I was not fishing for a free replacement. I was told you do replace "defective" ones but that you can do nothing for me because my book is now out of print. I knew it was out of print; I merely wanted something to hold the pages of my well-used cookbook together.
>
> I hate to bother a person in your position, but perhaps you would be able to furnish a satisfactory answer. Is it possible to buy such a cover, and if so, what would be its cost? And how would I go about ordering it?
>
> Very truly yours,

How would you have answered the letter from Mrs. Hamm if you had been Mr. Marshall? He decided that enough damage had been done by the incomplete explanation she had received previously and that a mere apology would not do the job. Here is the letter he wrote:

> Dear Mrs. Hamm:
>
> I am sending you a new Martha Johnson Picture Cookbook with my compliments. I realize, Mrs. Hamm, that this is not a completely satisfactory answer to your problem, since you obviously want the cookbook you now have but with a good binder. Because I can't find a binder that fits your book, this is the least I can do to prove that I am sorry I cannot be of more help to you.
>
> Perhaps this new edition, which is larger and more complete, will in time become just as valuable as the cookbook you are now using. I hope so.
>
> Sincerely yours,

GOING THE EXTRA MILE

We mentioned earlier that those who establish and maintain good human relationships are willing to extend themselves in order to be helpful. This means, of course, doing more than you really have to; and you will get many opportunities to go that extra mile. When customers complain about poor service or faulty merchandise, you search for explanations that will not only reassure the customers but also vindicate your company if possible. If you must say no to unreasonable requests, you offer reasons and possible alternatives. When questions are put to you that are outside your area of responsibility, you do all you can to find the answers.

Let's look at some examples of the "can-do" attitude.

Case Example 1: Elsa Maurat, manager of The Turntable Record Shop, received the following letter:

> Dear Ms. Maurat:
>
> During the past several months I have heard Aaron Copland's "Music From 'Our Town' " over a local FM station, and I am eager to have the recording. Unfortunately, none of the record shops in Broom County have it, nor can they find it in any catalog.
>
> Do you have a recording of this piece? If not, can you tell me how I can obtain one?
>
> Yours sincerely,

Unfortunately, the record referred to is not in stock, and no one in the record shop knows where it might be obtained. Because everybody is busy, there is a temptation to write a letter like this:

> Dear Mr. Kraft:
>
> I am sorry we do not have in stock the recording you asked about.
>
> Yours truly,

But if you want to win friends for the store and enhance the possibility of increasing its sales, you'll try to be more helpful, like this:

> Dear Mr. Kraft:
>
> I wish I could help you locate a recording of Aaron Copland's "Music From 'Our Town.' " Unfortunately, we do not have this recording in stock.
>
> I did find out that the recording was on the MGM label and went out of print about two years ago (it was part of an album, "Music From the Movies"). As far as I know, there are no plans to reissue this particular album.
>
> Have you tried the secondhand stores? Several carry a surprisingly large stock of old records, and many of our customers have picked up what they were looking for. In fact, Sullivan's, 416 Sheridan Road, Danville, has a good collection.
>
> Sincerely yours,

We can't say that every store or business can be as helpful to everyone who makes an inquiry, but if it is possible to respond at all, you won't need much extra time to extend yourself a bit.

Case Example 2: A college student is preparing a report and writes to a paper manufacturer to inquire about the booklet, *A Brief History of Papermaking in America,* which the firm published. The booklet is no longer in print, but that fact didn't prevent an administrative assistant from writing this helpful letter:

> Dear Ms. Kelly:
>
> Thank you for your interest in our booklet, A Brief History of Papermaking in America. We printed this piece several years ago and provided it free to thousands of schools and interested citizens. Unfortunately, our supply has long since been exhausted, and we have no plans to reissue the booklet.
>
> A couple of years ago, arrangements were made with Zion Press to use our material in a book they were publishing, The Romance of Paper. It is a paperback, and I believe it sells for about $3. You might try your local bookstore for a copy or write directly to the publisher—16 Oakwood Avenue, Fort Madison, Iowa 52627.
>
> Sincerely yours,

BREVITY VERSUS COMPLETENESS IN COMMUNICATIONS

Rarely is there any reason for a letter to exceed one page. Most letters can be cut about a third without suffering in meaning. The misconception therefore arises that short letters are the best letters. Not necessarily. In fact, brief letters can be harder to read than those that are too long.

Although brevity is a virtue when it means leaving out unnecessary words and phrases, irrelevant details, and muddled expressions, it is not a virtue when it interferes with the clarity or completeness of a communication.

If a furniture manufacturer has to tell a dealer that her order for a coffee table can't be filled because the company has discontinued a particular line, the objective of brevity could be accomplished with this letter:

> Dear Miss Meyer:
>
> We can't fill your order and are therefore canceling it. Sorry.
>
> Sincerely yours,

But this writer has left too many questions unanswered, the most important of which is "Why?" And the manufacturer has also passed up the opportunity to make or keep a friend—a friend who might be a customer for other products the company has to sell. Let's try again.

> Dear Miss Meyer:
>
> About six months ago we decided to discontinue our Conger red maple table line because most of our customers were not ordering it.

You can probably get the table you want, however, from the White Mountain Furniture Manufacturing Company, Plymouth, New Hampshire. At least they were able to fill a similar order I referred to them in November.

Good luck—and thanks for thinking of us!

Sincerely yours,

The second letter is longer, you will notice, but a lot more effective.

How long should a letter be? There is no better answer than "long enough to do the job it sets out to do." Some of the most successful sales letters written by *Esquire, Time,* and Haband (a mail-order clothing firm) have been four or five pages long. On the other hand, some very brief letters accomplish their mission in grand style. H. L. Mencken, the great literary figure, received many letters from people taking him to task about his newspaper and magazine articles on religion, women, politics, and other subjects. His answer to all these critics was very brief:

Dear Madam (or Sir):

You may be right.

H. L. Mencken

THE READER'S NAME AND TITLE

Someone has said that the sweetest music a person can hear is that sound of his or her own name. We might add, for the benefit of writers, that the most beautiful sight a person can see is his or her own name in print. But there is no music in a mispronounced name, and a misspelled or incorrectly typed name is offensive to the eye.

All of us want people to get our name right—and *right* means the way we like to see it. Everybody knows this simple fact; yet many people ignore it. When you make a mistake in a person's name, you are saying, to him or her at least, "Your name isn't important to me; therefore, *you're* not important to me."

A careless misspelling of someone's name can be forgiven if the receiver knows it's a typing error, such as *Lakw* for *Lake*. But it is not so easy to forgive misspellings that can't really be blamed on the typist: *Douglas* for *Douglass, Fisher* for *Fischer, Gunther* for *Gunter, Anderson* for *Andersen,* or *Thompson* for *Thomsen*. People are sensitive about their names, and although most of us are mature enough not to fume indefinitely about misspellings, we must all confess a certain disappointment when they occur. Indeed, a misspelled name, an incorrect job title, or the omission of a title of respect can start off a communication on the wrong foot.

Initials are important too. A man who likes to sign his name as *F. Donald Barnett* should be addressed that way—not as *Donald Barnett* or *Donald F. Barnett*. And if *Rebecca Finley Jones* signs all three names to her letter, she obviously expects to be addressed that way.

Watch, too, for the seemingly little things. *Lillie D'Asson* is not to be addressed as *Lillie Dasson*. The *O'Tooles, MacGregors* (or *McGregors*), *Van der Maarcks, von Hoffmans,* and *DeGrafs*—will want to see their name written exactly as *they* write it.

A man or woman who has worked hard to earn a doctorate, whether it is in medicine, science, or history, expects to be called *Doctor,* and Professor Brown likes to be addressed by that title. A sales manager who has just been promoted to marketing director winces every time he or she gets mail with the old title.

There are many ways to check on names and titles. Previous correspondence (the most recently received) is the best source. Then there are directories—telephone, business, and professional. If the correspondent is local or not far away, you can check the name and title by having your secretary telephone for accurate information. If you *know* you run a risk of being wrong, you can open your letter like this:

> Dear Mr. Rusmisel:
>
> I hope I have spelled your name correctly—this is the way the message was received by one of our telephone operators.

> ***Or:***

> Miss Purdue
> Lake Placid Supplies
> Lake Placid, New York
>
> Dear Miss Purdue:
>
> I'm sorry I did not learn your first name when you telephoned my office last week, and I hope you'll forgive this rather informal address.

TIMING OF COMMUNICATIONS

Executives often rant and rave at employees who don't answer their correspondence promptly. If you're dealing with customers or prospective customers, the reason for promptness is obvious—you want to prove your eagerness to have their business and to show your efficiency. Some firms try to enforce the rule, "Try to respond to all letters within 48 hours."

Generally, this is a good rule to keep in mind. All the writing skill in the world won't win or save customers whose letters go unanswered for long periods; and the well-organized correspondent sorts the material in the In box every day—maybe several times a day—to make sure that important correspondence gets priority attention. But even if you can't give a specific answer to the sender's questions or problems, because you don't have the information, you should acknowledge the letter and tell the sender when a reply can be given. Here is such a response:

> Dear Mrs. Krantz:
>
> Your request for information about Louis F. Foreman's employment here will be attended to just as quickly as possible. At the moment we are in the process of moving to a new building, and our personnel records are boxed for transfer.

We expect to be straightened out by the end of next week, at which time I will see that you get the information you need.

Sincerely yours,

The same type of response is appropriate for internal memos and reports that are delayed.

TO: Andrea Bardino   **FROM:** Fred Giles
SUBJECT: Space Needs   **DATE:** August 11, 19—

Just as soon as I received your memo of August 8, I began to talk to the department heads about their projected space needs for the next five years. They are now in the process of getting their figures together (a little complicated by the Ryerson acquisition), and I should have a full report for you by August 20.

There are situations, however, when a prompt response to a communication is *not* wise. For example, a person who lacks the necessary qualifications applies for a position or someone applies for a job that doesn't exist in your company; or an applicant for credit is sized up as a poor risk and must be told no; or an individual writes for special favors that will have to be denied; or an employee proposes sweeping changes in organization and procedure that are impracticable; and so on. In these situations, and similar ones where the respondent must convey disappointing news, it is often best to let the communication "season" a bit before replying to it. A quick response to such letters and reports is likely to produce the reaction, "They didn't even take the time to think about my request." Depending on the circumstances, a week or ten days may go by before a response is made, in which case the writer might begin the message in this manner:

Dear Mr. Harper:

I am late in responding to your letter of May 12 because I wanted to get all the background information necessary to evaluate your proposal intelligently . . .

GRAMMAR AND PUNCTUATION

Correct grammar and punctuation can be very important in achieving the favorable results you want from your communications. Poor grammar and punctuation can cloud your meaning and bewilder your reader, but equally important, they can destroy the reader's confidence in you and the company you represent. Whether we like it or not, educated people are offended when they see commas, periods, and other punctuation marks in the wrong place or missing entirely. They cringe when the subject and verb in a sentence are not in agreement, when participles dangle, when sentences are incomplete or run on, and so forth. The idea that it doesn't matter how you put your words together as long as people understand you has not been accepted in business.

One reason that errors in grammar and punctuation are frowned upon is that they distract the reader. Have you ever heard a speaker who, because of nervous mannerisms or slovenly posture or sloppy dress, diverted your attention so that you had trouble listening to what was said? See if you don't think poor grammar and punctuation in the following letter distract from the message.

Case Example: A member of the advertising staff of Berwyn Corporation writes to the director of a workshop, telling her who will attend and commenting on the program that is planned.

> Dear Ms. Grauer:
>
> I am delighted to tell you that everyone in our advertising department plan to attend the July workshop, in Columbus, some of them will be there for two days and others for all three. Sue Aiken our exhibit specialist will drive up with George Bok and I a day early to help us set up our display of point of sale posters.
>
> Concerning the program. We look forward to hearing Dr. Reinhart on research. He spoke at the Marshalltown conference a year ago and our people were unanamous in their praise saying "they would like to hear him again."
>
> Sincerely,

No doubt you discovered many mistakes, including a spelling error. Compare this revision:

> Dear Ms. Grauer:
>
> I am delighted to tell you that everyone in our advertising department plans to attend the July workshop in Columbus. Some of them will be there for two days and others for all three. Sue Aiken, our exhibit specialist, will drive up with George Bok and me a day early to help us set up our display of point-of-sale posters.
>
> Concerning the program, we are looking forward to hearing Dr. Reinhart on research. He spoke at the Marshalltown conference a year ago, and our people were unanimous in their praise, saying that they would like to hear him again.
>
> Sincerely,

Some prospective executives shrug off the importance of having strong language skills on the theory that they will have secretaries to polish the rough edges. Experienced executives will tell you, however, that not all secretaries are expert grammarians. Nor does every young executive have his or her own secretary; the newcomer often has to write communications in rough draft (or use a dictating machine), and the messages are transcribed exactly as they were written or dictated, with no "touch-up service."

If you feel insecure about your grammar, there is still time to do something about it. Several good self-study books are available at your library or bookstore. In addition, a good reference book (such as *The Gregg Reference Manual,* Fifth Edition, by William A. Sabin, Gregg Division, McGraw-Hill Book Company, New York, 1977) will also be very helpful. And on the job you can make it your business to study the communications of those who are skilled in business writing.

APPEARANCE

Some communications turn off readers because of their appearance. Poor typing (bad erasures, strikeovers, smudges), unbalanced margins, inconsistent spacing—all lessen your chances of making a favorable impression on the reader.

Case Example: The person to whom the following letter is addressed had sent a check for $8 to a magazine publisher for a subscription to a magazine. But the subscriber fogot to mention which magazine he wanted (the publisher issues several).

Dear Mr. Wright:

I'm sure if someone sent you a payment of $8 you'd want to know what it was for. So do we.

We received this among on 1/26/78 but allthough we have written to your twice, you have not as yettold us how to apply it. Apparrently it is intended for a subscription to Garden Week, but we have no openaccount fore that magazine in your name.

In the m antime, I fear we may be sending you bills...or that you are not getting a servicd to which you are intitled. So would you please let me know if your payment is to cover a bill..to enter a new subscription...to renew a subscription..or for any other purpose. MOST IMPORTANT; please tell us the exact mailing address.

Your prompt answer, jotted on this letter and returned in the enclosed envelop will be most welcome, Then we'll be able to straighten out the matter in a hurry.

Most cordially,

Sue Donahue

Sue Donahue
Circulation Credt

After reading the letter carefully, you will probably agree that the writer is capable of writing a good letter. The tone is pleasant enough; even though this is the third time Miss Donahue is writing to the addressee, she shows no irritation or anger. The writer obviously means well. Unfortunately, she could hardly have been more careless in attending to the important details of grammar, punctuation, and typing. Such imperfections insult the reader by implying that poor quality won't be recognized. (As a point of interest, because this letter was so carelessly written, the addressee sent it to an executive in Miss Donahue's company, a publishing house, with a bitter denunciation of the firm's correspondence standards. You can imagine the repercussions!)

Projects

(A) Rewrite the following so that each conveys a "you" emphasis.

1. We have just sent you several pieces of promotional literature, which we think will be effective for your back-to-school theme.
2. As we look at the calendar, we realize that there are only two weeks left in which dealers can take advantage of our special low prices on carpeting.
3. I noticed that you failed to sign the check in payment of Invoice 415-T, and I am returning it to you for that purpose.
4. We have spared no expense in designing these posters, and if they are properly used we think they will increase business.
5. I am especially interested in a job in advertising copywriting because this is where I have the most experience.

(B) The following letter was received by Edna Brower, manager of the Monkton Falls Furniture Store.

Dear Ms. Brower:

Can you please tell me how to remove stains from marble?

About six months ago I purchased a marble-top DuBois Coffee Table (Model 661) from your store, and recently I noticed that it was stained in several places—mostly rings left by glasses and cups. Although I have tried several cleaning fluids and detergents, nothing seems to work.

I would appreciate your advice.

Sincerely yours,

Mrs. Anna Klein

Here is the response Mrs. Klein received:

Dear Madam:

Re your inquiry regarding the removal of stains from marble, we are extremely sorry about this difficulty. As you perhaps have discovered, marble stains very easily and once the stains are allowed to penetrate, they are very difficult to remove—often impossible. People should be warned not to set wet glasses or cups on marble surfaces.

I am making inquiries about methods that may be used to remove the stains, and I will let you know when I have obtained the information. In the meantime, I am sending you a copy of Caring for Your Marble, which has been recently published. I believe it will be exceedingly helpful.

Yours truly,

Criticize the response to Mrs. Klein in terms of appropriateness and helpfulness. What would you have written?

(C) The Lorick Manufacturing Company manufactures air-conditioning and refrigeration equipment for industrial use only. Lorick's assistant marketing manager, Janice Lupo, received the following letter.

Dear Ms. Lupo:

I am building a beach house near Red Bank, New Jersey, which I am planning to air-condition throughout. Please send me full information on your air-conditioning systems.

Sincerely yours,

Here is the response that Ms. Lupo sent.

Dear Mr. Shuster:

Unfortunately, we do not distribute our products to individual consumers. We sell only to business and industrial users.

Thank you.

Very truly yours,

Rewrite the response, supplying whatever details you need to give Mr. Shuster the help he wants.

(D) The following letter was written to School and College Charms Inc. by the president of a college students' organization.

Dear Mr. Allenbough:

About a month ago I wrote for a free catalog, but I have not received it. I am particularly interested in the college pennant charm for William and Mary.

Is this charm available? If so, how much will it cost, including postage?

I would still appreciate having your catalog.

Very truly yours,

Here is the response as it was actually written (at the bottom of the student's letter).

```
Under sperate cover we are sending you a catalogue.  Please be
advised that we can give you a pennant with WM on it for William
and Mary.  If you want it in gold it will cost you $8.00 and 3.50
in sterling.  The pennant will be in color and the WM will be in
either gold or sterling according to  what you order it in.
```

Criticize the response and then prepare the one you would have written.

(E) Rewrite the letter at the top of page 44, eliminating the negative and accentuating the positive.

Dear Mrs. Lopez:

I am sorry to be so late in answering your inquiry about the availability of Monarch Cork-Prest bulletin boards, but because you addressed our Memphis office, your letter was delayed in reaching me. In the future, please address all such inquiries to the Neosho office, which serves your area.

The information you require is contained in a small catalog which I am sending you. Please read it carefully, and if you find that it does not contain the information you want, don't hesitate to write.

Yours very truly,

(F) Rewrite the following sentences, putting the messages in positive terms.

1. If you don't remit by August 14, you will not receive the 5 percent discount.
2. If the foregoing explanation is not clear and you feel that you need additional clarification, kindly advise.
3. We must know the exact size and color you desire in order to get your order to you by October 22.
4. Although I have no actual experience in writing advertising copy, my very thorough college training in advertising, plus my willingness to learn, leads me to believe I could handle your copy in a short time.
5. We cannot send the tarpaulin by parcel post as you requested since it is too bulky; instead, we are sending it by freight.
6. If, in the future, you will address your orders to this office instead of to the Racine office, you will not experience the delays that you complain about.
7. Because the building is over 40 years old, we could probably get no more than $75,000 for it.
8. Unfortunately, about 5 percent of our shipments in February were delayed because of a local transportation strike.
9. Are you handicapped in your business for lack of capital?
10. You may not have expected to hear from me, but I have been requested by Mr. Meell to answer the letter you wrote to him about our new discount policy.

(G) On January 12 Cynthia Noblett ordered 50 reprints of an article, "Mutual Funds and How They Work," which appeared in the February issue of *Financial Journal*. The reprints are for use in an investments course that Miss Noblett is teaching in a community college; the class begins February 16. It is now February 6, and there has been no response from *Financial Journal*. Here is Miss Noblett's follow-up letter.

Dear Mrs. Cohen:

The 50 imprints that I ordered have not been received, and I need them urgently. Please advise.

Sincerely yours,

Criticize the letter; then rewrite it, being careful to include everything you think the publisher should know.

 **(H)** Correct the errors in the following letter, which was sent by a furniture store chain to people who have just moved into the community.

Hello Neighbor!

As a newcomer to Cranbrook, we welcome you to this fine community. We know your going to enjoy living here.

Maxwell Furniture has served this community for over 50 years, we have three outlets—downtown Cranbrook, Park Village, and Ridgecrest. Each store fully stocked with the finest furniture for the most discriminating buyer.

If you will stop by one of our stores you will find a free gift waiting for you. To get your's you need only present this letter.

Cordially yours,

UNIT 4

MAKING YOURSELF UNDERSTOOD

"I must write with pains so that my reader may read with ease," said Robert Louis Stevenson. That's an important guide for business writers. Those who can put their ideas into crisp, clear language are much appreciated in business—not only by management but by everyone who has to do a lot of reading. So try to write so that busy people can read on the run with immediate understanding.

The best way to achieve immediate understanding is to choose words that readers are likely to be familiar with, comfortable with. Enemies of clear writing are big words, words that take up space but add no meaning, jargon, outmoded terms, and roundabout expressions.

BIGWORDISM

Most people believe that the size of a person's vocabulary is a measure of education—the larger the vocabulary, the better-educated that person is. We won't argue with that. We strongly recommend that you constantly strive to increase your word power. When you come across strange words in books, newspapers, and magazines, look them up and make them your own. If you are "word poor," you won't have much variety in your writing.

But don't use business communications to display your big vocabulary. You should know that business writers with the largest vocabularies are often the very same people whose communications are easiest and most interesting to read. They may know but would never use such show-off words as *bellicose* (hostile), *monition* (warning), *veridical* (truthful), *mansuetude* (meekness), *draconian* (cruel), *benignant* (gentle), or *synergic* (cooperating). Nor would they say "conflagration" when they mean *fire,* "edifice" for *building,* "expostulate" for *discuss,* "pedestrian" for *commonplace,* or "domicile" for *residence.* The best writers know that it is usually the simple, everyday word that expresses a thought most forcefully. Compare the examples that follow:

Precipitation in the Spanish region remains principally in vast, unwooded tracts.

(The rain in Spain stays mainly in the plain.)

Kindly extinguish the nocturnal illumination.

(Please turn off the light.)

Notice how much easier it is to read and quickly understand the examples in parentheses. So, when you can, choose the simple word over the showy word. (You won't always be able to do this. Sometimes there is no simple synonym for a showy word.) And don't be afraid to use two or three simple words in place of one showy word. Here are some examples:

Showy word	*Simpler*
cogitate	think
cognizant	aware
compensate	pay
comprehend	see, understand
comprise	make up
conjecture	guess
consummate	finish, complete
contemplate	consider
corroborate	confirm
deliberate	think about
disburse	pay out
increment	increase
initial	first
maximum	most, greatest
minimum	least
nominal	small
obviate	make unnecessary, prevent
originate	start, begin
proclivity	leaning
ratify	approve, confirm
rationale	basis
remunerate	pay
scrutinize	examine, inspect
transpire	happen
ultimate	final

Remember, though, that the shorter word isn't always simpler. For example, more people understand the word *beneficial* than the word *salutary*; the word *negligent* is more common than the word *derelict;* and *think* is usually a better word than *deem*.

And don't sacrifice precision. When you are trying to find a simple substitute for a big word, make sure it conveys the exact meaning you want. For example, if you are discussing salary administration, you will no doubt find the term *employee compensation* more appropriate than *employee pay*.

Some writers justify their use of big words by saying they can save space as well as the reader's time. But remember: Brevity is not a virtue when it is at the expense of completeness or clarity. We may save space, but we certainly don't save the reader's time, with a message like this:

> It is imperative, for reasons of product availability, that receiving personnel expedite delivery of all incoming shipments of merchandise to inventory.

Compare the above message with the one that follows.

> When we receive merchandise from our suppliers, let's not leave it lying around on the loading dock. It is important that we get those goods into the stockroom so that they can be sold.

DEADWOOD

A fault of many writers is that their communications are full of deadwood— words that occupy space but add nothing to meaning. For example:

> In the event that you can attend the meeting, plan in advance to offer some concrete suggestions on how to reduce the cost and expense of overtime in the Office Services Department.

Let's eliminate some of the deadwood.

In the event that. A roundabout expression. You can say the same thing with the word *If.*

plan in advance. The word *plan* is sufficient—*in advance* is deadwood since *planning* is something that is done *in advance.*

concrete suggestions. Why do suggestions have to be *concrete?*

cost and expense. Here the words *cost* and *expense* are redundant; since they mean the same thing, one is deadwood.

Now we can arrive at a simple, direct message that anybody can understand immediately. In this case, brevity *is* a virtue!

> If you can come to the meeting, plan to offer suggestions on how to cut overtime expense in the Office Services Department.

Roundabout Expressions. In the above example, we substituted the word *If* for the longer *In the event that* because *In the event that* is a roundabout expression—it uses more words than are needed to express an idea. Other examples are *It is my opinion that* for *I think* and *A large majority of the employees expressed the opinion* for *Most employees think*. Here is a list of some commonly used roundabout expressions:

Roundabout	Direct
we are at the present time	*we are* OR *we are now*
at this point in time	*now,* OR *today,* OR *at this point*
we are not in a position to	*we cannot* OR *we are unable to*
held a meeting	*met*
during the period of May 5 to May 12	*from May 5 to May 12*
during the time that	*during,* OR *while,* OR *when*
we seldom ever	*we seldom*
in the amount of $10	*$10* OR *for $10*
in view of the fact that	*since* OR *because*
in compliance with your request	Omit or say *as you requested* OR *here is the . . . .*
on or before September 30	*by September 30*
meets with our approval	*we agree* OR *we approve*
I regret to inform you that	*I'm sorry* OR *I regret*
I would like to call your attention to	*please note that*
due to the fact that	*because*
for your information	Omit; it says nothing.
subsequent to	*after*

Redundancies. Often, deadwood is simply words that say the same thing twice (such as *cost* and *expense* in the example on page 47). Even though redundancies are frequently seen in business and government writing, they only decrease the effectiveness of communications. Here are some examples of redundant expressions:

Redundant	Improved
attached hereto	attached
bank loan obligation	bank loan
basic essentials	essentials
big in size	big
budget forecast	budget OR forecast
consensus of opinion	consensus
dollar amounts	dollars OR amounts
gold in color	gold
irreducible minimum	minimum OR least
massively large	massive OR large
meet together	meet
prompt and speedy	prompt OR speedy
rules and regulations	rules OR regulations
substantial and significant	substantial OR significant
true facts	facts
vitally essential	vital OR essential

Try this experiment: The next time you write something, read it carefully to see how many deadwood words and phrases you can edit out.

Original

> In accordance with your request, attached herewith is the surplus inventory report. Included in the report is a valuation figure on each item, based on the FIFO method of inventory valuation.
>
> If you need more information, please don't hesitate to ask for it.

Edited

> ~~In accordance with your request, attached herewith~~ Here is the surplus inventory report. ~~Included in the report~~ you asked for, including ~~is~~ a FIFO valuation ~~figure~~ on each item~~,~~ ~~based on the FIFO~~ , Is there anything else I can do? ~~method of inventory valuation.~~
>
> ~~If you need more information, please don't hesitate to ask for it.~~

Final

> Here is the surplus inventory report you asked for, including a FIFO valuation on each item. Is there anything else I can do?

JARGON

Every area of work has its own technical terms, or jargon, which are perfectly clear to specialists in that area but which may be Greek to nearly everybody else. An accountant who is writing to another accountant can be almost certain that the reader will understand such terms as *monthly variance analyses, overhead control accounts,* and *ROI,* but if the writer is addressing, say, the factory superintendent, no such assumption can be made. Nor should the factory superintendent take for granted that the accountant will understand such terms as *wide span of control, the Flood method for job assignments,* and *economic lot units.* Even words that are fairly simple to you can bewilder a reader who does not hear them as often as you do. A loan agency correspondent wrote to a borrower about "the above-captioned loan," which drew the irate response: "Who captioned my loan and why?" Obviously, the word *captioned* was not understood (it referred to the loan number), and the borrower concluded that something bad had happened.

No matter where you work—personnel, finance, marketing, production, accounting, etc.—you will quickly pick up words that are the jargon of that field. As long as you are communicating with your colleagues, you're probably safe, but be very careful to avoid jargon when you write or talk to people outside your particular area of work.

VOGUE WORDS

Not long ago it became fashionable, especially in government circles, to tack the suffix *-wise* onto certain words—*businesswise, profitwise, policywise,* and so on. These very same people also like "ize" words—*optimize, maximize, definitize, finalize,* and *circularize.* These monstrosities not only do great harm to our language, but they obscure meaning. Compare the Federalese example shown below with the revised Plain English version that follows.

Federalese

> To optimize the utilization of the equipment available, it seems appropriate, both costwise and profitwise, to maximize the option of overtime.

Plain English

> I think it is a good idea, in terms of cost and profit, to make full use of this equipment, even if it means having our people work overtime.

Some words are fad words or buzzwords. A speaker or writer of national prominence uses a certain word, and people everywhere pick it up and start to use it to prove they are "in." Some of the current fad words are *viable, synergism, rhetoric* (for "hot-air oratory"), *rip-off, construct* (as a noun), *scenario, polarize, interface, in-depth* (study, interview, etc.), *dichotomy, dysfunctional, symbiotic, overkill, parameter, charisma,* and *cognitive.* Such words may be all right if the user is certain the reader or listener will understand them; but too often the words aren't understood—indeed, even the user may have only a vague idea of a word's meaning. Take the word *parameter,* for example. Many (perhaps most) people use it as a synonym for *perimeter,* which it is not.

Some people seem to work very hard to find words that hide what they really mean. Instead of putting something into effect or causing something to happen, they say *effectuate* or *actuate.* When something gets in the way of efficiency or works against an objective, it is *counterproductive.* Military personnel who guard our defense installations are said to have a *readiness posture.* Sociologists and educators like to speak of a conversation as *information transfer.* And business and government people like to tack *situation* onto statements, presumably for emphasis: *a high employee turnover situation, an economic recession situation,* and *a surplus inventory situation.*

HORSE-AND-BUGGY WRITING

Every bit as bad as using terms that are too mod is using terms that are as dated as the horse and buggy and high-button shoes.

My dear Sir:

Yours of the first received and contents duly noted. In reply would state that as per agreement the undersigned agrees to perform indicated services in accordance with prior instructions.

Thanking you for past favors, I remain,

Yours truly,

Would you ever write such a message? Of course not. But many people still cling to the "grand style" of the horse-and-buggy era. Wouldn't you write the message this way?

Dear Paul:

I was glad to have your letter and to know that we've come to an agreement. You can count on our living up to our part of the bargain.

Thank you for giving us this chance to work with you.

Sincerely,

Following are a few of the horse-and-buggy expressions that are still with us. Use their up-to-date replacements to keep your messages clear and direct.

Horse-and-Buggy	Up-to-Date
advise	tell
at hand	I have
beg to advise, state, suggest, etc.	Omit.
favor us with a reply	please write
has come to hand	has arrived
hereby advise	Omit.
herewith rendered	here is
I deem	I think
I seek your kind indulgence	I hope you understand
in due course	by next Monday
kindly	please
order has gone forward	order was sent
under date of	July 12
under separate cover	separately
up to this writing	until now
with your kind permission	may I
your kind (OR esteemed) favor	your letter

CLICHÉS

A cliché, as you know, is a phrase or expression that has been worn out through overuse. Following are some of the most common clichés:

neat as a pin	clean as a whistle
pure as the driven snow	poor as a church mouse
good as gold	Old Man Winter
light as a feather	abreast of the times
checkered career	sadder but wiser
staff of life (bread)	Father Time
Mother Nature	crack of dawn
bolt from the blue	beat a hasty retreat
herculean effort	goes without saying
reigns supreme	sigh of relief
easier said than done	green with envy
the worse for wear	wee small hours
Founding Father	burning issues
troubled times	clear as day

And of course there are hundreds more. The trouble with such expressions is that they mark the writer as unimaginative, verbally lazy. But even more important, because the reader or listener has been exposed so often to these tired expressions, they have little, if any, impact. Avoid them. When a phrase or expression comes to you automatically, you should strongly suspect that it is a cliché. For example, if you are tempted to say, "I view with alarm the rapid increase in manufacturing costs," stop right there. "View with alarm" is a cliché. How about this: "The increased manufacturing costs are playing havoc with our pricing formula"? That won't be much of an improvement because "playing havoc" is also a cliché. So you have to reach— and it isn't always easy. You might come up with something like this: "Manufacturing costs are rising so fast that we've got to change our pricing formula if we expect our usual 48 percent margin." Not sparkling, to be sure, but original.

SLANG

There is no question but that slang has enriched our language. "Right on," "cool it," "tell it like it is," "uptight," "nitty gritty," "hang-up," and "no way" (for "certainly not") are examples of current slang, and new slang expressions enter the language constantly. But slang is better spoken than written, and you're better off avoiding it—even in written communications to close business associates. To many people, slang sounds impertinent and juvenile. Imagine telling a customer, in response to an order that your firm cannot fill, that that particular product is not your "bag"!

OTHER WRITING FAULTS THAT FOIL YOUR PURPOSE

In addition to bigwordism, deadwood, jargon, vogue words, outmoded words, and clichés, some writers are guilty of other faults that hinder their effectiveness. These faults—exaggeration, excessive modesty, sarcasm, talking down, lecturing, euphemisms, and negative words—have a direct bearing on your ability to build and keep a rapport with your reader.

Exaggeration. The regional marketing director meets the vice president in the corridor and rushes jubilantly up to him. "Frank, I've just seen the March sales figures for my region, and they're fabulous!" The remark is accepted for what it is—an impromptu burst of enthusiasm. In writing, however, the word *fabulous,* which means "incredible," would seem irresponsible. Thus in a written report the marketing director would temper his enthusiasm and might start off like this: "We had a healthy sales gain in March—20 percent over last year."

In our hard-sell society we are accustomed to such terms as *a fabulous selection, sensational styling, dramatic advancement, dynamic achievement, unmatched performance, incredibly low-priced, unbeatable deal, revolutionary breakthrough, terrific values, unique* (or the illiterate "most unique") *features, tremendous savings, unbelievable bargains, once-in-a-lifetime opportunity,* and *fantastic offer.* And we have learned to live with such superlatives as *most exciting, most unusual, most beautiful, most impressive,* and so on. When we *hear* these terms, we quickly dismiss them as "sales puff" and let them slide by. But when they are used in written communications, they destroy credibility.

Closely related to exaggerations like the ones mentioned above is the use of *more than* for emphasis:

> We are *more than happy* to refund your money. (Ecstatic?)
>
> I am *more than willing* to do my share. (Stubbornly determined?)
>
> I shall be *more than grateful* for your support. (Humbled?)
>
> Rankin's is *more than concerned* about the delay. (Distraught?)

Another form of exaggeration is flattery. While some flattery is all right—in expressing appreciation, bestowing a compliment, offering congratulations, and so on—it can be overdone.

Expressing Appreciation

Overdone

> No one is more aware than I am of the tremendous sacrifices you made to complete construction of the Benton warehouse on time, Phil. Without your unflagging efforts and strong determination, that impossible date of May 1 would have been just a dream. Thanks to you and your wonderful colleagues, the dream became reality.

Revised

> All of us are grateful to you and your colleagues for giving our Benton warehouse top priority and meeting the very tight May 1 deadline. The Grand Opening came off very nicely, and we thank you for making it possible.

Bestowing a Compliment

Overdone

The success of the Materials Handling Seminar is a tribute to your genius as an organizer, speaker, and moderator. Everything came off magnificently, and only you could have done it.

Revised

I want to compliment you on the success of the Materials Handling Seminar. The programs were excellent, and I feel sure that everyone who attended came away as pleased as I was about the whole affair.

Offering Congratulations

Overdone

Your selection as president of the Society of Credit Managers for the coming year is a signal honor, Carolyn, and I couldn't have been more pleased to see this recognition of your imagination, dedication, and talent. Surely the Society is on the threshold of its greatest year ever.

Revised

I think the Society of Credit Managers chose well when they made you president for the coming year, and I congratulate not only you on this achievement but the officers for their good judgment. I predict that you will bring strong leadership to that organization.

Another form of exaggeration is the overstatement. For example:

Believe me, Ms. Forbes, such an error will not happen again. (The promise of perfection is hazardous; all too often, the same mistake *will* occur.)

Come in, and you'll see: A-1 Supermarket bags everything for less. (A catchy slogan, but in all probability untrue.)

Everyone stands ready at all times to make your shopping at Kahn's a thoroughly delightful and long-remembered experience. (Perhaps, but highly unlikely.)

Nothing is more important to Lipman's than a satisfied customer. (Not even a healthy net profit on operations?)

Everything that can be done will be done to guarantee your entire satisfaction. (Rubbish. How about pricing the merchandise or service below cost?)

Our greatest asset is our reservoir of dedicated, happy employees. (A nice thought if the management really believes it and conducts its affairs accordingly, but more often than not it is a homily.)

The success of our enterprise depends on customers like you. (True, to a certain extent; but success also depends on good management, favorable economic conditions, etc.)

When you say Budweiser, you've said it all.

And:

When you're out of Schlitz, you're out of beer.
(Somebody here is exaggerating.)

Excessive Modesty.   We have talked about the danger of coming on too strong in business communications—with exaggeration, effusiveness, and so on. At the other extreme is the self-put-down, which is just as bad. There is nothing wrong with humility (some braggarts could use a sizable dose of it), but too much humility can give your communications a phony ring. For example:

> In a large firm such as Tyndall Corporation, you probably don't have time to deal with my particular problem, but . . .

> I am not an accountant; therefore, my proposal for a new stock control system may seem a little ridiculous. However . . .

> I appreciate your nice comments about my presentation at the Suggestion Committee meeting. As you probably noticed, I am very uncomfortable in front of an audience . . .

> You might wonder what right I, as a relative newcomer, have to suggest a different orientation procedure . . .

> Forgive me for intruding on your time, but I have an idea for . . .

> I realize that my lack of experience as a programmer is a strike against me, but I think I could learn . . .

> Your preeminence in the field of public relations makes it awkward for me to venture a recommendation. Yet . . .

Sarcasm.   As mentioned earlier, sometimes in business situations our patience wears so thin that we are tempted to let someone "have it." But use the hard line only when you have exhausted every other alternative in trying to solve a difficult problem. Certainly you won't solve it by making sarcastic statements such as:

> Congratulations! This is the fifth month in a row that you have gone below your production quota. This must be a new record.

> Am I reading your company slogan, "Where Service Comes First," correctly?

> Sales figures for September show an industrywide growth of 10 percent. Our 12½ percent decline makes the other fellows look pretty silly, doesn't it?

> Who else but Walton's could manage to substitute 25 boxes of stenographers' notebooks for the accounting pads we ordered!

> Has it occurred to you that we are in business to make a profit?

> Apparently, some great brain there assumed that we use overhead conveyor equipment in our Manhattan offices instead of in the Newark warehouse.

Talking Down.   Another way to irritate readers and foil the purpose of your message is to talk down to them. Examples are given on the next page.

When you have been in the business as long as we have, you will learn that . . .

It seems unlikely that the mistake could have occurred at this end. Our insistence on the highest standards of quality control assures the efficient . . .

As large and successful as we are, we make no distinction between small customers, such as you, and giant corporations.

It is natural that you should assume that because of our position in the industry, we are insensitive to suggestions for improving our products and services. However . . .

I appreciate your efforts to research material for my "Trends in Fringe Benefits" article, Sara—even more so when I realize this is not your forte.

Lecturing. Some writers can't resist the temptation to lecture their readers—subordinates, customers, suppliers, and others. Beware of such preachments as these:

I am sure it is obvious to you that we . . .

Surely you know that . . .

You should be able to understand that . . .

For best results, you should . . .

Obviously, if you want to achieve growth you can't afford to . . .

It should be no surprise to you that without a profit we couldn't stay in business.

And avoid statements that tend to insult the reader's intelligence:

It is important to your business to attract and hold customers.

With spring coming on, you will be getting requests for grass seed and fertilizer.

You want to get the most from every dollar you spend for advertising.

The reputation of your business is very important.

Employee morale is difficult to measure.

A productive work force is a happy work force.

When expenses exceed income, there's no profit.

Insinuations and Accusations. Another way to enrage your readers and destroy your rapport with them is to make insinuations and accusations.

You claim that these electronic parts left your warehouse in perfect condition. (*You claim* is an insinuation that the reader is not telling the truth.)

It is hard to believe that your *Encyclopedia of Mayan Art* could be, as you put it, "coming apart at the binding." (*It is hard to believe* insinuates that the reader is stretching the truth. Too, the phrase *as you put it* is an obvious attempt to ridicule the customer.)

It is surprising to me that you did not understand the terms of our agreement. (The writer is saying, in effect, what are you trying to pull?)

You say that you did not receive any of our previous statements, and I am at a loss to understand why. (*You say* is another insulting insinuation.)

You neglected to sign the second and third copies of the contract. (Instead of saying *You neglected to,* why not say this: "You will see that the second and third copies of the contract were not signed. Would you please sign them and . . .")

It seems to me that the fair thing for you to do is to pay all crating and shipping costs. (An intimation that the recipient of the message is contemplating an unfair act.)

The packaging protection for our clocks is certainly adequate for ordinary handling, as our many customers will attest. (A veiled accusation that this particular customer was careless.)

Projects

 Rewrite the following in simple, easy-to-understand language.

1. In a subsequent memo, we will evaluate the relative desirability of various and sundry investments in effectuating the overall objectives of the company.
2. It is apparent and obvious, therefore, that sound knowledge of letter composition and cultivation of the accurate thinking by which it must be accompanied should constitute an exceedingly worthwhile accomplishment.
3. Verification that functional requirements of products are satisfied at minimal cost is established by design value reviews prior to final engineering release.
4. A number of business decisions are capable of easier resolution as a consequence of advance cost estimates.
5. Many top-management groups seek to inject more incentive into pay practices by gearing increases to differences in performance.
6. Business failure itself is an everyday occurrence in our country.
7. The two most important considerations in determining the internal communications system or systems that will be most appropriate for a given organization are speed and cost.
8. Mere availability of potential statistical method has not led automatically to practical applications.
9. What is the receptivity of the organization to change?
10. Clear-cut job descriptions, preferably in writing, for all supervisory personnel are indispensable to manager development.

B Reduce the number of words in each of the following, at the same time making each statement clearer and more to the point.

1. We are making this analysis for the purpose of providing a basis for improving the sales picture.
2. In the majority of instances, we ship goods to our customers under a c.o.d. arrangement.
3. In view of the foregoing facts and figures, it seems appropriate to suggest an entirely new customer service policy.

4. I have your letter of September 14 before me and am happy to tell you that we will be able to supply the uniforms you want in the colors and sizes you requested in your letter.
5. Would it be possible, do you think, for you to engage the Crown Room for our use as the meeting place of our task force on May 19?
6. It is the consensus of opinion of our Personnel Relations Committee that work stoppages would decrease impressively and substantially if the equipment were kept in constant and complete repair.
7. Are you sending the invitations out in the mail in plenty of time so that those who are being invited will have sufficient advance notice in which to respond?
8. The accountants in our department individually and collectively agree with the decision arrived at to cease and desist the practice of amortizing product-development costs over a five-year period.
9. The regional managers held a meeting for the purpose of discussing the distribution of sales territories in the various geographical areas.
10. Mr. Collard gave a talk on the growing increase in the popularity of bonus compensation systems for personnel in management positions.

C Suggest one or two words that can be substituted for each of the following expressions. Indicate whether the expression can be omitted altogether.

1. in regard to **OR** in reference to
2. along the lines of
3. due to the fact **OR** for the reason that
4. in favor of
5. in order to
6. in the majority of instances
7. in the neighborhood of
8. in view of the above
9. on behalf of
10. Hoping to hear from you, I remain
11. with the exception of
12. attached (**OR** enclosed) please find
13. enclosed herewith
14. continued patronage
15. I have your letter
16. subsequent to
17. taking the liberty of
18. would like to state (and all the would-like-to's and wish-to's)

D Tell why each of the following expressions is redundant.

1. new innovations
2. absolutely necessary
3. ask the question
4. consensus of opinion
5. enclosed you will find
6. necessary requirements
7. other alternative
8. reasonable and fair
9. temporarily suspended
10. totally unnecessary

E Study the following; then rewrite each, removing unnecessary words. In some cases, you may wish to substitute a different term.

1. exactly identical
2. basic fundamentals
3. connect up
4. free gratis
5. repeat back
6. past experience
7. four in number
8. at a distance of 40 miles

9. at a price of $175
10. the color of the Gizmo is dark green
11. round in shape
12. throughout the entire year
13. during the year of 19—
14. came at a time when
15. if it is possible, please
16. the reason is due to
17. in view of
18. according to our records
19. at all times
20. during the time that
21. held a meeting
22. in this day and age
23. made the announcement
24. at an early date
25. due to the fact that
26. a substantial number of people are of the opinion
27. fully cognizant of
28. encounter difficulty in

(F) Can you think of a simpler word for each of the following? (For some, you may need more than one word.)

1. acquiesce
2. aggregate
3. apparent
4. approximately
5. ascertain
6. assist
7. commensurate with
8. communicate with
9. conclusion
10. construct
11. demonstrate
12. difficult

13. discrepancy
14. disseminate
15. equitable
16. equivalent
17. expiration
18. initiate
19. inquire
20. interrogate
21. modification
22. permit
23. preclude
24. predisposed

25. previous to
26. procure
27. provided
28. purchase
29. render
30. submitted
31. subsequent to
32. sufficient
33. terminated
34. transmitted
35. utilization
36. verification

(G) Rewrite the following letter, using today's language.

Dear Madam:

Yours of February 1st at hand and contents noted. In reply would wish to state that your order for 20 Executive Desk Planners will be shipped to you in due course. It is anticipated that you will have receipt by February 11 or at an earlier date; if not, I beg your indulgence.

In this connection, would state that you will be billed at the price of $3.20 each, less trade discount of 30 percent. Hoping this is satisfactory and thanking you in advance for your esteemed patronage, I remain,

Yours truly,

(H) Rewrite the following cliché-ridden message.

The staff made a herculean effort to finish the inventory by January 3, but it was not in the cards—too many unforeseen difficulties. It goes without saying that we will leave no stone unturned to see that the job is done by January 5, even if it means working into the wee small hours.

I The writer of the letter that follows overdid it when he acknowledged a big order that a good friend and customer placed at the end of the year. Rewrite it so that it is more believable.

Dear Wally:

That was a really sensational order you just gave us, Wally. $46,000—wow! We are more than grateful for this fantastic business, friend. Thanks to you, we're going to have an incredible year, and everybody's rushing out to buy the biggest Thanksgiving turkey around.

Gracias, amigo!

Very sincerely,

J Rewrite the following so that they are free of excessive modesty, sarcasm, preachments, and insinuations.

1. I realize that I am not a systems expert, but perhaps you will allow me to venture some suggestions about simplifying the receiver report form.
2. When will you understand that we are Harrelson's—not Harrison's? We received their statement again, and presumably they received ours.
3. It is quite unlikely that the cartons were damaged when they left our warehouse. Our rigid inspection standards were designed to prevent this kind of thing from happening.
4. I was amazed to learn that you received only 36 copies instead of the 48 we sent you.
5. You say that you reported this difficulty to our representative on several different occasions. This seems strange, since we can find no record of any kind.

UNIT 5

KEEPING YOUR READER WITH YOU

Business writers always have to be conscious of time—the reader's time. Letters and reports should be constructed so that the reader can grasp the message quickly—on the run, so to speak—and with full understanding. Yet business writers want to make their communications so persuasive that the reader will think, feel, or do as the writers intend.

This is quite an order, and since it may be hard to dictate or write exactly what you want to say the first time, be prepared to rewrite. Even veteran writers often redo an especially important letter, memo, or report several times before they are satisfied with it.

If you dictate your communications, you may find it wise to ask for a typewritten draft first, double- or tripled-spaced so that you can make changes. Or you may prefer to write your message on a ruled pad and rethink it before you release it for typing. This may sound like a waste of time for both you and the secretary, but it can be much more efficient than allowing the material to be transcribed in "final" form and then deciding to change it.

In this unit we will emphasize some of the principles of construction that you will need to master if you are to keep your reader with you.

SENTENCES

If words are the individual components of a communication, then the sentence is the motor. A business message has power only when its sentences are clear, correct, of appropriate length, and properly structured for maximum impact.

Sentence Length.   Probably no other single writing fault hinders readability so much as the long, rambling sentence.

> Because of our limited warehousing facilities, we are studying the possibility of contracting with public warehouses, of which there are several in this area, that offer storage and handling facilities, charging their customers only for the space occupied by the goods and for the time during which the space is occupied.

The above sentence contains 51 words. With only slight adjustments in wording, we can make the author's ideas much easier to grasp:

> Because of our limited warehousing facilities, we are studying the possibility of using public warehouses. Several in this area offer storage and handling services. Most charge only for the cubic space occupied and the time the goods remain in storage.

There are no rigid rules about sentence length, although we recommend that you try to keep most of your sentences under 20 words—17 is average.

Of course we don't mean that every sentence should be 17 words long. Such a pattern would get pretty monotonous. Some sentences may be 20 + words in length, some 11 or 12, and some even 3 or 4. Just remember this: Look for ways to break up longer sentences. It is very easy to do.

> One of the greatest advantages of the photocopier lies in its ability to make reduced and enlarged copies, but it has disadvantages, too, such as its bulkiness in terms of space required and possible high cost if its use is not strictly programmed.

A period following the word *copies* will improve readability greatly. But by breaking up the second sentence and doing a little editing, we can make the ideas much more forceful, as shown at the top of page 62.

One of the greatest advantages of the photocopier is its ability to make reduced and enlarged copies. But it has disadvantages too. For one thing, the equipment is bulky and takes up space. Also, the process can be costly if its use is not strictly programmed.

Often, a long sentence can be simplified by breaking down the thoughts into a list. For example, read the following paragraph:

The drawbacks of combination compensation plans for salespeople are that they are more complex, require more time to invent, are harder to administer, are more difficult for people to understand, and are often felt to be unwieldy. Certainly they require constant review.

Now see what happens when the main ideas in this paragraph are enumerated as follows:

The drawbacks of combination compensation plans for salespeople are that they:

1. Are more complex.
2. Require more time to invent.
3. Are harder to administer.
4. Are more difficult for people to understand.
5. Are often felt to be unwieldy.

Certainly, such plans require constant review.

Occasional very short sentences can be highly effective. It is said, for example, that the most powerful sentence in the English language is "Jesus wept." And grammatically incomplete, short statements (called elliptical expressions) can occasionally be used with good results.

We certainly can, Miss Nottenberg.

We promise—October 3 at the latest.

Mail it today. Please.

I agree.

When?

Right!

When you use too many short sentences or elliptical expressions, however, your message becomes choppy and disconnected.

Dear Mrs. Talbot:

The error in your June statement was ours. No question about it! A corrected statement is enclosed. Your records and ours agree. Thank you. We appreciate your help.

Sincerely,

This is better:

Dear Mrs. Talbot:

You are right—the error in your June statement is indeed ours. Enclosed is a corrected statement, which brings our record into agreement with yours.

Thank you!

Sincerely,

Sentence Connectors.   The skillful business writer takes readers by the hand and leads them carefully from one thought to another—that is, from sentence to sentence from paragraph to paragraph—never turning loose of the hand. One way to make sure your reader is always with you is to use *transitional expressions*. Transitional expressions are words that help to link your thoughts together. If you don't supply them, your readers will have to think about where you're taking them. Not only does this take up valuable time but also it increases the risk of misunderstanding.

In the following two paragraphs, the writer has not connected the sentences. Note how difficult it is to understand what she is trying to say.

Most personnel managers think supervisors should show employees their merit ratings. There are several reasons why this is a good idea. Many supervisors resist showing employees their ratings when the ratings are unfavorable. They are put on the defensive. They also dislike confrontation with vocal employees. When the supervisor can show that the worker has been carefully rated on each facet of the job and can point out specifically where the worker has fallen down, the supervisor can use this conference as an instructional medium.

When management is trying to get an appraisal of the relative value of several persons for possible promotion, a more impartial picture is likely to be presented if the supervisor does not have to defend the ratings given the employees. It may be even better to have a collective rating of those being considered—a rating from the immediate supervisor, the department manager, and a representative of the personnel staff.

Now let's try that same message, this time with transitional expressions.

Most personnel managers think supervisors should show employees their merit ratings. There are several reasons why this is a good idea. *However,* many supervisors resist showing employees their ratings when the ratings are unfavorable. *One reason is* that they are put on the defensive; *furthermore,* they dislike confrontations with vocal employees. *Yet* when the supervisor can show that the worker has been carefully rated on each facet of the job and can point out specifically where the worker has fallen down, the supervisor can use this conference as an instructional medium.

On the other hand, when management is trying to get an appraisal of the relative value of several persons for possible promotion, a more impartial picture is likely to be presented if the supervisor does not have to defend the ratings given the employees. *Thus* it may be even better to have a collective rating of those being considered—*for example,* a rating from the immediate supervisor, the department manager, and a representative of the personnel staff.

Do you see how the italicized words help to guide the reader from sentence to sentence and from paragraph to paragraph? There are many transitional expressions that will help to keep your reader with you. Following are some of the most common ones.

To Add Something to What Has Been Said

also, besides, further, furthermore, in addition, in other words, moreover, too, what is more

Example: Such a reorganization will reduce costs by about 50 percent; *moreover,* it will increase efficiency.

To Show Cause or Effect

accordingly, as a result, consequently, hence, therefore

Example: The results of the employee survey indicate a strong preference for biweekly pay periods; *therefore,* this policy will go into effect on July 1.

To Show Exceptions to What Has Been Said

but, conversely, even so, however, nevertheless, on the contrary, on the other hand, otherwise

Example: The availability of skilled labor makes Pineville attractive as a possible location. *However,* water and electric power in that community appear to be inadequate for our needs.

To Indicate Time, Place, or Order in Relation to What Has Gone Before

above all, after all, again, finally, first, further, in summary, meanwhile, next, still, then, too

Example: I don't think we need to be sensitive about canceling the contract with Hobbs Associates; *after all,* they have been given numerous opportunities to perform. *Meanwhile,* we are losing valuable promotion time.

To Introduce Examples

for example, for instance, namely, that is

Example: The salespeople gave several good ideas for livening up our exhibit at the Business Show—*for example,* films showing how our products are made.

Sentence Faults.   Several types of sentence faults can trip the unwary writer and lose the reader. These include putting in more than one thought, fragments, run-ons, imbalance in construction, errors in singulars and plurals, omission of words, and dangling modifiers.

More Than One Thought.   Make certain that you separate distinct ideas into separate sentences, as in the "stronger" sentences below.

Weak: Thank you for sending a corrected invoice, and our check for payment is enclosed.

Stronger: Thank you for sending a corrected invoice. Our check for payment is enclosed.

Weak: We appreciate your comments on the new displays, and we hope you will let us know what results you get from them.

Stronger: We appreciate your comments on the new displays. Please let us know what results you get from them.

Weak: After bringing down the new balances on the stock cards, I made spot checks against actual merchandise in the warehouse, and I found all of them in agreement.

Stronger: After bringing down the new balances on the stock cards, I made spot checks against actual merchandise in the warehouse. I found all of them in agreement.

Weak: One of the advantages of the salary plan as compared with the straight commission plan is that sales representatives can be held directly responsible for results, and also the representatives can more easily identify with the company.

Stronger: One of the advantages of the salary plan as compared with the straight commission plan is that sales representatives can be held directly responsible for results. Another is that the representatives can more easily identify with the company.

Fragments.   In general, each sentence should be able to stand on its own—that is, it should make sense without leaning on what has gone before.

The committee agreed to postpone a decision until its next meeting. Which will probably be held in September.

As you can see, "Which will probably be held in September," is not a complete sentence (it has no subject). The solution here is simply to use a comma instead of a period after "meeting." Or the writer could have used two sentences:

The committee agreed to postpone a decision until its next meeting. This meeting will probably take place in September.

There are times, however, when a sentence fragment is perfectly all right. In fact, sometimes it can have more power than a complete sentence. Some examples follow.

You'll want to be among the first to sign up for this unusual service. Why not right now?

The most-frequently mentioned criticism of our annual report is that it is almost impossible to understand. Amen!

Some employees even think we have too many holidays. Not many, to be sure, but a few.

We ought to get started on this research as quickly as possible. Next week?

So much for plant costs. What about general overhead?

If you will send us your invoice, we will make payment promptly. In triplicate, please.

Run-Ons. Run-on sentences are just the opposite of sentence fragments. The writer of a sentence fragment stops too soon; the writer of a run-on sentence doesn't stop soon enough. Note the different ways in which you can correct run-on sentences.

Run-on: We will add two new parking lots this year, the third will be added next year.

Correct: We will add two new parking lots this year. The third will be added next year.

Or: Two new parking lots will be added this year, but the third will have to wait until next year.

Or: Although we will add two new parking lots this year, the third will have to wait until next year.

Run-on: I will ship the cabinets this week, in the meantime, I am back-ordering the tables.

Correct: I will ship the cabinets this week. In the meantime, I am back-ordering the tables.

Or: I will ship the cabinets this week and, at the same time, back-order the tables.

Or: Although I can ship the cabinets this week, the tables will have to be back-ordered.

Imbalance.   If you want to write clear, forceful sentences, make sure that the parts are balanced.

Wrong: The new advertisements *reduced* inquiries rather than *increasing* them.

Right: The new advertisements *reduced* inquiries rather than *increased* them.

Wrong: We expect to *exhibit* in Milwaukee as well as *exhibiting* in St. Paul.

Right: We expect to exhibit in Milwaukee as well as in St. Paul.

Wrong: They are *not only* anxious to make *these panels* for us *but also in making* the hardware as well.

Right: They are anxious to make *not only these panels* for us *but also the hardware*.

Errors in Singulars and Plurals. Although you can use singulars and plurals in the same sentence, make sure you don't mix them.

Wrong: Both retirees will receive a gold watch.

Right: Both retirees will receive gold watches.

Or: Each retiree will receive a gold watch.

Wrong: Every sales representative should have their own income and expense budget.

Right: Every sales representative should have his or her own income and expense budget.

Or: All sales representatives should have their own income and expense budgets.

Wrong: I was pleased to have a report from both you and Ms. Steinkraus.

Right: I was pleased to have reports from both you and Ms. Steinkraus.

Omission of Words. A common fault is the omission of certain words.

Wrong: This $15 calculator is as good, if not better than, the $50 one.

Right: This $15 calculator is as good *as,* if not better than, the $50 one.

Or: This $15 calculator is as good as the $50 one, if not better.

Wrong: Representative Atkins made more calls last month than any salesperson.

Right: Representative Atkins made more calls last month than any *other* salesperson.

Wrong: The programmers had little knowledge and sympathy for the proposed changes.

Right: The programmers had little knowledge *of* and sympathy for the proposed changes.

Wrong: The walkways have been repaired and the sign replaced.

Right: The walkways have been repaired and the sign *has* been replaced.

Dangling Modifiers. The dangling modifier is an all-too-common error in sentence structure. Look at these examples:

Wrong: After having written three collection letters, the customer finally paid his account in full. (In this sentence, it appears that the customer wrote collection letters to himself. Obviously, he did not.)

Right: After having written three collection letters, *I* finally received full payment from the customer.

Wrong: In order to become a top accountant, accruals and deferrals must be thoroughly understood. (Here, one would think that accruals and deferrals aspire to become top accountants.)

Right: In order to become a top accountant, *you* must understand accruals and deferrals thoroughly.

Wrong: Upon entering the building, the smoke blinded me. (The writer, not the smoke, opened the door and entered the building.)

Right: Upon entering the building, *I* was blinded by smoke.

PARAGRAPHS

Each paragraph you write should have one purpose—no more—and each sentence in the paragraph should contribute to the accomplishment of that purpose.

Automatic typewriters are ideal for limited reproduction, especially of letters that are being sent outside the company. Since each letter is individually typed, the effect is highly personal. Automatic typewriters are commonly used for "form" correspondence—that is, for letters that are identical in content. The letterhead is inserted into the typewriter, and the operator types in the name and address. After this is done, the machine takes over and automatically types the body of the letter, stopping at predetermined points for insertion of special data. The mechanism is usually controlled by either a perforated record roll or a perforated paper tape.

In the example above, the writer has combined two distinct thoughts: uses of the automatic typewriter and how it works. The description would have been more readable, however, if the writer had stopped at "that are identical in content" and started a new paragraph with "The letterhead is inserted . . . ."

If you have ever been reluctant to start a book because the first few pages were entirely descriptive, with no dialogue or paragraphing, then you know how important it is to give your reader a visual breather. Solid blocks of type are hurdles for any reader, and you should look for ways to break up long passages.

Here is another example:

Some dictators simplify their planning by sorting incoming correspondence according to some particular plan—for example, by subject matter. All letters that pertain to one topic are dictated before the dictator moves on to another topic. These writers say that separating the correspondence by subject matter improves their concentration and enables them to achieve the proper mood for each particular type of letter. Other successful dictators prefer to sort their correspondence according to difficulty. Some take the easy ones first; others, the tougher ones. There seems to be no hard-and-fast rule about this. And still a third method of sorting mail to be attended to is according to urgency—the most pressing items first, regardless of subject matter or level of difficulty. Executives who are frequently interrupted in their dictation maintain that this type of sorting is a must.

The writer of the above has put three distinct ideas in the same paragraph. Notice how much easier the material is to read when it is properly paragraphed.

Some dictators simplify their planning by sorting incoming correspondence according to some particular plan—for example, by subject matter. All letters that pertain to one topic are dictated before the dictator moves on to another topic. These writers say that separating the correspondence by subject matter improves their concentration and enables them to achieve the proper mood for each particular type of letter.

Other successful dictators prefer to sort their correspondence according to difficulty. Some take the easy ones first; others, the tougher ones. There seems to be no hard-and-fast rule about this.

And still a third method of sorting mail to be attended to is according to urgency—the most pressing items first, regardless of subject matter or level of difficulty. Executives who are frequently interrupted in their dictation maintain that this type of sorting is a must.

DISPLAYING YOUR MAIN IDEAS

Often you can make your communications easier for your reader by itemizing information that lends itself to 1-2-3 listings. This is frequently done in longer memorandums and reports, but it is also a good idea for certain business letters.

Case Example: The office services manager of Chadwick Corporation responds to an inquiry from Miss Michele Hardaway about Chadwick's experience with centralized files.

Dear Miss Hardaway:

Our experiment with centralized files pointed up three basic problems which caused us to abandon the idea in our company. The physical difficulty of employees' getting to and from the files was a serious drawback. The distance was sometimes great, and the result was a considerable amount of traffic and delay. Messenger service didn't solve this particular problem either.

Another problem was that different departments have different needs. Where one department called for information in terms of geographical location, another asked for the same information by subject. This created much confusion and resulted in duplication of files. Interestingly, one of the most serious problems (and this surprised us) was that some departments didn't want other departments to have access to their records. While it was unlikely that one department would have need for another department's confidential files, the suspicion prevailed nevertheless that people were getting information they were not entitled to.

If you get to Cleveland sometime soon and have a little time, I'd like to show you the setup we have now. It works like a charm and has solved most of the problems referred to above.

Sincerely yours,

Now let's see how the letter to Miss Hardaway can be improved by using enumerations and headings.

Dear Miss Hardaway:

Our experiment with centralized files pointed up three basic problems which caused us to abandon the idea in our company.

1. <u>Physical Problem</u>. The physical difficulty of employees' getting to and from the files was a serious drawback. The distance was sometimes great, and the result was a considerable amount of traffic and delay. Messenger service didn't solve this particular problem either.

2. <u>Varying Needs of Departments</u>. We learned very quickly that different departments have different needs. One department called for information in terms of geographical location; another asked for the same information by subject. Such variation created much confusion and resulted in duplication of files.

3. <u>Departmental Access to Records</u>. Interestingly, one of the most serious problems (and this surprised us) was that some departments didn't want other departments to have access to their records. Although it was unlikely that one department would need another's confidential files, the suspicion prevailed nevertheless that people were getting information they weren't entitled to.

If you get to Cleveland sometime soon and have a little time, I'd like to show you the setup we have now. It works like a charm and has solved most of the problems referred to above.

Sincerely yours,

Some writers prefer to number every paragraph in a memorandum in order to make follow-up references easier. For example, it is handier to refer to "item 4 in your July 21 memo" than "your statement concerning back-ordering procedures in the Connecticut and Massachusetts offices in your July 21 memo." However, enumerations tend to clutter correspondence when they are overused; they should be used only when they will help the reader stay on course.

Here is another example of how headings and subheadings can be used effectively to guide your reader:

Case Example: Susan T. Frey, a personnel specialist, prepares a report for the director of marketing on her visit to the three Western regional offices to study their personnel problems.

TO:	Daniel L. Haskell	**FROM:**	Susan T. Frey
SUBJECT:	Sales Personnel Study in Branch Offices	**DATE:**	January 27, 19—

As you know, I recently spent a week in each of the three Western regional offices, talking with the managers and their field supervisors about their personnel turnover problems. Here is a brief report.

LOS ANGELES

Los Angeles is short two sales representatives (and has been since October), and the Bakersfield and Riverside territories have been left virtually uncovered since that time. One other sales representative, Arnold Hooper (San Diego), is on the verge of resigning.

The Problem

The reasons given for the resignations of Alger (Bakersfield) and Hughes (Riverside) were just about identical: dissatisfaction with basic salary, inequitable incentive arrangement, and low mileage allowance. I understand that both received a substantial increase in salary from Jefferson Life, our major West Coast competitor.

While Hooper does not emphasize money as the basis for his unrest, it is certainly a major factor. Hooper's problem seems to be his inability to accept supervision, at least from the present field manager.

Recruiting

The Los Angeles office has found no effective sources of recruitment of new sales representatives, relying almost entirely on newspaper ads in the Sunday Times and word-of-mouth recommendations of other sales representatives. There do not appear to be any likely candidates on the horizon.

PHOENIX

Phoenix is fully staffed at the moment, although a couple of people are unsettled about their jobs (Millard in Phoenix and Carpenter in Flagstaff). The district manager told me that neither is performing up to capacity and that their loss would not be a serious blow.

Recruiting

Phoenix seems to have no difficulty obtaining highly qualified candidates for sales positions. As a matter of fact, several applicants there look quite promising. This office has established exceptionally good relations with several colleges and universities in the area and obtains many candidates from these institutions.

SAN FRANCISCO

The San Francisco office is short one sales representative; however, they have had several promising interviews and believe they will fill the vacancy before the end of the month. The situation here, however, is not so rosy as might be imagined.

The Problem

While San Francisco seems to have little trouble in filling their vacancies, the turnover rate is extremely high. Of the fifteen sales representatives in this office, seven have been with the company less than a year, four less than two years, and only one more than five years. According to the exit interviews, most of those who leave the company do so because of dissatisfaction with salary and incentives. However, a number seem to have some difficulty getting along with their field managers.

RECOMMENDATIONS

I believe that we are in serious trouble in the matter of hiring and retaining an effective sales staff. Even among those people who choose to remain with the company, morale is low. To overcome the situation, I recommend the following:

1. Salary Study. That a study of salaries of our sales representatives as compared with those in the industry as a whole and with several similar firms within each geographical district be undertaken.

2. Supervisory Training. That a how-to-supervise training program be established for district managers, field managers, and sales supervisors.

3. Personnel Recruitment. That a conference be held in each district under the supervision of our personnel department, instructing managers and field managers on the techniques of recruiting, testing, interviewing, and hiring sales representatives.

4. Management Contacts. That more frequent contacts with management be provided all sales representatives, through more frequent district and national conferences.

5. Field Memo. That a "field memo" or some such news-inspiration piece be distributed every month to field sales representatives.

After you have read this report, I would like to talk with you further about some of the problems I found and enlarge on the recommendations I have made.

STF

The style of headings shown in the memo report above is most common but may vary considerably, depending upon personal preferences. Some writers prefer to put major headings in the left margin, as shown in the following excerpt from the same report.

TO: Daniel L. Haskell   **FROM:** Susan T. Frey

SUBJECT: Sales Personnel Study in Branch Offices   **DATE:** January 27, 19—

As you know, I recently spent a week in each of the three Western regional offices, talking with the managers and their field supervisors about their personnel turnover problems. Here is a brief report.

LOS ANGELES   Los Angeles is short two sales representatives (and has been since October), and the Bakersfield and Riverside territories have been left virtually uncovered since that time. One other sales representative, Arnold Hooper (San Diego), is on the verge of resigning.

The Problem   The reasons given for the resignations of Alger (Bakersfield and Hughes (Riverside) were just about identical: dissatisfaction with basic salary, inequitable incentive . . . .

Displaying statistical data—no matter how simple—in tables increases the readability of letters and reports. Tables help the reader to understand at a glance information that might be quite difficult to grasp in narrative form. An example of statistical data in narrative form follows:

As to advertising expenditures by media, in 1978 we spent $15,000 on newspapers and magazines; $8,500 on radio and television; $18,000 on direct mail; $7,700 on transit advertising; $17,000 on premiums; and $6,400 on billboards. In 1977 we spent $18,000 on newspapers and magazines; $10,000 on radio and television; $21,000 on direct mail; $3,500 on transit advertising; $12,000 on premiums; and $9,800 on billboards. For all media, in 1978 we spent a total of $72,600 as compared to $74,300 in 1977.

Compare this narrative style with the following table:

ADVERTISING EXPENDITURES, 1978 AND 1977

	1978	1977
Newspapers and Magazines	$15,000	$18,000
Radio and Television	8,500	10,000
Direct Mail	18,000	21,000
Transit Advertising	7,700	3,500
Premiums	17,000	12,000
Billboards	´6,400	9,800
Totals	$72,600	$74,300

Would you agree that the information is easier to read in table form and that comparisons of yearly amounts are also easier?

LOGIC IN COMMUNICATIONS

Many people have the habit of jumping to conclusions and making statements that are untrue or that are based on whim. This is a particularly bad practice for writers because words on paper are permanent and may come back to haunt them. Consider these statements:

This is the second time this year we've had trouble getting a shipment from Louden Supply. They certainly don't care much about their customers.

The check to Murchison's was mailed four days ago, but they still haven't received it. What's wrong with our mailing department?

November was a bad month for employee absences, but of course the weather has been beautiful.

During April we had 24 resignations—16 women and 8 men—but of course it is well known than women are not satisfied here.

You have ignored our last two statements and obviously have no intention of settling your account.

Don't be guilty of making fast assumptions as the writers of the above statements have done. Every assumption may be true, but the chances are equally good that the assumptions are false. Nothing will destroy your credibility—as an employee or a writer—more than the use of faulty logic.

Also beware of non sequiturs. The term *non sequitur,* meaning "it does not follow," applies to situations where the writer omits steps in his or her reasoning and makes it difficult or impossible for the reader to see the connection between statements.

Example 1: What do you think this writer meant:

Our company is moving out of this building to Lafayette Street, and I am planning to buy a Buick.

Let's fill in the steps in reasoning that were omitted.

Our company is moving out of this building to Lafayette Street. Since there's no bus or subway service from my house to Lafayette Street, I'm going to need a car to get to work. I'm thinking of buying a Buick.

Example 2:

Non Sequitur: Because of the transportation strike, the cafeteria will be closed until further notice.

Clear: Nearly 70 percent of our cafeteria employees depend on public transportation to get to work, and because of the bus and subway strike next week, we expect to be hit hard by absenteeism. Therefore, the cafeteria will be closed for the duration of the strike.

Some writers can best be described as fuzzy thinkers. Following are two examples.

Case Example 1: Charles Renault, a retail furniture dealer, wrote to a wholesaler asking for an extension of 30 days in paying his invoice for goods purchased a couple of weeks ago. He also requested the usual discount of 4 percent, even though he knew he wasn't entitled to it. The wholesaler, although willing to grant the 30-day extension, felt that a discount could not be allowed because the purpose of a discount is to encourage prompt payment. If an exception were granted, the wholesaler's other customers would also have to be given the same privilege, and the whole idea of discounts for quick payment would be lost. The account supervisor who wrote to Mr. Renault said:

Although we will be pleased to grant you an extension of 30 days in paying your account, I must tell you that the discount is not permitted. Discounts are given only to our prompt-paying customers, and it is they whom we must favor.

The writer is not logical in implying that Mr. Renault is not a prompt-paying customer simply because he asked for an extension and a discount to which he was not entitled. Mr. Renault was presumptuous, perhaps, in asking for this special favor—he knows the rules too—but that is no reason to brand him a slow-paying customer. The two issues are the purpose of a discount and the fair and equal treatment of all customers—not who is a prompt-paying customer and who is not.

The account supervisor might better have written this:

Dear Mr. Renault:

Of course we're glad to give you an extra 30 days on your account.

We've had to make a hard-and-fast rule about discounts, however, giving them only when payment is received within the allowed 10-day period. If we made exceptions, a lot of our customers whom we've denied discounts would be unhappy; and at the same time, those who are entitled to discounts would feel we were penalizing them. Possibly you've experienced this situation in your own business and know why we cannot change our discount policy.

Sincerely yours,

Case Example 2: A mail room supervisor, angry because many employees brought mail to her department after the announced closing hour of 4:30 and expected it to be sealed, stamped, and mailed the same day, issued this memorandum:

TO:	All Employees	**FROM:**	Jane Dobson
SUBJECT:	Mail Deadline	**DATE:**	May 5, 19—

This is to inform all parties that mail cannot be accepted after 4:30 each day. This policy has been in effect for over two years, but it is still being violated by many people. Only special-delivery letters will be received.

What's wrong with this thinking? In the first sentence the supervisor said that mail cannot be accepted after 4:30, but in the last sentence she said that special-delivery letters would be received. What the supervisor probably meant was that ordinary mail received after 4:30 would not be sealed, stamped, and sent out that day (presumably, it would lie in the mail room until the next morning); however, special-delivery letters would be sent out after 4:30.

And what was meant by "but it is still being violated"? Probably that nobody paid any attention to the policy when it was announced two years ago. The mail room supervisor might have been more successful if she had issued the much more logical message that follows. People tend to cooperate more readily when they understand why they are asked to do things.

TO:	All Employees	**FROM:**	Jane Dobson
SUBJECT:	Mail Deadline	**DATE:**	May 5, 19—

Will you please help us?

A couple of years ago, we set a policy that when ordinary outgoing mail is received in the mail room after 4:30, it is held for processing and mailing until the next day. The reason is that our employees leave at 5 and we are not authorized to keep them beyond that hour. Therefore, we set 4:30 as the cutoff point for ordinary mail, to allow ourselves a full 30 minutes to get everything processed.

Of course you may bring your outgoing mail to us up to 5, and we'll put it in safe-keeping. But we won't try to get it to the post office until the next morning.

Special-delivery letters are exceptions to this policy. We will get those out the same day we receive them, even if they arrive in the mail room after 4:30.

Projects

A. Correct any errors you find in the following.

1. Be sure to stop in when you are in the Edwardsville area, and remember that our prices are the lowest in southern Illinois.
2. The new computerized system of stock control will be activated with the opening of the Kearney distribution center. Which probably means March 15.
3. Our aims at all times are these to give our customers the best service, to keep prices as low as possible, and making a modest profit for ourselves.
4. The schedule suggested by Bates was not satisfactory, it did not take into consideration our seasonal ups and downs.
5. Electronics, in addition to computer programming and refrigeration, are being offered by our training department.
6. An art book or a one-volume encyclopedia seems to be appropriate gifts for subscribers.
7. We received a bid from both Kimberly and Gilman-Jordan.
8. Rifkin's price is as low, if not lower than, Kelly's.
9. Arriving at 8:30, the building was completely deserted.
10. I did not attend the labor-management discussions therefore I am not certain of the outcome.

B. Rewrite the following, making any changes you feel will improve clarity.

1. Since an approved idea will win you a cash award, the amount depending on the value of your suggestion to the company, write your suggestions and drop your ideas in one of the suggestion boxes, and particularly welcome are suggestions that lead to improved quality or quantity of work, to reduced costs, or to improved relations with customers.
2. At a meeting of the board of directors, Miss Ames, the corporation treasurer, brought an important problem to the attention of the board, pointing out that so far the company has been moving ahead haphazardly, with no blueprint or plan for its future operations and without control over its business costs, and contending that the corporation would be even more successful if it paid more attention to estimating, planning, and analyzing its costs and profits.
3. Actual costs are essential factors in income determination, but they leave much to be desired for other management purposes, as they reflect the inefficiencies of the period's operations are subject to seasonal fluctuations, and show the influence of unusual and nonrecurring events and thus they are decidedly poor guides for planning, control of costs, product costing, and establishment of selling prices.
4. About half of the fifty states have merit systems which require competitive examinations, New York being the first state to introduce the merit

system and for over 75 years applicants for New York State employment have been required to pass tests other than those of political loyalty, so that today 70 percent of all jobs in the executive branch of the New York State government are filled through competitive examinations.

5. Salaries vary in different parts of the country and at different times, depending upon business conditions, the cost of living, and the supply of available trained office workers, being frequently determined by the ability and experience required by the position, but they have improved each year and, with more liberal allowances for sick leaves and vacations, are becoming quite respectable.

6. At a very minimum, the marketing organization should embrace such activities as sales, advertising, sales promotion, and market research, which is being "broken out" as a separate function in more and more companies and in many firms including the Central Electric Company, product planning is also considered a marketing function as well as product service, especially where it is a factor in maintaining customer goodwill.

(C) Rewrite the following, aiming at better variety of sentence length and paragraphing as needed.

1. The company contributes to still other benefit plans on your behalf. Because these plans bear no direct relationship to your employment with Polson's Inc., they are given only brief mention here. These are state unemployment insurance, social security, and medicare.

2. He called in his chief accountant. He discussed the situation and his concern over his precarious profit position. The chief accountant pointed out that on several occasions he had recommended that the president establish a profit plan. He made it clear that this profit plan should be implemented by a detailed budget. The president countered with the opinion that the company was too small to warrant such elaborate procedures. He added ironically that the cost of such a program would probably wipe out the small profit which remained.

3. The next cause of delinquency in our customer accounts is laziness. Laziness is one of the most difficult causes of delinquency we have to cope with. Laziness is hard to grasp adequately. This is so because people who pay slowly through laziness are difficult to identify. Eventually we have to resort to harsher collection procedures. This is necessary simply because we have to show people that there is something worse in store for them if they don't pay their bills. This refers only to extreme cases.

4. Enclosed for your review and comment is a brief proposal from Denise Markham. She has set up Personality Plus Institute. The purpose of this institute is to develop innovative programs on personal growth. In short, what must an individual do to sell himself or herself? Ms. Markham is a full-time employee of Horizons Unlimited. She is also a part-time teacher at Ketchum College. I think you will be interested in this proposal.

5. There is a simple way to control the cost of telephoning. It is to schedule as many of your calls as possible in the evening. Many of your customers will be available to you in the evening. Evening rates for long-distance calls are lower than day rates. A great deal of money can be saved by telephoning your customers in the evening.

(D) Some of the following sentences contain more than one idea. Rewrite them.

1. I look forward to our meeting in March, and in the meantime, I hope you will give some thought to the selection of a new agency.
2. It should not be necessary to assign guards for Saturdays and Sundays, and I suggest that we eliminate this expense.
3. We want you to come to see us in our new location, and I hope you will be completely satisfied with the Crawford-Gill line of maple tables.
4. I have clerked in stores, solicited door-to-door, and sold products on established routes, and I hope you will grant me an interview.
5. Fill in and return the card today, and remember that you get an additional 10 percent discount on all orders placed by August 1.
6. Won't you make use of Rayford's offer of a 10-day free examination by mailing the coupon today?
7. We want to congratulate you upon your successful completion of the Minnehaha Housing Project, and we hope the enclosed description of our expansion plans will encourage you to come to Des Moines to talk to us about our new shopping mall.
8. Employees have been particularly successful in making suggestions that bear some relation to their own work rather than to the work of others, but not eligible to receive awards are members of the methods staff and also those department heads and executives who are in a position to authorize the adoption of their own suggestions.
9. Here's a copy of Jefferson Brown's write-up and appraisal of the El Tiempo project, and you will notice that they have converted pesos to dollars.
10. Financial security for you and your family need no longer be a dream, and we hope you will stop in this month to learn firsthand how our Master Annuity can solve your money worries.
11. At any rate, I'm going to telephone you within a couple of weeks to see if you won't let me tell you more about Tuff Track tires.

(E) Read the following and see if you can supply connectors to bridge the gaps.

1. The language used in business communications obviously calls for precision. The word *nice*—what does it really say?
2. When you buy from a reliable merchant, you are encouraging good business practices. When you buy from an unethical dealer, you are approving his way of doing business.
3. If Winston Churchill, instead of speaking about "blood, toil, sweat, and tears," had used such dreary words as, "We shall all face difficult times," he probably would have made little impression. He would have had little success with big, fancy words.
4. A Federal Reserve bank does not provide service to the general public. It is a bank for banks; it provides the same services for its members that commercial banks provide for their customers.
5. About 90 percent of the goods and services produced in this country are produced by privately owned business enterprises. To a large extent, it is the owners and managers of business who are responsible for economic growth.

6. It has always been the first task of management to make profits for the company. And in their desire to increase the firm's income, managers are often thoughtless in handling employees, treating them as though they were just so many machines. Consideration is often given only to minimizing costs, no matter what effect such action may have on the income of the workers.

   Workers usually see only one side of the picture. They believe all too often that the major purpose of the business is to provide them with jobs and are uninterested in and unsympathetic with management's desire to keep costs down and to make a profit.

7. No one knows for sure how much of our economic growth is the result of our having a free enterprise system. No one would deny that freedom to make our own economic decisions has contributed greatly to our economic progress.

8. Automation is eliminating two kinds of jobs in our company, the kind that does not require a great deal of skill, sometimes called semiskilled, and the monotonous kind where the worker performs the same task over and over.

(F) You can make the following report easier to read by tightening up the wording and providing four headings: *Procedure, Results, Analysis,* and *Recommendation.*

TO: J. N. Carey

FROM: (Your name)

SUBJECT: Customer Complaints on Elimination of Delivery Service

You asked for a report on the complaints of customers because of our elimination of delivery service. As you know, this new policy went into effect March 1, and we have had three months in which to assess its impact on our customers. As soon as the decision was made, I asked all employees who have contacts with customers—either by telephone or in person—to fill out a customer complaint slip (see attached) when the matter of delivery service was introduced.

At this time we have received 27 complaints. Six were from customers who have long-established charge accounts and are rated A-1. Seven were from newly established charge accounts (less than six months). Twelve were from customers who could not be identified from our records and are presumed to be occasional cash shoppers. Two were from charge customers who have owed us money for 90 days or more and are rated as risky. Our total number of charge customers at this time is 7,003, and we estimate our cash customers each month to be about 35,000. If only 27 out of 42,003 have complained, we must assume that our new policy has had virtually no negative influence on customers and that we have weathered the initiation of this new policy well. Of course, we don't know how many customers opposed this policy and said nothing. However, it is significant that new charge accounts have not diminished during the past three months and store traffic is up slightly.

I recommend that we continue to keep records of customer complaints for three more months, say until September 15. At the end of that period if nothing more significant develops than we have already experienced, we can probably consider the matter closed.

(G) Each of the following contains faulty logic. See if you can find the flaws; then rewrite each.

1. The Manchester terminal is no longer adequate for our West Coast needs; therefore, we are considering enlarging the Haleyville plant.

2. DAILY CAFETERIA HOURS
   Breakfast — 7:30-8:30
   Lunch   — 12:00-2:30
      Closed Mondays

3. To All Sales Representatives:

   All credit cards bearing the company name must be surrendered to the accounting office immediately. In the future, if you wish to have credit cards, you must apply for them individually, paying the membership dues yourself (the dues are *not* legitimate company expenses).

   You may retain the Air Travel and Hertz cards issued by the company.

UNIT 6

PLANNING FOR CLEAR WRITING

No matter what you are writing about or to whom, you should have a plan. This means thinking hard about what you want your letter, memorandum, or report to accomplish and then organizing your thoughts and facts in such a way that you achieve your purpose. Writers who don't take the time to plan often wind up with a communication that has one or more of these faults:

- The purpose is not clear to the reader.
- Points that are essential to clarity are left out.
- Irrelevant material is included.
- The message is a hit-and-run affair; that is, the writer flits from one subject to another and back again.
- The message is overwritten.

MAKING THE PURPOSE CLEAR

The first step in planning is to satisfy yourself that the communication you are about to write is really necessary. This is not to say that you should look for reasons *not* to write—too many people don't put things in writing when they should, using the excuse, "There's already too much paperwork in the office." That is not a good excuse. But there are people who make a fetish of "covering" every action they take by writing a letter or memo, claiming that it is "good protection." A person who needs this kind of protection can't be very secure in his or her job and ought to find a position where there is less suspicion and intrigue.

Once you decide that you should put something in writing, ask yourself the question, What is the purpose of this communication? Your answer will guide you in planning what you will say, how much you will say, and how you will say it.

Case Example: Suppose your company is a longtime customer of the Hyatt Supply Company. In a recent closeout sale, Hyatt offered a special 20 percent discount on all its merchandise, and you placed an order amounting to $400. However, the invoice you received was for $400—the special discount had not been allowed.

Obviously, you will want to let Hyatt Supply Company know that an error was made and that you expect to be given credit for $80 (20 percent of $400). Thus the purpose of your letter might be stated as follows:

> To send a check for $320, pointing out that the 20 percent promised discount was taken.

With that purpose in mind, you would not be likely to write a letter like this:

> Gentlemen:
>
> I was shocked to receive your invoice for $400. The only reason I placed an order with you at this time was because you promised a 20 percent discount, and I don't intend to pay the full amount. What are you trying to pull?

The purpose of the letter shown would seem to be this: to show anger and let those people know that I won't stand for this kind of treatment.

The purpose, however, is to send a check for $320 to Hyatt and point out that the promised 20 percent discount was taken. Thus a letter similar to the one that follows would probably have been the result of your stated purpose:

> Gentlemen:
>
> Here is our check for $320 on Invoice 467. You will see that we took advantage of the 20 percent discount that we were promised but that was not figured in—obviously, an unintentional oversight.

Do you see the importance of stating, at least mentally, the purpose or objective of each communication? Doing so forces you to think about the results you want and keeps you on track. Let's take another example.

Case Example: As manager of the Data Processing Department of Wardman Products, you want to write an interoffice memorandum announcing the appointment of Jennifer Webb to the position of senior systems analyst. Ms. Webb replaces Dennis McCloud, who has resigned.

What will be your purpose? Probably this: to announce JW's appointment and mention her qualifications for the position. If you stick to that purpose, you will *not* produce this announcement:

> I am sorry to announce that Dennis McCloud has resigned as senior systems analyst in the Data Processing Department. Dennis has accepted a position in Morrisville, which is near his home.
>
> Dennis has been with Wardman Products for the past five years and was the principal architect of our very effective data processing operation. We shall miss him greatly.
>
> Dennis will be succeeded by Jennifer Webb.

The purpose of the above memorandum, as you see, is to lament the exit of Dennis McCloud and laud his work—not to announce the appointment of Jennifer Webb. Here is the kind of memorandum that you will probably write if you want to achieve your original objective:

> I am pleased to announce the appointment of Jennifer Webb to the position of senior systems analyst in the Data Processing Department. Jennifer replaces Dennis McCloud, who has resigned to accept a position near his home.
>
> Ms. Webb brings a wealth of experience to her new position, having been a programmer for 3 years prior to joining Wardman and a systems analyst in this department for the past 18 months. Jennifer designed the highly effective inventory system and assisted in a number of other successful conversions. She is a graduate of Morningside College.
>
> Tom Farley, Melissa Jantzen, Phil Brisson, and Linda Parr, all of whom previously reported to Dennis McCloud, will now report to Ms. Webb.

More Than One Purpose?   A business communication may have more than one purpose. For example, a letter's principal purpose may be to convince a customer to buy in greater quantities in order to take advantage of special new discounts, but at the same time the letter can reinforce the ideas of product superiority, rapid and dependable service, and national advertising tie-ins. The secondary purposes are closely allied to the primary purpose and indeed give it support. However, it is unwise to treat two quite different subjects in the same communication. For example, price changes should not be announced in the same memorandum in which cooperative advertising policies, or sales territory realignment, or automobile leasing arrangements for salespeople are also discussed. Each of these subjects is distinct and should be treated in a separate memorandum.

Also, in instances where two closely allied subjects could logically be covered in the same communication, it is best to write them up separately when one would weaken the impact of the other. Take the promotion of Jennifer Webb to the position of senior systems analyst (see above), which came about because of the resignation of Dennis McCloud. If the writer wants to announce McCloud's resignation, tell people where he is going, and commend him for faithful service, this should be done in a separate memo. To cover this information in the announcement about Ms. Webb would weaken the impact of her promotion.

INCLUDING ESSENTIAL DATA

If you plan your communications before you begin to write, you are not likely to leave out information that is essential to clarity. For example, you would not:

- Apologize to a customer for the delay in filling an order but neglect to say when shipment will be made.
- Announce a change in the time and place of an employee meeting but forget to mention the new place (or time).
- Accept a new dealer's request for credit on a large order without mentioning terms.
- Describe a new line of merchandise to prospective dealers without including prices.

Look at the following memorandum:

TO: All Departments   **FROM:** O. V. McGrimmon
SUBJECT: Transfer of Stock   **DATE:** August 17, 19—

The decision has been made to close down the Manchester distribution center and transfer that inventory to the Torrance branch. This move will bring all our merchandise under one roof, so to speak, and will simplify stock control as well as speed up deliveries to customers.

OVMc

What questions might the recipients of O. V. McGrimmon's memorandum want answers to? Of course, the most obvious one is, When? Without this information, the message confuses rather than enlightens. Even if McGrimmon does not have an exact date, he could have given some indication of time, such as "by the end of the year," or "around October 1," or "within the next month or two."

Mention might also have been made of the plans for the closed-down Manchester distribution center. Is it to be put up for sale? Used for another purpose? Even the statement, "We don't know what we will do with the Manchester distribution center," would be better than nothing.

Planning forces a writer to think through a communication before it is written and reduces the chances of leaving out important data.

AVOIDING IRRELEVANCIES

Another reason for planning your communications is that it will help you to avoid irrelevancies—material that gets in the way of, rather than adding to, your main message. For example, look at the following memorandum from a top executive to his employees. Its purpose is to discourage people from using the company's library staff to do their work for them.

TO: Staff   **FROM:** E. Dwight Vaughn

SUBJECT: Use of Library Personnel   **DATE:** January 6, 19—

I mentioned in a recent memorandum that our library staff is competent and willing to assist employees in locating information needed for various research reports. Unfortunately, a great many people think this means using library personnel to do their research for them—a sort of "information please" service.

Although library personnel will gladly recommend sources of information, they don't have time to answer such questions as: When was the first newspaper published in the United States? Which is the leading state in the production of soybeans? Where does direct mail rank among advertising media? (These questions were actually asked.)

We have one of the best business libraries in the industry. Engineers, business executives, research specialists—even college professors—make frequent requests to use our facilities. One professor recently told me that our petroleum engineering section is the best he has seen in a company library.

Remember, then, to restrict your requests to *sources* of information; don't ask for answers to specific questions that you can look up for yourself.

EDV

The memorandum from Mr. Vaughn is fine with one exception. Remember that the purpose of the communication is to stop people from abusing their library privileges. Paragraphs 1, 2, and 4 do the job nicely. Paragraph 3, in which Mr. Vaughn praises the library's collection, is irrelevant.

AVOIDING THE "HIT-AND-RUN"

Without a plan, a writer is apt to flit back and forth from one subject to another, never landing long enough in any one place to make a point. Let's look at an example of the "hit-and-run" technique of writing. The author of the following letter is responding to a customer who ordered a copy of the book *Handbook of Antiques,* which is no longer in print.

Dear Mrs. Moser:

We do not have copies of the book Handbook of Antiques, which you asked about.

I assume you have checked with your local bookstores. The book was declared out of print several months ago, and there are none left in our warehouse.

Perhaps you could find a copy by writing to Book Locators, 1902 Kenny Road, Columbus, OH 43210. Some local bookstores, however, particularly those that handle used books, may still have copies.

In any event, if you don't find a copy locally, I am almost certain that Book Locators can help you.

Sincerely yours,

Although the writer has tried to be helpful to Mrs. Moser, he has "jumped all over the lot." A cardinal rule in business writing is to *put like things together,* and a preliminary plan would have helped the author to do that. Compare the first letter to Mrs. Moser with the one that follows.

Dear Mrs. Moser:

The book Handbook of Antiques was, unfortunately, declared out of print a few months ago, and we have no copies in stock.

I assume that you have checked your local bookstores. If you cannot locate a copy (don't forget to try stores that handle used books), I would suggest that you write to Book Locators, 1902 Kenny Road, Columbus, OH 43210. I am almost certain these people have or can find this book for you.

Good luck!

Sincerely yours,

AVOIDING OVERWRITING

The old admonition "Don't beat a good horse to death" has special application to business writers. Some don't realize when a point has been made and literally beat the subject to death before they leave it. Read the following—a letter to a customer who has taken a cash discount to which he is not entitled.

Dear Mr. Falkenberg:

I have received your check for $304 in payment of Invoice A703 ($320). I notice that you took advantage of the 5 percent discount even though the bill went seven days beyond the ten-day limit.

Cash discounts are offered to our customers to encourage prompt payment, and the terms 5/10, n/30 on the invoice meant that you had ten days from the invoice date (October 8) to make payment and receive the 5 percent discount. The full amount was due in thirty days. However, since you did not pay the invoice until October 25—seven days past the deadline date—you are not entitled to receive the 5 percent discount, which amounts to $16.

I am sure you know that we must enforce our discount policy in all cases; otherwise, there would be no reason to offer such an incentive for prompt payment. If we allowed one customer to ignore the rules, then others would have the same right, and soon those who pay promptly would have the same privileges as those who do not. This, I am sure you will agree, is not good business practice.

Given the above explanation, I am sure you will promptly send me an additional check for $16 to cover the net amount on Invoice A703.

Cordially yours,

Besides being a rather condescending letter, bordering on insult, it is overwritten. The writer obviously gave little time to planning what to say. Indeed, the purpose of the message is obscure. Surely the writer's purpose was not to annoy Mr. Falkenberg by giving him a lecture; yet that seems to be the result.

Here is a revision of the letter:

Dear Mr. Falkenberg:

Thank you for your check for $304 in payment of Invoice A703.

If you will look at the terms of the invoice, you will see that the 5 percent discount ($16) was deducted in error. This discount is allowed only when the invoice is paid within ten days—October 18—and your check was dated the 25th.

Would you like to send us your check for $16 now, or would you prefer that we add it to your next order? Either way is fine with us.

Sincerely yours,

MAKING A PLAN

Once you have your purpose clearly in mind, you need to think about how you will achieve it. This requires a plan. Every good writer has some sort of plan in mind before beginning to write or dictate. The veteran writer may use only a "think plan." First, the writer will think about what the communication should accomplish—to say no without creating ill will, to say yes in a way that will bring the most benefits to the company, to create interest in a product, to sell an idea to top management, to achieve agreement on a controversial matter, to obtain payment of a bill, and so on. Then, with this objective in mind, the writer will think through the entire message before starting to write or dictate. The writer will recite to herself or himself the things to be covered and will think hard about what the reader's reaction will be to the various points.

The novice starts with a think plan too but, in addition, prepares a written outline before beginning to write the communication. The outline may be in the form of jottings on a sheet of scratch paper, or if the writer is answering a letter or memo, he or she may jot notes in the margins of the incoming message. As we mentioned earlier, some writers plan by writing or dictating a complete rough draft, which they then edit and revise. The latter method is slow and costly, but it can be worth the time when the message is important and one's writing ability is not yet fully developed.

In any event, a plan must start with the writer's thinking through the entire message before putting a word on paper. This may appear obvious; however, many communicators don't do it. When criticized for their efforts, they fall back on the excuse, "I never was a good writer." This is simply an alibi. A person endowed with a flair for writing can still produce unintelligible communications if they are not planned; conversely, a person with only a modest talent for writing can overcome this weakness by intelligent planning and organizing. "Genius is the art of taking infinite pains," said Thomas

Carlyle, essayist and historian. And taking pains is perhaps the chief distinction between those who communicate effectively and those who don't.

Case Example: In the Receiving Department of Benson Plastics Inc., one of the most important pieces of equipment is the photocopying machine. It is in constant use for making copies of purchase orders, invoices, bills of lading, receiving reports, and letters. But it is old, and you want permission to buy a new one. Requests of this type must be in writing. Look at the following memorandum:

TO:	Stacy L. Harvey	**FROM:**	John R. Holley
SUBJECT:	New Photocopier	**DATE:**	January 16, 19—

We need a new photocopying machine in the Receiving Department. May I have your permission to purchase one?

JRH

The trouble with this memo is that the writer didn't do much thinking before he wrote it. If he had, he might have asked himself, "What will my boss need to know in order to authorize this purchase?" And putting himself in the boss's position, he probably would have said, "I'd want to know what, why, when, and how much."

Before attacking even this simple communication problem, the writer ought to devise a think plan that will help him cover all the necessary points and organize these points in the right sequence.

A think plan for this situation might look like this:

1. *Present machine (Tru-Copy) NG—slow, faint copies, breaks down, costly.*
2. *Work piling up—need dependable machine.*
3. *Suggest F-87 (Keen-Fax). Cost, trade-in, etc.*
4. *Purchase order; demonstration?*

From such a think plan, the following memorandum results:

TO:	Stacy L. Harvey	**FROM:**	John R. Holley
SUBJECT:	New Photocopier	**DATE:**	January 16, 19—

Our photocopier, Tru-Copy, is no longer adequate for our needs, and I'd like your authorization to buy a new one. The Tru-Copy is now four years old and very slow. The copies we get from it are faint (see sample attached). What's more, the machine breaks down constantly, and while we're waiting for it to be repaired, we have to use the photocopier on the 16th floor. This puts us behind in our work.

Last week the representatives from Keen-Fax demonstrated their new F-87 model to several of us, and we are very much impressed with it (a description is attached). I'm convinced that this machine would pay for itself within two or three years. During the past year we spent over $100 in repair bills on the Tru-Copy, and the wasted time, effort, and paper would probably be double that figure. The cost of the F-87 is $600, and Keen-Fax would allow us a trade-in of $50 on the Tru-Copy.

Just in case I have convinced you, I'm attaching a purchase order for your signature. If, however, you would like to see the Keen-Fax F-87 in action, I am sure I can arrange a demonstration.

JRH

Case Example: You work as a customer account manager for the Drummond Supply Company. You have received a letter from Graham Matthews, manager of accounting services for Houghton Incorporated, one of Drummond's good customers. Mr. Matthews is out of patience. He has received a statement of the amount he is said to owe Drummond, and he is sure the statement is in error. He has tried several times to straighten out this matter, exchanging several letters with various people in your company, but has received no satisfaction. He wants this matter cleared up—now—and you must respond to him. He says he owes Drummond nothing.

The mission of your response is to get the situation squared away and give Mr. Matthews the satisfaction he deserves. How will you go about achieving your objective? Obviously, the first thing you have to do is get the facts. You will get the correspondence Mr. Matthews refers to, talk to the people who keep the Houghton Incorporated account, study these records, discuss the situation with the sales representative who calls on Houghton, and talk to anyone else in the company who might have had a hand in this particular problem. By the time you are finished with your investigation, you may have a page or two of notes. You study all the data you have collected until you know exactly what the problem is. Only after you have gathered all the facts and reached some definite conclusions about them will you be able to plan what you are going to say to Mr. Matthews when you write to him. If the story cannot be pieced together in such a way that you are sure of your ground, you may have to go back to all your sources and recheck everything. You might even have to write Mr. Matthews for clarification on certain points.

Let's say you uncover all the evidence you need to convince yourself that Mr. Matthews is right—he owes your company nothing. Now you are ready to start to plan your letter.

The plan starts with the question, What does Mr. Matthews want to know? The answer is simple: he wants to know if he is going to get what he asked for—a clean bill of health. The first item in your think plan will be something like this:

He's right on all counts. He owes us nothing.

You could stop there, of course, and write your letter. But if you do, the customer might think you look upon such mistakes as run-of-the-mill in your company and that he can expect more of the same in his future dealings. So the next item in your think plan might be this:

I should explain how these errors happened, even though some of them are minor. I won't duck the responsibility for them, but I don't want to give the impression that we do this sort of thing routinely.

Is there another point that ought to be covered? Yes. You will want to try to build goodwill and resell Mr. Matthews on your company. Your think plan continues:

Houghton is a good customer, and these people don't deserve the kind of run-around we gave them. At the same time, I hope Mr. Matthews won't hold this one experience against us and put us in bad with his purchasing office. We want their business.

If the foregoing think plan is put in the form of a written plan, it might look something like this:

1. Right--he owes us nothing. New stmt.
2. Explanation:
   #763--error in ext. (should have been $433.40).
   #877--discount of 2% ($6) should have been allowed.
   Ret'd shpmt.-- Accounting not notified by whse.
3. Apologies (runaround).
4. Special attn. on next order.

Such a plan is likely to produce a letter like the following:

Dear Mr. Matthews:

You are absolutely right—you owe us nothing. I'm enclosing a new statement which provides the details, but the important thing about it is the "00" balance!

As you will see, we made an error in our extension on Invoice 763. The figure should have been $433.40 instead of $466.40. For some reason, the discount to which you were entitled on Invoice 877 wasn't given you; this amounts to $6. And credit for $888.80 for the returned shipment was not given because our warehouse didn't notify the accounting department that it had arrived.

I am very sorry about these mistakes, Mr. Matthews, and I can't imagine why they all happened to you. Nor can I explain why you got a runaround when you tried to get the matter settled.

We've made such a fuss here about the treatment you received that I think it's safe to say that your future transactions with Drummond are going to have special attention from everyone. In fact, I look forward to your next order so that I can prove that statement!

Thank you for your patience.

Sincerely yours,

Suppose the customer is right on two points but wrong on one. How will your plan differ? Probably you will take the opportunity to deliver the favorable news first, telling where the customer is right and apologizing for the mistakes. Then you will gently explain where he or she is wrong and why; here you will offer a fuller explanation because the customer will want to know precisely what the error was.

Case Example: You are supervisor in the Order Services Department of West Fairfield Aluminum Company. You have received a letter from Donna Follett, manager of the Lone Star Department Store, saying she is returning a shipment of lawn chairs. The manager claims that the chairs received are not the ones she ordered, and she requests a credit memorandum for the total of the order, $477.80, plus shipping charges of $43.20.

Your investigation shows that the chairs sent to Lone Star are the ones that were ordered. Since you do accept shipments returned in good condition, there are no problems about giving Lone Star full credit. At the same time, you do not feel that it is fair for the manager of Lone Star to ask you to pay the shipping charges. It's against company policy to do so unless an error was made by West Fairfield Aluminum, and in this case the error is the customer's.

This letter requires two answers—yes on the credit memorandum for the returned chairs and no on the shipping charges. But you decide to check on that latter point; company policy is often loosely interpreted, depending on the customer and the circumstances. Lone Star happens to be a new customer—a potentially big buyer—and getting her on your side could mean several hundred thousand dollars' worth of business a year. Your boss might think $43.20 is a small price to pay for keeping a customer as large as this one.

If such a concession sounds inconsistent—and unfair to customers who do not receive such privileges—it is nevertheless realistic. Making such a decision, however, requires a thorough knowledge of one's job as well as sound business judgment.

Your think plan might be as follows:

1. *Certainly, we are willing to accept the chairs and give full credit.*
2. *But I think I should let her know that the chairs shipped were the ones she ordered; otherwise, she might think we usually get orders mixed up.*
3. *As a special favor to her, we'll pay the return shipping costs, but she ought to know that it's an exception.*
4. *I wonder why she didn't say anything about placing another order for lawn chairs? Did she forget? Does she want information about other styles? I'll try to get an order from her.*

Once you have thought through all the problems, you are ready to put your plan in writing.

1. Credit memo for $521, incl. shipping charge of $43.20.

2. Sorry about mix-up, but these appear to be chairs ordered. Copy of order encl.

3. Important thing is to place new order. Catalog section.

Here is the letter that might evolve from such a plan:

Dear Miss Follett:

Here is our credit memorandum for $521, which covers the returned shipment of Compac lawn chairs ($477.80) and shipping charges ($43.20).

Although the chairs we sent you seem to be the ones listed in your April 7 order, perhaps they are not what you had in mind. I'm sending you a copy of your order, together with a tear sheet of the Compac line, so that you may check. Because we think there might have been some misunderstanding, we are paying the return shipping charges, which we don't ordinarily do.

The important thing, of course, is that you have a stock of lawn chairs to meet your summer needs. Be sure to place another order soon so that you may have them for the first warm day. Separately I am sending you a section from our general summer furniture catalog; you might be more interested in the new Ezy-Fold line (pages 18-22), which is fast becoming our best seller.

Let me know, please, how I can be of further help. By the way, we can ship your next order the same day it is received.

Sincerely yours,

Whether you have only a "think" plan or jot down major points on the incoming letter or memo or prepare an outline on a separate sheet or write a rough draft, you will have to have *some* kind of plan if you expect to produce clear, complete, and well-organized communications. Too many writers start to compose their communications without having thought beforehand about the result they expect to achieve. This is a primary reason that so many unnecessary letters and memorandums are written and why so many that *are* necessary are rambling, disjointed, and overwritten.

Projects

 Communications that are not planned often contain irrelevant details. Identify the irrelevancies in the following letter; then rewrite it.

Dear Ms. Farnham:

I have received the original and one copy of the lease for the Bushnell property. You will see that Mr. Sontag has signed the document, and it was witnessed by our attorney, Mrs. Haig.

The original is being returned to you, and we are keeping the copy for our files. I hope everything is in order.

Thank you for your prompt attention to this matter.

Sincerely yours,

(B) Marathon Plastics Inc. of Memphis is planning to build three new warehouses in Indiana—one each in Indianapolis, Fort Wayne, and Gary—and management is talking with Brady Construction Company about building them. Representatives of Brady have been invited to visit Marathon the week of April 11 to discuss warehouse space needs with those responsible for receiving, storing, and shipping goods. R. J. Maxwell, executive vice president of Marathon, must write to the appropriate executives in the company, asking them to make sure they and their key people are on hand the week of April 11 and, in the meantime, to update information on space needs they previously reported. Mr. Maxwell asks an assistant to prepare a draft of the memorandum to the executives, and here is the result:

TO: Keith Wilson, Rachel Conover, Gary Himmel, and Roy Gagne

FROM: R. J. Maxwell

SUBJECT: Visit With Brady Construction

DATE: March 12, 19—

To alleviate the shortage of warehouse space, Mr. LeFevre and the writer have initiated preliminary negotiations with Brady Construction Company for the construction of three new warehousing complexes in Indianapolis, Fort Wayne, and Gary; and it is mandatory that we must know the requirements for space needs no later than March 16. Representatives of Brady plan to visit our premises during the entire week of April 11 to contact each one who has responsibilities for Receiving, Storing, and Shipping Departments, and you must check your calendars now immediately, informing the writer of plans you may have arranged to be absent from your desk during that period.

Brady appears to be eminently qualified to undertake the design and construction of these facilities; our previous meetings with their representatives were encouraging.

RJM

cc: Mr. S. LeFevre

Read the memorandum carefully, noting roundabout expressions, showy words, overlong sentences, and poor organization. Prepare a plan; then rewrite the memorandum.

(C) The home office of the Champion Sporting Goods Company has recently had several complaints from customers (schools, retail stores, government agencies, etc.) that refunds due them for overpayments or for returned merchandise are very slow in reaching them. These customers say that Champion's competitors are much faster. The six district offices of Champion are also aware of this problem, and they too want to see something done. The controller decides that each district office should prepare its own refund checks so that customers will get them quicker, and she writes to the district managers telling them about the new procedure.

TO: All District Managers **FROM:** Eileen Barnes
SUBJECT: Refunds **DATE:** March 19, 19—

Effective June 1st and thereafter issue all checks for any amount written out to customers for overpayment of their accounts or for returned merchandise from your office directly to the customer without having to go through the home office.

We feel that this plan and procedure will not only help to improve customer relations substantially but will also close the gap on one of the important areas where our company compares unfavorably with other companies in its contacts with customers.

However, you may or may not find in your previous or committed routine that this is feasible. This new practice may be too time-consuming. Comment on same at the bottom of this memo and return it to me. Please do this by return mail, as we hope to effectuate this new procedure immediately. Thank you for your cooperation.

The memo from Miss Barnes contains errors, deadwood expressions, and meaningless phrases. See if you can improve it.

D The president of Cowan Manufacturing Company is annoyed that some of the firm's major suppliers have been badly treated by employees, and he "fires off" the following memorandum:

TO: Purchasing Department Staff **FROM:** Walter J. Fong
SUBJECT: Relations With Suppliers **DATE:** April 1, 19—

Within the past few days, I have had letters from three of our major suppliers in which they complain about the treatment they have received from some of our people. One supplier was angered by an insinuation that he pads his prices; another, by the unreasonable demands for product delivery; and the third, by failure to obtain information she asked for again and again.

Our suppliers are, in many respects, just as important as our customers. We need them. Good suppliers—those who can be depended upon in any emergency—are not easy to find. It took us years to acquire our present suppliers, and we are proud of the relationship we have built up with such people as Lawson Brothers, Holtz and Brenner, Argo-Day, Crandall Inc., Mata, and others, and we owe all of them a great debt of gratitude for their good service and loyalty. In the early days of our company, some of these suppliers literally carried us when our cash inflow was considerably less than our obligations. We therefore owe them a great deal. Suppliers are people, just as customers are, and I urge you to give them the same courteous treatment. The thing to remember is this: Treat your suppliers well; you never know when you will want them to do you a favor.

Although we can understand the president's concern, he is guilty of overwriting in the second paragraph. Write a new second paragraph that conveys the same message without wearing out the reader.

THE FORM OF LETTERS AND MEMORANDUMS

Written communications tell a lot about a writer and the organization he or she represents just from the way the messages are set up. Just as a good picture can lose much of its impact on the viewer if it is improperly framed, an expertly written letter or memo can lose a great deal of its effect if it is set up badly. And, on the other hand, good form and arrangement can make a business message seem much better than it really is.

Even if the letter writers are top executives, their responsibility extends to making sure that their letters and memos appear in an attractive and appropriate form. Of course, a good secretary is half the battle. But let's take a rundown of the essentials of appropriate letter style and format.

LETTERS

Stationery.   For general business use, the most popular size of stationery is 8½ by 11 inches. The paper should be at least 20-pound bond with about 25 percent rag content to assure acceptable quality. The letterhead and the paper used for second sheets should be of the same weight and quality.

In addition to the standard 8½-by-11 size, top executives often use a distinctive size, such as Monarch (7¼ by 10½ inches) or Baronial (5½ by 8½ inches), for personal-business, social-business, and professional correspondence.

Within the next few years, metric-size stationery will be used more and more frequently. The two most common metric sizes are A4 (210 by 297 millimeters, or 8¼ by 11¾ inches) and A5 (148 by 210 millimeters, or 5⅞ by 8¼ inches). As you can see, A4 stationery is nearly the same size as standard 8½ by 11 stationery, and A5 is nearly the same size as Baronial stationery.

Letterhead.   Since the company letterhead is intended to project the "company image," its design is usually entrusted to a specialist in graphic arts. The best source is usually an art agency that specializes in this kind of graphic presentation, since creating a distinctive letterhead requires a knowledge of typefaces, layout, color, and other artistic factors. In any case, unless you have your own business or are permitted your own letterhead, you won't

THE **Art**
Collector's
Guild _____
3120 Market Street • Youngstown • Ohio 44501

November 16, 19--

Mr. Anthony Russo
6020 Bannockburn Drive
Bethesda, MD 20034

Dear Mr. Russo:

You are invited to join a small group of discriminating people who truly
appreciate fine original art. These are people who, like yourself, are
aware of its artistic and economic worth. As the accompanying folder
shows, you may acquire individually signed and numbered, authenticated,
and framed original lithographs and etchings by outstanding artists at
less than half their appraised value.

I'm sure you will also enjoy the framed original I would like to send as
a membership gift. Each is independently appraised at between $40 and
$70.

Our Board of Advisers seeks out only those living artists whose works
have already been accepted by respected critics, galleries, and museums.
Each large, original, full-color lithograph and each etching is chosen
both for its artistic beauty and for its financial potential.

Obviously, Mr. Russo, The Art Collector's Guild--by its very nature--
must choose its members carefully.

Please note that you risk nothing at all by joining. You will never be
required to make a single purchase. Your $10 membership fee is a one-
time payment, for which you will be billed only after you have received
and approved your free, framed original etching or lithograph. Please
act quickly--return the enclosed postage-paid form today.

Sincerely yours,

Phyllis Lowe Bradshaw

Mrs. Phyllis Lowe Bradshaw
Membership Director

PLB/sc
Enc.

Blocked Letter

have much to say about letterhead design or color. And if you do have the
responsibility for letterhead design, we recommend you have it done by a specialist.

Letter Styles. A few companies adopt one letter style and require all the
people in the company to use it. Most, however, leave the selection of format
to the executive or the secretary.

The two most popular letter styles—the *blocked* and the *semiblocked*—are illustrated above and on page 96.

The Bellevue—Netherlands
360 Seventh Avenue
New York, New York 10036

April 20, 19--

Mr. Philip J. Landers, President
Larchmont Industries Inc.
3224 16th Street, N.W.
Washington, DC 20010

Dear Mr. Landers:

You will, I think, enjoy the accompanying
brochure, <u>Fit for a King</u>. In the past six months
every suite and room at The Bellevue-Netherlands
has been completely refurnished and redecorated in
a most elegant fashion. All our rooms and suites
now have air conditioning and television.

Our location is second to none: We're at 59th
Street and Seventh Avenue (opposite beautiful Central Park)--close to magnificent shops, the theater
district, and the Coliseum.

Let me assure you that even though the
Bellevue-Netherlands has a new look, our policy of
superior service still prevails. I look forward to
the pleasure of welcoming you to our hotel in the
near future.

Cordially yours,

Victoria R. Markovis

Ms. Victoria R. Markovis
Manager

VRM:ct
Enc..

Semiblocked Letter

Punctuation Patterns.   The most commonly used punctuation style for letters is the *standard*. This requires a colon following the salutation and a
comma following the complimentary closing. Another acceptable style is
open punctuation. This style omits all punctuation at the ends of display
lines (other than those that end with an abbreviation, of course).

Parts of the Letter.   Most business letters include at least these parts: letterhead or return address, date line, inside address, salutation, body, complimentary closing, and signature block.

Letterhead or Return Address.   A printed letterhead not only contains the company name and address, but it may also include telephone numbers, cable address, advertising slogan, names of major officers, and so on. The trend in letterhead design, however, is toward simplicity. Observe the uncluttered look of the letterheads illustrated on pages 95 and 96.

If you are not writing on behalf of a company, the heading consists of your return address and the date. This information is usually flush with the right margin, thus:

> 1224 Gatewood Avenue, N.W.
> Washington, DC 20016
> July 21, 19—

Date Line.   The date line may be centered or it may end even with the right margin. On standard stationery, the date line is usually typed on line 15.

Inside Address.   The inside address gives the name and address of the person to whom you're writing. When sending a letter to someone's home, list the person's name, address, and city, state, and ZIP Code on three lines, as shown on page 95. When sending a letter to someone's business address, include the person's name and title on the first line and the company name on the second line, as shown on page 96. (If the title makes the first line too long, place the title on the second line and the company name on the third.)

Salutation.   The salutation is typed two line spaces below the inside address. When addressing one person, it is traditional to include *Dear* in the salutation (*Dear Miss Cole, Dear Henry*). Some women, regardless of marital status, prefer the title *Ms.,* and their preference should be honored. In writing to a firm or an organization, the most common salutation is *Gentlemen* (not *Dear Sirs*), even when you know that some of the chief executives in the organization are women. An alternative to *Gentlemen* is *Ladies and Gentlemen.* If you know, however, that all the executives are women, the correct salutation is *Mesdames* or *Ladies.*

Body.   The body is, of course, the message itself. It is usually single-spaced with a blank line between paragraphs. Depending on letter style, paragraphs may be indented five spaces or may start flush with the left margin.

Complimentary Closing.   Tradition dictates that we close a letter with some kind of sign-off. *Sincerely yours* and *Cordially yours* are the most popular closings. *Sincerely* and *Cordially* may also be used for a personal tone. When you want to be more formal, you may use *Very truly yours* or *Very cordially yours.*

Signature Block.   Three typewriter spaces are left for the signature of the writer, and this space is followed by the writer's typewritten name and title. (See illustrations on pages 95 and 96.)

Reference Initials and Notations.   Usually, the initials of the dictator and the typist are shown at the bottom left, two lines below the signature block. This practice probably sprang from a desire to fix responsibility in case someone other than the signer actually dictated the letter and also in case the typist needed to be identified if some question arose. At any rate, identifying the dictator and the typist seems to be a fixed habit in most businesses, even though its actual value is questionable. A current practice is to show only the typist's initials in small letters at the bottom left. Since the dictator's name is typed under the signature line, it does seem a bit redundant to repeat his or her initials a line or two below. Also, if the dictator types the letter, no initials are used.

Following the reference initials, enclosure and carbon copy notations are used, where applicable, to establish a record. For example, *Enclosures 2* means that the writer has enclosed two documents and the recipient should look for them in the envelope. The notation *cc: Mr. T. R. Feldon* means a copy of the letter has been sent to Mr. Feldon, and *bcc: Mrs. R. Mullins* indicates that Mrs. Mullins is getting a copy of the letter but without the knowledge of the addressee (the notation *bcc,* which means "blind carbon copy," does not appear on the original).

MEMORANDUMS

The memorandum is used for interoffice letters and informal reports. On page 99 is a memorandum typical of those written in business. It is from the executive vice president of a corporation to the vice president in charge of operations.

Parts of the Memo.   The stationery on which memos are written contains printed headings that eliminate the need for formal inside addresses, salutations, and closings. Although memorandum forms differ, most of them contain at least four headings: TO, FROM, SUBJECT, and DATE. Other headings are added to speed delivery or establish identification; for example, DEPARTMENT, LOCATION (branch office, for example), FLOOR, TELEPHONE EXTENSION, ROOM, and so on.

The To *Line.*   The addressee is not usually given a courtesy title, such as *Mr., Miss,* or *Dr.* (A courtesy title is common, however, when addressing a person of much higher rank.) The job title (*Vice President, Operations*) may be used in very formal circumstances. If there is no provision in the form for the department, this may be indicated alongside the addressee's name; for example, *Barbara A. Lee, Personnel Relations.* Such an identification may be very important in a large company.

When the memorandum is addressed to several people, the "To" line may appear as follows:

TO: Publications Committee

TO: See below

(and the names or initials of the individuals addressed are listed at the end of the memorandum, thus: *Distribution: WIT, MRMc, LRB, RJH, FMS, TRR, CIG.)*

To: Susan Liu   **From:** Patrick Donnelly

Dept.: Operations   **Dept.:** Executive

Subject: Fourth-Quarter Expenses   **Date:** November 18, 19--

I have just finished my analysis of the October operating statement and would like to call some things to your attention.

As you have noted or will shortly note, October was somewhat disappointing. While our sales were slightly over budget, we missed our predicted operating profit by $370,000. This underage was a result of our going over budget by $397,000 in direct expenses and $119,000 in indirect expenses. Contrasted with October of last year, we produced $94,000 less net profit on increased sales of $1,400,000.

Obviously, if we are to produce the profit we expect and are capable of, we must make a special effort to hold down expenses for the remainder of the year. I urge you to make all managers aware of the problem, keeping in mind that next year's plans and budgets will not be finally approved for another four to six weeks.

Would you report to me by November 25 what steps you are taking to meet this problem.

PD

PD:am
cc: C. J. Moore

Carbon Copy Notation.   The name of the person receiving a copy of the memorandum may be placed below the addressee's name, but more usually it is typed at the bottom left margin. If several people are to receive copies, the notation is placed at the bottom of the memorandum:

cc: C. J. Moore   Amy Post
     Albert J. Elliott   Anthony Finletter
     G. M. Hotchkiss   Deborah T. Locke

The From Line.   Neither a courtesy title nor a job title is given to the writer of the memorandum. However, when the memorandum form does not provide for an identification of the department from which the message is sent, the writer should include this information beside or below his or her name; for example, *FROM: Peter A. DiSalle, Customer Relations.* This is especially important when the writer is a new employee in a large company or an employee who is not likely to be widely known in the firm.

The Department Line.   The department from which the memorandum comes and to which it goes is usually taken for granted. There is a chance, though, that the memo may be misdirected; there, it is wise to identify the department.

The **Subject** *Line.* Stating the subject of the memorandum enables the reader to know at a glance what the memo is about. The wording should be as short as possible but long enough to tell the reader what you're going to talk about in the memorandum.

SUBJECT: REQUEST FOR LEAVE OF ABSENCE

SUBJECT: Overpayment to Jackson Associates

SUBJECT: Comparative Study of Retirement Policies in Six Major Petroleum Companies

The Body. The body of the memorandum, like the body of a letter, is single-spaced, with paragraphs blocked.

The Signature. Many memorandum writers feel that their name on the "From" line makes a signature unnecessary, either typewritten or handwritten. Again, whether you initial or sign your memorandums is up to you. If you want to personalize your memos, either initial or sign them. The best place for a signature is at the bottom of the memo, although some people like to sign or initial below their typewritten name on the "From" line.

Projects

(A) Edit the following letter from HERITAGE RESEARCH ASSOCIATES, 245 Landis Lane, Deerfield, Illinois 60015, and rewrite it in proper form.

Mr. Marcus S. Gaines, 4740 Earhart Blvd., New Orleans, La. 70150. Dear Sir, Did you know that your family name was recorded with a coat-of-arms in ancient heraldic archives more than 7 centuries ago. My husband and I discovered this while doing some research for some friends of ours, who have the same last name as you did. We've had an artist recreate the coat-of-arms exactly as described in the ancient records and this drawing along with other information about the name, has been printed up into an attractive one page report. The last part of the report tells the story of the very old and distinguished family name of Gaines. It tells what the name means, the origin of the name, it's place in history and famous people who share it. The first part of the report has a large, beautiful reproduction of an artist's drawing of the earliest known coat-of-arms for the name Gaines and this entire report is documented, authentic, and printed on parchment-like paper suitable for framing. This report so delighted our friends that we have had a few extra copies made in order to share this information with other people of the same name. Framed these reports make distinctive wall decorations and they are great gifts for relatives and it should be remembered that we have not traced anyones' individual family tree but have researched back through several centuries to find about the earliest people named Gaines. All we are asking for them is enough to cover the added expense of having the extra copies printed and mailed. If you are interested, please let us know right away as our supply is very limited. Just verify that we have your correct name and address and send the correct amount in cash or check for the number of reports you want and we'll send them promptly by return mail. Sincerely, Mrs. Ruth P. Genesco. PS: If you are ordering only one report, send two dollars ($2). Additional reports ordered at the same time and sent to the same address are one dollar each.

(B) Edit the following letter and put it in proper form.

LAKESIDE HILLS INN
860 Lakeside Highway Northwest
Columbia, South Carolina 29202

Mr. Liborio M. Sanchez, Sales Manager, Allied Products Corporation, 1333 West 5th Ave., Columbus, OH 43212. Dear Mr. Sanchez, We would like to host your next meeting, conference, or seminar! Lakeside Hills Inn, a complete resort on blue Lake Murray, has the following attractions to accommodate your meeting: 80 luxurious sleeping rooms with private balconies (some with fireplaces) overlooking Lake Murray; 4 public meeting rooms, 3 carpeted—each with a lake view; 18 hole championship golf course, driving range; swimming pool, horseback riding, 3 tennis courts, shuffleboard; complete marina with boat rentals for fishing, skiing, sailing, and other water sports; a 1000 meter paved airstrip with Unicom communications to the Lakeside Hills Inn; the elegant Yacht Club for use of registered guests; our very capable, willing staff is another asset to Lakeside. While we want most emphatically to host you and your associates and to have you keep us on your mind, we do not want to send you unwanted literature and news of Lakeside. Thus if you will fill in and return the enclosed self-address, postage paid postcard, we will comply with your wishes. I look forward to hearing from you in the near.future and if I may be of any assistance to you or your association, please let me know. Cordially yours, (Miss) Elizabeth Newman, Seminar Sales Coordinator.

LETTERS AND MEMOS
NEARLY EVERYONE WRITES

YOUR JOB *You are assistant office services manager for the Far Western Insurance Company, San Jose, California. The Office Services Department, managed by Harold R. Prince Jr., has the responsibility for seeing that all incoming and outgoing mail is processed quickly and efficiently, that office space in the various departments of the company is properly utilized, that furniture and equipment are adequate, that appropriate supplies are available, that interoffice communication systems are effective, and that company records are properly maintained. The department also must constantly study the flow of paperwork in the company to see that it is handled with minimum cost and maximum efficiency. You and the supervisors in the department act as consultants to the managers of the other departments on such matters as dictation, typewriting, letter form, and records maintenance.*

Although your responsibility for written communications is not heavy, you do write letters to suppliers and vendors and memos to Mr. Prince and others in your department as well as to people in other departments.

CASE 1

REQUESTING FREE MATERIALS

PROBLEM

As assistant office services manager of Far Western, you must have on hand the latest catalogs, price lists, and other materials of major manufacturers and distributors of office furniture, supplies, and equipment. Since you have only a few of these items—most of them out of date—you need to write several suppliers requesting up-to-date catalogs and price lists.

BACKGROUND

Letters written by potential customers asking a supplier for free materials, information, or routine service are among the easiest to write. Obviously, they are in a position to receive what they are asking for since it is to the supplier's advantage to provide it. Thus little convincing is needed to write such requests.

Even though you are in the driver's seat when writing letters such as these, approach the task as though you were on the receiving end and think about the kind of letter *you* would like to receive if the situation were reversed. Of course you would grant the request because it is in your company's interest to do so. In fact, you would be willing to go out of your way to be helpful. You would ask only that the writer tell you everything you need to know—no more, no less. And you would prefer a letter that is courteous.

In writing routine request letters, then, you should plan to give all the information the supplier will need in order to be really helpful, keep your request as brief as possible without omitting important details, and express your wishes courteously and tactfully.

SOLUTION A

Gentlemen:

In consulting my files of catalogs of equipment and supplies and checking them off against various manufacturers, it was noticed that I did not have your most current issues, which possibly were received but if so I misplaced them, and I like to keep up to date on all manufacturer's catalogs and price lists.

For this reason I would like to request that you send me your latest catalogs of equipment and supplies (plus price lists) at your earliest convenience.

Thanking you in advance, I remain,

Yours truly,

Analysis of Solution A.　How many examples of the following did you spot in Solution A?

1. Incorrect grammar and punctuation
2. Misspelled words
3. Poor sentence structure
4. Roundabout expressions
5. Trite expressions
6. Unnecessary words
7. Irrelevant details

In writing even the most routine letters, some people seem to want to tell their life story, wasting time for everyone and obscuring the purpose of the message. The writer did not need to go into an involved explanation of why she wants a new catalog and price list; the reader is neither helped by it nor interested in the details.

Although this letter probably will produce the desired results, it marks the writer as muddleheaded, incoherent, bumbling. More serious, it wastes both the writer's and the reader's time.

It is generally unwise to open a letter with an "In" phrase (*In consulting my files, In answer to your letter, In response to your question*) or with words ending in "ing" (*Replying to your letter, Acknowledging your inquiry, According to our statement, Referring to your question*). Such poor openings are equally weak closings. Don't close a letter with *Thanking, Hoping,* or *Expecting,* for example. The sentence that begins with one of these words will not be complete unless you end with the old-fashioned and meaningless *I remain* (as shown in the example) or *I am.*

Too, most people consider it presumptuous to thank someone in advance.

SOLUTION B

Gentlemen:

Send me your latest price lists and catalogs.

　　　　　　　　　　　　　　　　　Very truly yours,

Analysis of Solution B.　Solution B may be perfectly satisfactory. Certainly it is brief. Yet, although the writer committed no serious faults, she might have spared a "please" or a "thank you" or some other expression of courtesy. Also, if the writer had thought carefully about the situation, she might have come to the conclusion that giving the purpose of the request would have been helpful (some companies, upon receiving requests for catalogs and other promotional material, are inclined to rush a sales representative out with the material). And the writer might have asked, "How can I be sure of receiving all new catalogs and similar materials as they are issued? If I could get on the mailing list to receive such information automatically, I wouldn't have to worry about remembering to write for them."

SOLUTION C

Gentlemen:

May I have your latest catalog and price list? I am setting up a product information file for reference by our supervisors and managers, who often need the latest data about office equipment and supplies.

Will you please put me on your mailing list for all your promotion and catalog
material?

Sincerely yours,

Analysis of Solution C. Solution C is an effective letter for these reasons:

1. The tone is appropriate. Even though the prospective customer could say
   almost anything in her letter and get what she wants, the writer wisely
   observes the rules of good human relations. She could have said in the
   first paragraph, "I want your catalog" or "Send me your catalog," but
   those are demands. "May I have your latest catalog and price list" is a
   courteous request, and the tone makes a world of difference. In the last
   paragraph, the writer could have written, "Put me on your mailing list,"
   but asking and using the word *please* changed a demand to a polite request.
2. The letter is brief but complete. It gives only the information the reader
   needs in order to help.
3. The reason for the request is clearly stated, even though it is not absolutely essential in this case.
4. The letter starts with a question. Of course, this isn't the only way to
   begin such a letter, but it did get the writer into the subject immediately.
5. The writer obviously thought about her continuing need for new materials (last paragraph); this request can save additional letters in the future.

Projects

(A) The June issue of *Modern Office Training* featured the article "Making
Films for Training," by Charles E. Wirtz, which you enjoyed reading. In the
article, Mr. Wirtz mentioned a booklet available from Amerigo Film Produc-
tions, Baltimore, Maryland 21202, *The ABCs of Making Motion Pictures,*
which is free to business firms. You're thinking of preparing your own motion picture films for training clerical personnel. Write for the free booklet.

(B) About a month ago, you ordered and received from Southern Manufacturing
Company, Decatur, Georgia 30030, its latest catalog, *Functional Furniture—*
an expensively produced booklet with transparent color overlays. You have
made good use of the catalog and have shared it with several others. Unfortunately, the catalog has disappeared and, although you've made a thorough
search, you can't find it. Write for a replacement copy.

(C) The personnel training director has showed you a copy of *Tips on Telephoning* and told you the booklet is available free from the New England Tele-

phone Company, Hartford, Connecticut 06103. You want 12 copies by May 1 for use in a special training class that you plan to conduct for secretaries and others in the Office Services Department. Write for them.

REQUESTING INFORMATION

PROBLEM

The Customer Accounts Unit is planning a new office layout in order to achieve better flow of paperwork, and you have been asked to help. One of the questions you must answer is, Is the available space adequate to accommodate the new layout? You know there are various devices by which the workableness of a layout can be tested without having to move furniture and equipment around to see whether it fits the space. These devices, include templates, planning boards, and three-dimensional models. However, none of your catalogs contains the information you want about these devices, nor can you find what you want in nearby office supply stores. You decide to write for information to one of the large dealers with whom you occasionally place special orders, the Pioneer Office Supply Corporation, Chicago.

BACKGROUND

Often you will write for information when you aren't exactly sure what you want or what the supplier has available. In these cases, you are asking the supplier to think through a problem with you and help you solve it. Obviously, to be of any assistance, the supplier must be told exactly what your problem is.

When you request information about a puzzling problem, be very specific. The supplier can't read your mind! At the same time, your request should be reasonable.

SOLUTION A

Dear Miss DiScenzo:

I am interested in layout devices. Please send me complete information.

Yours very truly,

Analysis of Solution A. Solution A might achieve its mission. If the correspondent for Pioneer Office Supply Corporation tries to put himself in the writer's shoes, he will probably come up with some kind of solution to the problem. But his job would be a lot easier if he had more information to go on. Besides giving too little information, the writer has committed two faults:

1. He has assumed that Pioneer carries layout devices even though they're not shown in the Pioneer catalog. The recipient of the letter is likely to think, "We don't handle layout devices. I'd better set this person straight."
2. His brevity and impersonal tone make the request seem unimportant. If Pioneer's correspondent is alert, however, he won't treat the request as routine (even though we tend to be influenced in what we are willing to do by the importance attached to the request by the person asking for help).

SOLUTION B

Dear Miss DiScenzo:

Will you help me? We are planning a new layout of our Customer Accounts Unit in order to provide for a more efficient flow of work.

The various devices used for making preliminary layouts, such as templates, planning boards, and three-dimensional models, are not available in the local stores, and I haven't found any in the dealer's catalogs. If you do carry them, I would appreciate having complete information about them, including costs, delivery time, and ordering procedures.

If you don't handle layout devices, can you refer me to a company that does? You may jot the name at the bottom of the enclosed copy of this letter and return it to me.

Sincerely yours,

Analysis of Solution B. Solution B is a much better letter than A for these reasons:

1. The writer frankly asks for help, telling his reader exactly what the problem is and how he has attempted (unsuccessfully) to solve it.
2. The tone of the letter is good; the writer is businesslike and, at the same time, courteous and appreciative.
3. All necessary background information is supplied, but the writer does not bury the reader in words.
4. The writer makes it easy for the reader to respond.

Projects

 As assistant office services manager, you are frequently asked by supervisors for advice on employee relations. You have learned that Ranier Films, Wilmington, Delaware 19801, distributes excellent motion pictures on the subject of supervision and human relations, and you decide to write for information. Prepare the letter.

(B) The catalog arrives from Ranier Films and contains descriptions of several interesting films that you are considering suggesting Far Western purchase for training purposes. There is also a list of new films under the heading "In Production—Soon to Be Released: *Motivating Employees, Group Dynamics, Communicating With Employees, Dos and Don'ts of Employee Ratings,* and *The Human Manager.*" No additional information is given for these new films, but you are interested in all of them. You would like to know when they will be available, whether they will be in black and white or color, the cost, and the running time of each. Write the letter.

(C) You plan to set up a small reference library for the secretaries in the Office Services Department who have requested source books on English grammar and style, word usage, secretarial procedures, and communications. You are not certain which books would be best for the purpose, and you decide to write the business books editors of several major publishing houses for their suggestions.

1. Criticize the following as to its effectiveness in obtaining the information you want.

Dear Sir:

Please send me all the information you have about setting up a reference library for our secretaries.

Yours truly,

2. Write a letter that will do the job better.

(D) The vice president has asked Mr. Prince, office services manager, to find out about accommodations at the Ridge Falls Hotel, near Santa Cruz, California, for a three-day conference of about 40 department managers and company executives. The date is not firm, but August 18–20 is being discussed. Mr. Prince asked an assistant to prepare a rough draft of a letter to Ridge Falls Hotel requesting the necessary information. Criticize the draft and then rewrite the letter.

Dear Sirs:

I would like to know about your facilities. Please send information about them, costs, etc.

Yours sincerely,

REQUESTING AN APPOINTMENT

PROBLEM

The Seattle branch office of Far Western Insurance Company has asked someone from the San Jose office to visit in Seattle for a few days to help straighten out a problem involving procedures for handling policyholders' changes of address. Mr. Prince has given you permission to go, and you already have your travel and hotel accommodations.

One of your equipment suppliers, VitaRecord Corporation, is located in Seattle, and while you are there, you would like to see the new line of visible indexing equipment the company has been advertising. You decide to call on some of the people at VitaRecord but need to make an appointment.

BACKGROUND

Those who "drop in" on a busy executive without an appointment are not only guilty of gross discourtesy but are likely to be disappointed because the person they want to see is not available. Just as many people resent relatives and friends who drop in for the weekend unannounced, many executives resent visitors—even potential customers—who show up without warning. Most executives operate on a tight schedule, and they like to plan their activities ahead of time. It is a good idea, then, to ask for an appointment in advance either by telephone or by letter. Letters requesting appointments should include the purpose of the visit, the date, and a suggested time. Obviously, such letters are requests, not demands.

SOLUTION A

Dear Mr. Rhodes:

I expect to be in Seattle two weeks from Tuesday. I want to see your filing equipment, and I will be at your office in the afternoon.

Very truly yours,

Analysis of Solution A.   Solution A violates most of the rules for effective request letters.

1. It is not specific—an exact date should have been given.
2. The purpose of the visit is not clear.
3. The time of the visit ("in the afternoon") is vague, and the writer would be presumptuous if she believes Mr. Rhodes will set aside an entire afternoon on the chance she will show up.
4. The letter lacks courtesy and tact; it demands rather than requests.

SOLUTION B

Dear Mr. Rhodes:

I expect to be in Seattle on Tuesday, June 8, to meet with some of our branch office people. While in Seattle, I would like to visit VitaRecord and see your complete line of visible indexing equipment.

Would you or someone else be available to show me the new equipment from two to about four on Tuesday afternoon the 8th and, at the same time, discuss my problem of maintaining visible records of policyholders?

If Tuesday is inconvenient, I might arrange to stay over another day. Let me know, please.

Sincerely,

Analysis of Solution B. What makes the second letter better than the first?

1. The writer is specific about the reason for a visit to Seattle—"to meet with some of our branch office people"—and Mr. Rhodes will understand that the trip is not being made for the specific purpose of visiting VitaRecord. The explanation tells Mr. Rhodes that the writer's time is limited, that he doesn't have to worry about entertaining her, and that there is nothing particularly urgent about her seeing the VitaRecord equipment.
2. The writer has included complete information as to the time and the things she hopes to accomplish on her visit. This information will give Mr. Rhodes an opportunity to prepare for the visit.
3. The letter is courteous in tone and makes no unreasonable demands.

Projects

(A) You are planning to attend the western zone meeting of the National Association of Office Supervisors in Denver, October 7–10, to be held at the Brown Palace Hotel. While you are in Denver, you want to visit the showrooms of the Rocky Mountain Office Furniture Company, a large manufacturer whose catalog of office furniture and equipment you have seen. The Sales Department of Far Western is considering modular offices for the sales representatives and their assistants, and you want to see the equipment for yourself. (Rocky Mountain's literature carries the invitation, "Visit our showrooms when you're in Denver—an acre of new ideas in office design.") Write to the sales manager for an appointment (you don't know the sales manager's name), suggesting a date and time for your visit.

(B) Mr. Prince is program chairman of the Western Accountants Society, which is considering holding its annual convention in Denver in December. He has had some correspondence with the Ski and Sun Motor Inn in downtown Denver and has received literature from the sales manager, Miss Claire Boudreau. Mr. Prince has asked you to visit Ski and Sun Motor Inn while you are in Denver to see its facilities and to talk with Miss Boudreau about the Society's particular needs for its convention. Write to Miss Boudreau for an appointment.

CASE 4

REQUESTING APPROVAL

PROBLEM

The Office Services Department subscribes to two magazines— *Management Science* and *Systems Digest*—which are circulated among those in the department who want to read them. A new magazine, *Forecast,* has come to your attention recently, and several people have said that they would like to read it regularly. Although the company library subscribes to *Forecast,* there is such a long waiting list for it that sometimes a month passes before a copy reaches your department. The magazine costs $12 a year, $20 for two years.

First, you must ask Mr. Prince for permission to subscribe to *Forecast* for departmental use. If he agrees, you must then write the publisher.

BACKGROUND: The Request Memo

When you request permission to do something that requires spending company money, it is wise to put your request in writing. In getting ready to write the memo to Mr. Prince about subscribing to *Forecast,* you will want to consider these think-plan questions:

1. What is my purpose?
2. What background information will Mr. Prince want?
3. On what basis can I justify this request?

SOLUTION A

TO: H. R. Prince Jr. **FROM:** Paul Brown
SUBJECT: Forecast Subscription **DATE:** April 24, 19—

Several people in the department want to read the new management magazine Forecast regularly. May we have your permission to subscribe to it?

Analysis of Solution A.   As you undoubtedly observed, the request memo does not contain sufficient information; the writer obviously did not think before he wrote. Management always wants to know *why* and *how much,* and Solution A does not provide these facts.

SOLUTION B

TO:	H. R. Prince Jr.	**FROM:**	Paul Brown
SUBJECT:	Forecast Subscription	**DATE:**	April 24, 19—

May I have your permission to subscribe to Forecast? It is a new management magazine that you may have seen (a copy accompanies this memo).

Several people in the department have asked to see Forecast on a regular basis. The library gets one copy each month, but often it is weeks before we see it; and sometimes we don't get it at all. Many have said it is the best management magazine they have ever read.

The subscription rate is $12 for one year and $20 for two years. I am thinking of a two-year subscription.

Analysis of Solution B.   This memo is effective because:

1. The writer indicated the purpose of the memo in the first sentence.
2. He sent a copy of the magazine to Mr. Prince. Attachments that assist in the selling job are always in order.
3. In the second paragraph the writer gave the necessary justification for a departmental subscription.
4. He stated the cost, always an important fact to the manager who has authority to spend company money.

BACKGROUND: The Subscription Letter

Mr. Prince writes the following on your memo and returns it to you: "OK. Subscribe in your name. Pay for it and put it on your expense account." You are now ready to write to the publisher, and the letter is a very simple one.

SOLUTION

Dear Ms. Hoitsman:

Here is my check for $20 for a two-year subscription to Forecast. Please address the magazine as follows:

Mr. Paul Brown
Office Services Department
Far Western Insurance Company
462 El Camino Real
San Jose, California 95120

Very truly yours,

Analysis of the Solution.   Observe these points about the letter requesting a subscription to *Forecast*:

1. The writer includes his name and address in the body of the letter. This is not always necessary, but some letterhead addresses are confusing, and Paul Brown wants to make certain the publisher knows who is to receive the magazine and how it should be addressed.
2. The writer tells the publisher that a check is enclosed. When sending a check or money order, always mention that fact and the amount. This information is valuable for your records and the recipient's as well.
3. The letter is brief and straightforward—very little needs to be said. If you wish, you can add something like this: "The people in the Office Services Department are delighted with *Forecast*. Most think it is the best management magazine available."

Projects

(A) You have been invited to become a member of the San Jose chapter of the National Association of Office Supervisors. The group meets monthly for dinner and a program that usually includes a speaker or a panel. You have attended three meetings during the past year as a guest, and you found them interesting and helpful. The annual dues are $10, which entitles members to a free monthly magazine, *Dynamic Supervision,* and to various reports and surveys published by the Association. The cost of dinner is $9.50.

   Write a memo to Mr. Prince requesting permission to join the Association.

(B) You receive an announcement (plus descriptive folder) of the Business Show to be held at the Fairmont Hotel in San Francisco. This show, which features exhibits of new office equipment, furniture, and supplies, will run for three days beginning Monday, April 11. You want to go for one day (it doesn't matter which day) and to take with you two supervisors (Mrs. Marple and Mr. Poirot) who have also expressed an interest in the show. You plan to drive up in Mrs. Marple's car and return the same day, and you estimate the total cost of the trip for all three of you will be about $25.

   Write the request memo to Mr. Prince.

(C) You received permission to attend the Business Show in San Francisco, but later you received a printed invitation to a special open house sponsored by Voca-Mation Inc., a company that recently entered the dictating machine business and has caused quite a stir with its new line. You want to go to the open house (the date is April 14), but you would have to stay over an extra day. You estimate the additional cost (hotel, train fare, etc.) will be about $45.

   Write the memo to Mr. Prince.

CASE 5 — REQUESTING AND ACKNOWLEDGING SPECIAL HELP

PROBLEM

Mr. Prince feels that there are too many different forms in use in the company. No one has made an effort to control the output of forms—in fact, anybody can make up his or her own forms and duplicate them in large quantity. The result is that supply rooms are overstocked with unused forms and files are bulging with duplicate records. Obviously, time and money are being spent foolishly. Mr. Prince is considering appointing one person, or perhaps a committee, to act as a clearinghouse for all new forms. He has asked you to make a study of practices concerning forms design and control in some of the leading firms in the country. You decide to write to office managers in 25 companies in various parts of the United States and to prepare an acknowledgment letter for all responses.

BACKGROUND: Requesting Special Help

The letters we have been talking about up to this point concerned requests for materials and information from people who find it to their advantage to grant the requests. Such letters require no particular persuasion or sales technique to get what is wanted.

Some asking letters, however, require a little different approach. These are the letters asking for favors that will benefit the writer more than the recipient. In writing such letters, keep in mind that the people with whom you correspond have little to gain from cooperating with you; thus you have a selling job to do.

When you write a letter asking for special help, make sure your letter measures up to these requirements: (1) Gives complete information about what is wanted and why it is wanted. (2) Makes it easy for the recipient to respond with a minimum of effort. (3) Is tactful, reasonable, and extremely courteous. (4) Conveys appreciation for assistance.

SOLUTION A

Dear Ms. Cortez:

Would you please tell me how you handle forms design, standardization, and control in your company. I would appreciate all the information I can get.

Sincerely,

Analysis of Solution A. Solution A is courteous and tactful and appreciative in tone. But it is not a good letter for these reasons:

1. It does not provide enough information. Ms. Cortez might understand what the writer wants to know, but there is a risk that she will not.
2. The response to such a letter will require much time and thought, and the writer has not made it easy for Ms. Cortez to respond. Thus the request borders on the unreasonable. When you are making a request of this kind, you should put yourself in the recipient's shoes and think hard about the difficulty you may be causing.

SOLUTION B

Dear Ms. Cortez:

Would you take just a few minutes to give me the benefit of your experience?

Our company is making a study of forms design, standardization, and control, and we are asking 25 top organizations to tell us how they handle the problem. I would be very grateful if you would answer the following questions in the space provided.

1. Is the responsibility for forms design, standardization, and control centralized in your company? Yes_____ No_____

   a. If your answer is Yes, what is the title of the person who has this responsibility?_____

   b. Does this person have management authority to approve or disapprove all forms used in the organization? Yes_____ No_____
   Exceptions:_____
   _____

2. Are most of your forms:

   a. Reproduced in the office?_____
   b. Done by a printer?_____

3. Have you used committees (representatives of various departments) to control forms usage? Yes_____ No_____ If your answer is Yes, was the plan:

   a. Satisfactory?_____
   b. Excellent?_____
   c. Unworkable?_____

4. What is the title of the person in your organization who is responsible for designing forms?

   _____

5. For which types of forms do you use inexpensive paper stock?

   _____

6. For which types of forms do you feel that rag stock is required?

   _____

If you care to make additional comments, I would be very pleased to have them.

An extra copy of this questionnaire is enclosed for your records. Please use the enclosed addressed envelope for returning the questionnaire to me.

Sincerely yours,

PS: Would you like to have a copy of the results of this study?
Yes_____ No_____

Analysis of Solution B. Observe the following characteristics of the letter to Ms. Cortez.

1. The purpose for which the information is needed is clearly stated.
2. The letter is complimentary to the reader ("benefit of your experience," "25 top organizations," and so on), but it is not effusive.
3. The questions are easy to answer; Ms. Cortez will not need to compose a letter.
4. A summary of the results of the study is offered. This courtesy is customarily extended to those who give such assistance.
5. An addressed envelope is enclosed. More often than not, a stamp is affixed to the return envelope.

BACKGROUND: Acknowledging Special Help

Courtesy demands that each response to a request for a special favor be acknowledged as soon as it is received.

The letter may be short; the writer should not try to lengthen a short, sincere message with a trite and stereotyped "Thanks again" in an effort to add another sentence or paragraph. If you can honestly and sincerely state how the reply has helped, you should do so and end the letter.

SOLUTION

Dear Ms. Cortez:

Thank you for completing the questionnaire concerning forms design, standardization, and control. I especially appreciate your added comments.

Just as soon as I have tabulated the results of the study, I shall see that you get a copy.

Sincerely yours,

Analysis of the Solution. The solution is courteous and appreciative in tone. It tells what the writer will do with the information and says that a copy of the results of the study will be sent when they are received.

Projects

(A) You are a member of the Employee Relations Committee. One of your assignments on this committee is to study the feasibility of publishing a magazine for company employees. You need to find out what type of magazine would be most suitable, how large it should be, how often it should be published, how much it will cost, and so forth.

You decide to write to 100 different companies throughout the country for help. You want sample issues from them (two or three different ones, if possible). You would like to know how often the magazine is published, whether the company has a professional staff of editors whose sole job is to publish the magazine, employee reaction to the magazine, the number of copies printed, and whether the magazine is restricted to employees or is available to others. You would also like a statement from each company as to the main purpose of the magazine (some magazines feature management information, others emphasize employee activities, and so on). And you would like to know the annual cost of publishing the magazine.

Prepare a letter to send to the 100 companies you have selected, making it as easy as possible for each recipient to respond.

(B) Several companies respond to your request (Project A) with very helpful comments, supplying much more information than you asked for. Write a thank-you letter.

(C) Mr. Prince has asked you to lead a management seminar, a monthly meeting of department heads at which company policies and practices are discussed. The theme of your meeting is "Simplification of Personnel Procedures."

The February meeting of the National Association of Office Supervisors featured Anna Robles, of Management Consultants Inc., a firm in Stockton, California. In making her presentation, Mrs. Robles used a set of flip charts showing, by means of diagrams and cartoon drawings, the process of recruiting, hiring, placing, training, and promoting personnel. You would like to use these charts in your meeting. Write Mrs. Robles (you met her after the NAOS meeting and learned that her firm has done consulting work for Far Western) asking if the flip charts might be made available to you.

(D) Mrs. Robles (Project C) sends the charts and tells you that you may keep them; she has several sets. Write the appropriate letter to Mrs. Robles, assuming that the charts were used with great success in your presentation and will be very useful in future management meetings.

(E) Your company is considering overhauling its pension plan for employees, and you have been asked to study the problem and prepare a preliminary set of recommendations. In a recent issue of *Employee Relations* there is an excellent article entitled "Trends in Pension Plans." You would like to quote from this article in your report. Write to Paul Bahnsen, the editor, for permission.

INVITING AND THANKING A SPEAKER

PROBLEM

You are program chairperson of the Western States Management Conference, which will hold its spring meeting at the St. Francis Hotel in San Francisco on March 25 and 26. The theme of the convention is "Management *Is* Communication," and you have been looking for a keynote speaker—one who can open the meeting dynamically and set the stage for the rest of the program.

Ms. Berna Tillstrom, of Portland, Oregon, is a well-known authority in management. She has written many articles on management communications and is a consultant to several large corporations. Your committee has selected Ms. Tillstrom as the keynote speaker, and you are to write asking her if she will accept the invitation.

After the conference is over, you are to write Ms. Tillstrom a thank-you letter.

BACKGROUND: Asking Someone to Give a Speech

Letters asking someone to give a speech, write an article, or perform some other special service are of the persuasive type. Although outstanding speakers and writers usually receive a fee for their work, often they are very busy or the fee offered is not enough to make the assignment worthwhile. In writing letters to people whose services are in considerable demand, you should emphasize the importance of the affair at which they are invited to speak and why they were chosen for the engagement.

SOLUTION A

Dear Ms. Tillstrom:

The Western States Management Conference will hold its spring meeting at the St. Francis Hotel in San Francisco on March 25 and 26. The theme of the convention is "Management Is Communication."

Would you be willing to keynote this conference? We will pay you an honorarium of $500 plus all expenses.

May I hear from you?

Sincerely yours,

Analysis of Solution A.   The writer of Solution A was not at all persuasive in the invitation. There is no information given concerning the nature of the meeting or any indication as to why Ms. Tillstrom was selected. Too, the details of the meeting (such as length of the keynote talk) are missing. The most serious fault, however, is the strong inference that Ms. Tillstrom will be more interested in the $500 fee than in performing a professional service. It is usually wise in such letters to mention the fee only incidentally— not to emphasize it.

SOLUTION B

Dear Ms. Tillstrom:

The theme of the Western States Management Conference this spring is "Management Is Communication." Our members would be greatly honored if you would deliver the keynote address.

Your pioneering work in employee communication and your excellent writings on the subject—plus your reputation for being able to capture and hold an audience—make you the unanimous choice of our program committee.

The conference will be at the St. Francis Hotel in San Francisco on March 25 and 26. The keynote address is scheduled for 7:30 on Friday evening, the 25th. We are allowing 30 to 40 minutes for it and are prepared to offer you an honorarium of $500, plus all expenses.

Can you be with us? All of us certainly hope you can. Just as soon as I hear from you, I will telephone and give you complete details. We expect an audience of about 300 from eleven western states.

Please let me know as quickly as you can. If you prefer, you can telephone me at (415) 555–4190.

Sincerely yours,

Analysis of Solution B.   You probably have already spotted the things that make the letter to Ms. Tillstrom an effective one.

1. It is persuasive. Ms. Tillstrom should feel that she has an important contribution to make to this conference.
2. It is friendly.
3. It supplies the basic information Ms. Tillstrom needs to either accept or refuse the invitation.

BACKGROUND: Thanking a Speaker

The quality of the speech given will, of course, determine the content of the thank-you. If the talk was well given and well received, the letter should be courteous, sincere, and appreciative. Any complimentary remarks made regarding the talk can be honestly stated.

SOLUTION A

Dear Ms. Tillstrom:

Your keynote talk, "What Is Your Communication IQ?" set exactly the right tone for our conference. You will be pleased to know that your remarks were referred to time and again by the speakers in the various group meetings, leaving no doubt at all that your message reached home.

I am sure you know from your long experience that a good keynote speech can make or break a convention. The fact that this was the most successful conference we have ever had should be ample evidence of the effectiveness of your presentation.

Sincerely yours,

Analysis of Solution A.   The letter is effective because it is courteous, sincere, and appreciative. The writer's comment regarding the speaker's ability to "reach home" is important because speakers recognize that their audience's understanding is important to their success.

SOLUTION B

If, however, the keynote talk was disappointing, the speaker still deserves a letter of appreciation for making the trip and participating in the program. Such a letter is tricky to write. You do not want to tell Ms. Tillstrom she was great when she was not. On the other hand, nothing will be gained by writing an unpleasant letter.

Dear Ms. Tillstrom:

You will be pleased to know that our Western States Management Conference went very well. The reaction of the various audiences was generally enthusiastic, and the conference members are already talking about another convention next year—possibly even this fall.

I hope your trip back to Portland was a pleasant one and that you made your early Saturday morning appointment without difficulty.

Thank you for your participation in our conference. I enjoyed meeting you, and I was greatly interested in your provocative remarks.

Sincerely yours,

Analysis of Solution B.   This letter shows appreciation to the speaker for making the trip and assisting in the program. It is honest in that it doesn't say that the talk was well given or well received—simply that the reaction to the conference itself was generally enthusiastic. All in all, this letter is a tactful, effective thank-you message to a speaker who, at least in the writer's opinion, did somewhat less than an outstanding job.

Projects

(A) The March 19 issue of *Personnel Weekly* featured an article, "A New Approach to Incentive Compensation," by Mrs. Phyllis Larsen, which you found highly provocative. The biographical sketch that accompanied the article mentioned that Mrs. Larsen travels widely speaking to management groups. As program chairperson of the National Association of Office Supervisors, you would like to book Mrs. Larsen for the evening meeting of October 17. You are authorized to offer an honorarium of $300 plus expenses. The dinner begins at 6:30, followed by the main speaker at about 8:30. The speaker is usually asked to speak for about 40 minutes and then to answer questions from the audience (20 to 30 minutes). Write the letter to Mrs. Larsen, assuming that details such as place, hotel reservations, and so on, will be supplied later.

(B) Mrs. Larsen's speech (Project A) was very well received. Although several people felt that her ideas on wage incentives were far out, the discussion following her presentation was very lively and ran twice as long as usual. You received telephone calls the next day from a number of those who were at the meeting, telling you it was the best meeting of the year. Write Mrs. Larsen an appropriate letter, enclosing a check for $300 and reminding her to send you a statement of her expenses.

(C) Mrs. Larsen returns the honorarium, saying that company policy prevents her accepting fees or travel expenses and thanking you for your hospitality. You are informed by the president of NAOS that the $300 check will go into the Association's scholarship fund for outstanding local high school students. Write Mrs. Larsen to that effect.

(D) In a course that you are conducting for supervisors at Far Western Insurance you have scheduled several guest speakers—men and women from the San Francisco–Oakland Bay area who have achieved distinction in their various specialities.

At last week's session, you had invited Blanche Bedell, vice president of California Consultants Inc., to speak on the subject "Evaluating Employee Performance." However, Mrs. Bedell was called out of town at the last minute and sent in her place Joseph Zincus, a member of Mrs. Bedell's firm. Unfortunately, Mr. Zincus had virtually no time to prepare for his presentation, and the result was disappointing. Several people in the course came to you later to say that the evening was a waste of time.

You must write an appreciative note to Mr. Zincus, however. After all, he gave up an evening for you and did the best he could under very difficult circumstances. Prepare the letter.

CASE 7

PLACING AN ORDER BY LETTER

PROBLEM

The Office Services Department is setting up a small reference library, and Mr. Prince has asked you to place orders for the books that have been recommended by the people in the department.

From the catalogs of various publishers you obtain the information you need to place your orders—titles, authors, prices, etc.

BACKGROUND

Orders can be placed in three different ways:

On a purchase order form. Prepared by the company's purchasing officers, the purchase order authorizes the supplier to ship merchandise and to charge the purchaser at the quoted price.

A purchase order may or may not be accompanied by a letter. If a letter is written, it merely identifies the enclosure without repeating the information in the form.

> Dear Mr. Rhodes:
>
> Here is Purchase Order 362-18-99 for the visible indexing equipment we discussed when I was in Seattle.
>
> Sincerely,

On an order blank. Some vendors supply printed forms for their customers' use.

By letter. Usually an order is placed by letter only when the company does not use purchase order forms or when there are no order blanks on hand from the vendor. In writing order letters, correspondents should first ask themselves these questions:

1. What specific information (quantity, color, and size) will the vendor need to have from me about the items I want to order?
2. Is a check to accompany the order or will the supplier bill me later for the merchandise?
3. How are the items to be shipped?

Assume that Far Western does not use purchase order forms and that you do not have order blanks from a publisher from whom you want to purchase books. You wish to place an order for six different titles from this publishing house.

SOLUTION

Gentlemen:

Please send me 2 copies of each of the following books:

Code No.	Author	Title	Price	Extension
06012	Day	The Writer's Source Book	$11.95	$ 23.90
07630	Stein	Handbook of Management	17.50	35.00
11020	Carter	Style Reference for Writers	6.95	13.90
17325	O'Hara and Fox	Office Cost Accounting	9.95	19.90
02111	Ortega	Computer Data Processing	11.50	23.00
83210	Pasquale	Dictionary of Business Terms	16.95	33.90
		Total		$149.60

Our check for $149.60, plus shipping charges, will be sent to you immediately upon receipt of these books.

Very truly yours,

Analysis of the Solution.   Observe these points about the foregoing order letter:

1. Complete information is given—publisher's code number, author, title, and unit price. Column headings, though not absolutely essential, guide the reader.
2. The extension figures are optional; however, they help to make it clear to the publisher that two copies of each book are being ordered.
3. No mention is made of the method of shipment. The writer assumes that the publisher will select the best method in terms of speed and economy. If, however, the books are needed at once and the writer is willing to pay extra for Air Express, this fact should be mentioned in the letter.

Projects

(A) Order these three books from Acropolis Publishing Company (make up an address) for the Office Services Department library: *Complete Handbook of Personnel Management* (by E. R. Chisholm), $17.50; *Color Guide for the Professional Designer* (by Steven Hotchkiss), $47.50; and *Readings in Modern Management* (by Smith and Wesley), $12.75. Assume that your company has established credit with Acropolis and that you will be billed. You need the books within two weeks and ask that they be sent by Air Express, for which you will pay the charges.

(B) The Reprint Service Department of *Lincoln Accounting Review* offers reprints of articles that have appeared in the magazine. In a recent advertisement, you ran across six articles that you would like reprints of: "Capital Budgeting," Reprint 16, 25¢ each, 50 copies; "Long-Range Forecasting," Reprint 24, 20¢ each, 50 copies; "Inventory Valuation," Reprint 33, 40¢ each, 25 copies; "Financial Ratios," Reprint 47, 15¢ each, 60 copies; "Financial Statement Analysis," Reprint 59, 50¢ each, 30 copies; and "Preparing Financial Reports," Reprint 63, 35¢ each, 40 copies.

Write a letter to the magazine, placing your order for these reprints. You will enclose your check for the total (the magazine pays the postage).

CASE 8

TRANSMITTING IMPORTANT PAPERS

PROBLEM

Recently the company entered into an agreement with the local office of a computer manufacturing company for service to be provided by data processing equipment and for consulting service on programming and systems analysis. Two copies of the contract, with one slight change which was agreed upon in a telephone conversation between C. J. Webb of the computer manufacturing company and R. C. Boswell, vice president and treasurer of your firm, have been signed by Mr. Boswell. One copy has been retained for Far Western's files and the other copy is to be returned to the computer manufacturing company. You are to write the letter transmitting the contract.

BACKGROUND

When you send a check, a contract, a report, or any other valuable or hard-to-replace document to someone outside your company, it is always a good idea to send a transmittal letter with it. Similarly, when you send such a document to someone within your own company, always write a transmittal memo to go with it. The main reason, of course, is to provide a record (your file copy of the letter or memo) of *when* you sent *what* to *whom* and, if appropriate, *why*. Another reason is to assure proper delivery of the document and to let the receiver know what action, if any, is expected of him or her.

SOLUTION

Attention: Ms. C. J. Webb

Ladies and Gentlemen:

Enclosed is a copy of the signed agreement covering services to our Data Processing Department for one year. We have retained the original.

Note the change in paragraph 1 (c) relating to minimum number of hours to be delivered under this agreement. This change was agreed upon by Ms. Webb and Mr. Boswell, vice president and treasurer of Far Western, in their telephone conversation on Wednesday, the 16th.

Yours very truly,

Analysis of the Solution. This is a good transmittal letter.

1. Although the letter is addressed to the computer company, the writer has directed it to the attention of the representative who negotiated the contract. This is not unusual because the contract is with the company, not with Ms. Webb. The letter could have been addressed personally to Ms. Webb, which is the more common practice.
2. The writer mentions the subject of the contract so that it can be easily identified.
3. The writer points out the change that was made, citing the authority for it ("agreed upon by Ms. Webb and Mr. Boswell, vice president and treasurer of Far Western, in their telephone conversation on Wednesday, the 16th").

INTEROFFICE TRANSMITTALS

When you transmit important papers to people in your own organization, you should write an accompanying memorandum. This puts the disposition of the papers on record and establishes responsibility for their ownership or safekeeping. For example:

TO: Therese Waddell   **FROM:** D. G. Crews

SUBJECT: Personnel Department Layouts   **DATE:** August 11, 19—

Attached are the final layouts for the following units of the Personnel Department:

A   Recruitment and Selection

B   Wage and Salary Administration

C   Training

D   Personnel Records

E   Employee Services

I have retained only the "roughs" from which these final layouts were made.

DGC

Projects

Ⓐ As president of the Western Accountants Society, Mr. Prince recently signed an agreement with Ski and Sun Motor Inn, Denver, for the Society's annual convention, which will be held December 2–5. The original of the agreement is to be sent to Miss Claire Boudreau, the sales manager of the motor inn. Write the letter of transmittal.

(B) You have written a report, "Cost Control in Office Administration," at the request of Mr. Prince. He has complimented you on the report and is eager for several people in other departments to read and react to it. Prepare a transmittal memorandum.

(C) The accounting department has sent you the check for the Acropolis Publishing Company for $82.35, which you are to transmit. The check is in payment for books ordered for the Office Services Department library (Project A, page 123), and the vendor's invoice number is PC 41913.

CASE 9

CONFIRMING ORAL AGREEMENTS

PROBLEM

Mr. Prince has arranged to have a local firm refinish and repair some of the office furniture in the Purchasing Department. He has had several conversations with Raymond Courtland, owner of a furniture refinishing company, and they have reached an oral agreement that you are to confirm in writing.

BACKGROUND

It makes good business sense to confirm in writing any important oral agreement. Too often people forget conversations or misunderstand the terms agreed upon. Then, when one person doesn't live up to the agreement, problems arise. Written confirmations of oral agreements should be specific as to who is to do what, where, and when—and, if appropriate, the terms of payment.

If proof of delivery is necessary, send the letter by registered mail—and if you want to go all the way, request that a signed receipt of delivery be returned to you. Another way in which you can make sure of delivery, as well as acceptance of the terms, is to type at the bottom of the letter "Accepted and agreed to," with space for the recipient's signature and the date. If you follow the latter procedure, you will need to send two copies of the letter and ask the recipient to sign both copies and return one to you.

SOLUTION A

Dear Mr. Courtland:

This will confirm our agreement whereby you are to refinish six executive chairs, eight double-pedestal metal desks, and six 4-drawer filing cabinets at a total of $1,320.

Very truly yours,

Analysis of Solution A. Solution A is inadequate because it describes too vaguely the work Mr. Courtland is to do. The word *refinish* could mean a number of things—simply repainting, for example. Where is the work to be done? When is it to be done? What is Mr. Courtland to supply?

SOLUTION B

Dear Mr. Courtland:

This will confirm the oral agreement we reached yesterday afternoon concerning the work you are to do on our office furniture.

1. Six Executive Chairs. You are to sand and refinish in walnut stain all exposed wood, replace all casters, and reupholster in Tufftex vinyl plastic (three in camel tan and three in blue spruce, for which you have samples). The price we agreed on is $100 for each chair, regardless of present condition.

2. Eight Double-Pedestal Metal Desks. Chips and cracks are to be smoothed out and each desk is to be painted metallic gray (two coats). No work is required on the Formica surfaces, except that they are to be cleaned. The price we agreed on is $60 for each desk, regardless of present condition.

3. Six 4-Drawer Filing Cabinets. Chips and cracks are to be smoothed out and each cabinet is to be painted metallic gray (two coats). The stainless steel handles are not to be painted. The price we agreed on is $40 for each cabinet, regardless of present condition.

All work is to be done on your premises, and you will furnish the paint, vinyl, casters, and all other materials. At your expense, you will pick up the furniture on July 10 and return it to us on or before August 12. Payment will be made on the delivery date.

Please write to me immediately if you have any questions about this agreement.

Cordially yours,

Analysis of Solution B. Solution B provides a written confirmation of what was actually agreed upon.

1. Notice the enumeration of the three types of equipment that are to receive attention from Mr. Courtland, with a description of what is to be done to each.

2. Because most controversies arise over money matters, the agreed-upon price is put in writing so that there will be no question later.
3. The last paragraph gives Mr. Courtland a chance to take issue if he does not agree. If he does not protest, he cannot say later that he did not understand the terms.

Projects

(A) The Program Committee of the National Association of Office Supervisors, of which you are a member, is planning an afternoon meeting and dinner on June 12 at Morningside Manor in Carmel, about sixty miles away. The committee chairman has asked you to make reservations. You talked to the assistant manager of Morningside Manor by telephone and made tentative reservations for (1) a private meeting room for ten people, (2) single sleeping rooms for six (yourself, Judy Patterson, Leo Frailey, Peter Musette, Jane Logan, and Morris Haritan) for one night, and (3) dinner (to be selected from the menu) for ten in a private dining room. The hotel is to supply the meeting room without charge and is to bill NAOS for the dinner. Each person staying overnight is to pay for his or her own room (the rate is $20). Confirm your reservation request by letter.

(B) This morning Marcia Stoll, the representative of Seaway Stationers, called on you to discuss your needs for stationery and supplies. You placed an order for 10,000 letterheads, 8½ by 11 inches, with 7,500 matching envelopes; 5,000 letterheads, 7¼ by 10½ inches (Monarch), with 3,000 matching envelopes; and 2,000 business cards for Mr. Prince and you. Although you gave Ms. Stoll this information, plus samples that she is to match exactly, you decide to confirm the order in writing. Prices are in accordance with Seaway's May 1 schedule.

CASE 10

FOLLOW-UP LETTERS AND MEMOS

PROBLEM

Over a month ago you asked Steelway Equipment Company to send you a price list on the Rock-a-Way Filing Cabinet line, and you haven't received either the price list or a letter of explanation. A letter from you asking for action is in order.

BACKGROUND

Follow-up letters and memos are commonplace in business. People fail to respond to communications for a number of reasons. They don't realize they are supposed to respond. They lose or misplace requests. They fall behind in their work and don't get around to writing. They simply ignore requests. Or they must give a "no" answer and don't know how to say it. There are any number of reasons and excuses—all of which lead to follow-up letters and memos.

Secretaries often keep a tickler file of requests their bosses have made (oral as well as written, and in-company as well as out-of-company requests). At the appropriate time, the secretary either follows up on the request or reminds the boss to do so.

SOLUTION A

Dear Mr. Luzinski:

I can't understand why you didn't respond to my request for a new price list on your Rock-a-Way line of filing cabinets. It has been over a month. Obviously, we're not going to place any orders with you until we can compare your prices with those of other manufacturers (all the others responded).

I hope you will be courteous enough to reply this time.

Very truly yours,

Analysis of Solution A.   It is readily apparent, of course, that Solution A reflects the writer's anger. Certainly it is annoying when your requests seem to be ignored, but a "mad" letter is not the answer. Threats and insults are unlikely to produce the desired results.

Such statements as "I can't understand why," "Obviously, we're not going to place any orders with you," "all the others responded," and "I hope you will be courteous enough to reply this time" are particularly offensive.

SOLUTION B

Dear Mr. Luzinski:

On August 12 I wrote asking for a new price list on your Rock-a-Way line of filing cabinets. I suspect that my letter did not reach you because I haven't received the materials or an acknowledgment.

We are getting together comparative prices on new filing equipment, and I don't want to place an order until I have prices of all leading manufacturers. May I have yours by September 20 at the latest?

Sincerely yours,

Analysis of Solution B.   Solution B is a better letter than A because it creates a desire on the part of the manufacturer to do the right thing and do it quickly. Note these features of Solution B.

1. The letter gives the recipient the benefit of the doubt insofar as the first request is concerned.

2. The second paragraph says in effect, "If you want a chance at getting our business, you had better give us the information we need," but of course the statement is much more tactful.
3. The specific response date—September 20—should be a red flag to the manufacturer.

INTEROFFICE FOLLOW-UPS

It is important to have some system for following up on interoffice requests. Some people make notes on their desk calendar; others use the same tickler file used for letters. Here is a typical follow-up memo from an administrative assistant.

TO:	Vera W. Fleming	**FROM:**	M. C. Harmon
SUBJECT:	Topics for <u>Executive Notes</u>	**DATE:**	February 15, 19—

In Mr. Werner's memo of January 24, he asked department heads to send him by February 15 news stories that he might include in <u>Executive Notes</u>. I have not received your copy, and I must have it by February 18 at the latest.

Projects

(A) Last month you filled out an advertising coupon from *The Administrator* in which readers were invited to send for a free booklet, *Communicating With Employees*. You affixed the coupon to the company letterhead and sent it to Lathrop Paper Company. The materials have not arrived, and you would like to have them for a report you are preparing on management-employee communications. Write a follow-up letter.

(B) On January 15, you wrote to all department heads, asking them to submit by February 15 a report on their equipment needs for the second quarter (April–June). It is now February 15, and several reports are still missing. Write a follow-up memo, mentioning February 17 as the final deadline.

(C) About three months ago you wrote the following letter to Tele-Media Communications Systems.

Gentlemen:

Please send me descriptive literature on your Speedi-Com Interoffice Communication Systems. We are considering installing an audio system sometime this year, and I am interested in Speedi-Com.

Do you also handle signaling devices? If so, I should like information about them as well.

Sincerely yours,

You received the following response.

Dear Miss Carpenter:

I am delighted to send you our most recent catalog describing our Speedi-Com Communication Systems. I think you will find among these various systems precisely the one that fits your special needs.

If you need further help, why not telephone or write our San Francisco distributor, Golden State Electronics Corporation. They'll be glad to send someone to talk with you at your convenience.

Yours sincerely,

The catalog describing Speedi-Com Systems arrived very shortly after you received the letter; however, no information was supplied concerning the signaling devices you asked about. Follow up.

WINNING AND KEEPING CUSTOMERS

YOUR JOB *You are assistant manager of Pickwick Manor, a large hotel in Pompano Beach, Florida. Although the hotel provides accommodations by the week to individuals, its principal business comes from firms, organizations, and associations who use it for meetings and conferences. The hotel provides regular room accommodations for the conference participants, meals, meeting rooms, and banquet facilities. Various recreational opportunities are available—swimming, golf, tennis, boating, surfing, and so on. Your job involves not only management of the daily activities of Pickwick Manor but also advertising and promotion, customer services and relations, and general public relations.*

CASE 1

SUPPLYING INFORMATION TO PROSPECTIVE CUSTOMERS

PROBLEM

Your manager, Chris Nettles, gives you the following letter from the Marlow Cement Manufacturing Company, signed by Carl E. Bigelow, executive vice president.

> Dear Miss Nettles:
>
> We are planning a conference of our regional managers December 3–7 and are considering the Pompano Beach area. Your place has been recommended to us by several people who have had successful meetings there.
>
> We will need 12 double rooms and 6 single rooms to accommodate a total of 30 people (12 managers and their families).
>
> Would you please supply information about your facilities and rates and let me know whether you could accommodate us on the dates indicated.
>
> Sincerely yours,

BACKGROUND

The request from Mr. Bigelow illustrates the type that every business depends on to survive. Such requests are the result of the expenditure of a great deal of money for advertising, sales representatives, and good service. And speaking of good service, the greatest compliment a business can receive is the recommendation of a satisfied customer.

Business spends millions upon millions of dollars every year on direct mail and other forms of advertising, sales personnel, and various types of promotion in order to attract letters such as the one illustrated. Unfortunately, many of the people who handle such inquiries do not realize the effort and money that have been expended to generate these sales opportunities, and they make the mistake of treating them routinely.

To supply information to prospective customers, most commercial firms prepare special booklets, often printed in color. Depending upon the number of inquiries they receive, they send the booklets to prospective customers with a personal letter, a form letter, or a printed acknowledgment memo or card. Obviously, a well-written personal letter is most effective, but when hundreds of responses to inquiries must be prepared each month, the cost of such personal messages is usually prohibitive.

Pickwick Manor is a relatively small enterprise, however, and its staff answers every inquiry with a personal letter.

SOLUTION A

Dear Mr. Bigelow:

Enclosed is our colorful brochure describing the facilities of Pickwick Manor. We can accommodate your group nicely December 3–7.

Sincerely,

Analysis of Solution A.   Solution A may do the job if the brochure accompanying it is sufficiently impressive. But the writer has obviously treated the request routinely, saying in effect, "We don't care whether you choose Pickwick Manor or not." And when one thinks of all the effort that has been expended to generate this kind of sales lead, such a response seems a very feeble effort at this crucial moment.

SOLUTION B

Dear Mr. Bigelow:

It's good to know that you are thinking of Pickwick Manor for your regional managers conference December 3–7. We will be very glad to have you.

The enclosed brochure was prepared especially to give you the information you will want. Please note that you will be entitled to our summer rates (the winter rates, which are considerably higher, go into effect December 15).

Although Pickwick realizes the importance of your conference and makes sure you have the best possible facilities for that purpose, we expect you will find time for relaxation too. Our tennis courts, golf course, swimming facilities, and indoor game rooms are the finest in this area (we can arrange for deep-sea fishing expeditions too!).

Our social director, Mrs. Mary Glendenning, considers it an essential part of her job to see that the conference participants' families are happily occupied during the day. Mary arranges for sight-seeing tours, boat trips, fashion shows, and bargain-hunting excursions for those who want to be on the go; but she realizes that some guests will want no more than a beach chair, a book, and someone to bring them a cool drink from time to time.

With the hope you will choose Pickwick Manor for your conference, Mr. Bigelow, I am tentatively holding accommodations for you. May I suggest that you let me know your plans by September 14—reservations for December are filling up rapidly.

Sincerely yours,

Analysis of Solution B.   Solution B will do a better job than A for these reasons:

1. The letter is personal. Although many business firms prepare form letters for the purpose of answering inquiries, such letters can, with only slight adaptation, be individualized. In solution B, for example, note:

a. The specific reference in the first paragraph to the date of the conference and the group (regional managers).
b. The description of special activities for conference participants' families. (Mr. Bigelow's letter mentioned that families would be included.)
2. The writer does not repeat the information contained in the accompanying brochure but merely emphasizes some of the important points described in it—special rates, meeting facilities, and recreational opportunities.
3. The writer asks for action (last paragraph). One of the cardinal rules of selling is this: Try to get prospects to make a favorable decision—ask for their business.

Projects

The following letter from Arthur O. Lasser, executive secretary of the United Air Conditioning Institute, is given to you by your manager.

Dear Miss Nettles:

The United Air Conditioning Institute is conducting a three-day meeting March 16–18, and we are looking for an appropriate site. Your hotel has been recommended to us.

Do you have accommodations on those dates? We are expecting about 300 people to attend. We will need ten separate conference rooms for our section meetings, an auditorium for our general meetings, luncheon and dinner facilities (two luncheon and two dinner affairs are scheduled), and, of course, adequate sleeping accommodations.

Please send details, including prices. Incidentally, we are allowing a half day for recreation. Would it be possible to reserve exclusive golf accommodations for our party one afternoon (we would guarantee at least 100 players)? Also, what arrangements can be made to transport some of our people to and from Miami on that day?

Yours very truly,

Prepare a response, assuming that you can accommodate Mr. Lasser's group on the dates mentioned and that you will enclose descriptive literature on Pickwick Manor. Exclusive golf privileges can be arranged with Sunny Slopes Golf Club, the price of which is $1,000 regardless of the number of players (the Club also rents golf clubs and carts). Pickwick Manor operates its own bus service to and from Miami, as well as to all airports, at no charge to guests.

Shortly after you wrote to Mr. Lasser, you received the following letter.

Thank you for the information concerning Pickwick Manor. We are studying the materials you sent and will let you know our decision as quickly as possible.

I forgot to ask about the availability of audiovisual equipment for our meetings, and I did not find mention of them in your materials. We will need a 16mm motion picture projector, two or three cassette playback units, two Carousel slide projectors, screens, and perhaps other equipment. Will you be able to supply this equipment, or must we arrange for it ourselves?

Respond to the letter. Assume that you have the equipment he needs (or can obtain it locally) but that you would like to have a specific list so that you can make sure there will be no slipup.

FOLLOWING UP INQUIRIES

PROBLEM

Mr. Bigelow has not responded to the letter you wrote him about his December 3–7 conference (Case 1). It is now September 15 and you had asked for a reply by the 14th. You decide to write a follow-up letter.

BACKGROUND

Business firms are not satisfied when their first response to an inquiry produces no results, and they set up a system for follow-up. Some organizations write as many as four letters to the prospect in hopes of getting a favorable response. Others send telegrams (indicating urgency) to encourage response to an inquiry.

SOLUTION A

Dear Mr. Bigelow:

I cannot hold the tentative reservation I made for your group beyond September 25. Please let me know at once whether you intend to be with us.

Sincerely,

Analysis of Solution A.   Solution A will only annoy Mr. Bigelow. He did not ask that facilities be reserved—he merely inquired about them—and the writer seems miffed that she has not received a confirmation.

SOLUTION B (Telegram)

Hope you can still be with us for December regional managers conference. Reservations filling up. Urge you make yours right away.

Analysis of Solution B.   Telegrams may attract more than routine attention. On the other hand, a telegram used as a promotion device may nettle those who associate telegrams with crisis situations; they may consider it a false alarm, a hard sell. The sales correspondent, therefore, must weigh the telegram's merits against its shortcomings.

SOLUTION C

Dear Mr. Bigelow:

Your reservations at Pickwick Manor for 12 double rooms and 6 single rooms to accommodate a total of 30 people for your December 3–7 conference are still being held. Although you did not ask me to, I wanted to make sure we could accommodate you when you made your final plans. Unfortunately, Mr. Bigelow, I won't be able to guarantee accommodations for you beyond September 25. May I please know your plans by that date.

You will be interested to know that we have recently added a solarium with indoor pool at Pickwick. Now, no matter what the weather outside, you can always be assured of good swimming every day.

Sincerely yours,

Analysis of Solution C.   Solution C is a tactful and persuasive follow-up letter. Note that the writer mentions a new attraction at Pickwick Manor (the solarium with swimming pool), an effective method of reawakening interest in a cooled-off prospect.

Projects

(A) Mr. Lasser (Project A, page 135) has not responded to your letter. Write an appropriate follow-up letter, reinforcing Pickwick Manor's advantages and hinting that reservations should be made now while there is still space available.

(B) Two weeks have gone by since you wrote your follow-up letter to Mr. Lasser. Compose a telegram that you might now send as a last-ditch effort to get the business.

(C) Mr. Lasser responds at last, telling you that the membership has voted to hold its convention in the Pocono Mountains of Pennsylvania. He expresses his appreciation for your help and the hope that at a future date the United Air Conditioning Institute will come to Pickwick Manor. Write an appropriate response.

WRITING PROMOTION AND SALES LETTERS

PROBLEM

You have obtained a copy of the *Directory of Under-40 Presidents Association*—a list of 1,520 men and women who became the chief executive officers of their companies before reaching the age of 40. This is a new organization, and your boss at Pickwick Manor has asked you to prepare a letter that will sell these young executives on using Pickwick Manor for their away-from-home company conferences and meetings.

BACKGROUND

Every letter we write sells something, even if it's only a point of view or an idea. But the true sales letter has the primary objective of persuading people to spend money for a product or service immediately or of putting them in the mood to do so later.

Letters that attempt to make immediate sales, to get inquiries that may lead to sales, to determine interest in a new product or service, or to support other promotion efforts (for example, to "soften up" a prospect for a sales representative's call), all come under the heading of direct-mail promotion. Perhaps you have often wondered (as you threw away, unopened or unread, sales letters that you received) whether direct mail really pays off. It does—for certain organizations and products. You wouldn't use a sales letter to sell a package of gum or a tube of toothpaste because the letter would cost more than the profit on the item. But direct mail is used extensively to sell magazine subscriptions, life insurance, stocks and bonds, luggage, appliances, air travel, and other higher-priced goods and services. Every year many dollars are spent on sales letters of one sort or another because through direct mail you can select your audience and often get the most of each dollar spent.

In most organizations, sales letters are written by people who are responsible for advertising and promotion, which is where the responsibility belongs. Sales letters are a specialty all their own. Even experienced promotion people often turn to advertising agencies and direct-mail specialists for help with sales letters. Since letters can be extremely costly, advertising managers seek to make every carefully budgeted advertising dollar count by reducing the odds of producing a loser. The advertising manager who has a large mailing list may attempt to reduce the risk of wasting money by preparing two or three different sales letters and testing the pulling power of each by mailing them to small segments of the complete list. The one that gets the best response in the test mailing is chosen for the larger mailing.

What will be your responsibility for writing sales letters? If you work in the sales promotion department of a company or in the general field of advertising, you're likely to write many sales letters and other direct-mail pieces. Or if you manage a small business where you have to do a little bit of everything, you'll probably write some sales letters. If you become a sales manager or marketing director, you will have to evaluate the sales letters that others write. Chances are, however, that you won't be handed many sales-letter assignments. Even so, you should know something about how sales letters are constructed if only for the reason that the principles apply to all business letters.

PRELIMINARY PLANNING

Before you attempt to write a sales letter, you must be prepared to answer the inevitable questions a prospect will ask: Why should I buy a product like this? Why specifically *your* product? If you don't know everything there is to know about the item you are attempting to sell, you simply can't answer those two questions satisfactorily. Your product may be better-looking, lower-priced, sturdier, simpler and more economical to operate, easier to service, or better-known than that of your competitors. Every company can supply reams of evidence to support its claims of a superior product, and sales writers usually commit them to memory.

Once you know everything about your product, you must select a particular feature that you want to emphasize in your letter. You can't emphasize them all; most readers won't wade through endless "puffing," no matter how strongly you feel about the merits of your product. Besides, in putting down in a letter every detail about your product, you draw attention from the *principal* points that are most likely to convince your reader to buy. It's a good idea, then, to select one main feature of your product and pin your sales message on it. This is called the *central theme,* and it will vary according to what you can offer your readers and who your readers are. Generally, you have a special purpose for writing the sales letter (indeed, you may *create* a purpose for the occasion)—a big price reduction, a service never provided before, a special bonus offer, a new feature of an existing product, the introduction of an entirely new product—and you can use that as your central theme.

The kind of audience you are addressing will also have a bearing on your choice of a central theme. If you want to sell a house to young, middle-income couples, you're likely to emphasize economy, play space for children, ease of commuting to work, or quality and nearness of schools. If your list is made up of elderly people, however, your theme is bound to be different—convenient medical facilities or the fact that there is a minimum of walking, for example.

Mailing lists can be purchased from companies that specialize in compiling them; you can find their names in the Yellow Pages in all large cities. And, of course, you will have your own, developed from sales records, responses to advertising, sales representatives' reports, business directories, club and association rosters, and so on.

Wherever your list comes from, try to learn as much as you can about your readers so that you can choose the theme for your letter that is most likely to strike a responsive chord. You can't, of course, know precisely the key that will turn on *everybody's* buying mechanism. But you can reduce your chances of being locked out if you know such things about your readers as approximate age, income level, educational achievement, sex, professional status, and general interests. Even if you know only one or two of these things, you can select an appropriate central theme much more intelligently.

A list of members of a local parent-teacher organization will, of course, include people whose interests, income, and assets vary widely. But you can be pretty sure they share one thing in common: the education of their children. Thus if you're selling encyclopedias to parents, your central theme could logically be the value of your encyclopedias in helping children do better in school. If, however, your list is made up of socially prominent people, your theme is likely to be quite different—the craftsmanship and beauty of the volumes, for example. A letter selling a new typewriter to office managers will probably emphasize speed, economy, or quality (possibly all three). But if your list is made up of executive secretaries, you're more likely to talk about ease of operation ("Don't be all tired out at the end of the day"), beauty ("You can choose any color to match your office decor"), and/or performance ("Earn praise—and maybe a raise—from your boss").

Once you have selected your central selling theme, based upon a thorough knowledge of your product and as much information as you can get about your audience, you are ready to construct your letter.

Structure of a Sales Letter.   Let's admit at the outset that when we sit down to write a sales letter, we don't know exactly how it should be put together. Of course, we must have an opinion, but we will know whether it is the *correct* opinion only when we get the responses from our readers, in the form of reply cards, coupons, orders, letters asking for more information, and so on. If we knew precisely how to write a sales letter that would pull a 100 percent response, then just about everyone would use that letter. But we don't know. Given the same product and the same list of prospects, two different people will write entirely different letters. Each of us has a different idea as to what is most likely to "turn on" our readers. Sales-letter writing is not an exact science. Most organizations are very happy if they get a 5 to 10 percent return on their sales letters, ecstatic if they can get 20 percent or higher. You have to figure out beforehand the kind of response you are willing to accept in order to justify the expense of the mailing.

Yet there are elements common to all successful sales letters. Common sense tells us that if we want to sell a prospect we must first get our reader's attention. Then we must whet the reader's appetite for the product by building interest. Once we have done this, we convince our reader that he or she should have the product. And finally, we get the reader to take favorable action. A sales letter, then, should do four things:

1. Gain the prospect's *attention.*
2. Build the prospect's *interest.*
3. Create a *desire* for the product.
4. Get the prospect to take favorable *action.*

Attracting Attention.   The wastebasket is the archenemy of every sales-letter writer. The writer's first objective is to catch the reader's eye and cause him or her to want to read the message rather than toss the letter into the wastebasket. You can attract attention in various ways. The color and shape of the stationery itself can be an attention-getter. A coin, stamp, miniature art reproduction, swatch of fabric, gift certificate, facsimile check, film negative, plastic miniature musical instrument, mirror, key, pencil, dice, and so on—affixed to the letter—can be attention-getters. Admittedly, they are gimmicks. They attract attention only because people hate to throw anything away that looks the least bit valuable. But you have to accept the possibility that your readers will associate such razzle-dazzle devices with the hard sell, and you must decide whether it's worth the risk.

Above all, an attention-getting opening must be believable. Don't try to trick your reader with such an absurd statement as:

CONGRATULATIONS! You've just won $5,000!
Wouldn't you like to have someone tell you that?
Well, we can't promise that you will win $5,000, but . . .

Many different types of openings may be used to attract the attention of your reader. We will mention only a few.

A Special Offer

TWO FULL WEEKS TO ENJOY
  THE BEST OF IOWA'S DAILY NEWSPAPERS
    WITH OUR COMPLIMENTS

You'll save $26.50 if you order
Art Treasures of the Ancient World
before December 1 . . .

WITHOUT ONE CENT OF COST TO YOU . . .
We will mail you one of these
SPECIAL 7″ BLACK FOREST CLOCKS
Direct from Rotterdam, Holland

A Quotation or an Anecdote

Somebody once said, "The Greeks had a word for it," and I'm just beginning to understand what was meant.

May I borrow from an unknown author who wrote, "Though I have a thousand friends, I have not one to spare."

I WAS SITTING IN OUR SHOWROOM . . .
. . . The other morning when BANG, a firecracker exploded, a big puff of pink smoke appeared, and there stood a fellow with a rabbit in his hand.

It was Tuesday, May 12, when John and Sarah Beadling first came to see me. I remember it because it was a fateful day for me—and, as it turned out, for them.

A Provocative Statement or Question

Blackboards should be seen and not heard.

Did you ever split an axiom?

There is an "underground" in this country of about 20,000 men who use neither a safety razor nor an electric shaver. Yet they're the cleanest-shaven men in America.

Have you heard your baby cry since you left the hospital?

May we stick our nose in your business?

You are one in 60,000!

On page 143 is a sales promotion letter from an investment firm. Its purpose is to induce readers to send for a free booklet and eventually to buy the company's investment services.

Length of Sales Letters. Throughout this book we've emphasized keeping your communications as brief as you can without risking confusion and misunderstanding. That advice does not necessarily hold for sales letters. Some of the most successful sales letters written today run from four to six pages in length. Although we may argue that most people won't read such long messages, the companies that use them have discovered, through various tests, that they pull better for them than briefer letters. No doubt, readers take the position that if it takes six or eight pages to extol the many virtues of a product, it must be worth investigating—whether or not they actually read all those pages!

The letter on page 143 was processed—that is, duplicated rather than individually typed. Generally, you can afford to type individual sales letters—even by means of automatic typewriters—only when your list is small and the chances of getting a good return are very good.

When your mailing list is large, you also will usually find it too costly to insert the reader's name and address and a salutation (to say nothing of the problem of matching the typewriter type with the printed message). Many writers like to "fake" an inside address by means of a short message like this:

We pay the shipping costs
on any order
anywhere

Yes, we're so certain that you . . .

Preparation of the "Under-40 Presidents" Letter. We come now to the preparation of the sales letter to the Under-40 Presidents Association, referred to on page 138. Before you begin to structure the letter, you must first decide what you expect your reader to do. Is your reader to request a free booklet? supply information about himself or herself? send a check? invite a salesperson to call? In other words, you must decide what action you want the reader to take so that, in your sales message, you can lead up to it effectively. Let's assume that we are going to ask the reader to send for a free booklet, *Pickwick Plans a Meeting.*

In our letter to the Under-40 Presidents Association, what will be our central theme? How will we open? What ways will we choose to develop interest, build desire, and induce action? Before we try to answer these questions, let's try to determine what the members of the association are like. We know they are relatively young, reasonably affluent, probably physically active, dynamic, and aggressive. Probably, too, they are good business people, cost-conscious, eager to get their dollar's worth in behalf of their companies.

WALPOLE aNd FRIEDMAN
Investment Counselors
40 South Wabash Avenue • Chicago, Illinois 60603
Member New York Stock Exchange

DO YOU REMEMBER . . .

when Apex was selling for $120 a share back in 1970? Since
then the stock has split four times . . . and an original
$120 investment is now worth about $1,000.

and Conar, whose stock has split 15 for 1 since 1970, giving
its shareholders a profit of 50 times their original investment . . . in less than 10 years?

Why have companies like Apex and Conar been so profitable
for investors? The main reason is that our rapidly changing
world demands new technologies to solve problems faster
and more efficiently . . . and companies like Apex and Conar,
which provide industry with computers and other sophisticated
equipment and services, are riding the crest of what can only
be described as a technological revolution.

We can't guarantee that investors buying these stocks today
would realize the rate of profit we referred to earlier. Yet
we do think you should know more about the technological
changes that professional investors are watching so closely
today . . . the changes they feel will have enormous impact
on industry and society at large in the years ahead.

It's easy to find out about this technological revolution.
In fact, we've just published a study by that title . . . The
Technological Revolution. To get your copy, just mail the
enclosed card to me. There is no charge. We think that all
investors who want to make their capital grow should read
this study.

                    Very sincerely yours,

                    (Mr.) M. W. Friedman

                    M. W. Friedman
                    Executive Vice President

abf
Enclosure

The purpose of our letter is to induce these young presidents to select Pickwick Manor as the headquarters for their various away-from-home meetings and conferences. In selecting a central theme, we have several choices: luxuriousness of the accommodations, beauty of the surroundings, warm climate, superb cuisine, big-name entertainers, convenience to air transportation, complete sports and recreational programs, outstanding facilities for meetings, friendly atmosphere, fast and courteous service, and so forth. All of these things are important, but if you were to select one of them as a theme, which would you choose?

We would guess that these men and women would be interested, most of all, in making the most productive use of their time at a conference. Conferences away from home can be very expensive, and although most of them allow time for relaxation and fun, their main purpose is to transact business. We think the members of the Under-40 Presidents Association will insist on a place that can provide the facilities and services required for a productive conference. Certainly, such facilities will include some for fun and relaxation, but they become incidental to the primary purpose of the meeting. Our theme, then, would be the competence of Pickwick Manor to put on the best meeting possible in terms of facilities and services.

How would you open such a letter to attract the attention of your readers? Here are two possibilities:

1. "Thank you—

    for helping us put on the best conference we have ever had. Your superb facilities, the service, the know-how and helpful attitude of your staff—all add up to one word: Professionalism."

    Pardon us for crowing just a bit, but the above message was received a few days ago from the vice president of one of . . . .

2. KNOW-HOW

    That simple word is the difference between an outstanding company meeting and a merely passable one. That difference is Pickwick Manor. We know how.

    18 spacious, carpeted meeting rooms, each seating 25 + people; 2 large auditoriums, 1 seating 150 and the other 350 people; 3 special banquet rooms accommodating from 160 to 300 guests; 1,200 guest rooms, each sleeping two comfortably . . . .

    These are only a few of the physical facilities Pickwick Manor can offer you for your company meetings. You see, PM was designed expressly to handle meetings and conferences . . . .

Let's take the opening used in the first example and develop the theme.

SOLUTION

"Thank you—

for helping us put on the best conference we have ever had. Your superb facilities, the service, the know-how and helpful attitude of your staff—all add up to one word: Professionalism."

Pardon us for crowing just a bit, but the above message was received a few days ago from the vice president of one of the country's largest manufacturing firms. And it's typical of many we get from top executives who choose Pickwick Manor as their host for meetings, conferences, seminars, or conventions.

At Pickwick Manor we know how to help you make your meetings really successful. It's what we were designed to do, what we're still in business for, the reason we're beginning to be known as "convention host to the nation." Pickwick Manor is not just another magnificent resort center that offers everything any famous resort hotel boasts about (all sports, including a challenging 9-hole, par-36 golf course; a private beach plus two giant freshwater pools; outstanding cuisine; big-name entertainers; a climate that practically guarantees year-round "sun fun"; elegant shopping malls; horse racing; deep-sea fishing—you name it). We're all those things, of course, but we are more. We're professionals when it comes to arranging space for your specific needs and providing every personal service you require to make it the best meeting you have ever had. You'll find that we know what you expect to get from your meetings and conferences, and our entire staff is dedicated to seeing that you get it.

Skeptical? Do you think I may be promising more than we can deliver? Let me prove what I have been saying about our expertise in hosting successful meetings. First, look over the enclosed folder which tells something of our size and the beauty of our accommodations. Then, to learn more about our professional side—the <u>heart</u> of Pickwick Manor—mail the card for your free copy of <u>Pickwick Plans a Meeting</u>. This is all you'll have to do.

Sincerely yours,

Analysis of the Solution.   As you can see, the central theme is "getting the most from your meeting dollar," and that idea is a running thread throughout the letter. Attention is obtained by the testimonial excerpt. Interest is achieved by expanding on the excerpt and the idea that such letters are almost routine. We build desire by emphasizing that although Pickwick is a great resort hotel—with all the facilities anyone would need or want—it is a *professional* host to convention- and meeting-goers. We try to convince the reader that we know what he or she expects from meetings and conferences and that we will go all out to deliver. The final paragraph induces action, inviting the reader to make Pickwick Manor prove its claims.

We cannot say that the above will be an enormously successful letter, only that it has the ingredients. Assume that each letter costs about 50 cents to put in the mail; that's about $760. If you receive a 10 percent response (152) and 10 percent of them (15) eventually patronize Pickwick Manor at an average expenditure of $5,000 (a modest figure for most meetings), you've produced sales amounting to $75,000. Almost any business person is happy to spend $760 for $75,000 worth of business!

Projects

Ⓐ
The Southern States Kindergarten Teachers Association is holding its annual meeting at the Pompano Beach Civic Auditorium from August 11 to 14. You have obtained a membership roster of this group and plan to write a sales letter to the members encouraging them to stay at Pickwick Manor during the convention. Your special summer rates are in effect. Plan and write the letter.

(B) A new organization, the American Association of Administrative Assistants, has just been formed. It is made up principally of women who are essentially executive secretaries but have earned executive rank. Write a letter to the new president, Miss Jennifer Webster, inviting the group to consider Pickwick Manor as a place for their annual meetings. Assume that you can use this same letter for other similar groups.

CASE 4

GIVING CUSTOMERS THE VIP TREATMENT

PROBLEM

You have received word from Mr. Bigelow of Marlow Cement Manufacturing Company that Pickwick Manor has been chosen for the company's regional managers conference to be held December 3–7.

BACKGROUND

After expending considerable money and effort to "land" a customer—through advertisements, direct-mail promotion, personal calls by representatives, and so on—it is good business to give that customer the VIP treatment. Unfortunately, this doesn't always happen, because the people who assume responsibility for a customer after he or she has been won may not be the same ones who won the customer. It is a serious error to take good customers for granted—they are too hard to get. But many businesses do just that; they become so occupied with obtaining more and more new customers that they forget about the ones they already have.

Obviously, the most important thing you can do for your customers is to give them efficient service, products they can count on, competitive prices, and fair and courteous treatment. But it is also important to establish a good communication link with those VIPs you worked so hard to attract to your organization; for example, you should:

1. Give a special welcome to new customers.
2. Tell customers how much you appreciate their business.
3. Respond immediately and gratefully to customers who compliment you on your merchandise and/or service.

WELCOMING A NEW CUSTOMER

When you receive your first order from a customer—whether for merchandise or services—you should immediately acknowledge it with an expression of appreciation and assure the customer of your desire to be of service. The letter welcoming Mr. Bigelow and his regional managers can be very brief.

Dear Mr. Bigelow:

I was delighted to learn that you have chosen Pickwick Manor for your regional managers conference December 3–7.

We have already begun preparations for your conference, Mr. Bigelow, and you may be sure that we will all be ready for you. I would consider it a personal favor if you would ask for me when you arrive. I want to make sure that you receive the proper welcome and assure you that everything you need for a successful conference will be provided.

Sincerely yours,

THANKING A CUSTOMER FOR PATRONAGE

At the conclusion of the conference of the Marlow Cement Manufacturing Company, it is a goodwill gesture to write Mr. Bigelow to thank him for his business and to express the hope that he will choose Pickwick Manor again. If a firm has thousands of customers, it would be too expensive to write a personal letter to each of them thanking them for orders or patronage, so a postcard or form letter is often used. Although form letters are better than nothing, they can never be as effective as a personal letter.

Following is an appropriate thank-you letter to Mr. Bigelow. Note that it is very personal. Observe, too, that the writer has taken advantage of the occasion to do some subtle selling.

Dear Mr. Bigelow:

All of us at Pickwick Manor are delighted that you chose us as your hosts for your recent meeting. It was a pleasure having you. Mary Glendenning told me this morning she has never had a more enthusiastic group for the various social and recreational activities!

Please come back soon, Mr. Bigelow. Last week we had the pleasure of having 300 doctors at a medical convention. As you know, our main auditorium, the Beachcomber Room, seats 500 people comfortably.

Warm holiday greetings to you and your associates.

Sincerely,

RESPONDING TO A CUSTOMER'S COMMENTS

Letters complimenting a business for outstanding service are relatively rare—not because outstanding service is rare but because it is expected as a matter of course. When a business firm receives a letter of commendation, a quick response is a must. In replying to these letters, be careful not to be overly modest, but at the same time, do not display undue vanity.

Let's say you received a very warm thank-you letter from Mrs. Karen Ericksen, president of the Duluth chapter of the Association of Women in

Banking. Mrs. Ericksen expressed her pleasure with the excellent rooms, meeting facilities, food, and social activities, and with the friendly atmosphere. She said it was the best convention her chapter has ever had, and she gives Pickwick Manor a large share of the credit. How would you respond?

SOLUTION A

Dear Mrs. Ericksen:

How very nice of you to compliment us as you did for our part in the success of your meeting. Although you may have thought we went out of our way to serve you, we simply extended to you the Pickwick hospitality which all our guests learn to expect.

Please come again.

Cordially,

Analysis of Solution A. Although the tone of Solution A is generally good, the writer is guilty of smugness—indeed, of "putting down" Mrs. Ericksen for her well-intended compliment. The letter is not likely to achieve its mission: to reinforce a good feeling on the part of the customer.

SOLUTION B

Dear Mrs. Ericksen:

You were very thoughtful to compliment us for our part in the success of your meeting.

It was our pleasure to have you with us. Our people here who had a hand in providing service to the Duluth chapter of the Association of Women in Banking will be happy to know their efforts were appreciated. You may be sure that I will share your generous letter with them.

We hope you will come to Pickwick Manor again—soon.

Sincerely,

Analysis of Solution B. The writer of Solution B is neither too modest nor too vain. The letter is what it should be: a straightforward expression of gratitude for a compliment. Is the letter too brief? No. What is important is that everything that needs to be said is said.

Projects

Mr. Arnold T. Koenig, one of the members of the Under-40 Presidents Association who received the letter on pages 144–145, writes he has chosen Pickwick Manor for the annual meeting of the executives of his company, Blake Construction Inc. In a previous letter Mr. Koenig described his requirements for rooms, meeting facilities, and luncheons and dinners, to which you gave your assurance that all his needs would be filled. Write the welcome letter.

B The Association of American Composers has just completed a three-day convention at Pickwick Manor. Write to Ms. Emily Shoreham, president, expressing your pleasure in serving this group. Supply any details you believe appropriate.

C Prepare a form letter or postcard that may be sent to all guests of the hotel, thanking them for choosing Pickwick Manor.

D The following letter was sent by Mr. Edward Rivera:

Dear Miss Nettles:

Enclosed is my check for $294 in payment of my bill.

Thank you for a lovely week at Pickwick Manor—one of the most delightful vacations I have ever had. The people were extremely friendly and helpful; the room, quiet and comfortable; and the food, superb. I can't think of anything I could have wanted that was not provided.

                Appreciatively,

Miss Nettles asks you to respond to Mr. Rivera's letter.

E Develop a form letter that can be used as a general response to letters of commendation received by Pickwick Manor.

CASE 5

WINNING BACK FORMER CUSTOMERS

PROBLEM

Until two years ago, The Montrose Food Corporation had held its annual sales meeting at Pickwick Manor every March for five years in a row. Although you sent your usual promotional literature during the past two years, the company did not choose Pickwick Manor for its headquarters. You have decided to write a special letter to try to win them back.

BACKGROUND

"Once a customer, always a customer" is an axiom every business would like to make a reality. But in our competitive world, customers do stray. Sometimes they are lured away because a competitor offers better prices or service, or because another location is more convenient. Sometimes a customer strays because of downright dissatisfaction with the product or rude treatment at the hands of sales or service personnel. Whatever the reason, most businesses keep the names of their former customers and from time to time attempt to bring them back into the fold.

Many different promotional ideas are used to win back old customers: more generous credit terms, discount prices for a limited time, advance information about new styles and new merchandise, gifts, special buying assistance, and so on. One method is to write customers, inviting them to tell what went wrong and caused them to transfer their business elsewhere; another is to stress new products, new services, or a new appearance.

SOLUTION A

Dear Mr. Joplin:

You're missed, you know.

For five years in a row Pickwick Manor had the pleasure of being your host at your annual sales meeting in March. For this reason we had begun to think of you as partners of ours—we liked you and we think you liked us.

But for two years now you haven't called upon us. And frankly we miss you. In a situation like this, it is only natural for us to ask ourselves, What did we do to those Montrose folks that would cause them to stay away? But we can't come up with a reason.

If there was something at Pickwick Manor that did not measure up to your expectations, we'd like to know about it. Honestly. And while you're at it, look over our enclosed new brochure. We hope it will persuade you to come back.

Sincerely yours,

Analysis of Solution A.   Some promotion people object to the what-did-we-do-wrong theme because it is somewhat negative. There is no question that the writer invites criticism, encouraging the recipient to think of something wrong whether there is or not. Others believe such negativism builds a little sympathy for the company that has been spurned and at least gives the former customer a chance to blow off steam.

SOLUTION B

Dear Mr. Joplin:

You wouldn't recognize us! Since you were here last, we've added:

- 40 new luxurious sleeping rooms with private balconies overlooking the ocean.
- 4 meeting rooms—all carpeted—each with an ocean view.
- A 9-hole, par-36 golf course and a driving range.

- A complete marina with boat rentals for fishing, skiing, sailing, and other water sports.
- A solarium with swimming pool.

But there is one thing that hasn't changed: our friendly, superb service (except maybe it's better than ever!).

Why not make a reservation for your March sales conference right now while there's still unlimited choice of facilities? We want you back at Pickwick Manor. Let us show you we mean it!

Cordially yours,

Analysis of Solution B. This letter stresses the look-how-we've-changed theme in an effort to win back a former customer. It is a more positive but not necessarily a more persuasive letter than A. Such a letter is usually accompanied by a colorful folder or brochure that illustrates the "new look" talked about in the letter.

The writer of Solution B obviously feels that at least some of the additions to the hotel's accommodations will appeal to the reader (note the display arrangement that highlights each of them). And, as in Solution A, the letter closes with a request for action.

Project

Write two letters, each with a different theme, attempting to win back customers (organizations) who, after having been good patrons for several years, have not returned to Pickwick Manor for the past two years. Use your imagination in making the invitation attractive.

SOLVING CUSTOMER PROBLEMS

YOUR JOB *You are continuing as assistant manager of Pick-wick Manor, a hotel specializing in group meetings and conferences.*

CASE 1

TURNING DOWN REQUESTS FOR SERVICES

PROBLEM

Mr. Barry Lasky has written asking for accommodations at Pickwick Manor for 20 members of the Northeastern Antique Collectors Association for November 7–10. Pickwick Manor is sold out for those dates (his request for reservations arrived much too late), and you must tell him so.

BACKGROUND

Even though a request for a product or a service must be denied (the product is temporarily out of stock or is no longer being carried, or the service is not available on the dates requested), the letter writer must remember that the inquirer is still a prospect for a different product or for the same product or for service at another date. The writer also keeps in mind the advertising money and effort expended to generate interest in the product or service, and once the writer has a live candidate, he or she doesn't let go without a struggle. Even if there is no chance to land the prospect immediately, the writer keeps the prospect's name in an active file and sends letters and other promotional literature for several months—perhaps a year or more—until all hope is gone.

SOLUTION A

Dear Mr. Lasky:

You waited much too long to make reservations at Pickwick Manor, and we are filled up for November 7–10. If you had written a month earlier, we might have been able to help you.

I am sorry.

Yours very truly,

Analysis of Solution A.   Solution A is obviously a very poor letter. It is totally negative. If we want to get a prospective customer on our side, we don't start off with an accusation ("You waited much too long") and then say what he should have done ("If you had written a month earlier").

Although the writer could not provide the services requested, he could have tried to build goodwill so that Mr. Lasky might want to consider Pickwick Manor some other time. Solution A will succeed only in eliminating Pickwick Manor as a future meeting place for the organization Mr. Lasky represents.

SOLUTION B

Dear Mr. Lasky:

I wish it were possible for me to reserve accommodations for the Northeastern Antique Collectors Association for November 7–10. Unfortunately, Mr. Lasky, our facilities have been taken for those dates.

The only openings available in November to accommodate a group of your size at the Pickwick Manor are from the 16th to the 20th. If you would like to consider this date, please let us know by October 2.

In any event, thank you for considering Pickwick Manor. Perhaps before too long we may have the pleasure of being your hosts.

Sincerely yours,

Analysis of Solution B.   Solution B employs an effective technique for saying no to a customer: state your desire to provide the requested product or service before delivering the unpleasant news that you can't.

Observe that an attempt was made to save the sale, even though the writer knows that the chances of his changing Mr. Lasky's meeting date are very slim.

The closing is friendly and persuasive.

Projects

 Basil Milne, associate secretary of the Automotive Equipment Manufacturers Association of the U.S.A. has written the following letter:

Dear Miss Nettles:

The Automotive Equipment Manufacturers Association of the U.S.A. is looking for accommodations for its annual convention next April 12–16.

An important part of this convention is the display of equipment of the various manufacturers, which requires considerable space and special platforms on which to display very heavy machinery. It is estimated that about 600 square meters of space will be needed for this purpose.

Buyers as well as Association members will be attending the convention. We estimate that approximately 1,500 will register. We will, of course, require an auditorium large enough for this group as well as about 20 private meeting rooms to accommodate 75 in each room. Most people will want to stay at the hotel for the week.

Will you please send complete information about your facilities, including prices. Also, are we correct in assuming that luncheon and banquet arrangements can be made to accommodate our group?

Very truly yours,

You must turn down this proposal. Your facilities are not suitable for displaying heavy equipment, and you're afraid damage might result from moving, setting in place, and housing such equipment. Also, the group is too large for your hotel; you can accommodate only about 500 comfortably. Write the letter, choosing the reason you think most appropriate for turning down the request. Suggest an alternative to Mr. Milne.

(B) You received a letter from Pamela Lorenz of Dynamic Mail Promotion Inc., asking you for the list of registrants who attended a recent convention of purchasing agents. You must refuse because you don't have an official register; besides, it would not be wise to give out this information even if you had it (Ms. Lorenz obviously wants the list for promotion purposes). Suggest that she write the Bay State Association of Purchasing Agents, in Boston, for the information she desires.

RESPONDING TO CUSTOMERS' COMPLAINTS

PROBLEM

You received the following letter from Alice H. Thompson, president of the Capitol City Personnel Directors Association, whose members recently concluded a three-day meeting at Pickwick Manor.

Dear Miss Nettles:

Thanks to the inefficiency of your staff, the fall meeting of the Capitol City Personnel Directors Association was a big disappointment. As you know, the materials that were shipped to your hotel two weeks in advance for use in our group sessions were misplaced by someone there and were never found (they arrived here today from your hotel). The entire program was built around these materials; and as a result, we had to improvise, which proved to be a sorry mess.

Your statement for $988.65 arrived today, and I am tempted not to pay it. In any event, it would seem that we are entitled to some kind of discount for the inconvenience we were caused by your staff.

I expect an explanation from you before I make payment.

Yours truly,

You must, of course, answer Mrs. Thompson's letter.

BACKGROUND

Every business receives letters resembling the one illustrated. No matter how hard a business tries to satisfy its customers, mistakes are made. Orders are delayed, wrong merchandise is sent, errors are made in customer billings, a customer is offended by a salesperson, and so on.

Most businesses take the attitude that the customer is right—until proven wrong—but they carefully investigate each complaint before responding. If the customer is right, an apology is in order, along with the necessary adjustment. If the customer is wrong, he or she is usually told so gently and given a full explanation of the circumstances.

In the case of Mrs. Thompson's complaint, investigation showed that the materials in question arrived at the hotel several days before the meeting. A part-time janitor received the materials (they arrived in the middle of the night) and, not knowing where to put them, locked them up in the Lost and Found room. He left the hotel to go on vacation the following day and his whereabouts were unknown. Later, someone piled several pieces of luggage on top of the carton so that it was hidden from sight. Although the Lost and Found room was searched at the time people were looking for the Thompson materials, no one thought to lift the luggage to see if there was anything underneath it.

Although you are willing to offer Mrs. Thompson your sincere apologies, you are not authorized to give her a discount on her statement. The challenge, then, is to write a letter that will pacify Mrs. Thompson and at the same time induce her to pay the bill in full.

SOLUTION A

Dear Mrs. Thompson:

I am very sorry that the materials you say were sent here were not available for your meeting, but I do not believe this fact is justification for giving you a discount on your bill. We supplied you with meeting rooms, meals, and sleeping accommodations for your group, which is what we contracted to do, and you made use of our services. Therefore, I expect full payment of our invoice for $988.65.

Sincerely yours,

Analysis of Solution A. You don't have to be told that Solution A is an atrocious letter. The following errors are nearly unforgivable.

1. The writer, even though he knew that Pickwick Manor was at fault, failed to admit the hotel's error. Indeed, the expression "you say" implies that Mrs. Thompson did not tell the truth, which is devious.
2. The tone of the letter is sarcastic and rude. There is no excuse for the writer's assuming this defensive, officious attitude.

Although Mrs. Thompson will undoubtedly pay the bill after she licks her wounds for a time, she certainly will not return to Pickwick Manor—and what's worse, she will tell her associates to stay away too.

SOLUTION B

Dear Mrs. Thompson:

All of us are terribly embarrassed that the materials for your meeting were misplaced by a member of our staff and were not available to you.

Let me tell you what happened. A part-time janitor signed for the carton when it was delivered late at night and, not knowing what to do with it, placed it in our Lost and Found room for safekeeping. Later, several pieces of luggage were piled on top of the carton, hiding it from view. We tried in vain to locate the janitor, but he left on vacation the day after the materials arrived and could not be reached. Although several people searched the Lost and Found room, no one thought to look under the luggage that obscured the carton from view.

What can I say? If you are thinking that this mishap borders on the incredible, I would have to agree with you. But if you have had something similar happen in your company—something that really defies explanation—then you may know how I feel and can appreciate my deep embarrassment.

After such an experience here, you may feel it is presumptuous of me to suggest that you give us another chance to serve you. I sincerely believe we can convince you that we really are experts in the hospitality business.

Sincerely yours,

Analysis of Solution B. The writer of Solution B handled this difficult situation about as tactfully as it could have been done. He apologized, explained, and made the assumption that Mrs. Thompson is human enough to understand the hotel's position. If Mrs. Thompson does not understand or pretends not to (every company, including Mrs. Thompson's, experiences such moments of extreme embarrassment), there isn't much that can be done. Observe that the letter ends on a positive note—the give-us-another-chance theme. This is good psychology because it implies that Mrs. Thompson is big enough to forgive an unintentional mistake.

Should the writer have asked that the invoice be paid in full? Probably he was wise not to, letting Mrs. Thompson assume that she isn't going to get a discount. Leaving something unsaid is often stronger than an out-and-out "No."

Projects

Mr. and Mrs. Eugene Byram were recent guests of Pickwick Manor for three days. An unfortunate series of mishaps marred their stay. Their room, which had been reserved weeks before they arrived, was not available. They had specifically asked for and been promised an oceanfront room above the tenth floor, but because heavy rain and fog had closed down local airports, people who had expected to check out on the day of the Byrams' arrival were stranded, and the Byrams had to settle for a room on the third floor facing the street. A switch was made, but not until late afternoon of the second day.

Finally, when Mr. Byram received his statement (he had asked to be billed), he found an error. Because he was attending a convention, he was to receive the special convention rate of $30 a day for the oceanfront room, but he was billed at the rate of $40.

When sending his check (on which he made the adjustment for the room rate he was promised), he wrote that he had never seen such a "comedy of errors" and was bitterly critical of the hotel. Your investigation revealed that all the errors referred to by Mr. Byram were actually made and that he is due an apology. Write the letter. Assume that the street-front room, which the Byrams occupied the first night, was specially priced for the convention at $25 but that Mr. Byram made no mention of this in his letter.

B Miss Dianne Madison, who recently spent a week at Pickwick Manor and paid her bill in full when she checked out, wrote that upon examining the statement she found an error. She was charged for a dinner in the King Arthur Room for which she paid cash. According to Miss Madison, she signed the dining room check and entered her name and room number on it (which is the hotel's signal to place the amount on her bill). As she left the dining room, however, she decided to pay cash ($10.70) for the dinner. Upon investigation, you find that she is right. Write her, enclosing your check and apologizing for the error.

CASE 3

RESPONDING TO REQUESTS FOR ADJUSTMENTS

PROBLEM

You received the following letter from Carl Gabrini, treasurer of Quill International, a group of amateur writers who recently held a conference at Pickwick Manor.

Dear Madam:

I have received your invoice for expenses of our Board of Directors during our recent convention at your hotel, and I believe there is an error. The rooms for these six people are charged at the rate of $30 a day on December 15 and 16; the amount should have been $18 a day, as it was for December 13 and 14.

I am enclosing our check for $432, although your invoice is for $576.

Very truly yours,

BACKGROUND

Misunderstandings about prices often arise between customers and suppliers. In the case problem, the letter confirming the reservations of Quill International (addressed to Nicole Hawkins, president), specifically mentioned that winter rates of $30 per room a day would go into effect December 15 (the daily rate up to that time was $18). Possibly the treasurer, Mr. Gabrini, was not aware of the letter to Ms. Hawkins. In any event, Mr. Gabrini's request must be refused.

SOLUTION A

Dear Mr. Gabrini:

Thank you for your check for $432 in payment of the rooms for the six board members of Quill International.

When your president, Ms. Nicole Hawkins, originally made the reservations, I wrote her that on December 15 the winter rate of $30 a day a room would go into effect. She signed the agreement, and a copy is enclosed.

My calculations are as follows:

$$6 \text{ rooms at } \$18 \text{ a day for December } 13, 14 = \$216$$
$$6 \text{ rooms at } \$30 \text{ a day for December } 15, 16 = \underline{360}$$
$$\text{Total} \qquad \$576$$

Would you prefer to issue a new check for $576 or to prepare an additional check for $144?

Sincerely yours,

PS: It was a pleasure having Quill International at Pickwick Manor, and we hope that you will come to see us again.

Analysis of Solution A. Note the tactful manner in which this transaction was handled:

1. An expression of appreciation for the check, even though it was the wrong amount.
2. An explanation of a possible misunderstanding, including a copy of the agreement as evidence.
3. A detailed calculation of how the invoice was figured.
4. A subtle reminder (last paragraph) that the full amount of the invoice is due without the writer's actually asking for the money.
5. A friendly PS which says, in effect, "Let's still be friends."

SOLUTION B

Assume that there was a misunderstanding about the bill, and that special summer rates were extended to Quill International for December 15 and 16 but that this information somehow was not communicated to Pickwick Manor's billing clerk. Here's the letter you might write:

Dear Mr. Gabrini:

You are absolutely right—you owed us only what you paid us—$432. Although winter rates went into effect December 15, we gave Quill International our special summer rate for December 15 and 16. This fact was not taken into account, however, when the invoice was prepared. Please accept my personal apology.

It was a pleasure to serve you, and we thank you for choosing us as your conference headquarters. I hope you had a good meeting and that you will return to Pickwick Manor before too long.

Sincerely,

Analysis of Solution B.   Solution B is an effective response to a customer who was overcharged in error. When you are wrong, it is best to admit it immediately and say what you are going to do about it. It is important, however, not to overstress your error. You are not expected to go down on bended knee. And never say that such a mistake will not happen again. Everyone knows that an occasional error is inevitable. Observe the friendly closing which ends the transaction on a positive note.

Projects

 S. P. Cleveland, representing the Danforth Hog Breeders Association, objects to the gratuity charge of 15 percent that was added to the cost of the Association's banquet held recently at Pickwick Manor. In fact, Mr. Cleveland deducts the 15 percent ($108) from the total bill of $828, sending his check for $720.

Your contract with the Association specifically provided that a 15 percent gratuity charge would be made for the banquet, and Mr. Cleveland signed it. Respond to Mr. Cleveland, explaining that you cannot allow the deduction of the gratuity (such a charge is customary).

Three weeks have gone by, and you have had no response to your letter to Mr. Cleveland (Project A). Write a follow-up letter.

CASE 4

SAYING NO TO POOR CREDIT RISKS

PROBLEM

The Indian River Trotters, a folk-dance organization, held a three-day festival at Pickwick Manor two years ago. When a bill was submitted to the treasurer, Lorraine Schmidt, for $1,240 for hotel services provided the group, there was considerable haggling over the amount. Although Pickwick Manor finally collected in full, the bill was not paid for over four months.

You have received a letter from Mrs. Schmidt requesting a reservation for the group's semiannual meeting. She asks whether payment for the services can be postponed for 60 days after the meeting. Although you have space available on the requested dates and would be pleased to have the Indian River Trotters as guests of Pickwick Manor, you do not consider the organization a good credit risk and you feel you must deny the request for an extension.

BACKGROUND

Refusing credit is one of the most ticklish, if not *the* most ticklish, of all challenges to the letter writer. When you have to say no to a credit applicant, you are in effect saying that he or she is not to be trusted, that you don't think the applicant can or will pay. Such a serious indictment of a person or an organization must be handled with great delicacy and tact.

Some credit experts believe that a poor risk who must be refused credit need not be told directly that he or she is being turned down ("We lack sufficient information necessary to grant your request for credit"); others think it best to come right out with a no and give the reasons. Most agree, however, that if at all possible the customer should be "saved" and encouraged to buy on a cash basis. Obviously, this is quite a challenge, and the person who can bring off that kind of challenge is rare.

SOLUTION A

Dear Mrs. Schmidt:

I am sorry we cannot extend the 60-day credit privileges you asked for in connection with the fall meeting of the Indian River Trotters. We had an unfortunate experience with your group when you were here two years ago. You did not pay us for over four months, and we had to get very unpleasant about it before we collected. I am sure you will understand why we think you are not a good credit risk.

Very truly yours,

Analysis of Solution A. You will quickly agree that this is a wholly negative response. It is honest, and the writer may feel perfectly justified in stating the hotel's position in such hard terms. However, if she wants the Indian River Trotters to patronize Pickwick Manor on a cash-only basis, she has destroyed that possibility. The question that every credit person must ponder is: Is the customer worth trying to retain as a cash-only patron? Even if the writer of this letter felt that the customer was not worth the effort, she could have been more tactful.

SOLUTION B

Dear Mrs. Schmidt:

Thank you and your fellow members of Indian River Trotters for thinking of Pickwick Manor for your fall meeting.

Although it would be a pleasure to have you, I am afraid I cannot extend payment to 60 days. In other words, we would have to ask for full settlement at the time of checkout. This is our standard arrangement with similar organizations.

If you find it possible to accept these conditions, Mrs. Schmidt, you may be sure that we at Pickwick Manor will see to it that your group is extended every courtesy and service. Please make your reservations early so that you may be assured of getting the exact accommodations you want.

Sincerely yours,

Analysis of Solution B. The writer of Solution B, although straightforward, is tactful and sales-minded. Note there is no mention of the previous unpleasant experience with the Indian River Trotters. It is not necessary since the refusal itself implies a lack of trust. Note that the writer uses the last paragraph to soften the refusal of the credit request by implying that the group is still welcome at Pickwick Manor.

Projects

(A) Mr. and Mrs. Howard Kronefeld wrote for reservations for the week beginning December 20. They asked whether Pickwick Manor accepts U-Charge-It credit cards. You can accommodate Mr. and Mrs. Kronefeld for the week of December 20, but because this is the height of the winter season, you will require a $50 deposit in order to hold the reservation. Although Pickwick Manor accepts Diners Club and American Express credit cards, as well as personal checks, it does not accept U-Charge-It. Write the letter.

(B) John C. Helms, sales promotion manager of Pierson Camera Manufacturing Company, has written to reserve exhibit space at the November 16–20 convention of the American Photographers Association. The rental cost for the space Mr. Helms requested is $300.

Your records show that you are still trying to collect $120 from Pierson Camera for exhibit space rented at last year's convention (Pierson was billed for $280 but sent their check for $160, claiming they were overcharged). After numerous letters to the treasurer of the company, L. T. Pilosi, you have not settled the matter, and Pickwick Manor has threatened to sue.

The space Mr. Helms wants is available. However, you have been directed to ask for advance payment in full—no credit this time. Write the letter.

CASE 5

COLLECTING OVERDUE ACCOUNTS

PROBLEM

Mr. and Mrs. Aaron Trumbull, of Decatur, Georgia, engaged the Ponce de Leon Room on October 7 for a wedding reception for their daughter Alice. The cost of the reception, including dinner for 200 people, was $4,500. Mr. Trumbull signed a contract for this amount and was to pay for the reception within ten days. On October 17, an invoice was sent to Mr. Trumbull, and on October 25 a second statement (along with a printed reminder) was mailed. It is now November 3, and you have had no response from Mr. Trumbull. You must write to him to collect the amount due.

BACKGROUND

Most people pay their bills promptly. If this were not true, businesses couldn't afford to be as generous as they are about offering credit. If you consider that out of the millions of people who buy "on time" only a small percentage do not honor their bills, you will conclude that the majority are honest when it comes to credit. Yet, the small percentage of those who must be needled into paying represents a great deal of money, and credit managers in all commercial enterprises must everlastingly keep at them. Bad debts, even though they may represent but a fraction of the total sales, have sunk many a business.

Experience has proved that there are six basic reasons why people don't pay their bills:

1. *Overbuying.* Buyers have overextended themselves and don't have enough money to meet their obligations.
2. *Oversight.* People forget their bills or mislay them.
3. *Bad paying habits.* Some people apparently don't think it's important to settle their obligations promptly and relax into a you-can-wait attitude.

4. *Laziness.* A surprising number of customers think it is too much of a chore to sit down and write a check.
5. *Personal misfortune or disaster.* Fires, hurricanes, illnesses, accidents, and other misfortunes sap the resources of some charge customers.
6. *Customer dissatisfaction.* The customer didn't like the product or service and decides not to pay for it.

COLLECTION LETTER SERIES

Every organization goes about the task of collecting overdue bills in its own fashion. For example, firms that do considerable selling on credit, such as large department stores, furniture stores, appliance stores, and jewelry stores, may develop several different series of messages which they use over and over, constantly testing different combinations. Most businesses, however, develop a series along the following lines:

1. A statement which is sent at the end of the billing period.
2. A second statement, 20 to 30 days later, to which a sticker might be affixed with a message such as *Did you forget?*
3. One or two reminders, which are form letters, obviously duplicated so that they will appear to be routine and impersonal.
4. A personalized form letter, which is more urgent in tone than previous reminders. Three or four of these, each with a different appeal, may be sent. Four basic types of appeals are used to persuade people to pay:

Sympathy. Generally recognized as the weakest appeal, this one says in effect, "We need the money because we have to pay our bills," or "The company has put the blame on me for not having collected from you."

Justice. This appeal is to one's sense of fair play and duty. ("We did right by you; now you do right by us.")

Pride. Most people don't want to have their reputation tarnished, and an appeal to vanity is often very effective. ("A good credit reputation is a valuable asset; don't risk losing it.")

Fear. The appeal to fear is the strongest of all, and it is used only when all other appeals fail. ("We are considering placing your account in the hands of our attorney. Don't force us to do this.")

Practice varies from one business to another concerning collection procedures. Where one company will demand its money when a bill is not paid promptly on the due date, another will "baby" the customer along for months before getting hard-nosed. More often than not, the importance of a particular customer or the customer's record of meeting his or her obligations determines the collection procedures. Charge customers are often inconsistent; one customer will pay his bill with Company X but neglect Company Z; another will maintain a flawless credit record for years and suddenly default. Generally speaking, the ability to pay one's bills is no guarantee that one *will* pay—many people on a very tight budget are more reliable than others who are affluent. Thus collecting money from customers is a genuine art; credit managers must constantly study people and develop an extra sense that tells them when a person is or is not a good credit risk.

In any event, the purpose of all collection letters is to get the money and to do so without causing ill will—a big challenge to the collection-letter writer. Nobody likes to be dunned, and the typical recipient of a persuasive collection letter will cry "Foul!" automatically.

Following is a typical series of collection letters that a customer might receive after he or she has received one or two account statements.

First Letter—Gentle Reminder.   The following is a form letter, obviously duplicated, with blank spaces for fill-ins.

> Your account in the amount of $77.40 is now overdue. Perhaps your check is already in the mail; if so, please disregard this reminder.

Second Letter—Stronger Reminder.   The second letter may also be a form letter similar to the first one.

> Perhaps you did not receive the previous reminders about the outstanding balance of your account. Otherwise, I believe you would have sent us your check for $77.40 by this time. Your account is now 30 days overdue.

Third Letter—Appeal to Justice.   As you will notice, the following letter is a personalized, individually typed—rather than duplicated—letter.

> If a friend of yours borrowed money from you, promising to pay it back in 30 days, you'd expect him to keep his side of the bargain, wouldn't you? Or if he couldn't, you would expect him at least to tell you why, wouldn't you?
>
> That's the situation we are in. You bought a rug from us on credit, which is the same as borrowing money, and agreed to pay us $77.40 for it in 30 days. Those 30 days have come and gone and we still haven't received payment, nor have you told us why.
>
> Please use the stamped envelope to mail us your check for $77.40 right away.

Fourth Letter—Appeal to Pride.   If the customer still hasn't paid the account, another personalized letter similar to the one below would be sent.

> This morning I asked to see your account, and I have it before me right now. You have done business with us for over three years, and you have a fine credit record. Until now.
>
> I say "until now" because your good credit reputation is in danger of being damaged. And all for the small amount of $77.40, which you've owed us for six weeks.
>
> Probably you meant to settle your account long before this, but you simply have not got around to it. Or maybe there is another reason. Whatever it is, please take care of this obligation immediately. I don't want to see you labeled "Bad Credit Risk"—and this could happen if you delay longer. Please send me your check at once. Before it is too late.

Fifth Letter—Appeal to Fear. A letter similar to the one that follows gives the customer "one last chance" to avoid the unpleasantness and expense of having the account put in the hands of a lawyer or a collection agency.

> The last thing I want to do is to put your account in the hands of a collection agency. It's unpleasant business—unpleasant for us and unpleasant for you. But I will be forced to take this action unless I have the $77.40 in payment of your account by July 10.
>
> Help me to avoid this step by at least getting in touch with me and discussing your intentions. This is the last opportunity I can give you—the next move is yours.

What will you say in your letter to Mr. Trumbull about the bill for his daughter's wedding reception? Here are four variations of the first letter you might write (the previous communications were printed reminders). Note that none is demanding or threatening; yet each is a straightforward request for payment.

SOLUTION A

> Dear Mr. Trumbull:
>
> Funny how people forget.
>
> No doubt, before your daughter Alice's wedding all that you and Mrs. Trumbull could think of was getting everything done properly that had to be done. And if you're like most parents-of-the-bride, you often wondered if you'd hold up under the strain. Everything centered on giving the bride a wedding she would never forget.
>
> We were glad to have had a part in that memorable occasion, and we hope we were able to take some worries off your shoulders and help you to forget your responsibilities. It was, you'll agrée, a beautiful reception.
>
> Now that it's all over and, I hope, the bride and groom are happily settled, you have possibly forgotten the agonies of planning and the worries about whether everything would go off as you wished. That's only natural. But in the process have you forgotten us too?
>
> Your payment for the reception at Pickwick Manor has not been received, and we're betting that it slipped your mind. Unfortunately, it is something we can't forget. Won't you send us your check for $4,500 right away—today?
>
> Sincerely yours,

Analysis of Solution A. Solution A emphasizes a central theme (forgetting) throughout quite effectively. It is a tactful, reasonable appeal to Mr. Trumbull's sense of fair play. It should not offend the Trumbulls, and it should produce results—if the Trumbulls have a conscience (and the money!).

SOLUTION B

Dear Mr. Trumbull:

Your check for $4,500 is two weeks overdue now. It is very difficult for me to understand why it has not arrived.

I remember your saying to me that the reception for Alice's wedding was "beautiful" and "perfect"—we think it was one of the nicest affairs ever held here at Pickwick Manor. The orchestra, the florist, the caterer—all have been paid, but we haven't received our check.

Mr. Trumbull, please don't let this matter ride any longer. Mail us your check in the enclosed envelope today.

Sincerely yours,

Analysis of Solution B.   Solution B also emphasizes the fair-play appeal. It is an effective letter, and because the writer was more direct in asking for payment and stated Pickwick's position in fewer words, some would choose it over Solution A. Which do you think has the better chance of achieving its mission?

SOLUTION C

Dear Mr. Trumbull:

Here's the situation as I see it.

ONE: We provided a lovely reception for your daughter Alice's wedding, which your guests described variously as "superb," "elegant," "stunning" (you said "beautiful," "perfect").

TWO: We paid the orchestra, florist, caterer, and all the others who assisted.

THREE: We asked you for payment of the contract on October 17 and again on October 25.

FOUR: We have not received payment (the amount is $4,500).

FIVE: May we have your check by November 8.

Sincerely yours,

Analysis of Solution C.   Solution C reviews the history of the transaction and the writer displays each point tactfully and convincingly. Although the letter is not a hard demand, the writer makes clear that Mr. Trumbull's payment is expected by November 8.

SOLUTION D

Dear Mr. Trumbull:

On October 17, I sent you a statement of your account ($4,500) to which I received no response.

On October 25, I wrote you again reminding you that this bill had not been paid. Still no answer.

This is November 3, and I still have not received a check or an explanation from you.

Don't you think, Mr. Trumbull, that this account should be paid in full at once? Certainly I see no reason why it should not be, and I expect to have your check by November 8.

Sincerely yours,

Analysis of Solution D.   This is a variation of the history of the transaction used in Solution C. The writer is a little more demanding (last sentence), but the letter is still not harsh.

Projects

(A)   Lisa Jefferson, representing Party Time Novelties, was a recent guest of Pickwick Manor. She stayed two days and during that time incurred a bill of $275.70. At checkout time she paid her bill by check. However, the bank on which the check was drawn returned the check to you stamped "Insufficient Funds." Write Miss Jefferson, asking for payment.

(B)   Two weeks have gone by and you have not heard from Miss Jefferson (Project A). Write a follow-up communication that you think is appropriate.

(C)   Develop a series of four to six letters, from routine reminder to final notice, that might be used by Pickwick Manor to collect overdue accounts of individual guests who have been given credit privileges.

THE ADMINISTRATIVE ASSISTANT COMMUNICATES

YOUR JOB *You are assistant to the president of Peerless Publishing Company, Paul J. Weinberger. The company, located in Des Moines, Iowa, publishes professional and reference books, encyclopedias, trade books (fiction and biography, for example), textbooks for schools and colleges, and so on. You handle much of the correspondence addressed to Mr. Weinberger, preparing some letters for his signature and others for your own.*

CASE 1

RESPONDING IN THE EXECUTIVE'S ABSENCE

PROBLEM

Mr. Weinberger has received information that a small trade publisher in Orlando, Florida, is interested in selling his business to a major publishing house. Mr. Weinberger is eager to acquire this company because of its distinguished religious-books list, an area Peerless has long been interested in. He telephoned the Orlando publisher, who invited him to come to Florida to discuss terms. While Mr. Weinberger is away, you are handling his mail and now have the following letter from an executive in a large Chicago printing firm which manufactures books for many major publishers.

> Dear Paul:
>
> Would you be willing to act as chairman of the panel "The Publisher Speaks" at the National Book Manufacturers Association conference? As you know, this one-day conference is being held in Dayton on April 16; the panel is scheduled for 2:30 to 3:30.
>
> You are the ideal person to do this job for us. You have spoken very frankly and sensibly about the publisher's own responsibilities for good bookmaking, and I know most of our members would turn out for a panel discussion of this subject if you are the chairman. For the other panel members, I think we should have a manufacturer or two, a production manager, an editor, and possibly a marketing person. But you would decide what panel makeup would be best and the people you would like to work with.
>
> As soon as you accept this invitation, Paul, I will supply more details. Please say that you can find time to be with us.
>
> Sincerely,

BACKGROUND

The principal function of an "assistant-to" is to relieve a top executive of certain daily responsibilities. Assistants-to answer routine letters, see visitors to the office and screen out those whom the executive shouldn't take the time to see, arrange and report on meetings, and so on. The little word *to* in the title has a special meaning. Assistant general managers have direct responsibility for people, performance, and profits; but assistants to general managers usually have none of these responsibilities. They are the managers' eyes, ears, and right arm and speak not so much for themselves as for the executives for whom they work.

Assistants-to often walk a tightrope. Although they can make certain decisions for the boss, it is not always clear *which* decision it is safe to make.

Thus they have the task of doing everything possible to relieve the executive of detail without appearing to usurp the executive's authority. And they must always be discreet, always be on guard against revealing confidential information, always careful not to put the executive in an embarrassing position.

SOLUTION A

Dear Ms. Wolff:

Mr. Weinberger is in Orlando, Florida, talking with the Bennington Press people about a possible merger. He will return on February 16.

Although I cannot assure you that Mr. Weinberger will be able to accept your invitation to chair a panel at the NBMA conference, his calendar seems to be relatively uncluttered in mid-April, and I expect that he will be delighted to participate.

Very truly yours,

Analysis of Solution A. You will agree immediately that Solution A is unacceptable.

1. It reveals information that should be kept confidential. When the boss is away, it is wise to simply tell outsiders that he is away from the office, revealing nothing about where the boss is or what he is doing. Even though Mr. Weinberger and Ms. Wolff are friends, Ms. Wolff may have an even closer friend in another publishing house who would like to know about the Peerless negotiations with Bennington Press.
2. The writer practically commits Mr. Weinberger to accepting an invitation which, for any number of reasons, he may not be able to accept. Of course, we would have to know more about this particular situation before we could say definitely that the writer is in error. As a general rule, however, Mr. Weinberger himself should make a decision of this nature.

SOLUTION B

Dear Ms. Wolff:

Mr. Weinberger is away from the office for about ten days. He will, I am sure, let you know about chairing the panel at the NBMA conference at his first opportunity. In fact, I will be in touch with him by telephone late this week, and I will see if I can get an answer for you then.

Sincerely yours,

Analysis of Solution B. Solution B is much more effective than Solution A. Solution B reveals no confidential information, nor does it commit Mr. Weinberger to a speaking assignment or put him in a situation that would be hard to get out of. The writer, however, shows a can-do attitude, going the extra distance to be helpful.

Projects

(A) During your telephone conversation with Mr. Weinberger, he asked you to write to Ms. Wolff accepting the panel assignment at the April 16 conference of the National Book Manufacturers Association in Dayton (Case 1). Prepare the letter for your signature.

(B) The following is among the letters received in Mr. Weinberger's absence.

Dear Mr. Weinberger:

The Sioux City Uptown Association cordially invites you to be the luncheon speaker at our April 16 meeting.

The SCUA is a group whose aim is to promote the commercial and civic advantages of this community. Although our principal objective is to boost Sioux City, we also engage in a number of philanthropic activities in the community.

As head of a national publishing house located in Iowa, you would be an ideal speaker on the topic "Iowa Industry." We have featured this theme at this year's meetings because presidents of nationally known Iowa firms will talk about the advantages of having their headquarters in Iowa.

We would be happy to pay all your expenses in addition to an honorarium of $100.

Cordially yours,

Obviously, there is a conflict—Mr. Weinberger has already accepted an invitation to appear on the book manufacturers' panel in Dayton on April 16. You happen to know, however, that Mr. Weinberger likes to accept such invitations as the one from the Sioux City Uptown Association and that if a later date could be arranged, he would undoubtedly want to accommodate this group. Write an appropriate response for your signature.

(C) Following is another letter that arrived in Mr. Weinberger's absence (he is still in Florida for discussions with Bennington Press).

Dear Sir:

We would like you to appear on a panel at our Spring Career Conference on March 24 at Maryville High School. This citywide conference is held each year to acquaint high school students with career opportunities in various fields. Publishing is an area in which many of our students are interested.

Will you accept?

Very truly yours,

Although Mr. Weinberger feels that Peerless should participate in as many such conferences as possible, he is rarely able to do so himself. You are certain that he will decline this invitation (the week of March 24 promises to be hectic, with many appointments already scheduled) and will recommend as his substitute the Missouri sales representative, Melissa Lorenz. Mrs.

Lorenz does a fine job at these career conferences. Write the letter declining the invitation and suggesting the substitution of Mrs. Lorenz.

D Comment on the following response to an invitation to Mr. Weinberger, and then write one—for your own signature—that you feel is more appropriate.

Dear Mr. Phineas:

Your letter to Mr. Weinberger arrived while he is on a business trip to Florida.

As Mr. Weinberger's assistant, I must decline in his behalf your invitation for him to be a judge in the annual Mt. Tabor Mystery Writers Contest. Mr. Weinberger does not have time to participate in events of this nature. As president of Peerless Publishing Company, he is a very busy man; every week he receives dozens of letters inviting him to do this or that, and he must turn down most of them.

I am sure you understand the position Mr. Weinberger must take on such matters. Thank you, however, for writing.

Very sincerely yours,

CASE 2

USING DISCRETION IN EXECUTIVE CORRESPONDENCE

PROBLEM

Peerless is considering establishing a branch office which will include a book distribution center in the south Atlantic area. Executives are studying the advantages of each proposed site—Atlanta, Charlotte, Jacksonville, and Charleston—and the availability of suitable offices and other facilities. Until they have reached a decision, the subject is not to be discussed openly, particularly with people outside the company.

While Mr. Weinberger is out of the office, the following telegram arrives:

Have ideal warehouse and office space for south Atlantic branch in Brunswick, Georgia. Available immediately. Low, low price. Several prospective buyers, so you must act quickly. Prefer Peerless.

S. K. Vandergrift

As assistant to the president, you are to respond to the telegram.

BACKGROUND

When the boss is to be away for any length of time, it is generally understood that all important mail will be taken care of during his or her absence. If there are important decisions that only the boss can make, the mail is at least acknowledged and the writer told approximately when an answer can be expected.

The assistant-to must make decisions about responding to incoming letters. Some of the correspondence will be urgent enough to trigger a telephone call or a telegram to the boss, some will be handled directly by the assistant-to, and some will be referred to others to handle.

Unless the assistant-to has specific instructions, he or she must exercise judgment, making sure that nothing important is left up in the air. Failure to keep on top of things while the executive is away can be very costly in sales and public relations.

Some executives want to keep in constant touch with the goings-on back home, especially when their trips keep them away for several weeks. They may leave instructions with the assistant-to to send them a daily log of events as well as copies or digests (extracts of important points and the action taken) of important letters. Here are a few items that such a log might include.

February 10

1. Telegram from Holyoke Printers about quantity on reprint of This Is Peerless brochure. Checked with Mrs. Norris and confirmed 120M. Wire sent and confirmed by letter at price of 21 cents each. Dayton asked to send PO.

2. Memo from Mr. Granville asking for preliminary estimate of administrative personnel needs for next year; he needs it this week for space planning. Have sent your preliminary draft, explaining you would bring it up to date when you return.

3. Letter from Crofton Office Supplies, Inc., reminding us that our rental agreement expires 4/1. They sent new contract for your signature. Acknowledged, mentioning your probable return date (Feb. 16).

4. Telephone call from Mr. Abel (Gaslight Restaurant) about menu selection for April meeting of Franklin Book Group. I specified lobster as main course. OK? Also arranged for Davy Jones Room, microphone, raised dais, and photographer.

5. Proposal from Mid-America Advertising Agency saying how they would handle our advertising if they had the account. Acknowledged.

6. Miss Crowley's retirement luncheon to be held the 20th. Mr. Jacobs will present a cassette tape recorder and several operas on tape. Have drafted letter of congratulation from you (attached); they're putting all letters in a morocco-bound portfolio.

In the case problem, the writer must decide whether he will respond to the telegram for his own signature or for Mr. Weinberger's. Here we will assume that he will write for himself.

SOLUTION A

Dear Mr. Vandergrift:

Your telegram arrived while Mr. Weinberger is in Orlando, Florida. He will return on February 16.

Although Peerless is considering establishing a branch office (including a book distribution center) in the south Atlantic area, there has been no mention of Brunswick, Georgia, as a possible site. Locations being considered are Charlotte, Atlanta, Jacksonville, and Charleston. However, I will let Mr. Weinberger know about your proposal at the first opportunity.

Cordially yours,

Analysis of Solution A. You have already spotted the glaring mistake the writer made: confidential information has been revealed. Mr. Vandergrift should not be told where Mr. Weinberger is, and he is not entitled to know the locations Peerless is studying as possible branch office sites.

SOLUTION B

Dear Mr. Vandergrift:

Thank you for your telegram about the availability of your building in Brunswick, Georgia.

Mr. Weinberger is on a business trip until the middle of the month, but I shall let him know about your proposal when I next communicate with him. In any event, you may be sure that Mr. Weinberger will respond at the first opportunity.

Sincerely yours,

Analysis of Solution B. Solution B requires no comment. Although the tone is courteous and the writer offers help, the letter reveals no confidential information.

Projects

 The following letter, dated February 11, arrived during Mr. Weinberger's absence.

Dear Sir:

Through a business associate in France I have learned that Peerless Publishing Company is negotiating with D'Asson Press in Paris for the purpose of purchasing this French publisher.

I am acquainted with all the major publishing houses in Europe, and I consider D'Asson one of the weakest. Although this house has built a good reputation over the years, it has slipped badly during the past two years. I can bring to your attention a number of much better publishing firms that it would be to your advantage to investigate.

You may wish to have me come to Des Moines around the 15th to talk with you regarding this matter since I plan to be in the United States in May. May I hear from you—before you make any further moves.

Yours very truly,

It is true that Mr. Weinberger and others in Peerless have discussed a possible merger with the D'Asson people, but they have made no decision. Respond to the above letter (it is signed by Charles Lecquex).

(B) Refer to the daily log illustrated on page 175, and prepare the communications required in items 1, 2, 3, and 5.

(C) The consulting firm of Ferris and Borichaud, employed to design a new corporate symbol (logo) for Peerless, has sent a rough sketch to Mr. Weinberger for his comments. Since Mr. Weinberger will be out of the office for another two weeks, you decide to make a photocopy of the sketch for your records and send the original on to him since the matter is of some urgency.

You strongly dislike the symbol that Ferris and Borichaud has come up with, and you are convinced that Mr. Weinberger will not approve it. Acknowledge the materials in Mr. Weinberger's absence.

(D) While Mr. Weinberger is away, Ms. Sigrid Untermeyer writes to complain about the paucity of advertising and promotion of her new book, *A Fool's Folly,* which Peerless recently published. Ms. Untermeyer, an important new author who left her previous publisher to publish with Peerless, requests an appointment "right away" to discuss the matter.

You decide to telephone Earl Berenson, manager of the department that published Ms. Untermeyer's book, and he tells you that she has been in to see him several times about this matter. Although he tried to pacify her by showing her the extensive advertising and promotion that has been done, she left him, saying, "I'll write to Mr. Weinberger about this."

Acknowledge the letter from Ms. Untermeyer.

CASE 3

REFERRING COMMUNICATIONS TO OTHERS

PROBLEM

Here is a letter in the morning mail from Julio Gomez, a principal manufacturer for Peerless, that must be acknowledged in Mr. Weinberger's absence.

> Dear Mr. Weinberger:
>
> Have you reached a decision about the new shipping carton Frank Newhouse and I left with you on January 11? Our supply of the cartons you are now using is getting low, but before we put an order into our factory for an additional quantity, I want to make sure that you plan to continue to use it.
>
> Please let me know by February 14; I need to give our factory superintendent the decision within a couple of weeks.
>
> > Cordially yours,

You know that when the new shipping carton was left with Mr. Weinberger, he said he thought it was fine but that approval would have to come from Irene Currie, manager of the Shipping Department. Mrs. Currie would have to compare costs, see whether the size is appropriate for the various books Peerless publishes, and so on.

This situation calls for two communications: an acknowledgment of the letter from Mr. Gomez and a memo to Mrs. Currie.

BACKGROUND

A letter acknowledging correspondence that must be referred to another person within the company is prompt and courteous. It should not, however, commit the person who is to handle the matter to a specific course of action or time limit. Above all, it should not contain direct or implied criticism of a fellow employee.

It's a good idea to telephone in advance the individual to whom a letter is being referred so that he or she will know it's coming and can begin immediately to gather the information needed in order to respond.

SOLUTION A: Letter to Mr. Gomez

> Dear Mr. Gomez:
>
> Mr. Weinberger is out of the office this week, and I am handling his routine correspondence in his absence.

I am sorry you have not had an answer before this time to your question about the new shipping carton. Mr. Weinberger approved it at least two weeks ago and asked our Shipping Department manager, Irene Currie, to follow up with you. I am surprised that this matter was not settled.

You may be sure, Mr. Gomez, that you will have a decision from us this week. Mrs. Currie is attending to the matter at my instructions.

Yours very truly,

SOLUTION A: Memo to Mrs. Currie

TO: Irene P. Currie   **FROM:** Ralph G. McClain
SUBJECT: New Shipping Carton   **DATE:** February 11, 19—

Will you please attend to the enclosed letter right away. Apparently there was some kind of slipup. Note that the matter is somewhat urgent.

Analysis of Solution A. The letter to Mr. Gomez is faulty in several respects.

1. Although the statement, "Mr. Weinberger is out of the office this week," is entirely appropriate, referring to Mr. Gomez's letter as "routine correspondence" is very tactless. Beware of attaching labels, even though in your own mind they may be accurate.
2. The second paragraph implies some infighting in Peerless; the writer expresses open annoyance with a fellow employee for not doing what she was supposed to do. Although he may be put out with Mrs. Currie, he should not express his feelings to an outsider. Mrs. Currie will feel degraded, the writer will have made an enemy, and Mr. Gomez's problem will still be unsolved.
3. The statement, "Mrs. Currie is attending to the matter at my instructions," is officious. Flaunting authority, even when you have it, is in very poor taste.

The memorandum to Mrs. Currie will further annoy her and widen the human relations gap. It is abrupt and officious in tone.

SOLUTION B: Letter to Mr. Gomez

Dear Mr. Gomez:

Mr. Weinberger is not in the office this week, and I want to give you some assurance about the new shipping carton you wrote about.

I talked this morning with Irene Currie, our Shipping Department manager, who is doing some research on the new carton. She told me she plans to write you this week. I know that some of the information she requested from the various publishing departments about the size of the carton was late getting to her because a number of people have been out of the office.

Cordially yours,

SOLUTION B: Memo to Mrs. Currie

TO: Irene P. Currie   **FROM:** Ralph G. McClain
SUBJECT: New Shipping Carton   **DATE:** February 11, 19—

Here is a copy of the letter from Mr. Gomez that I spoke to you about this morning, along with my reply. Let me know if I need to do anything further on this.

Analysis of Solution B.   The Solution B letter to Mr. Gomez is appropriate. The writer did what he should have done—telephoned Mrs. Currie for up-to-date information before attempting to answer the letter. And rather than condemning Mrs. Currie, the writer explained the delay in a way that takes Mrs. Currie off the hook.

The memo is excellent for the purpose. The tone is businesslike but not officious, and the writer offers to cooperate if he is needed for anything else.

Projects

   The following letter, along with a manuscript, arrives while Mr. Weinberger is away.

Dear Sir:

I am sending you a collection of poems that I wrote in memory of my mother. Many people who have seen these poems, including a professor of English at Pythagoras College, have told me they ought to be published. I think Peerless would be a good publisher.

Please tell me how much I will be paid. I would also like a $3,500 cash advance. Please acknowledge this manuscript (it is the only copy I have), and let me know when you will publish my poems. I am thinking of the title "A Girl and Her Mother." What is your opinion?

Yours truly,

Several things about the letter concern you. The most important is that the author sent the only existing copy of her manuscript—a dangerous thing to do because manuscripts are sometimes lost in the mails or in the files of publishers. Also, you happen to know that Peerless does not publish poetry (except for the works of a few nationally known poets). In fact, there is very little market for poetry.

If Peerless were interested in this author's manuscript, which is highly unlikely, the Trade Department (Earl Berenson is manager) would publish it. Write the response (the letter is signed by Myrtle Parsons) and any additional communications that may be required.

(B) Dale R. Badham, a graduate student at Forseti University, has written to Mr. Weinberger requesting an interview. He is preparing a thesis on "The Economics of the Publishing Industry" and wants to get Mr. Weinberger's view of the subject.

Mr. Weinberger is often asked to participate in studies of this nature, and when he can find the time, he accepts. When he is especially busy, however, he refers the requests to Amy W. Zeigler, vice president for manufacturing of Peerless. You feel that he will want to have Mr. Badham talk to Miss Zeigler. Write the appropriate communications.

(C) Mrs. Sadie Warren, an important stockholder in Peerless Publishing Company, has written Mr. Weinberger about a biography she is having prepared about her father, R. D. VanSant, who was a pioneer in bridge construction. In her letter, Mrs. Warren states that she knows such a biography will not sell enough copies to justify its publication but expresses her willingness to subsidize the cost—that is, she will pay for all editorial, manufacturing, and promotion costs. She does, however, want the Peerless imprint on the book.

You do not know what Mr. Weinberger's reaction will be to such a proposal (Peerless does very little of this type of subsidized publishing). In any event, the matter would come under the jurisdiction of Ms. Charlotte Reichard, assistant manager of the Trade Department. Prepare the appropriate communications.

CASE 4

WRITING AND SIGNING FOR THE EXECUTIVE

PROBLEM

Before Mr. Weinberger left on his trip, he said to you, "Write to Professor Peter Himmel at the University of Houston, asking him if he would be willing to act as one of our consultants on the new ecology series. Since I know Professor Himmel pretty well, prepare the letter for my signature and sign it for me."

You know that the consultants on the ecology series usually receive a royalty of one-fourth of 1 percent on each book sold. You also know that Professor Himmel is one of several distinguished professors being asked to serve as consultants. Your search of files shows that there has been previous correspondence with Professor Himmel and that he and Mr. Weinberger are on a first-name basis.

BACKGROUND

Assistants-to often write communications and sign them with the boss's signature. Therefore, they quickly learn to make their letters sound as though the executive wrote them. To do this, they must know how the boss reacts to situations, the boss's style of expression (which can be learned by studying samples of his or her writing), and the boss's relationship with individual correspondents. The most important of these, of course, is the individual executive's relationship with each correspondent, for it determines the tone of the letters.

Writing *in behalf of* the boss is not the same as writing *for* the boss. Note that in the first example below, the assistant is signing the letter although it is written in behalf of the executive.

Dear Mr. Frantz:

Before Mr. Caine left for Amarillo this morning, he asked me to find out whether you have completed the tests you are making on tire mileage. He especially wanted to know how Super-Ms compared with the competing brands and whether you are planning further tests.

Mr. Caine spoke enthusiastically about his trip to El Paso. He was especially impressed with the new warehouse.

Cordially yours,

Now notice how different the tone is when the assistant writes about the same situation in the executive's name and for the executive's signature.

Dear Charlie:

When I was in El Paso, I forgot to ask you about the results of that tire mileage test you are making. How did our Super-Ms stand up against the competition? Are you planning more tests, or do you feel that you have all the evidence you need?

It was great being with you last week. Your new warehouse looks like a winner, and I hope we can automate the Duluth and Richmond warehouses to the same extent. With nothing to do but punch buttons, you're obviously planning to get in a lot of golf from now on.

Cordially,

SOLUTION A

Dear Peter:

Would you be willing to serve as a consultant on the new ecology series we are planning? We would be willing to pay you one-fourth of 1 percent royalty on each copy of the books that we sell.

I would appreciate your prompt reply.

Sincerely yours,

Analysis of Solution A.   Solution A is not an effective letter for the purpose.

1. The writer knows that Mr. Weinberger and Professor Himmel are on a first-name basis and have corresponded before, but the tone of the letter gives no evidence that they have ever met.
2. The letter is so lacking in necessary details that Professor Himmel will undoubtedly have to ask for more information.
3. If Professor Himmel is worthy of being asked to serve in a consulting capacity, something should have been said about why he was chosen.
4. The mention of money is too abrupt. Although Professor Himmel would be interested in the financial aspects of the assignment, he will want to know more about the series that is being planned, the names of others who are being considered as consultants, and other details.

SOLUTION B

Dear Peter:

When I talked with you at the American Geographical Society convention in Denver last November, I mentioned that we were thinking about publishing a new series of books for the ecology curriculum in colleges and universities. Since we have decided to go ahead with this series, we are now ready to engage several consultants to assist us in planning the materials, selecting the authors, and producing the books.

Naturally, you were one of the first people I thought of as those of us here talked about this project. Would you be willing to serve as a member of our consulting board? You're our first choice because I believe that once I have your acceptance, I'll have no difficulty in getting other distinguished scientists to join the board.

We are offering one-fourth of 1 percent royalty to each consultant on all the materials developed and sold in this series. If our projections hold up, you should receive from $2,500 to $4,000 a year for the life of the series.

Let me have your reactions, Peter. We are thinking about inviting Professor Laura Tyler, of Stanford, and Professor Arthur Matisse, of Duke, to act as consultants, but we will await your decision because we want your suggestions. At the moment, we're planning to have eight books in the series (each accompanied by laboratory manuals, films, slides, and so forth), but we can talk about this later.

Cordially,

Analysis of Solution B.   Solution B is an effective letter for these reasons:

1. The writer provides background information (previous conversation about the ecology series) so that Professor Himmel can quickly understand the purpose of the letter.
2. The writer acknowledges Professor Himmel as a distinguished scholar and indicates that is why he is inviting him to serve as a consultant.

3. The financial arrangements are explicit. (By mentioning them after issuing the invitation, the writer implies that Professor Himmel is more interested in educational leadership than in money. He may actually be more interested in the money, but it is better not to imply it.)
4. The tone of the letter, although professional, is friendly and personal.
5. The writer does not try to cover everything in one letter. He mentions decisions that can be deferred as points of reference only.

Project

Refer to the following projects, and prepare responses for Mr. Weinberger's signature rather than your own.

1. Project B, page 173.
2. Project A, page 177. Assume that Mr. Weinberger will be willing to see Mr. Lecquex when he comes to the United States but has no particular enthusiasm for a meeting. Suggest a date of around March 15.
3. Project C, page 181. Assume that Mr. Weinberger feels that Mrs. Warren's biography of her father is not suitable for Peerless. A small publisher, Bo-Peep Press, specializes in this type of publishing and would be a much better house for Mrs. Warren's book. Mr. Weinberger has telephoned the president, Clifton Bergstrand, and he would be pleased to hear from Mrs. Warren about the book.

PART

6

GENERAL MANAGEMENT
COMMUNICATIONS

YOUR JOB *You are continuing in the position of assistant to the president of Peerless Publishing Company, Paul J. Weinberger.*

CASE 1

HANDLING APPLICATIONS FOR EMPLOYMENT

PROBLEM

For several weeks Mr. Weinberger has been looking for a person to represent Peerless Publishing Company in Washington, D.C. This representative, who will be called "assistant to the president for Washington affairs," will have the responsibility for keeping in touch with important federal agencies, with the activities in Congress as they relate to budget appropriations for education, with the U.S. Copyright Office, with trade associations, and with VIPs in general. The job calls for someone with heavy experience in publicity and public relations, in education, and in publishing. Although the position has not been advertised (Mr. Weinberger is leaning toward selecting a person from within the company rather than going outside), word has gotten around and several applications have been received. Following is one of them:

> Dear Mr. Weinberger:
>
> I understand that you are looking for a person to represent Peerless Publishing Company in Washington, and I would like to make application for the position.
>
> For 12 years I have been a free-lance journalist in Washington and have had my articles published by several of the country's leading newspapers. I have also sold material to *Forbe's, Harper's, Fortune,* and several other magazines. Naturally, with my 12 years' experience, I have become acquainted with most of the "shakers and movers" on the Washington scene, and I am convinced that I can make this experience pay off handsomely for Peerless.
>
> Details are given in the enclosed résumé. May I come to Des Moines to talk with you? You can reach me at (202) 966-4343.
>
> Sincerely yours,
>
> Jean McNair

Mr. Weinberger, as mentioned, is responding directly to inquiries about the position in Washington. He is not impressed with the applicant whose letter appears above. The applicant is essentially a journalist and lacks the necessary experience in book publishing and education.

What response would be appropriate? Should Mr. Weinberger (or you, who must write the letter) tell the applicant about her shortcomings? Or should the response be simply "No," without giving reasons?

BACKGROUND

Company presidents receive many letters from people who believe they can get special attention and faster action by going straight to the top. Most executives acknowledge all mail addressed to them, but they often pass correspondence along to someone else in the company to handle. They generally refer applications for employment, particularly for other than top executive posts, to the personnel department, but the practice varies. If an executive refers the letter to someone, he or she usually simply expresses appreciation for the application and mentions that it is being referred to someone else; the executive does not offer an opinion about the applicant's qualifications or chances of getting a position. For example:

Dear Mr. Platt:

Thank you for your interest in a position as accountant with our firm.

I am forwarding your letter to Mrs. Gretchen Simms, our personnel placement specialist for accounting and data processing positions. You should hear from Mrs. Simms shortly.

Sincerely yours,

SOLUTION A

Dear Miss McNair:

This will acknowledge your letter in which you apply for a position as our Washington representative.

I am sorry that we cannot consider you for this position, but I appreciate your interest.

Very truly yours,

Analysis of Solution A. Solution A, as you have observed, is a tactless and rude letter. Miss McNair might be left with the impression that her character is in question. A flat turndown like this is unnecessary.

SOLUTION B

Dear Miss McNair:

Thank you for your interest in representing Peerless in Washington.

We are considering a number of applicants for this position, Miss McNair, and we are certainly glad to have your résumé in our hands. If we require additional information or think it would be to our mutual advantage to meet with you personally, you will hear from me or one of my associates by April 12.

Sincerely yours,

Analysis of Solution B. Solution B says no without bluntness or insult. Yet the writer has not played with the truth—everything in the letter is accurate. At the same time Miss McNair will notice that she has been given no encouragement—and probably will not expect to hear again from Peerless.

SOLUTION C

Dear Miss McNair:

Thank you for applying for the position as our representative in Washington.

The person hired for this job must have a great deal more experience in book publishing and in education than you have. Therefore, we consider you unqualified.

Your letter and résumé are enclosed.

Very truly yours,

Analysis of Solution C. This solution, although honest, is too blunt. The use of the term *unqualified* is totally unnecessary, and the return of the letter and résumé is insulting.

SOLUTION D

Dear Miss McNair:

Thank you for applying for a job as a Peerless representative.

For this position, Miss McNair, we are searching for a person with heavy experience in book publishing and in education. Although your qualifications in publicity and public relations are superb, we think your experience is light in these other important areas.

However, we certainly will give consideration to your application, along with the many others we have received. You may expect to hear from me by May 1 if we feel that there is an opportunity here for you.

Sincerely yours,

Analysis of Solution D. Solution D is the most effective because it tells the applicant that she lacks the desired qualifications without insulting her in the process. The final paragraph implies a "no," but that unpleasant and harsh word is avoided—and Miss McNair will understand what is meant.

Projects

(A) The following letter, addressed to Mr. Weinberger, is referred to you for reply.

Dear Sir:

I am writing to inquire about a summer job at Peerless Publishing Company.

At the present time I am a student at Brill College, where I am majoring in English. Upon graduation I hope to enter the field of book publishing as an editor, and I want to acquire as much experience as possible while I am still studying.

I would especially like to work on encyclopedias but would be willing to accept any editorial job that may be available.

A brief résumé is enclosed. May I hear from you?

Sincerely yours,

Nancy Rafferty

It is too early in the year to predict the need for editorial help during the summer months. However, each department is estimating its requirements for temporary people for the summer, and this information will be available about April 15—two months from now. You are impressed with Nancy Rafferty's qualifications. Write the letter for your own signature.

Ⓑ Respond to the following letter for Mr. Weinberger's signature. There are no openings in the accounting and financial departments, but even if there were, Mr. Moore seems to you (and Mr. Weinberger) to be an unlikely candidate.

Dear Mr. Weinberger:

I am offering you the opportunity to put on your staff the most knowledgefull financial man in the country today. I am throughly experienced in acct'g, finance, systems, and edp. I can begin work at anytime, and I will expect to hear from you very quickly that you won't me to go to work for you. I have had many offers, so you must act fast.

Yours truly,

L. Harvey Moore

Ⓒ Peerless hires several college graduates each year as editorial trainees. That is, ten to fifteen graduates with English majors are accepted and placed in a training program at a fairly good salary. Upon successful completion of training, they are eligible for promotion to the job of editing supervisor in one of the publishing departments.

There are many more candidates for these trainee positions than there are jobs. Each applicant must take a test designed to reveal his or her knowledge of English and general aptitude for editorial work. Many fail the test, but there are always more than enough who pass it to fill the training program quota.

Following is a letter written to an applicant who failed the test.

Dear Miss Gambrell:

You failed our editing test, and I cannot accept you as an editorial trainee. We have enough people who passed the test to more than fill our quota.

Cordially,

Rewrite the letter for Mr. Weinberger's signature.

RESPONDING TO UNREASONABLE REQUESTS

PROBLEM

Mr. Weinberger has received this letter and has handed it to you to answer.

ROCKLEDGE COLLEGE OF EDUCATION
Curriculum Library and Materials Center
Rockledge, Missouri 65741

Dear Sir:

I'd like to have a file in our Curriculum Center that contains information about professional educators, authors, and illustrators.

Would it be possible to secure from you descriptive literature, pictures, brief autobiographies or biographies, and brief reviews concerning your company's leading people in these fields?

And if you don't have such materials on hand but could tell me where to get them, I'd appreciate that too.

Such a file would be so helpful to us in many ways.

Sincerely,

Peerless publishes several hundred new books each year, many written by new authors. In addition, Peerless has over 5,000 different books in stock at the moment (representing more than 3,500 authors and several hundred illustrators). Although the publisher obviously has some data about most of the people who write and illustrate his books, he does not keep a systematic biographical file on them. Compiling such a file would be very costly and require months of work. Besides, the information would quickly become out of date since the works of new authors are being published every week.

You will have to turn down this request. The only suggestion you can offer to the inquirer is to consult professional directories (*Who's Who, Who's Who in Education,* etc.) to obtain the needed information.

BACKGROUND

Nearly every business receives requests with which it cannot comply. More often than not, the people making the requests are customers or potential customers. Perhaps because they think they are in a favored position, they believe they are entitled to receive almost anything they ask for. On the other hand, most of them probably don't realize that their requests are unreasonable.

SOLUTION A

Dear Mr. Kingston:

We find your request for biographical data on our authors, educators, and illustrators unreasonable. It would take us months to compile this information, and it would be out of date before we start because we are publishing books by new authors all the time.

Since you work in a library, you should be in a position to know about professional directories, such as Who's Who, and I would suggest that you do some research on your own.

Very truly yours,

Analysis of Solution A. Obviously, this is a very poor letter. In effect it calls the person asking for the information a fool and chides him for being so unrealistic. If the person is a customer, he will think twice before he buys anything else from the publisher. There is little doubt that the writer is annoyed—his annoyance shows through in every sentence, particularly the last one.

SOLUTION B

Dear Mr. Kingston:

Your letter to Mr. Weinberger has been given to me, and I am pleased to answer in his absence.

If it were possible, Mr. Kingston, to send you data on professional educators, authors, and illustrators, I would. Unfortunately, we do not have such information conveniently available, and it would be a formidable task to gather it. Every year Peerless publishes hundreds of new books; therefore, any biographical data we might assemble would become out of date quickly. For such information, we rely primarily on professional directories, such as Who's Who and Who's Who in Education.

Perhaps such directories will help you too. In any event, I hope you will be able to obtain the information you need without too much difficulty.

Sincerely yours,

Analysis of Solution B.   In Solution B the writer reasons with the correspondent, proving tactfully that the task would not be worth the effort since time would render the information almost useless in a short period. The tone is positive; the language, persuasive. Note that rather than saying, "Why don't you consult professional directories" (which would imply that the reader hasn't done so), the writer turned the phrase into a positive one: "we rely primarily on professional directories . . . ."

Projects

(A)   Ruth Baxter of Kansas City wrote Mr. Weinberger asking for copies of Peerless Publishing Company's annual reports for the years 1925 to the present. As a doctoral thesis, she is writing a history of annual reports showing how styles have changed over the years in financial reporting.

Peerless has in its archives one copy of every annual report issued since the company was founded in 1921. These copies are very valuable, however, and the company does not allow anyone to take them out of the building. Write Ms. Baxter (for Mr. Weinberger's signature), suggesting that if she can visit Peerless, you will make arrangements for her to spend as much time examining the reports as she would like. In addition, indicate that you can make a photocopying machine available to her for reproducing certain pages from the reports.

(B)   Respond to the following letter for Mr. Weinberger's signature.

Dear Sir:

Our Personnel Department is sponsoring a course for executives in how to listen, and we would like to borrow your excellent "Listen—and Learn" cassette tapes so that we can reproduce them for use in this class.

Since we are a nonprofit organization, our funds are limited, and I would hope that you could give us the privilege of recording these tapes without charge. We would, of course, return your tapes in excellent condition.

The course starts in two weeks, so I would like to have the tapes shipped immediately.

Thank you for what I know will be a favorable reply.

Yours very truly,

Dwight F. Menzies

The above request is an unreasonable one, and you must deny it. The price of the set of tapes is $120, and your agreement with the author is that he will receive 5 percent royalty on each set sold. If you permitted the tapes to be duplicated, you would not only establish a precedent whereby other organizations could ask for the same privilege but would also jeopardize your copyright and deny the author his royalty income.

WRITING LETTERS PERTAINING TO COMPANY POLICY

PROBLEM

The following letters, addressed to "President, Peerless Publishing Company," are on your desk:

Dear Sir:

The Glenwood Garden Club is trying to raise money in order to build a greenhouse. One of our members suggested that we sell cookbooks, provided we can purchase them at a price low enough to enable us to make a profit. We are especially interested in Margaret Langdon's Slow Cooker Guide, which you publish (it is listed in your catalog at $12.95). What would be the cost to us if we purchase, say, 400 copies?

An immediate response will be appreciated.

Very truly yours,

(Mrs.) Greta Wylie

Dear Sir:

One of your authors, Eric Calcaterra, has applied to us for a loan in the amount of $3,000. Please furnish us with information about Mr. Calcaterra's annual royalties on his book, Montana Horizons, so that we may assess him as a credit risk. Thank you!

Very truly yours,

QUICK-WAY LOAN AGENCY

BACKGROUND

Often, requests must be refused because they conflict with company policy. The letters above are good examples.

Peerless sells <u>Margaret Langdon's Slow Cooker Guide</u> primarily through retail bookstores, and if the Glenwood Garden Club were permitted to purchase the book at a discount and sell it in the community, the company would be undercutting its dealers. Therefore, the request must be denied.

Sometimes information requested by outsiders is confidential—personal data about employees, financial information concerning customers or the company itself, and so on—and is released only to people or agencies authorized to have it.

Requests such as those illustrated are so frequent in some companies that form letters are developed as responses. Usually, however, the answers are individually typed.

SOLUTION—Letter to Mrs. Wylie

Dear Mrs. Wylie:

We are pleased to know that you and your fellow members of the Glenwood Garden Club think so well of <u>Margaret Langdon's Slow Cooker Guide</u> that you wish to sell it as a means of raising funds. It is indeed a popular cookbook throughout the country.

Mrs. Wylie, I wish it were possible for us to assist you, but we can offer a discount only to bookstores through which our books are distributed. To do otherwise would place us in competition with our own customers—and that, we think you will agree, would not be fair.

The Glenwood Garden Club can, I hope, find another way to raise money for the greenhouse. Have you seen <u>Fund-Raising Ideas for Clubs and Organizations</u>? It is an inexpensive paperback (published by Five-Star Press) that contains a wide range of useful suggestions. Perhaps your local bookstore has a copy.

Sincerely yours,

Analysis of the Solution.   The letter to Mrs. Wylie is a good example of saying no tactfully. Note the three important points:

1. Expression of appreciation for her interest in, and apparently high opinion of, the book.
2. Explanation of why the request cannot be granted.
3. Suggestion of a possible solution to the problem.

SOLUTION—Letter to Quick-Way Loan Agency

Gentlemen:

I appreciate your inquiry concerning the royalties of Eric Calcaterra. I am sure you will understand, however, that such information is considered confidential and cannot be released.

Very truly yours,

Analysis of the Solution. You may consider the letter to Quick-Way Loan Agency abrupt, yet there is very little further to be said. As a business institution, Quick-Way should know that its request is unreasonable, and there should be no apologies for denying it.

Projects

(A) Miss Millicent Arness of the Hoopstown Public Library wrote asking for twenty copies of the Peerless general catalog. She said she gets many calls for publishers' catalogs and thinks it would be a good idea to have several handy so that they can be given to those who ask for them.

Ĺ The Peerless general catalog contains over 800 pages and costs $3.60 to produce. It is supplied in single copies free to large buyers of books—book dealers, librarians, school administrators, college professors, and others; but because of the cost of the catalog, copies are rarely given to individual consumers.

Ĺ Write the response for Mr. Weinberger. Assume that you will send two copies of the catalog to Miss Arness—not the twenty she asked for.

(B) Lloyd Demaret, office manager of a large printing house, wrote asking to be put on the mailing list for six copies of an employee publication, *Peerless Paragraphs*. This monthly monograph often contains confidential information and is restricted to employees. You don't know how Mr. Demaret got his hands on a copy. Write the response for Mr. Weinberger's signature.

CASE 4

RESPONDING TO CRITICS

PROBLEM

In support of bookstores that sell Peerless books, the company advertises its new products in several magazines. One of these magazines is *Quench,* a highly controversial monthly magazine that speaks boldly on all issues—political, social, educational, and scientific—often attacking public figures and social institutions.

Ĺ In Mr. Weinberger's absence, you are to respond to the following letter.

Dear Mr. Weinberger:

Why would a reputable company such as Peerless support, through advertising, a muckraking periodical like <u>Quench?</u> I cannot understand why you would assist in the desecration of our institutions and the character assassination of our national leaders, educators, and scientists. Your business and your profits depend on protecting and sustaining our American way of life—not on destroying it.

I expect to hear an explanation from you, Mr. Weinberger. It is not inconceivable that your products could be boycotted for such advertising practices, and if your explanation is not a satisfactory one, I shall take steps to see that Peerless books are not distributed—at least in this community.

Yours truly,

J. D. Douglas

BACKGROUND

All major companies receive letters from people who are highly critical of policies, activities, advertising, and so forth. Some writers are well-meaning and state their positions reasonably. Others are irrational and threatening.

Of course, the company should not panic in such situations, but at the same time, it cannot afford to ignore these critics. In the interest of good public relations, most critical letters require a response.

SOLUTION A

Dear Mr. Douglas:

I will not argue that you have a right to express your opinion, but perhaps you will give me the courtesy of allowing me to express mine.

If we listened to everyone who disagrees with our advertising policy, we wouldn't purchase any advertising. Nearly everybody, it would seem, has a list of publications whose editorial policy is at odds with his or her own. Obviously, we can't let these biases dictate where we place our advertising.

Your threat to boycott Peerless books in your area is carefully noted. This is not the first time we have been threatened, but so far they have been "full of sound and fury, signifying nothing."

Yours very truly,

Analysis of Solution A.   Obviously, the writer of Solution A is "hot" and the letter shows his anger. Although there is a temptation to let off steam at people who want to dictate company policies and practices, one must keep in mind the purpose of the response. This purpose should be to win over the critic to the writer's point of view—not to give her reason to write a second vitriolic letter. Convincing critics that they are wrong can be very difficult—often impossible. After all, how many times must the respondent turn the other cheek? Certainly, there is a point at which a persistent critic must be set down firmly or simply ignored. But that time comes only after at least one attempt is made at a reasonable solution.

SOLUTION B

Dear Mr. Douglas:

Thank you sincerely for your letter concerning our policy of advertising Peerless books in Quench.

I am sure you will agree, Mr. Douglas, that by placing advertising in Quench or any other magazine we are not necessarily endorsing the editorial policy of the magazine. By and large, we and other businesses select printed advertising media on the basis of readership. As is true with most companies, we are constantly experimenting with various media; whether we continue such advertising usually depends on the results it obtains. This is a standard practice of American business firms.

Peerless advertises extensively in all types of media. It would be presumptuous of us to adopt the policy of advertising only in those publications whose editorial policy we agree with. Some advertising managers have a personal editorial preference for publications that others find offensive. Yet none can afford to base business judgment on personal preference. As a business owner, you will understand, I am sure, the role that economics plays in such decisions.

Thank you for expressing your point of view so frankly, Mr. Douglas, and for giving us an opportunity to express ours.

Sincerely yours,

Analysis of Solution B. In Solution B the writer displays tact and courtesy even though it might have been hard for him to do so. Most important, he presents his position clearly, fully, and reasonably. This is the only effective way to handle such situations. Even if the writer agrees with the critic that the company should not advertise in a magazine like *Quench* (and he very well might), he must not say so openly. The point that even Peerless advertising people disagree on editorial policy should convince a reasonable person that readership and exposure are the primary criteria for selecting an advertising medium.

Projects

 Reply to the following letter for Mr. Weinberger's signature.

Dear Mr. Weinberger:

I am writing in behalf of the Pearl City Environment Association in protest of your support of a printing firm that pollutes our river and air. This firm, which prints many of your books, is the R. S. Ogle Company. Every day of the week we see dirty, black smoke pouring out of the company's plant, and the Langorous

River, on which the building is located, is fouled and filthy with the chemicals Ogle dumps into it.

Our group has protested to the mayor of Pearl City many times and has met with the Ogle bigwigs on numerous occasions about this matter. The only answer we get is, "We're working on it." Yet nothing happens—just more pollutants spill out to destroy the beauty of our city.

The only recourse left to us is to protest to those who support this company. As a large publisher, you have the obligation to take your business away from this irresponsible printer. I expect to hear from you.

Very truly yours,

Gardner V. Pritchard

Of course, Peerless has no control over the practices of its suppliers. Although Mr. Weinberger may deplore the situation (if the accusation is true), he must select his suppliers primarily on the basis of quality work, service, and price. Actually, Peerless is proud of its activities in environmental affairs. For example, one of the company's executives recently had his article, "The Book Manufacturer and the Ecology Movement," published in *Book Production* magazine. Too, this year Peerless published a series of ecology textbooks for college students and is now working on learning materials for elementary and high school students.

In your response, you may wish to make reference to the above. Also, you might want to mention the danger to the local economy if Ogle lost its publishing customers. Assume that you will send a copy of your response to Larry Whipple, president of Ogle.

(B) Prepare a response to the following letter for Mr. Weinberger's signature.

Dear Mr. Weinberger:

As president of the Lamonica Valley Concerned Parents Association, I must express my shock and disgust at Revolt of a Radical Realist, by Chauncey Arcane, that you recently published. How can a company with your reputation champion the cause of this bloody revolutionist—one who would destroy our sacred ideals and institutions?

This is an offensive and irresponsible act, Mr. Weinberger, and I protest strongly in behalf of mothers and fathers everywhere. The language is filthy and the ideas expressed by this punk Arcane totally un-American. If you do not withdraw this book at once, I will see to it that the schools and libraries of Lamonica Valley stop buying from Peerless and that your books disappear from their shelves.

Very truly yours,

Mrs. Mona Standish

Take whatever position you wish in responding to Mrs. Standish. It is true that Chauncey Arcane is a highly controversial figure. His ideas on social reform are somewhat radical—indeed, Mr. Weinberger does not agree with Arcane's position. Mr. Arcane is, however, a gifted writer (the reviews of his book have been highly complimentary).

CASE 5

SAYING NO TO REQUESTS FOR DONATIONS

PROBLEM

Almost every week Mr. Weinberger receives requests that Peerless contribute to this charity or that worthy cause. A majority of these requests must be refused—no company, no matter how large or how profitable, can afford to support every campaign for funds. A typical letter received at Peerless is from Ms. Frances Laytham, director of Clarkson Day-Care Center, which opened recently in your community. Ms. Laytham asks Peerless for a contribution toward the Clarkson fund drive. Because you have received a number of such requests, you have decided to develop two or three "pattern" letters that can, with slight adaptations, fit most situations.

BACKGROUND

Every business organization receives many requests for contributions. Although most organizations do contribute to various local campaigns, setting aside a percentage of profits for that specific purpose, they can never honor all the requests they receive. Some firms support only one united fund organization (called by that name, or Community Chest, or a similar name). Others give most of their contribution fund budget to a united fund group and, in addition, set aside money for other charitable organizations that do not share in the united fund.

In any event, requests for contributions must be screened very carefully. It is very hard to justify a no to one organization when you have just said yes to a similar one. More important, the charge of discrimination is always a possibility, especially among religious and ethnic groups. The subject of donations, then, is a very sensitive one in the public relations area.

Most large companies set up a special committee to study contribution requests, and the committee ponders over and discusses each request before reaching a decision. One purpose of such a committee is to share the responsibility for turning down a request. The negative decision of a group carries more weight than that of an individual; and certainly it is less painful to the person who has to convey the decision when he or she can say, "The Committee decided," rather than "I decided."

SOLUTION A

Dear Ms. Laytham:

Thank you for your letter in which you ask us to support your drive for funds for Clarkson Day-Care Center. Our Donations Committee, which has the responsibility for allocating our budget for contributions, handles all requests for funds. I am therefore referring your letter to that group. No doubt you will hear from the director soon after the Committee reaches a decision.

Sincerely yours,

Analysis of Solution A. In companies where all requests for donations are turned over to a special committee, a letter such as this is appropriate. Note that the writer is noncommittal but tactful.

SOLUTION B

Dear Ms. Laytham:

Thank you for writing us to request a contribution to Clarkson Day-Care Center.

Each year we set aside a generous budget for contributions to local activities. In fact, last year we gave to various organizations the largest amount in our history. Even then, we were able to give to only a fraction of the groups that sought our help. I am sure you will understand that we cannot give financial support to all.

Reluctantly, then, we must refrain from participating this year. In your case the decision is particularly painful for us because we are well aware of the fine public service you are performing.

Best wishes in your drive, and I hope that at some later date we may be able to share in this effort.

Sincerely yours,

Analysis of Solution B. This pattern letter emphasizes the we-can't-give-to-everyone theme. It is sympathetic in tone, tactful, reasonable, and friendly.

SOLUTION C

Dear Ms. Laytham:

Thank you for writing me about the need for funds to operate the Clarkson Day-Care Center you have recently established.

Certainly we at Peerless are sympathetic with your objectives, Ms. Laytham, and wish it were possible to participate in this endeavor. Because the requests for our financial support have become so numerous (last year we had over 120 requests), we have had to confine our company contributions to the three major community funds: Citizens All, Charity Council, and Givers Anonymous.

You will be interested to learn that we have a policy of matching contributions made by our employees to recognized charities and nonprofit institutions. Thus we undoubtedly will be contributing indirectly to Clarkson Center, which is, of course, on the approved list.

Sincerely yours,

Analysis of Solution C.   In the kind of letter represented by Solution C, the writer makes two important points: (1) company policy is to support only community funds and (2) the company has a matching contribution plan for employees.

SOLUTION D

Dear Ms. Laytham:

Thank you for writing us asking for support of Clarkson Day-Care Center.

Last year we had over 120 requests for financial aid. Fortunately, we were able to make contributions to nearly half of these organizations. One of the hardest decisions we have to make is determining which organizations do and which do not qualify for our support (we'd like to support every worthy cause). To help do this, we have established a point system to rate the various causes objectively. It's the only way we have found to bring objectivity into our decisions.

Although we cannot honor your request this year, I assure you that all of us at Peerless appreciate the valuable work you are doing. It is a great public service, and we wish you much success in your endeavors.

Cordially yours,

Analysis of Solution D.   Some companies are sensitive about the subject of how they select the organizations to which they contribute. Solution D explains one company's procedures.

Projects

 The Patterson Guild is a small, private art school near Lexington, Kentucky. Because of the high expense of operation, the administration has announced that the school must close its doors at the end of the current academic year. Although the students understand the problem and appreciate the administration's attempts to deal with it, they are not willing to accept the school's fate and have decided to solicit funds from various organizations to keep the Guild in operation. The Committee to Save Patterson Guild has written to Mr. Weinberger asking for financial help from Peerless (Peerless publishes art books that are used at Patterson Guild).

Although Peerless is sympathetic, the Donations Committee has voted not to make a contribution to the Patterson Guild students. The company cannot, according to the Committee, support "every cause, no matter how much we may sympathize with it." Write the letter for Mr. Weinberger's signature, and address it to Rachel DeVille.

(B) A local organization known as Patriotic Americans for Puritan Principles is soliciting funds to support its work. In his letter asking for money, the president (Roger Beckett) stated the objective of the organization: "To protect the American way our forefathers fought and died for."

After a thorough investigation, the Donations Committee found nothing favorable about the organization. Several civic leaders and local government agencies said they believe it is an extremely radical group with a platform of bigotry. Write the appropriate letter to Mr. Beckett.

(C) The Old-Timers Club of Racine, Wisconsin, wrote Mr. Weinberger asking for free copies of damaged and out-of-date books for its library. Peerless has made arrangements with a number of organizations throughout the country to supply such books to young people's libraries in especially needy areas and to philanthropic organizations concerned with the welfare of young people. The demand is, of course, greater than the supply. Write a response, addressing it to Mrs. Agnes H. Coltran.

CASE 6

SAYING NO TO ADVERTISING SOLICITORS

PROBLEM

Mr. Weinberger received the following letter. He asked you to draft a reply for his signature, saying, "We can't do it."

Dear Mr. Weinberger:

The Suburban Art League is having its annual ball in October at the Lakewood Club. The proceeds from the ball will go toward establishing a scholarship fund for gifted young artists.

In connection with the ball, we are printing a special souvenir program. This program is designed by local young artists and printed in four colors.

Advertising space is available in these programs ($200 for a full page, $130 for a half page, and $75 for a quarter page), and we hope you will want to be represented in the advertising pages. Hundreds of people will see your ad and know that your company supports this very worthy activity.

Another reason that I believe you will want to help us is that many of your employees are members of the Suburban Art League, and they will be proud to see their company's name in the program.

May I hear from you?

Sincerely yours,

N. A. Jurasek

BACKGROUND

Business firms receive many requests to purchase advertising space in school yearbooks, directories, programs for sports and cultural events, and so on. Although there is some advertising value in such publications, it is mostly "institutional" (public relations). Most businesses look upon such advertising as a contribution, and the printed advertisement often consists of just the simple message "Compliments of the ABC Company."

Although many business firms support local community activities by purchasing advertising space, such requests are often so numerous that many must be turned down. Refusing such requests is a delicate matter—every organization needs money to support its activities, and local business people are obvious sources. The solicitor's appeal is to the business peoples' conscience, their responsibility to the community they live in. Often, though, the solicitor emphasizes the theme "We keep you in business and you owe us something."

SOLUTION A

Dear Mr. Jurasek:

I am sorry that we are not able to buy space in the souvenir program of the Suburban Art League Ball. Our advertising budget is exhausted.

Very truly yours,

Analysis of Solution A.   Of course, Solution A won't be very convincing to Mr. Jurasek. He will accept the statement that the advertising budget is exhausted, but he won't believe that Peerless can't find the money elsewhere. More important, the letter does not achieve its real mission: to say no but to retain the friendly feeling of Suburban Art League members toward the company. Solution A is too cold, too curt—it will produce bad feeling.

SOLUTION B

Dear Mr. Jurasek:

A recent study made by our personnel department revealed that our employees hold memberships in 93 different organizations. Naturally, we are proud of the fact that our employees are active in their respective communities.

Because there are so many worthwhile organizations, we find it impossible to give financial support to all of them. This is why we must decline the invitation to advertise in the souvenir program of the Suburban Art League Ball. We think yours is an outstanding organization and are delighted that many of our employees are members; but if we were to favor the League while denying the solicitations of the many other equally worthy organizations, we would put ourselves in a most embarrassing—and indefensible—position.

Best wishes, Mr. Jurasek, to you and your colleagues in your efforts to raise funds for your scholarship program. It's a great idea!

Sincerely yours,

Analysis of Solution B. We do not claim that Solution B will make Mr. Jurasek happy (only a "yes" response would do that), but it is a tactful and reasonable "no" employing the fair-play theme.
Note the following:

1. The first paragraph—in a very positive manner—actually sets the stage for the refusal of Mr. Jurasek's request.
2. The second paragraph not only states the refusal but also gives a logical and defensible explanation of it.
3. The last paragraph attempts to retain Mr. Jurasek's goodwill.

Projects

You must refuse this invitation in Mr. Weinberger's name. Assume, however, that Mr. Weinberger will send a personal check for $25 as a donation.

Dear Mr. Weinberger:

The Willard T. Peck Memorial Committee is sponsoring a dinner dance at the Morristown Heights Country Club on May 17. The purpose of the event is to raise funds to carry on the work of this renowned ornithologist who has done so much to establish and preserve bird sanctuaries all over the state.

The special program is being printed, and we have decided to accept advertising in it. A full-page ad will cost you only $100 (we do not accept smaller ones). Naturally, we hope that you recognize the benefits of our work and will give us your support. Please submit the copy for the ad you wish to place, along with your check for $100, to me by April 20.

Very truly yours,

Andrew M. Wong

Peerless receives many invitations to advertise in high school yearbooks all over the country. Apparently, students are aware that they are using books published by Peerless and feel that since they help to "support" Peerless, Peerless should contribute to their causes.

Although the company frequently takes advertising space in year-books of high schools located in the Des Moines area, it cannot afford to advertise in all the thousands of annuals published throughout the country. Actually, the students themselves are not the buyers of the textbooks they use—local school boards purchase the books that teachers and administrators choose. Therefore, an advertisement would be more of a contribution than a promotion vehicle.

Write a form letter, as from Mr. Weinberger, to send those soliciting advertising for high school yearbooks. Use whatever rationale you think appropriate for refusing the invitation.

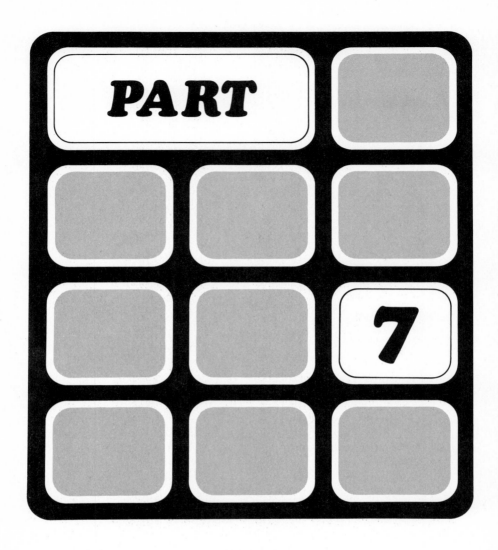

LETTERS OF APPRECIATION AND CONGRATULATION

YOUR JOB *You are supervisor of the Records Management Department of Keystone Designs Inc., Chicago, specialists in modern office furniture and interiors. You are responsible for seeing that the company's records are properly maintained, which means that you establish records systems, select equipment and supplies, maintain checkout and safekeeping procedures, determine when inactive materials are to be transferred or disposed of, and so on.*

CASE 1

EXPRESSING APPRECIATION FOR A FAVOR

PROBLEM

Recently you were asked to speak at the Tri-State Conference of the National Records Management Association on "Legal Implications of Records Disposition." Although your job requires a general knowledge of statutory requirements for certain records, you do not feel that you are an authority on the subject. You had to read as much as you could, therefore, in order to get ready to write your speech. Mrs. Abigail Parkington, assistant librarian of the company, helped you find materials on your subject and came up with several reports, reprints, and clippings that were extremely helpful to you. Your talk was enthusiastically received by those at the meeting. You feel that you should write to Mrs. Parkington and thank her for her help.

BACKGROUND

Almost every day in a typical organization there are occasions for writing messages of a personal nature—when someone does you a favor, is promoted to a new position, receives an honor, or accomplishes something worthwhile. We emphasized earlier the role of communications in establishing and maintaining good human relationships, and personal-business letters in the situations mentioned do much to make the occupational journey a little more rewarding for everyone. In some instances, such letters are simply good business.

For some personal-business communications you may use the company's letterhead stationery—for a letter to a customer, a supplier, or a business associate outside the company, for example. But when your letters go to personal friends with whom you have no business connections, you should use your own stationery or plain paper.

Some people write personal-business messages to fellow employees on the company's interoffice memo form. Although the memo form is perfectly acceptable for these messages, plain paper or a letterhead is better because it is less "mechanical" looking.

Although rules for writing personal-business letters are not rigid, there is one principle that should guide you in composing messages of this type: Be yourself, but don't get carried away. The use of superlatives, such as in the following examples, has a tendency to destroy believability.

> Your promotion to director of advertising research is the greatest thing that ever happened.
>
> The set of Audubon prints is the handsomest present I ever received.
>
> The dinner you prepared was just about the tastiest I have ever eaten. How did you do it?

Of course, if you are honest when you use words like *greatest, handsomest,* and *tastiest,* go ahead. Chances are, though, that in your eagerness to say the right thing you are overdoing it.

On the other hand, it is possible to pass over too lightly the occasion your personal-business letter is honoring, and the result can be worse than going overboard.

> Allow me to congratulate you on your promotion to director of advertising research.

> This will acknowledge the set of Audubon prints that I received recently.

> I had never eaten a real Armenian dinner before; so it was a new experience for me.

Somewhere between the two extremes lies the appropriate tone for personal-business letters.

> I was delighted to learn that you have been promoted to the position of director of advertising research. Congratulations!

> The Audubon prints are beautiful, and I can think of a dozen places where they will look mighty handsome on the wall.

> The Armenian dinner was a "first" for me, and I enjoyed it immensely.

SOLUTION

> Dear Mrs. Parkington:

> You'll be pleased to know, I think, that "our" speech at the National Records Management Association meeting in Omaha went over quite well. In fact, I had nine requests for copies of it—so somebody was listening!

> Thank you for all your help, Mrs. Parkington—I would have been practically lost without you. The Keystone librarians, particularly you, have won an ardent supporter.

> Sincerely yours,

> cc.: Miss Grace Garvin
> Head Librarian

Analysis of the Solution.   This letter is a good one.

1. The tone of the letter is friendly, conversational, believable. The writer expresses appreciation without becoming effusive.
2. Note the use of Mrs. Parkington's name in the body of the letter. Using the reader's name adds a personal touch as long as it isn't overdone.
3. Observe that a carbon copy of the letter was sent to Mrs. Parkington's immediate superior. This courtesy is always in order. Often this gesture means more to the recipient of the letter than the letter itself.

Projects

(A) Some of the people who heard the talk ("Legal Implications of Records Disposition") you gave at the National Records Management Association meeting feel that it should be published, and you have decided to submit it to *Records Management Journal*. Before doing so, however, you asked R. C. Garrison, the attorney for Keystone Designs, to read the manuscript. He agreed, and in his review he corrected a few minor factual errors and offered several good ideas for improving the material—for example, suggesting that you include a table showing typical state regulations pertaining to the statute of limitations. Write an appropriate thank-you letter or memo to Mr. Garrison.

(B) Recently you were at a luncheon for several people, most of whom were out-of-town guests, in one of Keystone's private dining rooms. The food and the service provided by the dining room staff were excellent, and you decide to drop a note to the manager, Larry Barstow, expressing your appreciation. Write the letter or memo, supplying details about the menu, special services, and so on.

(C) Professor Florence Wilford of Northhampton University recently spoke to a management training class at Keystone on the subject of organization planning. As a member of the class, you found the talk very helpful. For the first time you understood the need for clear lines of organization, delegation of responsibility, and individual authority to exercise assigned duties. Write Professor Wilford a letter of appreciation.

CASE 2

EXPRESSING APPRECIATION FOR A GIFT

PROBLEM

Paul Whitcomb, sales representative for Westline Lithographers, a company from whom you purchase printing, has sent you a beautiful lithograph of Wyeth's famous painting, <u>Christina's World</u>, suitable for framing. You plan to write Mr. Whitcomb to thank him for the gift.

BACKGROUND

The gift from Paul Whitcomb (actually a gift from the company for which he works) deserves a letter expressing appreciation. Such gestures have a commercial flavor, of course; a business organization that bestows favors on its customers and potential customers is obviously mindful of the promotional advantages. Some organizations (particularly government) have established strict policies against accepting gifts from suppliers. But where the gift is permitted, the donor is entitled to a thank-you letter even though both the giver and the recipient know that the transaction is more business than personal.

SOLUTION A

Dear Paul:

The print you presented to us is very much appreciated, and on behalf of Keystone Designs, I want to express our gratitude.

Sincerely yours,

Analysis of Solution A. One might admire the writer's restraint, but the letter is too cautious, too impersonal. There is no warmth, no friendliness—all in all, it is a poor expression of appreciation.

SOLUTION B

Dear Paul:

The beautiful lithograph of Christina's World came today, and I am delighted with it. How did you find out that I like pictures with people in them? You know, I think this is Wyeth's best.

As much as I hate to give Christina up, I think our department's reception room is the best place for her. At any rate, when you next visit us, you will find this beautiful reproduction in a prominent place.

Thank you, Paul, for this thoughtful and generous gift.

Sincerely,

Analysis of Solution B. Unlike Solution A, this letter shows genuine appreciation, friendliness, and personality. Paul Whitcomb is certain to get the feeling that he has done the writer a favor that will be remembered.

Note that the writer makes it clear that she considers this gift a business, rather than a personal, one by stating that the lithograph will be placed in the department's reception room. Many people feel it is unwise to accept gifts for their personal use only because they are in a position to buy the donor's products or services.

Projects

(A) In today's mail you received a copy of a 270-page book, *Office Guidebook,* published by Walsh-Hiller, manufacturers of office equipment. Attached to the front cover is a card which reads "Compliments of Norman Morrison." Mr. Morrison is the local representative of Walsh-Hiller, and he has apparently submitted your name as one who should receive this book, which contains facts and ideas about modern office equipment and its efficient use. Write a letter to Mr. Morrison expressing your gratitude.

Nancy Wicker, manager of Career Personnel Agency, sent you a desk calendar at Christmas. The calendar is handsomely bound in imitation leather, and your name has been stamped in gold on the cover. Write an appropriate thank-you letter. (You use the Career Personnel Agency often when you need temporary and full-time office help, and you have found the agency, especially Nancy Wicker, extremely efficient. Assume that you are on a first-name basis with Miss Wicker.)

CASE 3

EXPRESSING APPRECIATION FOR SPECIAL SERVICE

PROBLEM

You have been asked to speak at Creighton University, Omaha, Nebraska, on new developments in records management. One of your suppliers of filing systems has produced a film, *Filing and Finding,* which you would like to show during your talk. You find, however, that all copies of the film, except the reserve copy in the company's library, are out and none will be available in time for your presentation. In fact, you got your request in so late that it is doubtful the film could have been delivered in time even if it had been available.

Although the supplier has a rule of not releasing its library copy of a film, she has made an exception for you. In fact, she is sending it to you by Air Express to make sure you get it in time. You receive the film, make effective use of it, and now must write the supplier expressing your appreciation for this special service.

BACKGROUND

Customers expect to receive efficient service from those with whom they do business, and special citations are not necessary for routine transactions. Now and then, however, a supplier will go well beyond the call of duty for a customer, and in these situations it is wise to express special thanks. The problem described presents an occasion for a thank-you letter.

SOLUTION A

Dear Miss Norton:

The film Filing and Finding arrived in plenty of time for my guest appearance at the Management Institute of Creighton University. You would have been pleased by the audience's reaction to the film; as I explained, my entire talk was built around it.

You went to a lot of trouble in order to get this film to me—even to the extent of robbing your library of its last copy—and I appreciate your help more than I can express.

The film has already been mailed back to you, and you should receive it this week.

Thank you very much.

Sincerely yours,

Analysis of Solution A. The letter illustrated is only one version, since there is no one best solution to a letter problem. Note how the writer has stressed four points that he knows the reader is interested in:

1. The film arrived in time.
2. The audience reacted favorably to the film.
3. The writer appreciates what the supplier went through to get the film to him.
4. The film has been returned promptly.

SOLUTION B

Dear Miss Norton:

Filing and Finding was sent this morning by Air Express. With it goes my gratitude to you for getting it to me in time for my talk at Creighton University.

My presentation was extremely well received, and a number of people praised the high quality of the film. It certainly added drama and excitement to my talk.

Thank you, Miss Norton, for going out of your way to help me. I'm deeply grateful.

Sincerely yours,

Analysis of Solution B. There is no particular order in which points to be discussed must appear. Solution B, which covers the same points, is as effective as Solution A.

Projects

(A) On October 13 you placed an order for a Peerless C.O.M. (Computer Output to Microfilm) Reader with Micro Line Inc., Benton Harbor, Michigan. You were in a special rush for this reader and asked for delivery by October 20, even though the advertising literature mentioned that purchasers should allow at least 30 days for delivery. The reader arrived on October 19, and you realize that your order must have been given special attention. Write to the president (you don't know his name), expressing appreciation for this special service.

(B) About a week ago you wrote to View Gems Corporation asking for information about the cost of making color transparencies that you need for training new file clerks in the Records Management Department. You received a letter from Mrs. Bess Sarazen telling you that View Gems does not make transparencies. In her letter, however, Mrs. Sarazen listed the names and addresses of several companies that do this kind of work. She also enclosed a reprint of a magazine article, "Preparing Artwork for Color Transparencies," that she happened to see the same day your letter arrived. Write Mrs. Sarazen an appropriate letter of appreciation.

CASE 4

EXPRESSING CONGRATULATIONS AND APPRECIATION

PROBLEM

The training director of Keystone Designs Inc. recently ran a week-long seminar on human relations for supervisors. As supervisor of the Records Management Department, you felt that it was a profitable conference. You want to express your appreciation for the seminar and, at the same time, congratulate Mr. Breir, the training director, on the way it was conducted.

BACKGROUND

In the typical business firm hardly a day goes by that somebody doesn't receive a promotion or an honor or do something worthy of favorable comment. To write or not to write, as far as you are concerned, depends entirely on how you feel about a particular event. It is neither necessary nor appropriate to write congratulatory messages to people whom you've never seen and have no particular association with. In some companies, one could spend a considerable amount of time composing letters of congratulation. There is no rule either that says you have to write to people you do know but don't get along with very well or have no particular liking for. Some people write letters to all their business associates who have been cited for one thing or another, but you must decide whether you can do so without sounding forced.

The number of letters you write to people outside the company depends on your job and your own inclinations. If you work in advertising, sales, public relations, or publicity, you will probably write more congratulatory letters to customers, potential customers, and the general public than you would if you worked in the tax, accounting, insurance, production, or data processing department. Many such letters written to people outside the firm create goodwill. Even though they may also have a sales mission, they must be genuine. A congratulatory letter to a potential customer that smacks of commercialism is worse than no letter at all.

SOLUTION

Dear Mr. Breir:

Last week's seminar, "Human Relations in Management," was the best I have ever attended, and I want you to know how much I enjoyed it. Congratulations to you and those who assisted you in planning and staging the conference.

There were many highlights, but the things that helped me most were the "T" sessions run by Mr. Praeger, the group dynamics program you and Ms. McNally conducted, and the play Ishmael's Day in Court. The luncheon and dinner speakers were outstanding.

I sincerely hope we'll have more seminars along the same line. I'm already trying to put into practice what I learned last week, and a refresher course from time to time would be valuable to me.

Sincerely,

Analysis of the Solution.   When you are congratulating someone for an outstanding achievement, make sure you are specific about what you are congratulating that person for. In the solution above, the writer not only expressed appreciation but also cited a number of things that merited special mention.

Projects

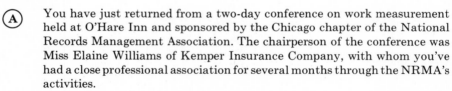

You have just returned from a two-day conference on work measurement held at O'Hare Inn and sponsored by the Chicago chapter of the National Records Management Association. The chairperson of the conference was Miss Elaine Williams of Kemper Insurance Company, with whom you've had a close professional association for several months through the NRMA's activities.

The conference was a huge success as far as you are concerned, and you know how hard Miss Williams worked to make it so. Write her a letter expressing your appreciation and congratulations. Supply your own details about the program, speakers, and so on.

You read in last night's paper that Dr. Louis Misa, a former professor under whom you studied psychology and with whom you had a special rapport, was selected to attend a White House conference on higher education. This is a great honor, and you know that Dr. Misa must be pleased. Write a letter of congratulation. Assume that although you have not seen Professor Misa for about a year, he will remember you well. Supply any personal details that you think would be appropriate.

CASE 5

CONGRATULATING AN EMPLOYEE UPON AN ANNIVERSARY

PROBLEM

The Personnel Department of Keystone Designs keeps a record of the anniversary dates of all employees. The personnel manual recommends that supervisors acknowledge anniversary dates upon completion of the first, fifth, tenth, fifteenth, etc., year of employment.

Mrs. Millie Cox is celebrating ten years with Keystone. She began as a file clerk in the Contracts Department and, through a series of promotions, is now section supervisor, Central Files. She is a most valuable employee—hardworking, pleasant, dependable. Although you are now her boss, she has been at Keystone several years more than you have. You are to write the congratulatory message to Mrs. Cox.

BACKGROUND

It is customary to acknowledge an employment anniversary by letter, even when employees have special luncheons and banquets given for them to celebrate a fifteen- or twenty-year anniversary. Of course, in such a letter, the emphasis is on the employee's contributions to the company; and, depending upon the rapport between the writer and the employee, a bit of reminiscing may be in order.

SOLUTION A

In the following solution, we are assuming that the writer and the employee enjoy a good rapport and have become friends.

> Dear Millie:
>
> You must know how much I value you and your work. It's hard to imagine what I would do without you.
>
> On the occasion of your tenth anniversary, I want to pay special tribute to you—for your support of my efforts, your efficiency, your cooperation, your dependability. No one has contributed more to this department than you have.
>
> Personally, I hope we'll be working together for many more years to come.
>
> Sincerely,

Analysis of Solution A. Solution A may strike you as an effusive—at least overgenerous—letter. In some instances it would be. As mentioned earlier, whether or not this is a good letter depends on the kind of person the writer is and the feelings he has about the employee.

SOLUTION B

Dear Mrs. Cox:

Congratulations on your tenth anniversary with Keystone.

In one way, it seems unbelievable that you could have been with us that long—unbelievable because I prefer not to admit that time can fly that quickly. On the other hand, when I look at the many important things you have done, I wonder if it hasn't really been longer.

On this occasion, one is tempted to reminisce about the past ten years and what they have brought in the way of progress, pleasure, and satisfaction. But I'd rather think about the future and the mountains we have yet to climb. I just hope you'll be here, doing your usual fine job, prodding us on, and helping the department reach the top.

Sincerely yours,

Analysis of Solution B. Some executives could not write a letter like Solution A because they prefer a more formal relationship between themselves and their employees. They would write a letter similar to Solution B, which is quite all right if it reflects the personality and feelings of the writer.

Projects

(A) Loraine Carlson, a clerk-typist in your department, is celebrating her first anniversary with Keystone. As her supervisor, you must write the customary letter of congratulation. Assume that Loraine is a personable, hard-working, efficient, and popular employee. You value her highly; in fact, you are thinking about promoting her to an assistant supervisor's job, but you are not yet ready to announce the fact. Write the letter, supplying your own personal details.

(B) Jack Kiley, a messenger in the Records Management Department, has just completed his fifth year with Keystone. Jack does not take his job very seriously (although he has had modest annual salary increases, he has never received a promotion), but he manages to do it just well enough to keep it. Jack is one of those people who do no more than they have to; yet he is agreeable and accepted by other employees, who refer to him as a "pretty good guy." Write an appropriate letter acknowledging Jack's anniversary.

CASE 6

CONGRATULATING AN EMPLOYEE UPON RETIREMENT

PROBLEM

The chief design engineer of Keystone Designs, Blake Baumgartner, is responsible for the company's design of office furniture and interiors. One of the most gifted of his furniture designers—the veteran of the department—is William Osler, who is retiring after forty years with the company. During this period, Mr. Baumgartner has seen the company grow from a small manufacturer of advertising-promotion novelties to one of the leading designers and manufacturers of office interiors in the industry.

Although Mr. Osler will be honored at special department luncheons and a company banquet, he will receive letters of congratulation when the story of his retirement is published in the company newspaper.

BACKGROUND

Letters to those who are retiring probably fall in the congratulations category, though to some, retirement is not a particularly joyous occasion. In writing such letters, however, you must assume that retirees are looking forward to the new leisure time and freedom to do what they have always promised themselves they would do if they had the time.

To many people who reach retirement age, letters of congratulation naturally are extremely important, particularly if the retiree's worth is emphasized. When employees have devoted many years to their jobs and are proud of their records, letters are evidence that their efforts were appreciated.

SOLUTION A

Dear Bill:

Congratulations on your retirement after forty years of service at Keystone. I am sure this is a happy occasion for you.

Best wishes for many successful retirement years.

Cordially yours,

Analysis of Solution A. The letter says nothing and will probably have very little meaning to Mr. Osler. Nothing is said about his achievements, and there is no indication he will be missed—only that "I am sure this a happy occasion for you," which it may not be. There is very little here that Mr. Osler can look at in his retirement with any pride or satisfaction.

SOLUTION B

Dear Bill:

As I look around my office, I can see the hand of Bill Osler everywhere. It should be a great source of satisfaction to you, as it is to me, that you have left so many magnificent creations for all to see and admire for years to come.

It is impossible to begin to count all the contributions you have made to our growth and prestige. Let's just say that I give you credit for putting us on the map and making our name favorably known throughout the country. That's a pretty sizable achievement when one considers that we could claim neither distinction until you came along.

May the years ahead bring rich and satisfying rewards to you—and all the fishing you have planned. But if I know you as well as I think I do, you will find time to continue your professional associations too.

Good luck, Bill. And come to see us often.

Sincerely,

Analysis of Solution B.   Solution B is much better than A for these reasons:

1. Mr. Osler is reminded that his contributions will be long remembered in tangible form ("As I look around my office, I can see the hand of Bill Osler everywhere").
2. Mr. Osler's impressive record as a designer is emphasized, a fitting tribute to a valuable employee.
3. A salute to the retiree's future and an invitation to come back for a visit put a personal capstone on the letter.

Projects

(A)   Homer Ault, supervisor of the Archives Section of the Records Management Department for the past fifteen years and a thirty-five-year employee of Keystone, is retiring this week at the age of sixty-five. Mr. Ault is practically an "institution" at Keystone—highly regarded by everyone for his knowledge, effectiveness on the job, and personableness. Although you are relatively new as Mr. Ault's boss, he has never resented you; indeed he has been your good friend and confidant. Mr. Ault has many hobbies, but the one that occupies most of his free time is stamp collecting. He and Mrs. Ault plan to move to Southern California later in the year and eventually to establish a small business, buying and selling rare stamps. Write an appropriate letter of congratulations.

(B)   Miss Grace Holden, manager of the Payroll Department, is a casual friend of yours (she serves on several committees of which you are a member). It has just been announced in the company newspaper that Miss Holden is retiring next month for reasons of health and is moving to Arizona. Miss Holden, sixty, has been with Keystone for thirty-three years and is highly regarded in the company. She insists that everybody call her Grace. Write Grace Holden an appropriate letter.

EMPLOYMENT COMMUNICATIONS

YOUR JOB *You are approaching graduation, and the time has come for you to begin to make definite plans for employment. You know, of course, that in order to enter the world of business you must first land a job. What you need now is the know-how to get the job you want. In fact, your first and most important job is to sell yourself.*

CASE 1

ASSESSING AND CONVEYING YOUR QUALIFICATIONS FOR EMPLOYMENT

PROBLEM

Before you start pounding the pavement in search of a job, you need to think through the answers to some hard questions: In what kind of job would I be happiest and most productive? In what location? What assets do I have—personal, professional, educational, and social—that I can "sell" to a prospective employer? How can I present these qualifications so as to gain a favorable response?

BACKGROUND

Most people, during their working lives, will write one or more of the following types of letters: an inquiry about a job opening in a business firm, a request for permission to use the name of someone as a reference, a response to an invitation from a company to apply for a position, a letter accepting or declining a position, a resignation letter, a recommendation of someone for a position.

Jobs and the Job Market.　The amount of effort you must exert to land the job you want will depend largely on the competition for that job. The employment market itself fluctuates. One year there may be a scarcity of engineers, and those who qualify can choose their own employer. The next year there may be an overabundance of engineers, and competition is tough.

Some jobs are always highly competitive—certain positions in advertising, for example. Even ordinary jobs that might be a dime a dozen in industry as a whole can become highly competitive in a certain company where the pay is high and the prestige great. For example, without too much effort you can usually get a pretty good job as a sales representative. But a sales position in some blue-chip companies is always hard to come by.

It's a good idea, no matter what the job market is like when you read this, to learn the principles of employment letter writing. Even if you don't need this know-how to get your first job, chances are that you can use it later. Many people change jobs several times during their working lives. They want to live in a certain section of the country, or they are dissatisfied with working conditions and opportunities for advancement in their present jobs, or they want to change to another kind of work. Often these people "prospect" by letter; that is, they send written applications to various companies, hoping to get a good lead on the job they want.

What Do You Have to Sell?　Your first step in getting the job you want is to determine what you have to sell. The business firm that lays out cash for your services is just as eager to get its money's worth as if it were buying, say, a computer installation. You can be sure that company executives think long and hard before buying a computer, looking at equipment from various manufacturers to compare cost, efficiency, and service. Most of them are equally cautious when hiring people, at least those with management potential. They make comparisons among the applicants available.

You can be sure, too, that the computer sales representatives know precisely what their equipment will do for a firm and why it would be a smart investment. They plan their sales strategy carefully in terms of the organization they hope to sell the equipment to. Doesn't it make good sense that you should plan just as carefully your sales strategy for the organization that is in the market for your services?

The first thing in planning your sales strategy—perhaps the only thing—is to answer the question, Why should a firm want to hire me? If you can show that you would be a good investment for an organization, you are well on your way to getting the job you really want.

You should know every bit as much about your sales features as the computer salesperson knows about the equipment's sales features. While the computer offers such features as greater speed, better customer service, and greater economy, your assets are education, experience, and personality. In answering the question, Why should a firm want to hire me? you should write down the things you have to sell.

But, first, let's look at what the employer wants when buying talent; then we can do a more intelligent job of sizing up ourselves in terms of the employer's needs. Every salesperson relates the features of the product to the needs of the customer, and you must do the same. You try to find out what the customer (firm) wants in the way of knowledge, attitudes, and skills and then emphasize them in your employment application. This is simply good selling technique. The personnel manager or other executive to whom you apply *expects* it.

What Do Employers Want?   The things employers want when they hire people are no different today than they ever were, and chances are that they will never change. They include, among other things, the following.

   A Return on Their Investment.   It is no secret that an employer expects every worker to produce a profit. This profit may be in the form of increased company revenue, more effective selling or customer service, savings on costs, greater production, and the like. Accountants are expected to produce several times their salaries by pointing out where money is being wasted, by establishing time- and people-saving systems, and by producing a financial records system that will guide management in long-range planning. Sales representatives are expected to produce net revenue for the company far in excess of their salaries. And corporation presidents earning $100,000 a year may be responsible for decisions that result in revenue amounting to a thousand times their salaries.

   If every worker produced only enough to pay for his or her salary, then there would be no profit. Let's be realistic: Effective executives never receive in salary all that they produce. Those who do take home more income than they produce for the company don't stay around very long.

A company expects to lose money on certain employees during the first year, especially management trainees. The cost of training and orienting the new employee to the job amounts to far more than he or she will produce for several months—maybe a couple of years. Sooner or later, though, the company expects to realize a profit on that investment through the employee's ability to make the right decisions, to improve operations and procedures, to increase production, to make more sales. That's the reason companies can afford to gamble on promising new employees—and it is the only reason.

Human Effectiveness. Business is essentially people; thus it is a team effort. Few college-trained people work all by themselves. They deal with many people who influence the firm's success—suppliers, customers, competitors, and the general public. If business is to succeed, its employees must work effectively with all these people. Internal employee relations are just as important; the outward impression a business makes depends largely on internal harmony or lack of it. It is equally necessary, then, that you get along well with fellow workers, managers, supervisors, and subordinates. Indeed, it is not enough merely to "get along" with them; often you must cooperate, lead, influence, motivate, and follow.

Business, therefore, is interested in knowing what kind of person you are when it comes to working with people. You may be a genius and have straight A's on your college transcript, but if you can't cope with the give-and-take of daily human relationships, you aren't going to be much good in a position that requires you to supervise, cooperate, and perhaps compromise.

If you're going to be happy operating a calculator, doing library research, or performing experiments in some hidden-away laboratory, it probably isn't important that you think about your effectiveness in human relationships. But such jobs are rare, and most of them don't pay much. The jobs that pay the most are those that require leadership—the ability to motivate others to get a job done or to accept a point of view. That's why a manager or a top sales representative gets more money than a machine operator.

The Right Job Attitude. Employers are interested in your attitude toward work. They expect you to have enthusiasm for your job, the company, and the people in the company. In fact, they want you to be so interested and enthusiastic that you will give them more time than they actually pay for.

The old slogan, "An honest day's work for an honest day's pay," does not apply to the ambitious person. It isn't strong enough! The employer would change it to read, "Give the job all you've got and don't worry about the pay." If this seems selfish and hard, then you must think about the problems that the typical business is faced with. Competition is keen and many businesses fall by the wayside because they are outsmarted or because their management simply isn't effective. Management wants people who are dedicated to the company's growth, who are keenly competitive, and who are success-conscious.

The greater your responsibility, the more hours you can expect to put in on your job. That's why people on the move take a briefcase full of work home on evenings and weekends. They don't think about how many hours they work or whether they are being paid enough; they think only of doing their job. It is a fact that those who work hard without worrying whether they're being paid enough usually get the plums in business. They earn them.

Imagination.   Business thrives on the imagination of its workers. That is why top management looks for the inquisitive person, the innovator, the thinker. The employee who thinks imaginatively about how to save money, increase production, compete more effectively, or get a bigger share of the market is highly prized. Of course, business doesn't expect you to turn everything upside down in your first month on the job, but most progressive firms won't expect you to settle comfortably in your job and continue to do things the way they have always been done. They want improvement, and improvement means change.

Of course, some executives won't reach out for new ideas because they don't want to rock the boat. If you run into one of them, don't get the idea that this is a typical attitude. The most successful companies have executives at the top who encourage innovation and creativity.

Knowledge.   No matter how skillful you are in human relationships, how imaginative in designing new systems or products, and how positive your attitude toward your work, there is no substitute for job knowledge. If you advertise yourself as an accountant, you are expected to know the fundamentals of accounting theory, cost methods, auditing procedures, modern data processing, and the like. A good secretary must, among other things, be able to take dictation no matter what the speed or the material and transcribe it into flawless letters and reports (perhaps doing a great deal of editing in the process). A sales representative must know markets, buying motives, sales psychology, and so on. In your job campaign, then, it is important that you emphasize the education that equips you for the job you are after.

Communicating Ability.   Because this is a book on communication, you may get the idea that communicating ability is listed as a "must" in self-defense. Not so. The truth is that one of the biggest complaints about those who aspire to management is that they are poor communicators. And we're talking not only about people whose primary work is writing communications but also about sales representatives, accountants, secretaries, market researchers, financial analysts, and others. If you have better-than-average ability to express yourself orally and in writing, emphasize this on your list of qualifications, for it is a fundamental requirement for management success.

Ambition.   Never was the demand for management talent so great as it is today. This demand is attested to by the fact that hundreds of large companies are forced to carry on expensive programs to train managers from the ranks. Obviously, in considering talent, management wants people who aspire to positions of responsibility, not people who lack either the interest or the talent to move up in the organization. Ambition is not a vice; it is a virtue. Don't be afraid to let people know that you don't want to sit still—that you want to grow in your job. Of course, you wouldn't be so foolhardy as to expect the vice president's job the first year, but at the same time you don't want to leave the impression you will always be satisfied with the job you begin with.

Assessing Your Qualifications. Now let's get back to the question, Why should an organization want to hire me? To answer that intelligently, you need to find out as much as you can about the employer's expectations.

If you know that, for a certain position, an employer prefers people with experience—and you have very little—you would be foolish to emphasize experience as one of your prime assets. Or if you learn that a position you want demands a good knowledge of Spanish and you've had only a couple of years of high school Spanish, you probably will want to emphasize your readiness to become fluent in the language rather than your proficiency in it. Try, then, to learn all you can about the prospective employer's preferences and requirements so that you can fit your presentation to the company's particular needs.

Suppose you are answering this advertisement that appeared in a metropolitan newspaper.

```
Management trainees in  marketing research.
Minimum two years of college, preferably in
marketing  and/or business  administration.
Heavy writing.    Apply Box 73, Times.
```

Not much here, you say? Actually, the ad says a great deal. It tells you that the employer:

1. Wants applicants with management aspirations ("management trainees").
2. Does not expect applicants to have work experience.
3. Wants people with at least two years of college (and you'll be favored if you have a marketing or business major).
4. Wants people with the ability to write well and handle a large volume of writing.

Given these clues, you are ready to match assets against requirements.

First, you will review your college work and highlight those courses and achievements that you think will impress the employer.

Second, you will emphasize your ability to express yourself in writing.

Then what? You will want to let the employer know what kind of person you are. Your activities in college, your work experience, your hobbies, your long-range goals—all help to reveal things about you that an employer will want to know.

Presenting Your Qualifications. After you have thought about the job, the employer's needs, and your fitness for the position—and only then—you are ready to summarize your qualifications in the form of a sales presentation.

The presentation of an applicant's qualifications may be called a résumé, data sheet, personal profile, or qualifications summary. By whatever name it is called, the résumé should enable the prospective employer to see at a glance the extent of the applicant's education and experience as well as something about him or her as a person. Suitable headings and an uncrowded appearance help the résumé do this.

Preparing a résumé will give you a head start on the application blank, which is usually required, and help you get ready for the job interview.

Since your résumé is your sales presentation, personalize it. Use your imagination (and good taste) in adapting the conventional headings and their sequence. The way in which you describe your qualifications will, of course, depend on the job you are applying for.

Make sure that the physical appearance of your résumé is top-notch: a good grade of bond paper; clear, clean typing; good spacing and arrangement; no misspellings or grammatical errors. If you are not an expert typist, hire one to do the job.

Your résumé will make a better impression if it is an original. Although preparing an original for each job you apply for can be costly in time and money, it obviously personalizes your application and may strengthen your chances in getting the position. A really sharp mimeographed sheet, an offset-printed one, or a professionally printed one is acceptable, but a carbon or a fluid-duplicated copy is not. A copy of a résumé, no matter how crisp, will imply that you are giving it wide distribution. That may be true, but each employer likes to think you have only one choice.

Keep your résumé to two pages if you can. In some cases one page may be enough, but don't squeeze and condense your story just for the sake of brevity.

Above all, don't be modest in stating your qualifications. The résumé is a sales presentation, and you are expected to point out your good qualities.

The one-page résumé on page 229 is what Martin T. Hammond's presentation might look like if he were answering the ad (page 227) for a management trainee in marketing research. Mr. Hammond rightly emphasizes his education, specifically those courses most relevant to the position he is applying for.

SOLUTION A

Analysis of Solution A. Now let's look at each part of a well-prepared résumé, such as that of Martin Hammond.

Heading. Whether you use the heading "Résumé of," "Data Sheet," etc., or just your name is optional. If you feel something is needed to head the form, here are several variations:

Résumé of

MARTIN T. HAMMOND
1977 DuBlanc Avenue
Monroe, Louisiana 71201

(318) 515-1234

MARTIN T. HAMMOND

Job Qualifications Summary

1977 DuBlanc Avenue
Monroe, Louisiana 71201

(318) 515-1234

Position Wanted. Personnel managers strongly urge applicants to specify the job they are applying for. If you do not know the title of the job— or indeed whether there *is* a job for you—identify the general area in which you are interested. Unless you apply for a job in the personnel department,

---

MARTIN T. HAMMOND
1977 DuBlanc Avenue, Monroe, Louisiana 71201
Telephone: (318) 515-1234

Position Wanted: Marketing Research Management Trainee

EDUCATION

Degree: B.B.A. (June 1978), Centenary College, Shreveport, Louisiana.
Major: Marketing

Marketing Courses:
Marketing Principles	Advertising	Retail Merchandising
Marketing Research	Sales Management	Fundamentals of Buying

Other Business Courses:
Business Communication	Accounting	Money and Banking
Business Statistics	Business Law	Government and Business

Comments: I maintained a B average in my business subjects and was on the Dean's List. I especially enjoyed my marketing courses. In Marketing Research, I made four A's and two B's on required research reports; two reports were exhibited as models of excellence.

EXPERIENCE

June-September, 1977	Warehouse clerk, Tracy's Discount Store, Monroe, Louisiana. Filled customer orders, maintained inventory, supervised two part-time helpers.
July-August, 1976	Delivery driver, Davey's Pharmacy, Monroe. Drove truck, assisted in stockkeeping, did some floor selling.
June-September, 1975	Sales representative, Cavell Home Products. Sold aluminum cooking ware from house to house.
1971-1974 (various dates)	Laborer (repaired city streets and helped with replanting city parks), filling station helper, paper carrier, lawn tender.

ORGANIZATIONS AND HOBBIES

Organizations: Debating Society, Marketing Club (treasurer), Tau Kappa Epsilon (social fraternity), Interfraternity Council, tennis team.

Hobbies: Building and flying model airplanes, tennis, writing short stories.

PERSONAL DATA

Birth Date: October 29, 1957 Weight: 170 Height: 6' Health: Excellent

REFERENCES

Dr. Christine Hale, Professor of Marketing, Centenary College, Shreveport, Louisiana 71104.

Mr. A. T. Mitchell, Manager, Tracy's Discount Store, Monroe, Louisiana 71201.

Judge R. N. Toffenetti, 1416 DuBlanc Avenue, Monroe, Louisiana 71201.

---

the personnel manager won't actually hire you. The personnel manager will simply screen your papers and forward them to the executive in whose department the vacancy exists. Naming the job you are after will make the papers travel faster to the person in the organization who should see them. Besides, your case is strengthened considerably when you know what you want and ask for it. Such vague generalities as "marketing work" and "general management" tell the prospective employer almost nothing.

Education. Most college students have only a modest amount of job experience; the main thing they have to offer an employer is their education. That part of your education which equips you to handle the job you are applying for should be emphasized so that it gets immediate attention.

In addition to the format shown in Martin Hammond's résumé on page 229, here are two other ways in which you could show your educational background:

EDUCATION

Three years at Centenary College, Shreveport, Louisiana (1974 to 1977), studying marketing and business administration. Had to leave school before graduation for financial reasons.

Major courses included economics, marketing principles, selling technique, business management, accounting (three semesters), business statistics, sales management, business psychology, and industrial relations.

A.A.	Norwalk Community College, Norwalk, Connecticut, 1976 Major: General Business
B.B.A.	Centenary College, Shreveport, Louisiana, 1978 Major: Marketing

Courses in Marketing and Related Fields:

Marketing Principles	Sales Administration
Advertising	Retail Management
Market Research	Merchandising Techniques
Selling Technique	International Marketing
Business Writing	Buying for Marketing

High School	Monroe, Louisiana. Graduated in 1974 Business courses included typewriting, general business, and business machines.

Experience. Employers are interested in almost any kind of work experience—it doesn't have to be specifically related to the job for which you are applying. Working for others shows a certain amount of independence and maturity. If you bagged groceries in a supermarket, sold magazines, or supervised young people at a summer camp, list these activities. Experience should be described in reverse chronological order—that is, the most recent job first.

In relating your experience, give the date, title of the job, name of the person or firm, and a brief description of your duties. If you have had actual experience in the type of job for which you are making application, enlarge on this with a longer description.

Organizations and Hobbies. The purpose of listing the organizations you belong to in college and your hobbies is to give the prospective employer some clues about the kind of person you are. Your out-of-class activities say something about your mixing well with people, your leadership ability, and your general personality. Note that Mr. Hammond mentions writing as one of his hobbies. Again, this supports his earlier statement about his writing ability. In another résumé for a different job, he might have, though not necessarily, omitted this activity.

Personal Data. There is no point in giving your life history under the heading "Personal Data." Sufficient vital statistics for the résumé are your age, physical facts, and general health. Elaborating on them will not help to sell you—and the résumé is a sales instrument. You will have ample opportunity on the application blank or in a personal interview to go into more detail. On their résumé some people include place of birth, national origin (Irish, for example), and religious affiliation. Such information is best omitted. In fact, many companies prefer that applicants do *not* list information that will reveal race or religion.

References. It is generally recommended that you list three references on the résumé, although it is acceptable to simply state, "References supplied upon request." Since education is your most marketable product, make sure one of your references is a dean, a professor, or other college person who knows you well. But don't force any references; the lady down the street for whom you mowed lawns when you were fourteen wouldn't make a very impressive reference.

Another person on your reference list should be someone who can vouch for your character. You can use the name of your priest, minister, or rabbi if you feel such a reference is appropriate. A prominent citizen or a local business person who knows you and your family will also serve the purpose.

It is no secret that you list as references only those who you know will say the right thing in your behalf. Obviously, employers do not expect you to list your enemies as references; they know that you have chosen references who think well of you.

It is a cardinal rule that you never use a person's name without first asking for permission. This can be done by a telephone call, a visit, or a letter. Such a letter might look like this:

Dear Judge Toffenetti:

Graduation is only a few weeks away, and if everything goes right, I will receive my B.B.A. degree from Centenary June 2. I don't know who will be happier—me or my dad!

Now I'm getting ready to look for a job. My interest is in marketing research, and I hope to find a management trainee position in some large company, preferably in New Orleans or Atlanta.

May I include your name as a reference on my application? If you will do this favor for me, just write your "OK" at the bottom of this letter and return it to me in the enclosed stamped envelope.

Best wishes to you and Mrs. Toffenetti. I will be in Monroe about June 8, and I hope to see both of you then.

Sincerely yours,

SOLUTION B

A variation in the presentation of qualifications is shown in the two-page résumé below and on the next page. This was prepared by Sara Jacobsen to support her application for an executive assistant's job she heard about from

```
                        Qualifications of
                          SARA JACOBSEN
                         17 Cayuga Lane
                    Fort Lauderdale, Florida 33308
                    Telephone:  (305) 936-4421


Position applied for:  Executive Assistant to Mr. Ronald Brewer
                       Vice President and Controller
                       Loughborough Paper Company

  EXPERIENCE

      At present       Administrative assistant to the Dean of Faculties,
                       Fort Lauderdale University.  In this position,
                       which I have held all this academic year while a
                       student, I have the following responsibilities:

                       1.  Take all the Dean's dictation (often heavy);
                           type her memorandums and reports, many of
                           which are statistical; receive visitors;
                           answer the telephone; keep the Dean's appoint-
                           ment calendar; and do the filing.

                       2.  Write many letters and reports for the Dean's
                           signature to job applicants, other deans and
                           administrators, faculty members, parents,
                           students, and others.  Assist the Dean in
                           research for reports and articles she writes
                           for publication.

                       3.  Supervise two part-time clerks.

                       4.  Assist in the preparation of budgets, personnel
                           reports, and financial proposals.

      1975             Clerk-stenographer, Florida Credit Corporation.
                       In this summer job, I took some dictation and typed
                       contracts, letters, bank documents, and financial
                       statements.

      1975-1976        Salesclerk (part-time after school and on Saturdays),
                       Craig's Variety Store.  In this job, I waited on
                       customers and assisted in the office and the stock-
                       room.  Did some light typing and filing of invoices.

  EDUCATION

      College

        Attended Fort Lauderdale University, 1976 and 1977, majoring in
        Secretarial Administration.  Will be graduated in June with A.A. degree.
```

the placement director of Fort Lauderdale University. The director shared with Ms. Jacobsen the notes she made during a phone call from Loughborough Paper Company.

Executive assistant to the controller. Must have secretarial skills, broad background in accounting, and ability to write letters and reports. Apply in writing. (Very good job.)

As Ms. Jacobsen studied these job requirements, she mentally noted what she should emphasize in her résumé: experience, secretarial skills, writ-

---

Qualifications of Sara Jacobsen   Page 2

Business Courses Completed:

Shorthand (120 words a minute; hold Gregg certificate)
Typewriting (78 words a minute; hold Gregg certificate)
English (composition, vocabulary, letter writing, report writing)
Secretarial Procedures
Accounting (principles, cost, and intermediate)
Data Processing (including computer programming)
Mathematics of Accounting and Finance (two semesters)
Economics
Business Machines

High School

Graduated from Fort Lauderdale High School, 1975. Took the business curriculum, which included shorthand, typewriting, secretarial practice, personal development, business English, office machines, and accounting.

Scholastic Honors and Activities

National Honor Society
Psi Beta Chi (social sorority), Fort Lauderdale University
Executive Secretaries Club
Fort Lauderdale Choral Society (Vice President)

OTHER INTERESTS

Sing with the Fort Lauderdale Choral Society and the First Baptist Church choir and play the piano and the guitar.

Swimming, water skiing, deep-sea diving.

PERSONAL DATA

Birth Date: January 1, 1958
Physical: Weight, 120; height, 5'5"
Health: Excellent

REFERENCES (by permission)

Dr. J. Frank Halderman, Chairman, Department of Secretarial Administration, Fort Lauderdale University. Telephone 462-1527 (Ext. 27).

Dr. Phyllis Tangerman, Dean of Faculties, Fort Lauderdale University. Telephone 462-1527 (Ext. 31).

Rev. Frank C. Carter, First Baptist Church, Fort Lauderdale. Telephone 847-4756.

ing ability, and knowledge of accounting. She recognized that as controller, Mr. Brewer was no doubt the chief accounting officer of his company, and she planned to use this clue to guide her in preparing her résumé. If the position had required outstanding shorthand and typing skill, she would have given more emphasis to these skills. If the ability to supervise people had been stressed, she would have provided more details about her experience as a supervisor.

Analysis of Solution B.   Unlike Martin Hammond, Sara Jacobsen presents her work experience first. In this way she emphasizes what she has actually done that helps her qualify for the specific job she is applying for. She also details college business courses she has completed.

Project

Prepare résumés for any two of the following twenty positions, emphasizing in each one the skills or abilities you possess that match the employer's requirements.

1. PERSONNEL ASSISTANT (Job Evaluation). Excellent opportunity for college-trained man or woman in Personnel Department of large advertising agency. Must have at least two years of college, preferably in personnel or business administration. We'll train you, and you earn as you learn. Write to Box M1465, Post. An equal opportunity employer.

2. PERSONNEL INTERVIEWER. We want people who are interested in a career in personnel administration, and interviewing prospective employees is an ideal place to start. Business training (some college) required. Must be able to speak well, present good appearance, write reports. In this job you will learn to interview, screen, and test applicants for jobs. Send résumé to Box 14, Times.

3. MANAGER TRAINEE. Publicly owned multimillion-dollar building company needs person to train for manager of new subdivision. Must have feeling for organization, marketing, sales/display, advertising, and public relations. Security, salary, and fringe benefits of major corporation. Excellent starting salary for the right person. Write Mrs. L. Jones, Suite 309, Bradley Building.

4. MANAGEMENT TRAINEE. Interested in finance? Our company has 3 openings for young college persons who have good training in finance and are interested in managing a finance or budget department. Excellent starting salary and fringe benefits. Nationally known corporation, excellent chances for advancement. Address Box 98-C, Star-Ledger. E.O.E.

5. HOSPITAL ADMINISTRATION. Want young man or woman to train as hospital administrator. Degree preferred but not essential. Applicant should have general knowledge of accounting. This job requires an individual who can work well with people and who is strong in communication skills. Modest beginning salary but outstanding opportunities for frequent financial and career advancement. Send résumé to J. I. Trumble, 2401 Blueridge Avenue, Morristown, New Jersey 07960.

6. MANAGEMENT TRAINEES—AVIATION ACTIVITIES. Firm dealing in aviation activities (we have several government contracts) desires to interview men and women who have management aspirations. Good benefits, fine starting salary. Address Box 123, Inquirer.

7. SALES CAREER. Century-old international financial institution has opening for 2 counselors in investment and insurance. Complete 2-year training program. Will consider those with no experience. For interview, send brief personal history to Box M1434, Chronicle.

8. SALES. Top opportunity for ambitious go-getter. Any good experience in auto or route selling will help. Salary plus commission. Write Cynthia Olwell, 217 Mayfair Building.

9. SALES. We are a nationally recognized sales and marketing personnel agency, and we are seeking an intelligent, motivated, people- and sales-oriented individual capable of justifying and maintaining a 5-figure income with consistency. Previous history of success in sales or personnel would be advantageous but will consider good college business administration background. Must be able to communicate effectively on all levels from recent college grad to executive. Ability to work successfully with a minimum of supervision a must. Candidate selected will take over currently productive desk. Call John Mulholland, Ajax Agency. Have résumé ready.

10. SALES OPENINGS. We have several excellent openings for people interested in selling. Our clients include food manufacturers, retail furniture dealers, magazine publishers (space selling), time-sharing firms, and many others. Name your interest—we have the job if you're qualified. Tell us about yourself. Box 0072, Times-Herald.

11. MARKETING/PUBLIC RELATIONS. Rare opportunity in education field. We are interviewing for several openings in our marketing management training program. If you like people, are ambitious, a hard worker, and college-trained, then you will be thoroughly trained in our successful marketing methods. Earn an excellent salary. Opportunity for advancement into management as fast as ability and performance warrant. Send résumé to Box 27, World Globe.

12. ACCOUNTANT—AUTOMOTIVE. Fast-growing auto dealership requires accountant to work closely with general manager in overall operations. Applicant must have strong background in accounting principles and be looking for a permanent position with a bright future. Some experience in automotive accounting preferred. Reply Box 2 (Mrs. Agnes Lawson), Examiner.

13. ACCOUNTING MANAGER. Growing firm has immediate need for fully qualified, aggressive accountant who can quickly develop to take full charge of general accounting and auditing functions. Knowledge of cost accounting and budgeting techniques desired. Excellent opportunity for the right person. Full package of employee benefits. Salary commensurate with education and experience. Submit résumé to Daily Blade, Box 47113.

14. ACCOUNTING—SYSTEMS AND PROCEDURES. Headquarters of national association has opening for a person with good background in accounting

and economics. This is a non-data-processing-oriented position. If you have initiative and imagination, a thorough knowledge of business procedures, and a better-than-average ability to express ideas in writing, please send us your résumé. Box C-40, Tribune. An Equal Opportunity Employer.

15. JR. INTERNAL AUDITOR. Office of controller in large expanding firm is seeking an individual in a full-time junior auditor's position. If you are a 2- or 4-year graduate or a student attending night school in accounting and want to earn while you learn, here is an excellent opportunity. No experience necessary. Salary commensurate with education. Write to Oscar Jesurun, Star Foods Inc., 6900 Landover Road. Equal Opportunity Employer.

16. ADMINISTRATIVE SECRETARY. No shorthand. For this spot you must be a thoroughly trained individual with emphasis in business administration, office procedures, and supervision. Lots of public contact, so you must enjoy working with all sorts of people. Can advance to department manager. Good typing ability, letter writing, routine reports. Pleasant private office. Assist president in public relations work. Résumé to Box 16, Clarion.

17. EXECUTIVE SECRETARY. Great opportunity for person with high level of stenographic skills. Work for V.P. of Marketing, assisting her in planning, research, contacts with sales representatives, advertising and promotion, and so on. General knowledge of accounting helpful but not necessary. Prefer some college. Good salary, with all benefits; sophisticated offices. Send résumé to J. T. Evans, Albert Gamble Building.

18. ADMINISTRATIVE ASSISTANT — INTERNATIONAL AND CRIMINAL LAW. Well-known lawyer seeks versatile person to be his right arm. You'll handle various administrative matters and may even attend court cases. Fast-paced and challenging opportunity, with typing and shorthand skills. No law experience needed. More of a management job than secretarial—managing the boss, supervising small clerical staff, etc. "Take-over" type desired! Write to Lawrence Applebaum, Box 4747, Center-town.

19. ADMINISTRATIVE AIDE—URBAN RENEWAL. As executive secretary to senior partner of firm dealing with urban renewal, you will be in a key administrative position where you can utilize your executive talents along with your shorthand and typing. Excellent future and benefits. Want to be "involved"? This is the place. Write to Betty Grayson, 1102 Riddell Building. An E.O.E.

20. MEDICAL SECRETARY. Medical secretary (work for Chief Medical Officer) with good skills and knowledge of medical terminology. Exciting opportunity. Write to Personnel Manager, Providence Hospital.

CASE 2

WRITING THE APPLICATION LETTER

PROBLEM

Let's repeat the advertisement for which Martin T. Hammond prepared his résumé.

> Management trainees in marketing research. Minimum two years of college, preferably in marketing and/or business administration. Heavy writing. Apply Box 73, Times.

What kind of letter would you write in answer to this ad?

BACKGROUND

The résumé is essentially a personal history which concentrates on dates and events. But even though it is an individualized presentation of one's qualifications, it is not intended to be a highly *personal* one. That is, there is little opportunity in the résumé to reveal one's sincerity, ambition, and enthusiasm.

The really personal document in employment communications is the letter of application. It may be written in answer to an ad, it may be written because the writer has been referred to a job opening by a friend, or it may be entirely unsolicited. In each case, however, the purpose of the application letter is to obtain an interview; it is therefore a sales letter. Its job is to attract favorable attention and to persuade a prospective employer that the résumé—as well as the applicant—is worth looking at.

The application letter is generally accompanied by a résumé; therefore, it does not merely repeat the dates, events, and achievements in the résumé. It *supports* that presentation by giving the employer a more personal statement of an applicant's interest in and fitness for a particular job.

You won't need a long letter to do the job—certainly not more than one page. If your résumé is complete, there isn't much to be said in the application letter. The letter should be built around one or all of these points:

1. Why I want the job and feel qualified for it.
2. What my interests, ambitions, and aspirations are.
3. What I expect to do for you, the employer.
4. When I'm available and how I can be reached.

We mentioned that the application letter is a sales letter. And so it is. But remember that you are not selling a bag of flour. For example:

> Wouldn't you like to have an eager, dynamic, resourceful college graduate working for you—a man with ideas, imagination, and ambition? I'm your man.

Such a beginning sounds bombastic—even laughable—to the typical executive who reads it. The applicant is likely to be put down as a know-it-all. While you don't want to hide your light under a bushel, neither do you want to give the impression that you have all the answers. Managers are well aware that the big talkers are rarely the big doers. Even old hands don't know all the answers. As they struggle with the brain-racking problems of their jobs, imagine how they feel toward the person who makes the work sound like a cinch.

Unless you are applying for a very competitive position that you know will require you to display your ingenuity, don't. Occasionally, tricky letters will work—in advertising agencies, for example, where shock effects are part of the game. For example, one applicant for an agency job affixed his picture to a cover of *Time* magazine, calling himself "Man of the Year." Inside was a biographical sketch, such as *Time* might publish, emphasizing the applicant's talents, ingenuity, education, and so on. For the purpose, it must have been effective, because he got the job.

For the typical job in business, however, you will want to strike a chord somewhere between the boastful and the modest. Certainly you won't approach an employer on your knees with "You probably wouldn't want to hire an accounting graduate with no experience, would you?" There is no harm in saying frankly what you believe you can do for a firm.

Above all, don't copy a letter someone else has written, no matter how good the author says it is. Your letter should be you—honestly you—and nobody else.

For your letter use a good grade of white bond paper (8½ by 11 inches) that matches the paper used for the résumé. Never use a company letterhead (believe it or not, some people have written application letters on hotel stationery) or tinted paper. Leave generous margins all around. You want your letter to invite reading.

Another point is worth repeating: Exhaust every source to find the name and title of the person to whom your letter should be addressed. Then be sure that the name is written the way the recipient likes it and that the title is accurate. If Mr. J. Walter Meade is Director of Marketing, don't address him as Mr. J. W. Mead, Marketing Department.

The first thing to keep in mind as you answer the ad in the case problem is that you are probably going to have plenty of competition. This is no reason to make your letter shout, but it *is* a good reason to make your letter good looking, accurate, and somewhat persuasive. By the way, if you consider yourself a little weak in grammar and punctuation, have an English major (or your instructor in business communication) check it for you.

SOLUTION A

> Gentlemen:
>
> I want to apply for the job in marketing research you advertised. My résumé is enclosed.

I very much want to work in Atlanta because I have relatives there. I need the job because I am helping to support my parents (my father is disabled).

I am sorry I don't have any experience, but I hope you will not hold that against me. College students don't have much of an opportunity to get experience, and we have to start someplace.

Sincerely yours,

Analysis of Solution A.   You don't have to be told that this is a very poor letter, assuming that the organization to which it is sent is not charity-minded (most aren't!). All you have to do is think how you would feel if you were doing the hiring and received such a letter.

1. The opening is trite and ordinary; probably a hundred others will say the same thing. Also, it is not clear where the applicant learned about the job (the *Times*).
2. The writer concentrates on why *he* wants the job—not why the firm might want to hire him. Beware of personal reasons for applying for a job, such as the fact that relatives are nearby. And never say you *need* work; this puts you in the position of a beggar, and you are expected to have some pride. Lots of people have financial problems—and young college graduates are no exception—but keep the problems to yourself.
3. Don't apologize for lack of experience. Someone getting started in business isn't expected to have worked at anything except part-time or temporary jobs, most of which are unrelated to the person's main interest.
4. The last sentence in paragraph 3 is sarcastic. If the reader gets this far, it will surely sink the applicant.
5. The writer offers no details about when he will be available, how he might be reached, whether he could come for an interview, and so on. The last paragraph should suggest action, leaving no doubt in the employer's mind that an interview is desired and giving details on how it might be arranged.

SOLUTION B

1977 DuBlanc Avenue
Monroe, Louisiana 71201
May 16, 19—

Atlanta Times
916 Peachtree Street, N.W.
Box 73
Atlanta, Georgia 30309

Gentlemen:

The position you advertised in the May 14 Times for management trainees in marketing research is exactly the opportunity I had hoped to find. As I read the ad, I felt that you were talking to me.

As you will see by the enclosed résumé, I will be graduated from Centenary College in June with a major in marketing. I feel that I have an excellent marketing education (21 semester hours in my major), supported by a broad program in business administration and liberal arts. Of special interest to me was my course in marketing research. Not only did we study modern techniques, but we were required to read and report on significant current books in the field—including two by E. B. Weiss and the highly controversial <u>Markets and Media</u>, by Marshall McGoogan. Writing those reports and others requiring the use of sampling techniques and interviews was the most interesting part of my work (and my grades in this course prove it).

In college I held several part-time jobs and was still able to maintain a good grade-point average while carrying a full academic load.

On June 7 I will complete my work here and can come to Atlanta any day after that. Will you allow me the privilege of talking with you in person and telling you why I believe I can be useful to your firm in the exciting field of marketing research? If you prefer to telephone me, you may reach me at (318) 515-1234.

Sincerely yours,

Martin T. Hammond

Analysis of Solution B.   This effective letter has features that you could give a similar letter of your own.

Heading.   Type your address and the date as shown. The address to which you expect a reply to be sent is a must, even though it is included in your résumé.

Inside Address and Salutation.   Some ads indicate the company's name and ask that the applications be addressed to "The Personnel Director." In this case, you will use the salutation "Dear Sir" or "Dear Sir or Madam." If the person's name is given, you will, of course, use it in the salutation. Remember, make every effort to learn the name and use it.

Opening Paragraph.   You can open your application letter in various ways. The one illustrated is effective for three reasons:

1. It comes right to the point; the writer doesn't beat around the bush in applying for the job.
2. It reveals that the writer is genuinely interested in the job.
3. It identifies the source of information about the job.

Here are other possible openings:

The enclosed résumé, I believe, will provide evidence that I am a logical candidate for the position of management trainee in marketing research that you advertised in the May 14 <u>Times</u>.

Will you please consider me an applicant for the position of management trainee in marketing research that you advertised in the May 14 <u>Times</u>?

My interest and specialized training in marketing make me an exceptionally well-qualified candidate for the position of marketing research trainee as described in the May 14 _Times_. Will you please consider me an enthusiastic applicant?

If the name of the company or the type of business is mentioned in the advertisement, the following would be effective openings.

Marcal is a name that I know very well, not only because you distribute your products nationally but also because you have an excellent reputation among marketing people for innovations in food packaging and distribution. I would consider it a privilege to work in your marketing research department (_Times_ of May 14) and would like to be considered a trainee applicant.

A genuine interest in food distribution, a desire to make a career in marketing research, energy and ambition, and a specialized college training in marketing—these are the things I can offer in response to your advertisement in the May 14 _Times_.

Some writers prefer the opening immediately above because it puts the applicant's primary sales features right up front.

Second Paragraph.   You will have to think long and hard about what goes into your second paragraph. The opening introduces you and gets the employer interested. The job of the second paragraph is to convince the reader that you have the qualifications needed for the job.

Ask yourself the question, "What human-interest features about my experience or education might the executive want to know that I didn't include in my résumé?" In Solution B, Martin Hammond has assumed that the progressive marketing manager knows who E. B. Weiss is and has at least heard about Marshall McGoogan. Even if she hasn't, it is probably worth taking a chance to show that Mr. Hammond is familiar with the current literature in the field. Note the emphasis on writing ability in this paragraph.

The second paragraph obviously is a good example of why you can't copy somebody else's letter. You need to single out your own special attributes for emphasis, and no two people have the same ones.

Third Paragraph.   It is a good idea to let the employer know that work doesn't scare you and that you like challenge. The employer will interpret this as willingness to apply yourself and to learn. Mr. Hammond got both points across.

Closing Paragraph.   The closing paragraph should be an action paragraph, telling the employer that you want an interview and suggesting ways in which it might be arranged. Of course, not everybody can travel several hundred miles for an interview, as suggested in Mr. Hammond's letter. If it is out of the question for you, then you can simply leave the matter open, hoping the company will be sufficiently interested in you to pay your travel expenses or perhaps suggest an interview with one of their nearby representatives. Or you might say something like this:

I hope you will allow me the privilege of an interview. Do you have a representative in this area with whom I might discuss my qualifications?

This statement implies that you won't be able to travel to the employer's headquarters at your own expense but are willing to go a reasonable distance.

Signature. Type your name exactly the way you sign it. And don't forget to sign the letter! It is surprising how many people, after struggling for hours or days over the contents of an application letter, spoil the entire effect by failing to sign it.

THE SALARY QUESTION

Some advertisements ask applicants to state the salary expected. Most advertisements don't. Never bring up the subject of money unless you are asked to or unless you have a burning financial problem and a few dollars makes a big difference. If you must have a certain amount in order to live and pay off your debts, then be frank and say how much.

As to salary, I feel that the minimum I could accept is $9,500.

If money is not the crucial issue (salaries for college trainees are surprisingly close in similar industries), don't even bring up the subject.

REFERRAL APPLICATION LETTER

The best entrée you can have to a job is when you are recommended by a person whom the employer knows and whose opinion the employer respects. For example, your major professor receives word from a personnel director that a certain type of person is wanted to fill a vacancy, and your qualifications happen to match the requirements. Such a recommendation gives you one leg up the ladder; the employer doesn't have to puzzle about who you are and why you are applying.

Such an application letter may be similar to the one addressed to Mr. Brewer, below. The main difference is that you will mention, in the opening paragraph, the name of the person who suggested that you apply. For example:

Dear Ms. Carlson:

Professor George T. Courtright, chairman of the Accounting Department at Monmouth College, has suggested that I apply for the position of cost accountant that you spoke to him about earlier this week. The job sounds very interesting to me, and I should like to be considered for it.

Or:

Dear Ms. Carlson:

Will you please consider me for the position of cost accountant about which you recently spoke to Professor Courtright? He recommended that I write to you and apply for the job.

The second and succeeding paragraphs will be similar to those you would write in answer to an advertisement. You would be wise, however, to capitalize on the name of the person who recommended you. For example:

I feel that I had excellent training in accounting at Monmouth (24 semester hours in my major), supported by a broad program in business administration and liberal arts. Of special interest to me was Professor Courtright's course in data processing techniques as they affect modern cost accounting procedures. Here we studied . . . .

Following is the letter Sara Jacobsen might write to apply for the position of executive assistant to Mr. Brewer (pages 232–233).

Mr. Ronald Brewer
Vice President and Controller
Loughborough Paper Company
320 Broadway
Miami, Florida 33142

Dear Mr. Brewer:

Mrs. Farnsworth, placement director at Fort Lauderdale University, has suggested that my qualifications are uniquely suited to the position as your executive assistant, and I should like to be considered for it.

Ever since I took a business curriculum in high school, I have had trouble deciding between secretarial work and accounting as a career. I did extremely well in these subjects in high school and college and have had experience in both areas during the past year. I made up my mind at the beginning of my second year at Fort Lauderdale University that I would make secretarial studies my major and accounting my minor. Since the position as your executive assistant offers an opportunity to work in both fields, it seems ideal for me.

A résumé is enclosed. I shall be pleased to provide further details at a personal interview, and I can come to your office when it is convenient for you.

You may reach me at 462-1527 (Ext. 31) until 3 p.m. each day and at 936-4421 after 4 p.m.

Sincerely yours,

Sara Jacobsen

UNSOLICITED APPLICATION LETTER

Sometimes you may have your heart set on a job in a particular section of the country but do not have any leads on jobs or firms. One way to get leads is to obtain newspapers from cities where you want to work and see if there are advertisements that appeal to you. Another way is to contact local firms that are likely to have a branch or main office in that city. In some cases, you will simply have to choose the type of firm you want to work for, obtain the addresses of several leading firms in the city of your choice, and write to the personnel directors. (In many cities you can obtain telephone directories of any city in the United States.)

Suppose you live in Charlotte, North Carolina, and want to work in San Francisco. If you're like most people, you can't afford to make the long trip from Charlotte to San Francisco, at least without some definite hope that you will have a job when you get there. Your interest is petroleum accounting, and you have selected five major oil companies to which you will direct your inquiries about job opportunities.

Following is a letter you might write. Of course, the letter will be accompanied by a résumé.

Mr. Eliot Skaff, Controller
Western Oil Company
1518 El Camino Real
San Francisco, California 94137

Dear Mr. Skaff:

Do you have a place in your department at Western Oil Company for a young man who:

1. Hopes to make a career of accounting—particularly in the petroleum industry?
2. Has a broad background in accounting but knows that he must prove himself by on-the-job training?
3. Is eager to learn and not afraid to dig in?

In June I will be graduated from King's College, Charlotte, North Carolina, and I am eager to find a challenging job in the San Francisco area.

My résumé is enclosed. Would you let me know, please, whether you are interested in my qualifications?

Cordially yours,

Projects

(A) Write application letters to accompany the résumés you prepared in Case 1, pages 234–236.

(B) Carlton J. Sibley, assistant personnel manager of the Jason Products Corporation, has informed your major professor of an opening in a certain department (choose the type of position in which you have an interest and the necessary qualifications). Your professor has suggested that you apply. Write an application to Mr. Sibley, assuming that you will accompany it with a data sheet.

(C) Select an area of the United States in which you would like to work (or a company with overseas operations). Write an unsolicited letter of application that you could send to several firms.

CASE 3

FOLLOWING UP
APPLICATION LETTERS

PROBLEM

You have received no response to your application for the position of marketing research trainee (Case Problems 1 and 2), and you decide to write a follow-up letter.

BACKGROUND

If you receive no answer to an application within a reasonable time—say, two or three weeks, depending on the distance the letter has to travel—it is wise to follow up. The objective of the follow-up letter is to remind the firm of your interest—not to show impatience or anger. Responses to applications may be delayed because the papers are being circulated among several people; if one of these people is away on a business trip or vacation, the decision is held up until that person returns. You should be notified, of course, that your application has been received and that there might be a short wait before you will hear anything definite, but don't count on it.

Your follow-up letter can serve to provide additional information that will help your cause. In fact, some authorities recommend that the applicant deliberately withhold a nugget or two from the original letter. But since you may not have a chance to write a follow-up letter, you naturally will not want to withhold your most important "sales features" from your application letter itself.

SOLUTION A

Gentlemen:

When can I expect to hear from you about the position I applied for as marketing trainee? I can only conclude that you are not interested in my qualifications; but if you are, I will need to know very soon, for I am considering other opportunities that have recently come up.

Sincerely yours,

Analysis of Solution A. If the applicant who wrote Solution A had been on the list of possible candidates, the letter would surely have taken him off. It reveals impatience and annoyance. Equally important, the applicant's suggestion that he is no longer in the running is too easy for the recipient to agree to. Negative suggestions rarely make sales!

SOLUTION B

Gentleman:

When I wrote you on May 16, applying for the job of marketing research trainee (your advertisement in the May 14 <u>Times</u>), I neglected to mention that one of my senior projects in marketing research was a report on recent marketing trends in the food industry. I think you might be interested in a brief summary of that report and am enclosing a copy.

When may I expect to hear from you concerning my application? I am eager to know whether I am being considered so that I may complete my plans.

Cordially yours,

Analysis of Solution B. Solution B is likely to get a favorable response if the position has not been filled. The writer uses a good selling technique by supporting his previous application papers with a sample of his work—a technique many people have found very effective.

Note that the writer asks about the status of his application, but he does not put the question in the form of a demand. Observe the phrase "so that I may complete my plans." This is more subtle and tactful than "because I am considering several other offers," which is a veiled threat.

Project

About two weeks ago you applied for one of the positions listed on pages 234–236, but you have not had a response to your application. In the meantime, you have been offered another position that you must accept or decline within two weeks. You would prefer the first position you applied for (salary is better and the opportunities are more attractive.) Write the appropriate follow-up letter.

CASE 4

THANKING THE INTERVIEWER

PROBLEM

You have been interviewed for the marketing research position that you applied for. You spent most of your time with the manager of marketing research, Martha Patton, but you also met her boss, Daniel Conrad, the marketing director, and Mr. Conrad's assistant, Regina Archdale. You believe it would be a good idea to write Miss Patton to thank her for seeing you and to restate your interest in the job.

BACKGROUND

A thank-you letter following a job interview will give you an advantage over applicants who don't think of writing (most people don't). Even though the firm to which you are applying is local, it is better to write than to telephone and to do so no later than a day after the interview.

SOLUTION A

Dear Miss Patton:

Thank you for allowing me to meet you this week to discuss the position of marketing research trainee.

The job is most attractive to me and offers the kind of opportunity that I am looking for. I know I would find the work challenging and rewarding.

Please express my appreciation also to Mr. Conrad and Mrs. Archdale.

Sincerely yours,

Analysis of Solution A. The type of follow-up letter you write will depend on how things went at the interview. If you feel that you were favorably received and that you have a good chance of getting the job, the solution above is fine. If your letter is friendly, positive, and sincere, you will reaffirm the employer's interest, saying in effect, "Now that I've met you, I know I want the job." And it doesn't hurt to mention the names of others with whom you talked besides the principal interviewer. You never know where the center of influence is.

Suppose you got the impression at the interview that you were lacking in certain desired qualifications. Your letter might then be somewhat different, as the following solution illustrates.

SOLUTION B

Dear Miss Patton:

Thank you for allowing me to meet with you this week and discuss the position of marketing research trainee.

The job is most attractive to me and offers the kind of opportunity that I am looking for. I know I would find the work challenging and rewarding.

After learning more about the job, I realize that my knowledge of advanced statistical methods may be somewhat light. The subject interests me, however (I did well in the elementary course in college), and I would expect to become more expert in it. Cole University offers advanced courses in statistics, and I would plan to enroll in its evening division.

Would you please express my appreciation also to Mr. Conrad and Mrs. Archdale for giving me so much of their time.

Sincerely yours,

Analysis of Solution B.   In this letter you are telling your interviewer that you recognize you are lacking knowledge of advanced statistical methods and you are honest enough to admit it to yourself and to the interviewer. A prospective employer would be impressed with your awareness as well as with your desire to gain expertise.

Projects

(A)   Assume that your follow-up letter in the project on page 246 resulted in an invitation to come for an interview. After the interview, you are more certain than ever that you want the position. Write a letter expressing your appreciation for the interview and reaffirming your interest in the job.

(B)   One of the letters you wrote for Project C (page 244) resulted in an invitation to come for an interview, expenses paid. The interview completed, you return home convinced that you would enjoy working for that particular firm. Write a thank-you letter.

CASE 5

ACCEPTING AND REJECTING JOB OFFERS

PROBLEM

You have been offered and have decided to accept the position with Marcal as marketing research trainee. Miss Patton gave you the news in a letter and confirmed the salary you are to receive and the date you are to report to work (you are to appear at 8:30 a.m. on June 16 for a physical examination). She also sent you a copy of Welcome to Marcal, a booklet for new employees describing various company policies, employee benefits, and so on.

Your decision to accept the job will call for three types of employment letters: (1) a letter of acceptance of the position offered, (2) a thank-you to those who permitted you to use their names as references, and (3) a notification to other prospective employers that you are no longer a candidate for a position with them.

BACKGROUND—Accepting a Job Offer

The person offering you a job will expect you to respond immediately to the offer. Although you could telephone your acceptance, you should respond in writing, particularly if the invitation you receive is in writing.

SOLUTION

Dear Miss Patton:

You don't know how delighted I am to accept the position of marketing research trainee with Marcal. As you suggested, I shall report to the Medical Department at 8:30 a.m. on June 16 for my physical examination and will come to your office immediately afterward.

The prospect of joining your team is exciting, and I look forward to the experience. You may be sure that I will read <u>Welcome to Marcal</u> from cover to cover!

Cordially yours,

Analysis of the Solution.   This promptly written response accepts the job, confirms all the requests made by your new employer, and tells her that you are enthusiastic about getting started.

BACKGROUND—Thanking Your References

Once you have obtained a position, it is important that you write those whom you listed as references on your résumé to thank them for their help. You have no way of knowing whether your prospective employer actually sought the opinions of your references, but it is safe to assume that they were contacted. Writing to thank those who helped you is the courteous and thoughtful thing to do, and it is also good insurance in case you want to use their names as references again.

Case Example: Judge R. N. Toffenetti, a family friend, and Professor Christine Hale, your marketing professor, were two of the references you listed on your résumé. During a telephone conversation with Professor Hale this morning, you mentioned that you had accepted a very good job offer. You haven't been in touch with Judge Toffenetti since you accepted the position as management trainee in marketing with Marcal Distributors, Atlanta, Georgia.

SOLUTION—Letter to Judge Toffenetti

Dear Judge Toffenetti:

Well, Judge Toffenetti, I have accepted a position as management trainee in marketing with Marcal Distributors in Atlanta. It looks like a great opportunity, and I couldn't be more pleased.

Next week I will leave for Atlanta and start searching for a place to live (I'm to report to work a week from this coming Monday). My folks think Atlanta is a long way off, but I think they're getting used to the idea of my living there.

Thank you for letting me use your name as reference in my application. You must have said the right thing!

Respectfully yours,

Analysis of the Solution. This letter courteously thanks the judge. It also says, "I am thoughtful enough to appreciate the privilege of using your name as a reference."

SOLUTION—Letter to Professor Hale

Dear Professor Hale:

As I told you on the telephone, I landed the job with Marcal and I start work June 16. I will leave here next Tuesday to try to locate a place to live—preferably in the suburbs.

You must know how much I appreciate your help in getting this position. Your letter of recommendation obviously carried a great deal of weight. Thank you for the confidence you have in me. I hope I can prove that I deserve it.

I'll write you a note when I get settled so that you may reach me if you ever get to Atlanta. You must drop in to see me—I'd like that.

Respectfully yours,

Analysis of the Solution. This letter is an appropriate and effective follow-up to a telephoned thanks to a reference.

BACKGROUND—Rejecting a Job Offer

Let's say the other company to which you submitted your application (see the project on page 234) has just made you a job offer, which, of course, you must decline. When you accept a position, you should notify the other companies to which you applied that you are no longer a candidate. Do this whether or not you have received a firm offer.

Following is an effective letter in which the applicant asks to have her name removed from the list of active candidates. Note the courteous and appreciative tone. The writer doesn't say, "I got a better job than you offered." Instead, she describes the job as one better tailored to her interests.

Dear Mr. Lyles:

Thank you for considering me for a position in your marketing research training program. However, I have accepted a similar job with Marcal Distributors, and I wish to withdraw my application with your firm.

While I know I would have enjoyed working at Midfair, I feel that the job I am taking offers a better opportunity to concentrate on packaging, which is of special interest to me.

It was a pleasure talking with you. I appreciate all your kindnesses.

Sincerely yours,

Projects

(A) You have received a letter from the person who interviewed you for a position (Project B, page 248), telling you that the job is yours. You are to report to work at nine on Monday, June 27, going first to the Personnel Department for a medical examination, an orientation session, and so on. Respond to the job offer, indicating your pleasure in accepting it.

(B) Select one of the references given when you applied for the position that was eventually offered you (A above), and write an appropriate letter of appreciation.

(C) When you made application for the position mentioned in A and B, you also applied for a similar one with the Dilworth Corporation (Mrs. L. G. Bouton, personnel manager) and received a favorable response though no job offer as yet. Write to Mrs. Bouton, telling her to withdraw your name as a candidate.

CASE 6

RESIGNING FROM A POSITION

PROBLEM

You have decided to resign from your position as assistant credit manager of Franklin Steel Company.

BACKGROUND

Although some people spend all of their working years with the firm that gave them their first position, most of us do not. We change employers for a variety of reasons: financial needs, distance from work, family problems, health, dissatisfaction with the job, lack of opportunity, and so on. And although we feel you should not stick with a job merely for the sake of "security," we also feel that spending a year here, six months there, a year and a half elsewhere—becoming a job-skipper—can be very damaging.

Before you change jobs, therefore, you ought to make sure that the cause of your dissatisfaction can't be eliminated. Sometimes a serious talk with your boss (or with your boss's permission, someone higher up) can result in a solution. If you feel that your situation is hopeless and that there is nothing left to do but resign, you should discuss your intentions with your immediate superior and then put your resignation in writing. In doing so, remember that it is customary to give the company at least two weeks' notice of your intention to resign.

Naturally, it makes good sense to scout around to see what is available in other companies before you make that final decision to resign from your present position. Most people make a thorough study of the job market—and even contact several prospective employers—before they take the leap. **Caution:** In making application for another job, it is best not to knock your present company or the people in it, no matter how you feel. When your prospective employer asks why you want to leave your present job, you are always safe in saying that it does not give you the opportunity you want.

A letter of resignation is a simple one to write if you are changing jobs for "nonpeople" reasons. If you are offered a job that pays better, if you must move to a more healthful climate, if commuting from your home to your present job location is inconvenient and expensive, or if the hours of work or the work itself are unsuitable, you simply "tell it like it is."

On the other hand, when your reasons for leaving a company involve other people—your boss, your fellow employees, or others in the firm—your approach may be somewhat different. Although you may still wish to "tell it like it is," doing so will create animosity (toward you more than toward anyone else) and might hurt (you more than anyone else). Proceed with caution, then, when writing a letter under such circumstances. Lambasting your adversaries will gain you nothing but the short-lived satisfaction of blowing off steam. Here's a resignation letter that's the result of a personality conflict.

SOLUTION A

Dear Ms. Jensen:

Please consider this my resignation from my position in Franklin Steel Company, effective August 1.

As I told you, I have decided to take a position in another company, although I have not made a firm commitment to any particular one. I do think I would be happier and more productive in publishing or advertising, and I expect to concentrate on firms that can offer me this opportunity.

Thank you for the help you have given me. I have learned a great deal from my job that should prove useful in my new work.

Sincerely yours,

Analysis of Solution A. Solution A is written on the assumption that the writer has not located another position but is considering several definite opportunities. Let's analyze it from that viewpoint.

1. The opening paragraph states the writer's decision to resign and gives the effective date of his resignation.
2. There is no evidence of bitterness anywhere in the letter. The writer skillfully avoids mention of dissatisfaction, even though he may have been unhappy with the person to whom the letter is addressed. You may feel that the writer did nothing but "cop out," but remember that when this particular job and employer are only dim memories, the writer probably will be glad that he did not spill out what was really on his mind.

3. In the last paragraph, the writer is noncommittal. He simply expresses thanks for the help he has been given (and he surely received *some* help), but he doesn't dwell on it. Nor does the writer say that he enjoyed working with Franklin Steel Company—simply that he learned a great deal that will be helpful later.

SOLUTION B

Dear Ms. Jensen:

Please consider this my resignation from my position in Franklin Steel Company, effective August 1.

As I mentioned to you, I have never really adjusted to life in a big city, and I have long wanted to get back to Vermont, where I was reared and where my family still lives. The position I have obtained in Bennington—managing a small travel agency—is the kind I have been hoping to find. So the new job and the location made the opportunity too hard to turn down.

At the same time, I have really enjoyed my work at Franklin Steel, and I hate to leave my many friends. I am especially indebted to you for training me. You are a great teacher, and I shall always be grateful to you for your patience and your inspiration.

Sincerely yours,

Analysis of Solution B. The writer of Solution B obviously had a nonpeople reason for resigning and a much easier task than the writer of Solution A. In this letter, too, the writer:

1. Stated his decision to resign and gave the effective date of his resignation.
2. Referred to his previous discussion of the situation with Ms. Jensen.
3. Gave his reason for resigning and, in this instance, told the reader some details of his new position.
4. Expressed appreciation for the help given him.

Projects

(A) You have held your first job two years. You have enjoyed the work very much and learned a great deal from your boss and others with whom you associated. However, you have received an offer of a much better position—one that offers greater responsibility, a more convenient location for commuting, and a higher salary. It is an opportunity you feel you can't afford to turn down. After discussing the matter with your superior, Lydia Morehouse, you have decided to resign and take the other job. Write the letter of resignation.

(B) Margaret Kincaid has decided to resign from her position as assistant training director. Her reason is that she has no freedom—her supervisor, Howard Frankenthaler, refuses to give her any real responsibility, hovers over her constantly, complains about the quality of her work without offering constructive suggestions, and goes out of his way to belittle her efforts. Although Margaret tried to be a conscientious worker, she couldn't seem to overcome the personality clash with Mr. Frankenthaler. When she tried to discuss the matter with him, he brushed her off with, "If you learn to do your work right, your chance for responsibility will come. You're nowhere near ready to take on anything bigger."

Margaret has looked around for other opportunities and has been offered a job as supervisor of word processing for the McGregor Company. Although it isn't exactly what she wanted, the salary is comparable and the opportunity for management seems much better. Write a letter of resignation that you would prepare if you were Margaret Kincaid.

WRITING REFERENCE LETTERS

PROBLEM

Frank McGrath was a copywriter in the Promotion Department under your supervision for about six months. Although a competent copywriter, McGrath proved to be undependable. He was constantly late for work, often called in "sick," and frequently missed important deadlines, which proved very costly. Numerous discussions with McGrath produced no results, and you finally had to let him go.

Frank has applied to another company for a copywriting position, and you receive a letter from the personnel director of that firm inquiring about Frank's employment record. You will have to decide what you want to say in behalf of Frank McGrath.

BACKGROUND

At some time in your life you will probably be asked to give a recommendation for someone who has applied for a job. Many large companies write to references listed by job applicants—usually it is a form letter, obviously designed to look "routine." As in the following example, the letter often is set up in such a way that the person sending it only types in the inside address, the name of the applicant, and the title of the position applied for.

> Mr. Edward B. Costello
> 910 Hewlett Street
> Franklin Square, New York 11010
>
> Dear Sir:
>
> Your name has been given as a reference in the application of
> Susan Wasserman

for the position of

Computer Programmer

Would you please give us your assessment of this applicant—work habits, ability, character, potential, personality, and any other traits and characteristics that would help us to evaluate her as a potential employee in our company? Your statement will, of course, be kept in strictest confidence. An addressed, stamped envelope is enclosed for your reply.

Very truly yours,

Responding to such a request can be very simple if you have a high opinion of the applicant and sincerely believe she would be an asset to the prospective employer.

Dear Mr. Seaton:

It is a pleasure for me to write in behalf of Susan Wasserman, who has applied for the position of computer programmer in your company.

I have known Miss Wasserman for over three years, first as a fellow programmer and later as her supervisor. I consider her an extremely competent person, completely dependable and extremely intelligent. She works well with people— she was always cooperative and pleasant. Her record here was outstanding.

When Miss Wasserman told me that she was leaving us (she had to return to Duluth to care for her invalid father), I was sad indeed. She will be missed here. Any organization that hires Miss Wasserman will be most fortunate.

Sincerely yours,

Writing a letter concerning someone about whom you are not so enthusiastic is more difficult. Here you must wrestle with your conscience. You could take the attitude that even though you consider the person incompetent or otherwise undesirable, it's of no concern to you—let the company to which the person applied take the risk. True, it is somewhat painful to assume the responsibility for denying a person a job. Yet you do well to remember that if you were a manager seeking information about a prospective employee, you would expect honesty from those who are asked to supply it.

SOLUTION A

Some people, rather than say something negative about an applicant whom they can't praise, resort to a noncommittal letter.

Dear Mrs. Phineas:

I do not feel competent to evaluate the qualifications of Frank McGrath for a position with your firm. He was under my supervision for a very short time.

Sincerely yours,

Analysis of Solution A. One could argue that the writer of Solution A has actually given a very negative report; that is, if she knew anything at all favorable about McGrath, she would have said it. In other words, what is left unsaid speaks as loudly as an outright denunciation. In our opinion, the writer of Solution A is somewhat less than honest; when the writer released Mr. McGrath, she was expressing her dissatisfaction.

SOLUTION B

Some people deliberately emphasize only the favorable qualities of the employee, ignoring the request for information about attitudes, character traits, and performance, in order to avoid a damaging statement.

Dear Mrs. Phineas:

Frank McGrath, about whom you inquired, was a copywriter under my supervision for about six months (March 15 to August 31 of this year). I found him to be a talented writer; the copy he produced for us was always sharp and persuasive. He was personable, and everyone here liked him.

I would recommend Mr. McGrath for a similar position in your company.

Analysis of Solution B. Solution B, although honest in some respects, is an example of what might be called a "half truth." Still, it is not an uncommon approach to such a sensitive problem. Those who favor it believe it is unfair to condemn a person when the fault may have been theirs; that is, they lacked the ability to motivate the person and should share the blame for his failure. Even so, the fact is that the whole story is not being told.

SOLUTION C

Dear Mrs. Phineas:

In the best interests of both you and Frank McGrath, about whom you inquired, I cannot give him an unqualified recommendation.

Mr. McGrath was a copywriter under my supervision for six months. While he is competent as a copywriter, his attendance was sporadic. He was absent from work a great deal, and for this reason and others frequently missed important deadlines. In spite of my having several discussions with him, the problem was never resolved, and finally I had to let him go.

Perhaps, Mrs. Phineas, the position Frank had here didn't challenge him enough—or perhaps he had personal problems he couldn't resolve. Certainly he is a likable fellow and seemed to get along well with his co-workers here. Unfortunately, however, I just couldn't get him going. Perhaps he will do better in a different working environment.

Sincerely yours,

Analysis of Solution C. It could be argued that the writer of Solution C has shot down Frank McGrath's chances at another job and, for that reason, is heartless. No one can say that such a letter is bad or that it is good. The writer apparently feels that she is placing her integrity on the line, and she must deal with her own conscience. She has, however, said some positive things:

1. Frank McGrath is a competent copywriter.
2. Mr. McGrath is likable and got along well with his co-workers.
3. The writer suggests the possibility that she herself may have been at fault because of her inability to motivate Mr. McGrath.

This case is a good example of the dilemma many business writers face: whether or not to tell the whole truth when to do so could be very damaging to an individual. Whether you select Solution A or B or C is a matter of personal judgment. Generally speaking, we prefer C, but it would have to be adapted to fit each specific situation.

Projects

(A) As administrative assistant to the vice president for public relations in Basel Corporation, you supervise two clerk-typists. One of these positions was until a month ago filled by Millicent Crater. Ms. Crater left of her own accord (her father was transferred to another city, and she wanted to go with her family), but you were about ready to release her. Her typing skills were very weak, and she never did catch on to the filing system. Also, her attitude was sullen, uncooperative—there was always a scene when she was asked to do a job over because of errors.

You receive a form letter from Mudville National Bank, asking you to assess Millicent's work record while in your employ. Write the letter.

(B) Another clerk-typist who once worked under your supervision, Barbara Cherner, was first-rate—a rapid typist, accurate, devoted to her job, and pleasant to be around. You were about to recommend her for a promotion to senior clerk when she left the company to be married. Four months after she left, you receive an inquiry from Jonesburg Realtors about Miss Cherner (now Mrs. Francis Donovan); she has applied for a position as clerk-typist. Write the letter.

BUSINESS REPORTS

YOUR JOB *You are assistant personnel manager of the Warner-Dennison Company, a manufacturer of desks, chairs, and other furniture for business firms, government organizations, schools, colleges, and other institutions. Your job is to determine company personnel needs, supervise recruitment and placement activities, establish and maintain job specifications and descriptions, operate orientation and special training programs for employees, and so on. Your boss is Barbara L. Haskell, the personnel manager.*

WRITING INFORMAL REPORTS

CASE 1

PROBLEM

Warner-Dennison publishes the booklet *This Is Warner-Dennison* and, as part of its orientation program, gives a copy to each new employee of the company. The booklet contains a brief history of the company, a description of its principal products, and information about such matters as work hours, vacation policy, insurance plans, and recreational programs. The booklet has 24 pages and is printed in two colors and illustrated throughout.

The manuscript for a new edition of the booklet is about ready to be released for composition, printing, and binding. Miss Haskell has asked you to get comparative cost estimates from three local printers and to give her the information in the form of a written report.

BACKGROUND

In every organization those responsible for managing the company's operations must have factual information about various subjects that they can use as the basis for making intelligent decisions. For example, marketing directors must have at their fingertips information about sales, personnel, competition, advertising media, budgets, customers, prices, transportation, and so on, to answer such questions as these:

How are sales going?

Should we add another field representative in the Twin Cities area?

Why did we lose the Tucker account to Consolidated?

How is Dave Faulkner working out in the Spokane territory?

How well did the full-page ad in the six metropolitan dailies pull?

Are we under or over budgeted expenses?

What changes should we plan in our rate schedule for next year?

Why are there so many back orders in the El Paso office?

How can we speed up shipping?

What can we do to decrease postal costs?

Marketing directors obviously could get the answers to some of these questions simply by picking up the telephone and asking various people for the information. In some instances, though, they cannot get the information they need in the form they need it through a phone call or even a personal visit. Thus they often must ask a responsible subordinate to "give me that information, please—in writing."

Although typical marketing directors or other business executives may give you some guidance in preparing a particular report, they seldom will "label" the kind of report they expect or tell you how to set it up. Even at the outset of your business career, the person asking you for a report will expect you to have an understanding of the mechanics of report writing and, more important, a fairly high level of skill in writing reports. Such an expectation may seem unreasonable, but it stems from a simple fact of business life: reports play a far more vital role in business management and involve more employees than do letters or other business communications. Many business workers, including high-level executives, who have limited responsibility for letter writing must write a great many reports of various types.

CLASSIFICATION OF REPORTS

Reports can be classified in a dozen different ways. In some reports the writer simply presents factual data, such as the inventory picture on a given date, and this is called an *informational report.* In other situations the writer analyzes a problem and offers recommendations for solving it—for example, data on high employee turnover and the writer's opinion as to what might be done about it. This type is usually referred to as a *recommendation report.* Some reports involve considerable research and investigation—perhaps requiring several weeks or months to complete—and the writer offers conclusions and recommendations based on the findings. This type of report is called an *analytical report* or an *investigation report* or a *research report.* An example is an in-depth market study to determine buying habits and preferences of customers in six regions of the country, with implications for future marketing strategy.

But to the typical business writer, classifications are meaningless, and we will discuss reports according to the form used in preparing them—informal and formal.

The following situations are examples of occasions for writing an informal report.

Case Example 1: Morrison Machinery Corporation pays its sales representatives a salary plus commission. The sales manager desires a monthly report showing commissions earned for the year to date compared with commissions earned during the same period of the previous year. At the top of page 261 is one such report. Though the writer used plain paper, an interoffice memorandum might also have been used.

Case Example 2: The president of the company likes to write a personal note to employees celebrating their fifth, tenth, fifteenth, and so on, anniversaries with the organization. At the end of each month, an information report (see bottom of next page) is prepared for him.

Case Example 3: In the first memorandum on page 262, the purchasing director, Alton T. Pratt, asks each department manager for a report on magazines received by employees for which the company pays the subscription.

Gathering the Information. To obtain the information she needs to write the report to Mr. Pratt, the Office Services Department manager (Jeanette Fordham) might write a memorandum to each supervisor in the department,

MORRISON MACHINERY CORPORATION

Summary of Commissions Earned
January 1-April 30, 19--

Sales Representative	This Year	Last Year	Increase	Decrease
Blank, C.	$4,657	$5,046		$ 389
Cord, L.	6,617	5,958	$ 659	
Dreyfus, J.	3,986	4,456		470
Espinoza, R.	5,566	6,437		871
Feingold, R.	7,094	6,493	601	
Tomaselli, F.	4,238	5,916		1,678
Young, R.	5,925	4,206	1,719	

Prepared by: *J. T. Williamson*
Distribution: C. T. Sousa, M. Blankenship, O. Flood, M. DeHarak,
R. P. Griffith, C. Lomax

Interoffice Memorandum

To	T. J. Courtney	From	Carmen Soriano
Dept.	Executive	Dept.	Executive
Subject	Employment Anniversaries	Date	March 20, 19--

The following employees will celebrate their employment
anniversaries during the month of April:

Name and Department	Anniversary
Collins, Andrew T. Payroll	April 4 (Fifth)
Holmes, Estelle (Mrs.) Executive	April 8 (Tenth)
Vincent, Carl Accounting	April 9 (Fifth)
Vincent, Pauline (Ms.) Marketing	April 16 (Fifth)

```
                                          Interoffice Memorandum
   _____

    To   Department Heads          From   Alton T. Pratt


  Dept.                            Dept.  Purchasing


  Subject  Magazine Subscriptions  Date   August 14, 19--



          Will you please help us make a roundup of the various magazines
          subscribed to by individuals in Morrison--that is, periodicals
          that are paid for by the company but received by individuals for
          their own use.

          Please give me the name of each periodical, the name of the sub-
          scriber, and the disposition of the magazine (retained by the em-
          ployee, thrown away, sent to the library, or whatever).  Do not
          include magazines that employees pay for themselves.

          Could I have the list for your department by September 1?

                                          ATP
```

adapting her memo from Mr. Pratt's. More than likely, though, she will simply photocopy Mr. Pratt's memo and write a brief covering memo such as this one:

```
                                          Interoffice Memorandum
   _____

    To   Mr. Prince   Mr. Cordoza    From   Jeanette Fordham
         Miss Welch   Mr. Yates
         Ms. Latham   Mrs. Zeldin
  Dept.                              Dept.  Office Services


  Subject  Magazine Subscriptions    Date   August 15, 19--



          Please read the attached memorandum from Alton T. Pratt, in which
          he asks for a report on paid magazine subscriptions for individual
          use.  Please let me have your list by August 25.

          I suggest that you use the following form.
```

		Disposition of Magazine			
Magazine	Subscriber	Keep	Discard	Library	Other

As soon as all the replies are received, Fordham will consolidate the information into a report like that shown on the next page.

Interoffice Memorandum

To Alton T. Pratt

Dept. Purchasing

Subject Magazine Subscriptions

From Jeanette Fordham

Dept. Office Services

Date August 27, 19--

Here is a report of the magazine subscriptions in the Office Services Department, which is in response to your memo of August 14.

Magazine	Subscriber	Keep	Discard	Library	Other
			Disposition of Magazine		
Administrative Aide	Barbara Latham			X	
Better Offices	Gabriel Cordoza			X	
Communication Digest	Barbara Latham				Cut up and filed
Computer News	Richard Yates H. R. Prince	X			Central files
Data Management	H. R. Prince		X		
Forecast	J. L. Fordham	X			
Management Science	J. L. Fordham Irene Welch	X	X		
Methods Analyst	J. L. Fordham Gabriel Cordoza		X X		
Modern Accounting	A. K. Zeldin H. R. Prince	X X			
Supervision	A. K. Zeldin				Ames Coll. Library
Systems Digest	J. L. Fordham	X			
Today's Secretary	Irene Welch			X	

You will see that there is some duplication of subscriptions. However, in those cases, the employee feels that it is important to have his or her own copy for clipping and for future reference. I agree.

JF

In gathering the information on production costs for the booklet *This Is Warner-Dennison* (see case problem on page 259), the writer sent the following letter to three different printing houses.

Gentlemen:

Would you please give me an estimate showing the composition, paper, printing, and binding costs for each copy of a new edition of <u>This Is Warner-Dennison</u>. Except as otherwise indicated by the following specifications, this new edition is to match the present booklet, a copy of which is enclosed.

1. 24 pages, 6 by 9 inches.
2. Line and halftone illustrations on each page (see present booklet for number and distribution).
3. Printed on 50-pound offset paper in two colors of ink.
4. Saddle-wire binding, 65-pound Monarch antique cover stock.
5. Printing quantity of 1,000 copies.

If you have questions about these specifications, please telephone me.

Sincerely yours,

SOLUTION A

Interoffice Memorandum

TO: Barbara L. Haskell   **FROM:** Nathan L. Frey

SUBJECT: Comparative Costs for Printing This Is Warner-Dennison   **DATE:** June 4, 19--

In answer to your memo of May 19, here are estimates of unit costs for composition, paper, printing, and binding of the booklet <u>This Is Warner-Dennison</u> submitted by suppliers Carleton, Froelich, and Rhodes.

	Carleton	Froelich	Rhodes
Composition	$0.492	$0.515	$0.541
Paper	0.015	0.020	0.025
Printing	0.112	0.121	0.130
Binding	0.072	0.081	0.090
TOTALS	$0.691	$0.737	$0.786

The specifications given to each printer were as follows:

1. 24 pages, 6 by 9 inches.
2. Line and halftone illustrations on each page.
3. 50-pound offset stock, printed in two colors throughout.
4. Saddle-wire binding, 65-pound Monarch antique cover.
5. Quantity of 1,000 copies.

Please let me know if you wish to have additional information or if you want me to get costs from other suppliers.

NLF

SOLUTION B

COMPARATIVE COSTS FOR PRINTING

THIS IS WARNER-DENNISON

PURPOSE

    To compare unit costs for composition, paper, printing, and binding of the This Is Warner-Dennison booklet as submitted by suppliers Carleton, Froelich, Rhodes.

SPECIFICATIONS

    Estimates were based on the following specifications:

1. 24 pages, 6 by 9 inches.

2. Line and halftone illustrations on each page.

3. 50-pound offset stock, printed in two colors throughout.

4. Saddle-wire binding, 65-pound Monarch antique cover.

5. Quantity of 1,000 copies.

COSTS

	Carleton	Froelich	Rhodes
Composition	$0.492	$0.515	$0.541
Paper	0.015	0.020	0.025
Printing	0.112	0.121	0.130
Binding	0.072	0.081	0.090
TOTALS	$0.691	$0.737	$0.786

Analysis of the Solutions. Either solution is satisfactory. Of the two forms shown, A is more common for an informational report. B will require a transmittal memo, addressed to Miss Haskell, like the one shown at the top of page 266.

TO:	Barbara L. Haskell	**FROM:**	Nathan L. Frey

SUBJECT: Comparative Costs for Printing **DATE:** June 4, 19—
This Is Warner-Dennison

The subject report is attached. Let me know if you need additional information.

Notice the following things about Solution A:

1. The clear statement of the subject in the heading and in the first paragraph and the reference to Miss Haskell's memo.
2. The description of the specifications each printer was supplied with (next to last paragraph), indicating the estimates are based on identical data.
3. The display of the three estimates so that Miss Haskell can quickly compare figures.

An Informal Recommendation Report. Employees are often asked for their suggestions for making the company a more efficient organization—recommendations for improving personnel practices, saving time and effort, cutting costs, serving customers more effectively, and so on. Often such reports are quite informal.

Case Example: The editor of Warner-Dennison's magazine, *Intercom,* has written a memo to all department heads asking for suggestions for improving the publication. There has been considerable criticism of the magazine, and the editor, Julia Sanchez, seeks recommendations for making it better.

SOLUTION A

TO:	J. R. Sanchez	**FROM:**	S. Colfax

SUBJECT: Suggestions for Intercom **DATE:** May 27, 19—

Although I have never been an editor or publisher, I hope you will permit me to offer suggestions for improving Intercom. I would leave the title as it is, but there ought to be more photographs, a "Letters to the Editor" column, a new masthead, a better typeface, more stories about typical workers, and a gossip column. Also, I think you might consider an Employee of the Month Award.

I hope these suggestions will be helpful.

SC

Analysis of Solution A. Solution A has several shortcomings:

1. The writer is guilty of excessive modesty in the opening sentence. There is no reason to make such a confession, especially since opinions were solicited by the editor.
2. The report starts off negatively. Although the request was for recommendations for improving *Intercom,* there would be no harm in starting off with some positive points.

3. The report is too general, too sketchy. Sanchez will be bewildered by some of the recommendations; they should be expanded.
4. The eight different suggestions would be more effective if they were grouped by subject and these subjects displayed as headings.

SOLUTION B

TO:	J. R. Sanchez	**FROM:**	S. Colfax
SUBJECT:	Intercom	**DATE:**	May 27, 19—

I am pleased to respond to your invitation to offer suggestions for Intercom.

First, let me say that there are many good things about Intercom. I like the informal style, the editorial quality, the "Shop and Swap" column, the "What's New in Books" feature, and many other things. But I know you want suggestions rather than praise, and mine follow.

Title

Although a new title for the magazine has been suggested, I believe it would be a mistake to change it. Everyone recognizes the publication by the name Intercom, and it still seems to me to be entirely appropriate.

Design

A new masthead would help, and I would like to see us engage a professional designer to do one. Indeed, this designer might be asked to give a new look to the entire magazine.

Photographs

More photographs would help—photographs of employees celebrating anniversaries, participating in athletics and hobbies, receiving special recognition, and so on.

Features

1. A "Letters to the Editor" column would be especially popular. It would have good readership and, at the same time, give employees a chance to "sound off" on their pet likes and dislikes.
2. After studying the issues for the past year, I feel that we have too many management stories and too few stories about the typical worker. It seems to me that this should be principally a publication for and about employees—not a management PR magazine.
3. I recommend that the magazine establish an Employee of the Month Award. A committee of employees would select this person on the basis of recommendations of supervisors and department heads. You might run the employee's picture with a brief biographical sketch and story about his or her special recognition.
4. Finally, I suggest that a monthly gossip column be added. This column would be light and whimsical—nothing scandalous, of course, but fun to read and laugh about.

If you wish, I'd be glad to discuss these recommendations further with you. Certainly, Intercom is an excellent instrument for communicating with employees, and I'm all for experimenting with ideas that will help to make it even better.

SC

Analysis of Solution B.   Obviously, Solution B is much better than A. Note how the writer has grouped the suggestions under four separate headings—Title, Design, Photographs, and Features—and has provided clear descriptions of each recommendation.

Projects

 Your boss, Barbara L. Haskell, has asked for a report on the number of physically handicapped people employed by Warner-Dennison and how their performance is rated by their superiors in terms of safety, attendance, and job performance. This information has been requested by the executive vice president, Calvin Gilmore, for a talk he is planning to give to a local civic organization. You are to supply whatever data you think will be helpful.

To get the information you need, you sent a questionnaire to all executives and department managers in the company asking them to give you the total number of handicapped workers employed in five categories—professional and technical, supervisory and management, clerical, craftsmen, and laborers—and to rate those in each category as above average, average, or below average. Following is the information you obtained.

Professional and technical: Total employed: 82. In terms of safety, 40 of these were rated above average, 41 average, and 1 below average. In terms of attendance, 33 were rated above average, 40 as average, and 9 below average. As to job performance, 32 were rated above average, 45 average, and 5 below average.

Supervisory and management: Total employed: 38. In terms of safety, 22 were rated as above average, 16 average, and 0 as below average. In terms of attendance, 16 were rated above average, 20 as average, and 2 below average. In job performance, 15 were rated above average, 21 average, and 2 below average.

Clerical: Total employed: 65. As to safety, 34 were rated as above average, 30 as average, and 1 below average. In terms of attendance, 35 were above average, 25 average, and 5 below average. In job performance, 27 were rated above average, 32 average, and 6 below average.

Craftsmen: Total employed: 110. In safety, 39 were rated above average, 67 as average, and 4 below average. In attendance, 40 were rated above average, 52 as average, and 18 as below average. As to job performance, 30 were considered above average, 60 as average, and 20 as below average.

Laborers: Total employed: 14. As to safety, 3 were rated above average, 10 as average, and 1 as below average. In terms of attendance, 4 were rated above average, 9 average, and 1 below average. Concerning job performance, 2 were rated above average, 8 average, and 4 below average.

Many of those reporting made enthusiastic comments about their handicapped workers. The most consistent reason given for the outstanding performance of these people is that they have a higher degree of motivation, presumably because they appreciate the opportunity to work.

Included in the handicapped category are people who are blind, partially sighted, and deaf, as well as amputees, paraplegics, and others crippled from various causes—polio, accidents, birth defects, etc.

Prepare the report as a memorandum.

(B) Following is an accountant's statement concerning financial operations of the Caldwell and Bonelli Company. Put the statement in the form of a report to the Executive Committee (a group of top executives).

Operations of the company for the month of March produced total revenues of $1,890,000, over budget by $147,000. Net operating profit was $289,000, over budget by $114,000. Almost all categories of expenses are performing more favorably than budgeted, resulting in favorable comparisons for gross margin and operating profit. Comparison with the same period last year reflects a sales increase of $314,000 and an NOP increase of $93,000, a rate which is 5.3 percent higher as a percentage of sales than the previous year.

Accumulative performance for the first quarter shows a slight under-budget condition of $58,000 in revenue. However, a revenue increase of $382,000 is shown when compared with the previous year. Net operating profit is $120,000 over budget and is $32,000 ahead of the previous year.

At March 31, Caldwell and Bonelli assumed complete responsibility for servicing both the Pump and Water Softening Divisions in all matters relative to purchasing, production, warehousing and shipping, and common accounting services activities. Common personnel administration also became effective during March. It is anticipated that significant dollar savings and higher levels of efficiency will be realized.

In the Pump Division, March revenues amounted to $940,000, which is $85,000 over budget. General Sales contributed $66,000 of the increase, with the balance of $19,000 coming from Service Contracts. Net operating profit of $109,000 is $84,000 over budget. All categories of expense performed as expected in relation to total revenue levels. Provision for uncollectible contracts reflects the monthly adjustment necessary to amortize the deferred expense created at the end of last year. Manufacturing costs appear high in relation to budget; however, we anticipate that a reasonable adjustment will be made as a result of a physical inventory taken at April 3. The physical inventory provides the basis for transfer to a perpetual system.

In the Water Softening Division, revenue exceeded budget and previous year by $34,300 and $162,565, respectively. The superior revenue performance can be attributed to a continuation of the interest of customers in the ecological and environmental factors that distinguish our line.

Expenses for March were well in line with budget except for advertising, factory wages, and dealer service. Although these expenses were well ahead of budget, comparable reductions in expenses of maintenance, overtime, and breakage brought the total to a favorable figure.

© You have been asked to write a memorandum recommending certain changes in company policy, practices, or procedures. The following subjects are possibilities. Make your own assumptions as to the current status in the company.

Improving Facilities and Services in the Company Library
Improving the Handling of Mail for Executives
Revising the Guide to Writing Company Letters
Boosting Employee Morale
Improving the Company's Public Relations
Improving the Company's Accounting System (or Marketing, Advertising, Data Processing, etc.)

You may wish to choose a subject that relates to the college you are attending—the bookstore, cafeteria, parking facilities, enrollment procedures, athletic program, student government, campus regulations.

Make your memo at least two pages long and supply visual guidelines.

© The senior personnel clerk has been complaining to you, her boss, about the need for all new typewriters in the department (there are seven). According to your records, four are three years old, two are two years old, and one was purchased eight months ago. You ask the clerk to give you a report on the condition of the typewriters so that you can make a decision about replacing them. Her report is as follows:

You asked for a report on the condition of the seven typewriters in my department. They are all old and inefficient. We are wasting time with this old equipment; there are new models available now that would pay for themselves in the increased speed and quality of work. I recommend that we buy all new typewriters.

What is wrong with the report?

CASE 2

WRITING MORE FORMAL REPORTS

PROBLEM

The executives of Warner-Dennison are constantly faced with the problem of locating people in the company who are qualified for management positions that become vacant. The firm has a strict policy of trying to promote people from within the company, rather than recruiting from the outside. All too often, however, when a management position becomes vacant, there is no one on hand who is really ready to fill it. The answer, nearly everyone believes, is an ongoing management development program.

The Long-Range Planning Committee, of which Miss Haskell is chairperson, has asked for a study of the situation and specific recommendations as to what should be done. Miss Haskell has asked you, as assistant personnel manager, to undertake such a study. You are to interview key executives in the company for their assessment of the problem and their ideas for solving it, look at management training programs in several other companies, and investigate training opportunities in nearby educational institutions. You will prepare a complete report, which will include your recommendations.

BACKGROUND

The situation described in the case problem is not unusual in larger organizations. Management constantly seeks information as a basis for making sound business decisions. For example: Should Warner-Dennison set up facilities to manufacture its own products, or should it continue to contract with outside manufacturers? Should the company try to market its products in foreign countries? What are the advantages of furnishing sales representatives with leased automobiles as compared with having them buy their own cars and be compensated on a mileage-rate basis? Is Warner-Dennison's retirement plan fair compared with the plans offered by similar companies? These are only a few of the big issues that arise constantly, and their answers must not be guessed at. They deserve careful investigation that will turn up hard data, thoughtful analysis of that data, and a plan of action based on the findings.

Topics of such weighty concern call for more than short memorandum reports. Often several weeks or months will be required to research and analyze such problems and present the results in a carefully written analytical report, which is somewhat formal in organization and content.

PARTS OF THE FORMAL REPORT

The typical formal report contains the following parts:

1. *Purpose*—why the report was prepared.
2. *Procedure*—how the data for the report was gathered.
3. *Body*—the "meat" of the report (what was found).
4. *Conclusions*—what the information presented means.
5. *Recommendations*—actions suggested by the writer as a result of the findings.

Some reports will have more than the five parts shown, and others will have fewer, depending on the nature of the study, the depth of the research, and the implications of the findings. Nearly all formal reports, however, will answer these questions: Why was it written? Where and how did the writer obtain the information? What did the writer find out? What are the implications of the information given?

DEFINING YOUR PURPOSE

The purpose of your report should, of course, be clear to you before you begin to gather your data. To make absolutely sure, state the purpose in your own words. After doing so, check it with the person who asked for the report, to make certain your objectives are in agreement. Too many writers fail to do this, and after they have completed their work, they find out that they didn't really understand what was wanted.

Generally speaking, under "Purpose" you will state why the report was written, for whom it is intended, and who authorized it. Thus:

PURPOSE

This report, prepared for the Long-Range Planning Committee (Barbara L. Haskell, chairperson), assesses management training needs in Warner-Dennison, presents possible sources of such training, and suggests courses of action for executives in the company to follow to meet the needs for management personnel.

GATHERING YOUR DATA

Once you are certain that you and the person who requested the report agree on what the objectives are, you are ready to think about gathering the data. After a second discussion with Miss Haskell, you decide that you will obtain information from four different sources:

1. Chief executives in the major divisions of the company who are most concerned with the subject of your report.
2. Others in the organization who are likely to have important input.
3. People in other companies who have operated successful management education programs.
4. Training specialists in nearby colleges, universities, and other educational institutions where such programs are likely to be available.

Reading. Your first step in gathering information is to do some reading. Find out if other studies have been made in the company and, if so, read them. Look for articles in professional journals and for textbooks and handbooks on the subject. Check footnotes and bibliographies for additional sources of information.

As you read, make notes on cards (4- by 6-inch cards are fine). By using cards, you can easily add new material, and you can organize your material in different ways. Be sure to identify the source of the material; you may want to quote from it, in which case you should give credit to the author and publication.

Interviewing. Once you have soaked up some learning on the subject of management training and have an idea of what you want to find out by talking to other people, you are ready to start your interviews. It's best to give advance notice to these people—either by memorandum or letter—setting a specific time for the interview.

In preparing for interviews, you may also want to design a brief questionnaire—either to leave with the interviewee or to use as your guide in asking questions. Certainly, you will want to have clearly in mind the type of information you seek, for you will be the "manager" of that person-to-person situation.

Again, be prepared to make notes. You won't be able to remember everything that is said; besides, by making notes you indicate to the interviewee that what he or she thinks is important to your study.

OUTLINING YOUR REPORT

Assume now that you have collected the information you need for your report. You have a small stack of cards on which you made notes from your reading, a larger stack (or a notebook) of notes taken from your discussions with various people, and perhaps a batch of completed questionnaires. After you have reread all these materials, you are ready to prepare a tentative outline of your report. Although you might have made an earlier rough outline to guide you in your reading and interviewing, you'll now have a better idea of what will go into your report, so you can be more specific.

Your very broad outline for this particular report might look something like this:

1. Purpose
2. Need
3. Scope
4. Procedure
5. Findings (the body)
6. Conclusions and Recommendations

Of course, you can't begin to write using such a general outline, but it is a good guide in arranging your materials. Eventually, you will want to set down a more detailed outline of the topics to be covered under each main heading. How detailed should this "final" outline be? Some writers work best when they make an exhaustive outline before they start to write; others claim that they work best from a broad outline—that the topics fall into place only when a rough draft of the narrative has been attempted. In any event, don't be a slave to any preliminary outline; all good writers change their minds many times as writing proceeds.

And it's a good idea to outline your material again after you have finished a rough draft of your report. Doing so will tell you whether your report is logically organized. Many report writers discover, after completing their writing and wrapping up the job, that some topics don't fit the headings or are out of sequence.

Purpose.   The purpose of your report should now be reviewed in the light of what you discovered in your investigation and, if necessary, revised. You shouldn't have to change it, however; and we will assume that the purpose stated earlier (page 272) is still all right.

Need.   In a situation such as this one, you will probably want a special heading, *Need*. After all, the circumstances that brought about the request for this study were based on the company's need for training programs to prepare people to accept management responsibility. We hasten to say that not all formal reports will require such a heading—for example, comparing three possible sites for a manufacturing plant. The report to Miss Haskell, however, will be more convincing if need is emphasized. For example:

NEED

Warner-Dennison is constantly faced with the problem of finding from among its employees people who are ready to accept management responsibility. Positions that are vacated because of promotions, transfers, retirement, and resignations often have to be filled with unqualified people. Time and again executives in the company, eager to adhere to the promote-from-within policy, have found a serious shortage of candidates and have been forced to recruit from the outside.

If the company is to continue with its present promotion policy, then a ready reservoir of talent must be available to fill management positions. In order to solve this problem, it seems likely that we must attack it as an educational problem. The company has many potential candidates for management, but most of them need additional education and training in order to compete with outsiders for these good jobs.

At the present time, management training at Warner-Dennison is a hit-and-miss proposition—left up almost entirely to individual executives and department heads, most of whom . . .

Under *Need,* as you see, we provide an appropriate setting for the discussion that is to follow. Once the recipients have read such a background statement, there should be no reason for them to ask the question, Why are we concerned about the subject of this report?

Scope.   The scope of the study refers to its boundaries—that is, the subjects it covers as well as the subjects it does not cover. (In scholarly papers this is sometimes called *limitations*.) Again, you won't always need this section, but in this situation it will be helpful. For example:

SCOPE

In this report we concentrate on the education and training of managers and executives—the areas where present needs seem to be most serious. Other types of training are important too—for clerical personnel, receptionists, correspondents, secretaries, sales representatives, and so on. However, training at these levels is not within the limits of this study.

Procedure.   Under *Procedure* you include background information such as the gathering of the data you will present. Here also you may wish to define some of the terms that you will use in the report. A possible outline of the *Procedure* section follows.

PROCEDURE

    Methods of gathering the information

        Library research
        In-company interviews
        Outside interviews (business firms)
        Outside interviews (educational institutions)
        Company reports
        Meetings, seminars, and conventions

    Definition of terms

        Education versus training
        Indoctrination programs
        Orientation programs
        Simulations
        Vestibule training
        The case method in management training
        Apprenticeship in management

As you prepare the outline of the material you want to present, you may decide that *Procedure* isn't the best heading—that perhaps *Introduction* is a better one, under which you would put all the material that was previously planned under the four separate headings, *Purpose, Need, Scope,* and *Procedure.* The point is that nothing is "fixed" until you have put your entire rough draft together; it is at that stage that you will sift your ideas and arrange them in the best sequence and under the most appropriate headings.

Findings. Outlining the findings—the body of your report—will be a little more challenging. Here you will draw upon all the notes you made, arranging and rearranging them in various topical sequences until you have a plan that suits you.

Here is a possible outline for the body of your report.

FINDINGS

    Status of training at Warner-Dennison

        Indoctrination
        Orientation
        Refresher
        On-the-job
        Supervisory
        Managerial

    Training needs in various divisions

        Corporate offices
        Marketing
        Manufacturing
        Finance and Accounting
        Personnel
        Purchasing

Management training in other companies

    American Safety Razor
    Westinghouse
    Firestone
    American Seating
    General Foods

Sources of management training

    In-company programs
    College and university courses
    Home study
    Apprentice opportunities
    Meetings and conventions

Conclusions and Recommendations. Depending on how you treat the *Findings* section of your report, you may decide to make your next heading *Conclusions.*

CONCLUSIONS

    Definite need for management training
    Approaches to solving the problem
    Opportunities in the company
    Opportunities outside the company

The conclusions may stand alone or be combined with the final heading in your report, *Recommendations.* The outline for the *Recommendations* section might look like this:

RECOMMENDATIONS

    Establishment of a company "attitude" and policy
    Appointment of a training director
    Specific training programs recommended
    Procedures for selecting trainees
    Enlargement of training facilities
        Classroom space
        Equipment
        Instructional staff
    Use of outside facilities
    Assessing the results

A portion of the recommendations for this report might appear as follows:

RECOMMENDATIONS

It is recommended that:

1. A genuine company commitment be given to the establishment of management training programs. This might begin with a meeting, chaired by the president, in which all operating executives would participate. Here the pro-

gram would be fully explained and the various problems discussed. From this meeting might evolve a written policy statement, so that all executives are aware that the program has top-management backing.

2. A training director be appointed. This individual should have a great deal of experience in management education (preferably in a business organization). It would be his or her job to coordinate all education efforts, organize and administer the program, select the faculty, evaluate results, and so on. This individual should report directly to the president.

3. Three separate management education programs be established: Principles of Effective Management, Operations Management, and Advanced Management.

Principles of Effective Management. This would be the basic program for everyone selected to participate in management education. Included in the curriculum would be such courses as Principles of Management, Marketing and Sales Management, Financial Management, Personnel Management, Basic Communications (including both writing and speaking), Supervision, and Production Management.

Operations Management. Those who have successfully completed the Principles program above (or who are qualified by previous experience) would be admitted to this program. Included in the curriculum would be such courses as Management Organization and Planning, Advanced Communications, Systems, Advanced Management Concepts, and Advanced Financial Management.

Advanced Management. This program would be restricted to those who have completed the two programs mentioned above. It would be operated by the case method. That is, complete cases of complex business situations would be presented, and in a seminar-type atmosphere, the participants would discuss the problems and arrive at various solutions. (There are several good case books written by graduate business school professors—Harvard, Stanford, Chicago, and so on.)

4. The following system be established for selecting management trainees in the . . .

INDUCTIVE VERSUS DEDUCTIVE ORGANIZATION

The outline we have just presented is called an *inductive* plan of organization. That is, we state the problem, show how we are going to approach it, discuss the problem in detail, and suggest ways in which it might be solved. In other words, we proceeded from the particulars to the general statement or conclusion.

A second plan of organization is *deductive*. The writer first states the results (summary, conclusions, recommendations) and then proceeds to present the back-up material that supports the results. Thus:

Inductive	*Deductive*
Introduction	Summary (conclusions and recommendations)
Body of the report	
Summary (conclusions and recommendations)	Introduction
	Body of the report

The deductive pattern is preferred by many executives, particularly those who must read many long reports and who want to get the main point quickly without having to wade through all the details first. Those who prefer the inductive pattern say that the conclusions reached by the writer may be so startling that the reader may develop a negative bias before learning why those particular conclusions were reached.

OTHER PARTS OF FORMAL REPORTS

Some formal reports have four additional parts: title page, table of contents, appendix, and bibliography.

Title Page. The title page typically contains four things: the title of the report, the name and title of the person or organization for whom the report was written, the name of the writer, and the date. The title page for the report we have been discussing might appear as shown on the next page.

Table of Contents. A table of contents is very helpful when your report is quite long and/or has several sections. It includes the major headings and important subheadings, along with page numbers. (See the table of contents illustrated on page 280.)

The Appendix. The appendix of a formal report contains supplementary documents that some readers may wish to see but which, if placed in the body, would hinder easy reading and reference. The appendix of our report might contain the following items:

1. Questionnaires used.
2. Additional tables, charts, and illustrations.
3. Copies of relevant letters written and received.
4. Excerpts from reports and other documents (such as curricula from college catalogs, pictures and descriptions of equipment, and classroom layouts).

Each item in the appendix should be labeled. For example:

Exhibit A. Questionnaire sent to company executives.

Exhibit B. Reprint of ''The Coming Crisis in Education'' from Forward, March 1976.

Exhibit C. Management curriculum from Creighton University catalog.

Exhibit D. Advertisement of Electron-Tutor (Educorporation).

Labeling appendix items makes it easy for the writer to refer to them in the report. For example:

Professor Becker of Harvard cites the universal problem of recruiting management talent (Exhibit B), suggesting that . . .

If the appendix contains many documents, the items should be listed as in a table of contents and placed in front of the exhibits.

```
          MANAGEMENT TRAINING IN WARNER-DENNISON

          An Assessment of Management Training Needs With
                 Recommendations for Executive Action






                          Prepared by

                       Richard C. Lennox
                    Assistant Personnel Manager
                     Warner-Dennison Company








                             For

                The Long-Range Planning Committee
                 Barbara L. Haskell, Chairperson

                        May 5, 19--
```

Bibliography.   The bibliography is a list of books, newspapers, magazines, reports, monographs, etc., that the author consulted when gathering the information for the report. It has two purposes:

1. To provide readers with additional references in case they would like to read further.
2. To acknowledge the work of the authors whose writings are listed.

The bibliography for our report might look like the one on page 281.

CONTENTS

ii

TIPS ON WRITING FORMAL REPORTS

The skillful report writer pays particular attention to tone and writing style, objectivity, specificity of data, and readability.

Tone and Writing Style. There is no hard-and-fast rule about tone and writing style in formal reports. Some people maintain that the use of the term *formal* as a classification implies an objective, impersonal style. Look at these two versions of the same idea:

```
                              BIBLIOGRAPHY

       Archibald, Oscar, "What Is a Manager?"  Management Digest, January
              1977, p. 46.

       Becker, Brenda T., and C. S. Silver, "The Coming Crisis in Education,"
              Forward, March 1978, p. 7.

       "The Great Rip-Off" (editorial), Management Science, May 2, 1977,
              p. 4.

       "Everyone Profits," The Wall Street Journal, September 16, 1978, p. 4,
              col. 2.

       Management Occupations, U.S. Department of Labor Publication No. 18,
              Washington, July 1978.

       Scott, W. C., et al., Education for Leadership, 2d ed., McGraw-Hill
              Book Company, New York, 1976.

       Trenier, Sara M., Rewarding Employees, LaSalle Press, Boston, 1978.
```

Informal: I heard over and over from the executives whom I talked with the complaint that the company doesn't seem interested in doing anything about education.

Formal: The executives interviewed expressed the opinion that there does not seem to be a genuine company commitment to management education.

The "informal" writer has made the statement very personal, while the "formal" writer is more objective.

What is the right tone and general writing style for a formal report? The only accurate answer to that question is, It all depends. Who is going to read the report? How important is the subject? What is the writer's position or authority? These questions must be answered before the appropriate style can be determined.

We can give you three generalizations about tone and general writing style in formal reports:

1. Reports on matters of great importance or that are based on considerable research and investigation are more formal in tone than those concerning routine matters.
2. Reports that travel upward, especially to top management, generally call for a more formal tone than those that travel laterally or downward.
3. Reports that are to be circulated outside the company are usually more formal in tone than those kept within the "family."

Your position in the organization and your authority to offer personal opinions on a given subject will have a bearing on style. The corporation treasurer, for example, can say something like the following with complete authority:

> There is no doubt in my mind but that another stock issue at this time would seriously weaken our position in the market. Therefore, I vote against it.

An assistant analyst in the financial division, however, lacking the treasurer's "muscle," would probably say something like this:

> Under the circumstances, it would seem unwise for the corporation to issue additional stock at this time, since doing so could weaken our position in the market.

In other words, the faith that readers have in the writer's opinion—based on his or her position, knowledge, and experience—will often determine style.

You will notice that in our various examples in the preceding pages we have leaned toward an impersonal style. This is because the writer, the assistant personnel manager, is presumed not to be an authority in management education and is carrying out an investigative assignment for the boss. The writer, then, is more likely to concentrate on evidence rather than opinion.

We mentioned earlier the trend toward an informal writing style, and we stand by our statement that in most of your communications you should inject your own personality. Formal reports, however, are usually an exception—at least for the beginner. But even in formal reports, you don't have to be dull and stodgy.

> ***Businessese:*** Articulation between the classroom and the employees' realm of responsibility is mandatory if management objectives are to be realized.

> ***Plain English:*** In order to reach our objectives, it is important that every trainee sees a definite relationship between classroom training and the job itself.

Objectivity.   No matter what tone you decide on for your reports, it is important that you let your reader know when you are stating a fact and when you are offering an opinion. Assume that during the week of the World Series, department managers reported 212 employee absences—three times the rate in a typical week. You are pretty certain that the reason for so many absences is that the World Series "interfered" with attendance, but you don't really know. You would *not* write:

> During the week of October 3, there were 212 employee absences. This is three times the rate in a typical week, and it is because the World Series was being played and the employees stayed home to watch it on television.

In the absence of hard data, you would probably write:

During the week of October 3, there were 212 employee absences—three times the rate in a typical week. The fact that the World Series was being played that week probably accounts for a number of these absences.

Although in the second example you have offered an opinion, it is stated as an opinion by use of the word *probably*. Yet the above example is not satisfactory either, because we don't know whose opinion it is. If it is solely the writer's, he should have said in the last sentence:

It's interesting to note that the World Series was being played that week, and I suspect this would account for a number of these absences.

If the writer was expressing opinions offered by the department managers reporting the absences, he would have said in the last sentence:

It's interesting to note that the World Series was being played that week, and most department managers think this accounts for a number of these absences.

Specificity in Reports.   Writers often confuse their readers when they are not specific in the facts or opinions offered. Let's take the example of the 212 employee absences during World Series week. Suppose you had reported the following:

During the week of October 3, there were 212 employees absent from work . . .

If this is true, there is nothing wrong with the statement, of course. But the phrase "212 employees absent" does not mean the same as "212 employee absences." The first phrase means that 212 different employees failed to show up for work some time during the week; the second allows for the possibility that some people were absent for more than one day and that only 50 or so different *people* were absent.

In the matter of specificity, make sure you avoid generalizations when you have specific details that you can use. If you are writing a report to your boss about the status of job descriptions in the Personnel file, don't say:

Most of the positions in Warner-Dennison are covered by job descriptions. Of these, some are satisfactory and some are not. But where descriptions are either inadequate or nonexistent, we are attempting to correct the situation.

when you can say:

There are 133 different positions in Warner-Dennison. Of these, 100 are covered by what I would call accurate job descriptions. Of the remainder, 20 positions have descriptions in various "states of inadequacy" (some don't show the changes in jobs since they were prepared; others were written poorly in the first place). Within the past 22 months, 13 new positions were created but lack specific descriptions. All in the last two categories mentioned are being worked on now, and I expect they will be finished by February 17.

Readability of Reports.   In writing your report, make it as easy as possible for the reader to grasp, with conviction, what you have to say. Following are suggestions for making your report readable.

Organization and Headings.   We have already looked at the essentials of choosing an organization plan (deductive versus inductive) and outlining the content of your report (pages 273–278). Remember, then, to organize your report in such a way that your readers are constantly with you. Visualize yourself as taking your readers firmly by the hand, guiding them from point to point, never letting go. Don't lure them into uncharted byways.

To make sure your readers stay with you, be generous with headings in the report. And make sure the headings show proper subordination. Minor points are correctly shown *under* major headings in the following:

POPULATION
> Total Population
> Regional Distribution
> Urban, Rural, Suburban, and Interurban Distribution

CONSUMER INCOME
> Nature and Scope of Income
>> National Income
>> Personal Income
>> Discretionary Income
> Income Distribution

When you have several minor headings under a major heading, it's a good idea to introduce them—in other words, tell your readers what you're going to tell them and then tell them. Thus:

METHODS OF APPRAISING MORALE

The generally recognized methods of appraising morale include:

1. The supervisor's or executive's impressions
2. The guided interview
3. The unguided interview
4. Analysis of production
5. The ''listening-in'' process
6. The questionnaire

The Supervisor's or Executive's Impressions
Relatively few supervisors or executives are trained observers of morale. They usually know how to get things done . . .

Pay particular attention to parallelism in headings. For example:

Right	Wrong
Major Causes of Turnover	Major Causes of Turnover
Reduction of Turnover	How to Reduce Turnover
Results of Reduced Turnover	Reduced Turnover Saves Money

Word Choice. Keep it simple. Don't try to exhibit the breadth of your vocabulary in your report. Choose the plain words and straightforward expressions that nearly everyone understands.

Sentences and Paragraphs. Keep your sentences relatively short and uncomplicated. Avoid the extremes of too many short, choppy sentences on the one hand and, on the other, long, involved sentences that demand the reader's utmost concentration.

Don't be afraid to paragraph. Practice varying the length of paragraphs, remembering that a fairly brief opening and a short closing paragraph are more likely to gain the reader's attention.

Coherence. Your report will hang together for the reader if you provide transitional words and phrases between sentences and paragraphs. Your reader is more likely to stay with you if you use such bridges as *in addition, too, on the other hand, moreover, in the second place, therefore, however, yet,* and so on.

Margins and Spacing. Be generous with your margins. Allow at least 1 inch for the top and bottom margins, but start chapter or section headings 2 inches from the top of the page. For generous side margins, type the copy to a 6-inch line length. And make sure to use the same margins consistently throughout a report.

Because double spacing is easier to read, we recommend that you use it for most of your reports—even longer ones. Indent paragraphs at least five spaces.

Pagination. Number all pages except those that precede your introduction (such as a title page). Place the number on the seventh line at the right margin.

Illustrations. Provide illustrations (maps, charts, tables, graphs, drawings, diagrams, etc.) when they will help your reader understand what you are talking about. When your report contains a great many figures, try to find ways to put them in tables and charts. Your report will be hard to read (and dull to most people) if your narrative contains a great many figures. Compare the narrative presentation below with the tabular arrangement that follows.

As to advertising expenditures by media, in 19— we spent $15,000 on newspapers and magazines; $8,500 on radio and television; $18,000 on direct mail; $7,700 on transit advertising; $17,000 on premiums; and $6,400 on billboards. In 19— we spent $18,000 on newspapers and magazines; $10,500 on radio and television; $21,000 on direct mail; $3,500 on transit advertising; $12,000 on premiums; and $9,800 on billboards.

Advertising Expenditures	19—	19—
Newspapers and Magazines	$15,000	$18,000
Radio and Television	8,500	10,500
Direct Mail	18,000	21,000
Transit Advertising	7,700	3,500
Premiums	17,000	12,000
Billboards	6,400	9,800
Totals	$72,600	$74,800

Binding the Report.   Formal reports are usually bound. The elegance of the binding depends on the importance of the report and the impression you want to make. Some short reports are not bound at all but merely stapled at the left side (at least three staples, affixed vertically, are recommended). Others are housed in an elaborate cover and bound with comb plastic; and still others are hole-punched and placed inside a folder-type report binding. Stationery stores stock a wide variety of bindings, and companies that prepare a great many reports for clients develop their own special bindings.

Letter of Transmittal.   Generally speaking, bound formal reports will require a letter of transmittal.

INTEROFFICE MEMORANDUM

TO: Long-Range Planning Committee (see below)   **FROM:** Barbara L. Haskell

SUBJECT: Management Education Report   **DATE:** May 6, 19—

Here is a copy of "Management Training in Warner-Dennison," a report prepared by Richard C. Lennox at my request. I urge you to read it carefully, for I consider it an excellent study.

Please be prepared to discuss this report at the June 16 meeting of the Long-Range Planning Committee. In the meantime, if you have comments or suggestions, I would be pleased to have them.

                                            BLH

Distribution: Knudsen, Louderbush, Katz, Pico, Wojinski, Meagher

Projects

(A)   The following report was prepared at the request of Charles S. Fauxhall, president of Romeo Spice Company. Mr. Fauxhall said to the sales manager, Marion T. Hotz, "How is the new car-leasing arrangement working out?

Please give me a report on your experience to date (including costs) and your opinion on what the future looks like. I want several people in the executive group to have this information."

Hotz prepared the following report. Organize the information as a formal report, making whatever changes in content you think appropriate. The style should be somewhat casual since the report is fairly routine and comes from a responsible executive.

INTEROFFICE MEMORANDUM

TO:	Mr. Charles S. Fauxhall	**FROM:**	Marion T. Hotz
DEPT:	Executive	**DEPT:**	Sales
SUBJECT:	Car-Leasing Plan— A View of the First Eight Months	**DATE:**	May 16, 19—

At the conclusion of our first eight months in operation, we have 305 cars on lease from Lacy Corporation (302 are in operation and 3 are surplus—1 in St. Louis, 1 in Los Angeles, and 1 in Memphis). As far as we can determine, only three were lemons—an Indomitable, a Fearless, and a Mariah. Our relations with Lacy are excellent. They handle our requests rapidly and we have had a barely noticeable number of complaints from the field. In the case of the three lemons, information was forwarded immediately to district warranty people or to the service dealer who quickly corrected whatever was wrong.

During the first eight months, the average mileage per person per month was 1,625 on business and 368 personal for a total of 1,993. Annualized, that would be an equivalent of 19,500 business miles and 4,400 personal miles per car.

The running expense per car-month, including gas, oil, maintenance and repairs, tires, and tire repairs, was $68.50, or 3.43¢ per mile. The standing expense, including rental less depreciation, provision for depreciation, depreciation adjustment on cars sold, licenses, and taxes, insurance, accident and theft loss, and some miscellaneous items, is $115 per car-month, or 5.80¢ per mile. For instance the cost of parking, storage, washing, and tolls was $15 per car-month, or 0.75¢ per mile. The total cost of the operation, as credited to us after payment made by drivers on their personal use of the cars, was $177 per car-month, or 8.87¢ per mile. The cost per mile for business usage was 10.9¢. An added item of interest—these 300 cars averaged 13.3 miles per gallon of gas; 1,250 miles per quart of oil; or a cost per gallon of gas of 61.6¢ and a cost for a quart of oil of 81.5¢.

Looking ahead to the coming year, our rental will decline by 6¼% or so per month due to aging and our fixed charges will be less. The maintenance will probably go up as the cars become older. We are told that the new models will be approximately $150 more per car and that the manufacturers have discontinued their fleet allowance of $50–$150. This additional cost would be offset by lower cost of money—thus we will be saving on interest and a higher trade-in value on more expensive cars.

We propose to change the reimbursement plan to take care of the increased operating cost for those people driving their own cars. This plan, you will recall, was effective for those driving 5,000 miles per year whose jobs required them to do so. The present plan provided 4¢ per mile for the first 14,000 miles, 5¢ per mile for the next 4,000 miles, 6½¢ per mile for everything over 18,000, plus $720 a year for depreciation and actual insurance costs.

We plan to introduce a change which would eliminate the 4¢-per-mile bracket and would pay 5¢ per mile for 18,000 miles. Such a plan would cost the company, based on current travel in this class, approximately $17,000.

That expense may be offset by a proposal that the members of the Lacy car-lease plan who are now paying the company 4¢ per mile for private use of the car have that charge increased to 5¢ per mile, which is a more realistic figure. Based on personal travel in the range of one million miles, it will reduce the cost of the paragraph above in the amount of $10,000 and result in an overall cost to the company of $7,000.

We are planning to establish a new account on the monthly statement of expense for car expenses. This will carry the actual expenses during 19—, moving them from the Travel and Entertainment account. It isn't possible to budget this in 19—, and, therefore, it will show expenses only. With that experience behind us, we will be able to budget for 19— at the appropriate time.

Ⓑ Educademy offers educational programs by means of correspondence (home study). Last year the school launched a new Computer Programming course (COBOL Language), placing advertisements for the course in eight men's and women's special interest and general consumer magazines. By the end of March 19—, over a thousand inquiries (coupons) had been received from readers who wanted additional information about the course. After mailing a catalog and other promotion literature, Educademy turned over the coupons to its sales representatives who were to contact in person the people who responded to the advertisements. However, there were 682 respondents who did not enroll, and Educademy was curious as to whether they had received satisfactory information about the course from the school; whether they were actually called on by an Educademy representative, and if so, whether the representative was courteous, informative, and helpful; why the respondents failed to enroll for the course; and what the respondents were like—occupation, age, income, education, etc. This information, it was felt, would be helpful to Educademy in learning something about the people who responded to the ads, in determining whether it had chosen the appropriate media for advertising the course, and in evaluating the efficiency of its follow-up mail and direct selling efforts.

The decision was made to send a questionnaire on April 15 to each of the 682 people who responded to the advertisements but failed to enroll, in an attempt to get answers to those four questions. The mailing consisted of a covering letter, a two-page questionnaire, and a stamped return envelope. The cutoff date of May 30 was established for the return of the questionnaires, and by that date 114 questionnaires had been completed and returned to Educademy (nearly 17 percent!).

The eight magazines used for advertising were *Redbook, Popular Mechanics, Modern Romances, Cosmopolitan, Sporting News, Popular Science, Esquire,* and *True Story.* The rate of return varied considerably for each magazine. The returns for three of the magazines—*Modern Romances, Sporting News,* and *Esquire*—were too few to allow Educademy to draw any conclusions.

Following are the details of the study. Each figure in the Percent Returned column has been rounded off to the nearest whole number.

Magazine	Total Questionnaires Mailed	Total Questionnaires Returned	Percent Returned
Redbook	153	34	22
Popular Mechanics	123	15	12
Modern Romances	109	2	11
Cosmopolitan	99	17	17
Sporting News	20	5	25
Popular Science	108	18	17
Esquire	74	9	12
True Story	86	14	16

Of the *Redbook* readers who responded to the questionnaire, 88% received literature from Educademy about the Computer Programming course. An Educademy representative had contacted 56%; the representative was generally rated as courteous, informative, and helpful. The primary reasons for not enrolling in the course were: (1) "Can't afford the course right now" and (2) "Not enough spare time." Of the total respondents, 61% were between 19 and 34 years of age, 28% between 35 and 44 years of age, and 11% over 44. As to education, 77% were high school graduates, 15% were college graduates, and 8% did not complete high school. Of the respondents, 54% were married and many had 1, 2, or 3 children at home; 70% were female. The most common responses to the question, "What is your occupation?" were "student," "secretary," and "homemaker." As to income, 38% had an income under $7,500, 39% between $7,500 and $10,000, and 23% over $10,000.

Of the *Popular Science* respondents, all received literature from Educademy about the Computer Programming course; half of them had been called on by an Educademy representative, who was rated as courteous, informative, and helpful. Primary reasons for not enrolling were: (1) "Not enough spare time," (2) "Want resident course rather than correspondence," and (3) "Want FORTRAN language instead of COBOL." Of the respondents, 45% were between 19 and 34 years old, 27% between 35 and 44, and 28% over 44. All were male. Of those who answered the questionnaire, 76% had a high school education, 12% were college graduates, and 12% did not finish high school; 51% were single. Occupations listed included student, bookkeeper, laborer, computer programmer, mechanic, and military serviceman. As to income, 38% received an income under $7,500, 31% between $7,500 and $10,000, and 31% over $10,000.

Of the *Cosmopolitan* readers who responded to the questionnaire, 94% had received literature from Educademy about the Computer Programming course, and 65% were contacted by an Educademy representative. The representative was generally rated as being courteous, informative, and helpful. Reasons given for not enrolling in the course were: (1) "Can't afford the course right now," (2) "Want a resident course," and (3) "Don't have the time." Of the respondents, 59% were 19 to 34 years of age, 26% were between 35 and 44 years old, and 15% over 44; 67% were female; 59% had a high school education, 23% did not finish high school, and 18% were college graduates; 62% were single. The most frequent occupations listed were homemaker, secretary, teacher, and student. As to income, 23% had an income of less than $7,500, 37% of between $7,500 and $10,000, and 40% of over $10,000.

All *Popular Mechanics* readers who responded said they had received literature from Educademy about the Computer Programming course. Of those who responded, 67% had been called upon by an Educademy representative, who was rated as courteous, informative, and helpful. Primary reasons given for not enrolling in the course were: (1) "Can't afford the course right now," (2) "Want a degree program," and (3) "No help to future ambitions." Of the respondents, 67% were between 19 and 34 years of age, 23% were between 35 and 44, and 10% were over 44. As for education, 87% had a high school education, 7% were college graduates, and 6% did not complete high school; 40% were single. Occupations mentioned were clerk, store manager, secretary, technician. As to income, 33% earned less than $7,500 a year, and the same percentage had an income between $7,500 and $10,000. The rest (34%) earned over $10,000.

Of the *True Story* respondents, 85% had received literature from Educademy about the Computer Programming course. Only 21% of the respondents were called on by an Educademy representative, who was generally rated as courteous, informative, and helpful. Reasons given for not enrolling were: (1) "Can't afford the course right now," (2) "Course not fully explained," and (3) "Didn't receive enough information about the course." Of the respondents, 90% were between 19 and 34 years of age, 10% were between 35 and 44; 94% were female. Of those who answered, 85% had a high school education and none were college graduates; 63% were married; several had children at home. Occupations mentioned were homemakers, clerk, and stenographer; several were unemployed. As to income, 64% had an income of less than $7,500, 25% had an income between $7,500 and $10,000, and 11% over $10,000.

From these data, the advertising manager of Educademy concluded that although the returns were not heavy, from them she got a better "feel" for the prospect. She also believed that the five magazines represented in the final tabulations were good media to use for the Computer Programming course. Her analysis of the demographic factors (age, education, income level, etc.) led her to believe that the group was appropriate for the course advertised.

She was encouraged that the representatives were rated by everyone as courteous, informative, and helpful. She gathered from this that they had the necessary knowledge and enthusiasm to sell the course.

The advertising manager was surprised at the percentage of women who responded to the advertising. She and others had felt that the primary market was male.

She was most distressed by the fact that so many prospects were not being called on (in one case, only 21%).

Based on her analysis, the advertising manager felt that several proposals could be made. In the first place, she wants to continue to advertise in the five magazines from which she made tabulations but to give up the others. Even those five, however, she wants to evaluate constantly for results. She thinks that follow-up studies such as this should be conducted periodically to guide the school in the future, for changes not only in the product but also in promotion methods.

She wants to slant future advertising and promotion to women.

Finally, she feels strongly that the school should reemphasize to its representatives the importance of calling on prospects and wonders if a monthly bulletin on the subject should be issued to the representatives.

Prepare a report from the data given. Assume that it will be given to the Director of Marketing, Kenneth L. Bradshaw.

What format will you use? Either of those discussed and illustrated in Case 1 would be appropriate—the decision is yours.

(C) Write the following in a more formal, impersonal tone.

1. I think we should first find out why dealers are returning so many lawn mowers this spring.
2. Of course, we will look only at people who have the experience these jobs call for.
3. It's clear to me, based on the interviews I've had with top people here, that we've got to find a better way to compensate our executives.
4. I think the first step we should take is to make a careful audit of our supervisors to find out what they think the needs are for a training program.
5. I will continue my daily check on the efficiency of this new installation and report to you at the end of October—earlier if something important develops.
6. Would you like a further breakdown on the inventory situation in Dayton and Chattanooga? I have the information and can get it to you quickly.
7. When the figures arrive from Harrison, I'll be in a better position to make an accurate long-range forecast for you.
8. This is about as far as I can go until our committee meets again in December, after which I will report in more detail.

REPORTING MEETINGS
AND CONFERENCES

PROBLEM

Miss Haskell has suggested you as a member of the Forms Standardization Committee, a group recently formed to study ways of saving time and money through more intelligent design, use, and distribution of company forms. At the first meeting of the committee, you were appointed secretary, with the responsibility for making sure the meeting place is properly arranged, each meeting is announced, and minutes are distributed after the meeting is over.

BACKGROUND

Although meetings are often joked about as necessary evils—nearly all executives think they attend too many—it would be difficult, if not impossible, to run a business without them. Often meetings provide the only face-to-face opportunity for key people in an organization to communicate with each other.

A meeting can be any kind of get-together—from a conversation between two people to a convention attended by thousands. An executive who refers to "those meetings," however, is probably talking about meetings of committees he or she belongs to, usually made up of from half a dozen to twenty or so people.

Nearly every organization has several committees that meet frequently. These committees are of two types: standing committees and ad hoc committees. Standing committees are permanent; the membership changes from time to time, but the committee stands. Ad hoc committees are formed to do a specific job and are dissolved when that job is over. Typical of an ad hoc committee is one appointed to direct a company drive for Community Chest funds. When the drive ends, the committee disbands.

Planning the Meeting. When meetings are unpopular with the people who attend them, the reason is probably poor planning in the first place. Everyone resents wasting time, and some meetings are notorious time wasters. A meeting worth being called is worth being planned. Planning includes (1) keeping each participant informed about time and place of the meeting, (2) preparing and distributing an agenda, (3) setting up the meeting room, and (4) seeing that the necessary materials and equipment are provided.

Keeping Participants Informed. Everyone who is to attend a meeting must be informed about the time, place, and program. The effective chairperson will give special attention to those who have an assigned part in the program and will review each presentation in advance. In reviewing the presentations, the chairperson will check how long each is likely to take, whether discussion will follow the presentation and who will moderate it, the types of visuals and other audience aids that may be used, and how the meeting will be run. If nothing else, such a premeeting conference will let each program participant know that the chairperson is in command and expects all participants to do their part.

Alerting each participant is not a one-shot affair that takes place the day before the meeting. It should start right after the previous meeting—or as soon as the planning of the next program begins—and continue right up until the day of the meeting. A final check by telephone—"Are you all set for the meeting this afternoon?"—is quite in order. The chairperson can't forget that people get so wrapped up in their own jobs that a meeting seems an interruption in their regular routine, even when they are to have an important part in it.

The Agenda. Every meeting that is held on a regular schedule should have an agenda—that is, a list of topics to be discussed and the names of those who are to present them. An agenda gives purpose and direction to a meeting and gives a meeting more importance in everyone's eyes.

The agenda for a typical committee meeting can be an informal document, taking any form the chairperson or committee secretary chooses. Here is one type.

FORMS STANDARDIZATION COMMITTEE

Agenda for October 29, 19—

Skyline Room, 10:30 a.m.

1. Data processing installation study
   R. C. Cox

2. Personnel forms
   Sol Slater

3. Stock-control forms simplification study
   C. R. Wilkes

4. New letterhead design
   Nina Bracher

5. Reduction of composition costs
   Tom Curtis

6. Filing problems created by new forms
   Millie Fein

7. Carbon packs vs. padded forms
   Arthur Hobbs

8. Visit to Pitney-Bowes
   R. C. Cox

R. C. Cox, Chairperson

The Meeting Room. Meetings of standing committees are usually held in the same place each time, and it isn't necessary to remind people about it. However, when there is a change, it's up to the chairperson or the committee secretary to see that everyone is notified in advance. One way to do this is to put the new meeting place on the agenda and call attention to it by some device such as an arrow or the words "Note new meeting place."

Obviously, the place for a meeting should be well-suited to the purpose. But if the room isn't suitable, there is not much anyone can do about it in a business office—one has to take whatever is available. (Hotel and other commercial meeting rooms are another matter; usually something *can* be done about it.) The chairperson or committee secretary can see to it, however, that there are plenty of chairs, that all the lights are working, and that the room is well-ventilated. By inspecting the room an hour or so before the meeting (or as soon as it is vacant), the chairperson can check that there are clean ashtrays in ample quantity, a dust- and litter-free table, a clean chalkboard with plenty of chalk and an eraser, and so on.

Materials and Equipment. When special equipment is needed for a meeting, it is usually up to the person who is going to use it to look after these needs. Even so, the committee chairperson should volunteer to help. Film projectors, tape recorders, and other equipment requiring electric outlets will deserve special attention. The distance between the machine and the nearest outlet has often created havoc until someone dug up an extension cord. Many a meeting has been spoiled because the outlet was DC and the equipment for AC. Some visual aids require a darkened room, and the person who wants to show a film freezes in discovering too late that the windows have no blinds. Users of projection equipment often discover to their dismay that there is no screen or that the room is too small for the equipment. Even worse is the discovery that the operator engaged to run the film projector forgot to show up, whereupon several self-styled experts hover over the machine trying to thread the film and get "the thing going." And so on. Any crisis can happen when visual equipment is to be used, and the alert chairperson or committee secretary plans ahead to see that it doesn't!

Most meeting rooms have a chalkboard, and chalk and erasers must be on hand. It is not easy to predict whether the chalkboard will be used during a meeting—it's a spur-of-the-moment visual aid—but it is amazing how many meetings are held up while someone goes in search of chalk or an eraser.

The committee secretary should supply writing paper and a pencil or two for each participant in a meeting and should distribute other materials that will be needed—reports, books, and other printed materials.

Taking the Minutes. The secretary usually records the minutes of meetings of important committees. Minutes furnish a record of decisions reached and action taken, remind participants of things to be done, provide a historical record for the company, keep top management and others informed, and pinpoint responsibility for recommendations and actions.

If you are to take the minutes, it is wise to study the agenda carefully beforehand and to learn the names of the committee members. If the people in the group are strangers to one another, try to get the names of the participants beforehand, and then prepare stand-up name cards and arrange them at various places. (A sample stand-up name card is shown at the top of the next page.)

If you are unable to get the names of the people beforehand and the group is fairly small, make a rough seating chart after you get to the meeting; then fill in the names as quickly as you hear them.

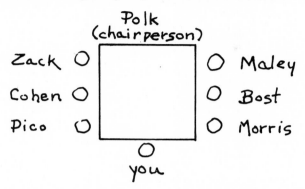

If the group is very large and it is important to know who said what, ask the chairperson to have each person identify himself or herself when making a statement.

Recording the Minutes.   The recorder must be a discriminating notetaker, listening for key ideas and writing just enough to get the main points the speaker is making. For example:

What the Speaker Said	*What the Recorder Wrote*
I see very little to recommend a change in policy that requires committee approval of all forms before they are printed. People have a natural tendency to develop a form for every purpose, and it isn't very long before we've got a stockroom full of forms that nobody uses. Just to let people know that any form they design for official use must be approved by a committee is a healthy thing and serves three basic purposes: it helps to cut down the number of forms designed in the first place, it simplifies the filing problem, and it saves time and money.	RCC: No need to change policy requiring committee approval of forms. Committee approval accomplishes three purposes: 1. Cuts down number of forms 2. Simplifies filing 3. Saves time and money

Writing Up the Minutes.   Minutes of meetings can take several different forms.

The Heading.   There are only two rigid rules about the heading of the minutes: it should contain the date of the meeting and the name of the committee or group. Here is one type of heading:

Warner-Dennison Company

Minutes of Meeting, October 29, 19—

Here is another. Note the omission of the company name; it really is unnecessary since minutes are usually distributed only within the company.

MINUTES

Forms Standardization Committee

October 29, 19—

Minutes are often prepared on interoffice memorandum forms, in which case the heading might appear as follows:

WARNER-DENNISON COMPANY
Interoffice Memorandum

TO: Forms Standardization **FROM:** R. C. Cox,
Committee Chairperson
cc: L. Nugent, P. Weinberger
S. Ellis, J. Katzenbach

SUBJECT: Minutes of Meeting, **DATE:** October 30, 19—
October 29, 19—

The Body.　The style of the minutes themselves is also a matter of individual preference. In choosing the style, the recorder must consider the form that will be most useful for reference purposes.

Obviously, the topic discussed and/or the name of the person presenting it should be displayed in some way. By and large, the topic is more important than the person, but there may be exceptions. The safe way is to display both the topic and its discussion leader. It is also a good idea to number the topics so that they may be easily referred to by number in any subsequent communications (you may remember that the topics on an agenda are numbered). Some recorders like to identify the topic in the margin like this, because it stands out.

1. Data Pro- Ranier Consultants' report on data processing will be com-
cessing pleted by December 12. The preliminary report indicates they
Installa- will recommend a computer installation for customer billing
tion Study and payroll. RCC will give full report . . . .
(R.C.Cox)

But because this arrangement eats up space, others prefer a regular heading like this:

1. Data Processing Installation Study (R. C. Cox)
Rainer Consultants' report on data processing will be completed by December

12. The preliminary report indicates they will recommend a computer installation for customer . . . .

Even in meetings where there is no set program and the discussion is free-for-all, it is wise to assign topic headings to major issues being discussed. Remember that minutes ought to be useful for reference purposes.

When discussion follows a presentation, its summary appears below the presentation like this:

1. Data Processing Installation Study (R. C. Cox)   Rainer Consultants' report on data processing will be completed by December 12. The preliminary report indicates they will recommend a computer installation for customer billing and payroll. RCC will give full report . . . .

Discussion   Mr. Hobbs asked how much time would be allowed for converting present procedures to computers. Mr. Cox estimated six months to a year.

Miss Fein's question about provisions for training present personnel in the new procedures was answered in this way: Training sessions will be set up, by department, and these will continue for as long as they are needed. Special instructors from IBM will be engaged.

SOLUTION

The minutes of the meeting of the Forms Standardization Committee are shown on pages 298–299.

Analysis of the Solution. Note the following points concerning the minutes illustrated:

1. The items that were listed on the agenda (page 293) are given the same numbers on the minutes.
2. Names of people who made presentations or who contributed to the discussion are given.
3. Note that Item 3, although not discussed at the meeting because of department reorganization, is accounted for.
4. Observe that all assignments given out at the meeting are carefully documented.
   a. Item 1 (RCC will prepare a full report and present it at a meeting of all department heads.)
   b. Item 3 (CRW promised a report for the December meeting.)
   c. Item 6 (Mr. Cox will issue the invitation.)
   d. Item 7 (Mr. Hobbs is to gather data and report at the January meeting.)
   e. Item 8 (CRW, NB, RWZ, and RCC will drive their cars.)

```
                          MINUTES
                Forms Standardization Committee
                       October 29, 19--

 1.  Data Processing      Ranier Consultants' report on data processing will be
     Installation         completed by December 12.  The preliminary report in-
     Study                dicates they will recommend a computer installation
        (R. C. Cox)       for customer billing and payroll.  RCC will give full
                          report to department heads when study is completed.

     Discussion           Mr. Hobbs asked how much time would be allowed for
                          converting present procedures to computers.  Mr. Cox
                          estimated six months to a year.

                          Miss Fein's question about provisions for training
                          present personnel in the new procedures was answered
                          in this way:  Training sessions will be set up, by
                          department, and these will continue for as long as
                          they are needed.  Special instructors from IBM will
                          be engaged.

 2.  Personnel Forms      All personnel forms have been standardized.  All
        (Sol Slater)      department managers solicited suggestions on the new
                          forms and composite forms submitted in Varitype
                          form.  The most controversial form was the Personnel
                          Change Notice (5090) and especially the items under
                          "Separation."  However, the revision seems to be
                          generally acceptable.  Not everyone agrees on the
                          form and content of all the newly designed forms,
                          but all agreed to experiment with them and keep a
                          record of their suggestions.

 3.  Stock-Control        Department reorganization caused the delay of the
     Forms Simpli-        study.  CRW promised a report for the December meeting.
     fication Study
        (C. R. Wilkes)

     Discussion           Mr. Cox asked whether a methods analyst is being con-
                          sidered as a staff addition, and CRW replied that
                          Miss Ethyl Aschner, formerly of Data Control Inc.,
                          has been employed.

 4.  New Letter-.         The new letterhead design was displayed and enthusi-
     head Design          astically endorsed by the Committee.  NB indicated
        (Nina Bracher)    that a second color, in addition to black, is still
                          to be chosen and several are being considered.  Gold
                          seems to have the edge at the moment.

 5.  Reduction of         We should consider cold type (Varitype) for all forms
     Composition          composition.  It is about half the cost of machine
     Costs                composition and is quite attractive.  We accepted the
        (Tom Curtis)      Varitype composition shown.  The easily adjusted type
                          line for typewriter spacing is the biggest advantage.
                          Another way to cut composition costs is to reduce the
                          number of typefaces.
```

5. The minutes show the plans for the next meeting, a good way of giving advance notice.

6. The names of all committee members should appear somewhere. The minutes on this page and the next illustrate one way of listing them. Here may also be noted those who were absent from the meeting.

Before the copies of the minutes are distributed, the committee secretary can underline or circle in red on each member's copy that person's assignments. For an example, see the illustration at the bottom of page 299.

Discussion	Mr. Hobbs asked about flexibility in terms of composition schedules, and TC said that assurance has been given by Foley Letter Shop that schedules will definitely be met.
	Mr. Wilkes feels that the readability of Varitype is not so good as machine composition. (The Committee felt that this was not a problem since there is no "continuity reading.")
6. Filing Problems Created by New Forms (Millie Fein)	Most people who design forms do not consider the problems created for Records Maintenance when forms are improperly designed. Size of the form and layout of the top portion of the form are particular problems. MF suggested that Mrs. Roach, in Records Maintenance, be invited to inspect and approve all forms when they are designed.
Discussion	It was recommended by Mr. Cox, and approved by the members, that Mrs. Roach be invited to become a member of this Committee. Mr. Cox will issue the invitation.
7. Carbon Packs vs. Padded Forms (Arthur Hobbs)	Recent studies in the company have shown that carbon packs are definite time-savers over padded forms. AH recommends that all frequently used forms be printed in carbon packs.
Discussion	The Committee feels that we do not have sufficient cost information on which to base a decision. Mr. Hobbs is to gather data and report at the January meeting.
8. Visit to Pitney-Bowes (R. C. Cox)	The visit to Pitney-Bowes is scheduled for December 8. CRW, NB, RWZ, and RCC will drive their cars; the group will be at the Ash Avenue entrance at 9:30 a.m.
9. Other Business (R. C. Cox)	Mr. Cox announced that he will represent the Forms Standardization Committee at a special meeting of the Management Council on November 14 at which various company committees will report on their activities during the past year.
NEXT MEETING:	The next meeting will be held November 30. We have invited C. A. Kiernan, of Moore Business Forms, to speak on trends in forms design.

                              R. C. Cox, Chairperson

Distribution

    Members of the Committee: Bracher, Cass, Curtis, Fein, Hobbs, Johnson,
                               Moskowitz, Slater, Wilkes, Zelden (absent)

    Others: Mr. S. Ellis, Mrs. Katzenbach, Ms. Nugent, Mr. Weinberger

7. Carbon Packs vs. Padded Forms (Arthur Hobbs)	Recent studies in the company have shown that carbon packs are definite time-savers over padded forms. AH recommends that all frequently used forms be printed in carbon packs.
Discussion	The Committee feels that we do not have sufficient cost information on which to base a decision. Mr. Hobbs is to gather data and report at the January meeting.

Project

You are secretary of the Employee Activities Committee of Warner-Dennison Company. This committee is made up of seven people, and the chairperson is Mary Beth Rooney. The group was formed to deal with such matters as planning recreational activities, recognizing employee achievements and anniversaries, operating an employee suggestion system, and so on. The following notes were made during the meeting of April 3.

Catherine Vining recommended that the profits from vending machines in the building ($2,440.55 last year) be used to establish a scholarship fund for children of employees. The members of the committee participated in a full discussion of this suggestion. There was one dissenting voice. Bert Whelan raised the question as to how the recipient or recipients would be chosen for the scholarship, and he pointed out the difficulties of administering such a program. He wound up by saying that the program would create ill feelings among employees whose children were not selected—that it would not accomplish what it set out to do. On the other hand, Paul Zackowitz felt that the suggestion was a worthy one. He said that an independent committee (outside the company) should be appointed and that candidates for the scholarship award should be recommended by their high school principal, based on scholarship, leadership, and need. Helen Chu agreed with Mr. Zackowitz and further suggested that two scholarships of $1,000 each be awarded each year rather than one. The group agreed on the two-scholarship idea and also endorsed Mr. Zackowitz's suggestion about administering the program through an outside committee. Amy Rhodes felt that the scholarships should be limited to those who are interested in a career in publishing, citing the need for editors and expressing the feeling that such scholarships would fill not only a need insofar as the students themselves are concerned but a publishing need as well. This idea was rejected by other committee members. The general consensus was that the scholarship idea was good enough to be thoroughly explored. Paul Zackowitz and Amy Rhodes were asked by Chairperson Rooney to find out how other companies, particularly competitors, handle scholarship programs. She further recommended that committee members talk with local high school principals and perhaps some teachers to see what criteria might be set up for the scholarships and to get ideas for names of people who would make the final judgment on winners of the scholarships. A full report will be given by Zackowitz and Rhodes at the next meeting on April 27.

Concerning the formation of a Bowling League, Bert Whelan reported that 17 employees have signed up as interested in participating. He is having a meeting of these people Monday, April 7, to organize the teams. He has made arrangements to purchase bowling shirts with the Warner-Dennison emblem imprinted on the back (the employee is to pay half the cost of the shirt). The shirts will not be ordered until after the first organization meeting.

Chairperson Rooney announced that suggestion boxes have now been installed on each floor of the building and forms for making suggestions distributed to each department manager. The policies and procedures concerning employee suggestions will appear in the next printing of the *Employee Handbook*. She also reported that the balance in the treasury of the Employee Activities Committee now stands at $3,426.17.

Amy Rhodes reported that 300 copies of the anniversary brochure of the 25-Year Club will be published in June. The printing cost per copy is $1.85, and Mr. Mullen, the president, has said that the cost can be assumed by the company.

The meeting adjourned.

Prepare minutes of the meeting, condensing the discussions as appropriate and setting up the minutes in a form of your own choosing. These are unedited notes, so watch out for poor grammar, word choice, and so forth.

PART

10

COMMUNICATIONS
PROJECT

YOUR JOB *As sales manager of the College Department in the Dallas regional office of the Merit Publishing Company, you supervise ten field representatives who call on professors and others at colleges and universities in Texas, Oklahoma, Arkansas, New Mexico, and Arizona. Your duties also include corresponding with professors, authors, bookstore managers, and others; seeing that customers' orders are shipped promptly; attending educational conferences; and keeping in touch with your boss, Stanley G. Wright, and others in the New York office.*

During the week of October 4, you receive the correspondence reproduced on pages 305-341. Study each piece of correspondence in each of the 33 situations and the notes about each situation. Solely on the basis of these, decide the action to be taken and then prepare the necessary communications.

ABOUT THE MERIT PUBLISHING COMPANY

The Merit Publishing Company has its headquarters in New York City and six regional offices in various parts of the country. The company publishes dictionaries, encyclopedias, technical handbooks, and other reference materials; children's books, novels, biographies, and other trade books. The company derives the largest share of its income, however, from the sale of textbooks, filmstrips, and other educational publications.

The Dallas office, which is the headquarters for the Southwest Region, receives and fills orders from customers in Texas, Oklahoma, Arkansas, New Mexico, and Arizona. However, the New York office handles the collection of customer accounts and other financial records, the advertising of the company's products and services, the editing and manufacturing of books and other items, and similar matters.

As regional sales manager, you obviously receive a large volume of mail and therefore must devote much of your time to reading and answering it—with an absolute minimum of delay. And, as you might expect, the letters, memos, and other items that you receive run the gamut as far as writing style is concerned. Consequently you will not be surprised to find that in this project you must work with letters and other communications that are not necessarily model examples of "good" business writing.

Another Merit "First"
... in Marketing

Illustration—Cover of text

F O R E S T   P R O D U C T S   M A R K E T I N G

By STEVEN T. McCAUGHEY

Professor of Marketing

University of the Northwest

Seattle, Washington

A new college textbook designed for forestry and business school students who aspire to marketing or general management positions in the forest industries.

As forest products companies become increasingly concerned with finding and serving markets for the finished output of the mills, more and more forestry school graduates will have to be knowledgeable in the field of marketing. (David J. Keane)

Send for your examination copy today!

Merit Publishing Company
1640 Stemmons Freeway
Dallas, Texas 75201

Gentlemen:

Please send me an examination copy of Steven T. McCaughey's FOREST PRODUCTS MARKETING for consideration for adoption.

Name (Please Print).......................................

School..

City..................... State................ ZIP.......

NOTES: *Merit has just published a new book,* Forest Products Marketing. *Rough copy for an advertisement to appear in the* Southwest Journal of Marketing *is given above, and descriptive material concerning the book appears on pages 306–307. The objective of the ad is to encourage instructors to send for the book, examine it, and order it for use in their classes. In anticipation of receiving many cards from instructors as a result of the ad, you are to prepare a follow-up sales letter that you can send to all those requesting an examination copy.*

NEW BOOK INFORMATION

erit publishing company

TITLE: FOREST PRODUCTS MARKETING

AUTHOR: Steven T. McCaughey
Professor of Marketing
University of the Northwest
Seattle, Washington

SIZE: 6 3/8 x 9 1/4, 384 pp.

PUBLICATION DATE: March 19--   PRICE: $10.00

TEXT

Written for students in forestry schools or in business schools who aspire
to marketing or general management positions in the forest industries, the
book may also be used in management training programs or for general
reading by executives in the forest industries. It has a managerial, or
decision-making, focus, particularly in the cases it contains. This focus
will help train the student for any type of administrative job, not only
marketing. Policy decisions in any functional area are likely to have
major marketing implications, so that even the students who remain in
timberlands management or in production will find that some knowledge of
marketing is essential.

This book provides an economic, historical, and institutional background
against which the reader can assess the trends taking place in the forest
products industries today. While the book assumes no prior knowledge in
marketing or in the forest products industries, both the text material
and the cases are presented in such a way as to provide challenging
material for readers who already have backgrounds in these fields. The
34 cases, for instance, are of a fairly wide range of difficulty and
have been successfully used in both graduate and undergraduate teaching
and in management training programs. Concepts presented in the product
planning, distribution, and selling areas should provide new insights
into the many changes taking place in these fields.

In Part I of the book, containing Chapters 1, 2, and 3, the reader learns
what marketing is about and what role it plays in the forest industries.
The technique of analysis and solution of cases is explained, and an
approach to the understanding of market demand and customer buying habits
is presented.

Part II deals with the four basic elements of the marketing mix--product
policy, pricing, channels of distribution, and promotional programs--plus
marketing organization and marketing research. The material in these
chapters, both text and cases, is presented in terms of the marketing of

lumber and wood products, with an emphasis on the marketing function as playing a central role in the total operations of the forest products enterprise.

Part III also deals with the elements of the marketing mix, plus marketing organization and marketing research. The setting here, however, is in the pulp and paper segment of the forest industries. The reason for this division is that the markets and customers served, and the marketing problems involved, are rather different in pulp and paper, as compared with lumber, plywood, and other panel and wood products.

Finally, Part IV, with its concluding chapter (Chapter 16), provides the capstone to the structural sequence of Parts II and III. Throughout the earlier chapters the author has emphasized the importance of setting goals and objectives, determining marketing strategy and tactics to achieve the objectives, planning the marketing program to carry out the strategy, and developing an appropriate marketing organization to put plans into effect. In the concluding chapter, methods for the control and evaluation of marketing performance are described. These methods may be used by marketing executives to gauge the effectiveness of their companies in performing the essential parts of the marketing function.

SPECIAL FEATURES

34 major Harvard Business School-type cases based on actual company situations and successfully proven in use in both graduate and undergraduate teaching and in management training programs.

An Instructor's Manual containing teaching notes and solutions to the cases.

Full text coverage of all major aspects of marketing as applied to the forest industries.

Emphasis on a managerial approach to marketing in forest products companies, supported by a description of the economic, historical, and institutional background of the forest industries.

Explanation of the use of the case method of teaching.

Alpha University

ENID, OKLAHOMA 73705

October 1, 19--

Merit Publishing Company
1640 Stemmons Freeway
Dallas, Texas 75201   OCT 4   RECD

Dear Sir:

Would you please send me a copy of CHEMISTRY
FOR EVERYONE, by Kevin Burgess, which I would
like to consider for use in my general chemistry
course for nonscience majors.

Your attention will be very much appreciated.

Sincerely,

Carla J. Schweitzer

Carla J. Schweitzer
Assistant Professor

CJS:cw

NOTES: *Merit does not publish the Burgess book (it is published by First-Rank Press, a competitor). However, Merit has just issued a new book,* Chemistry for General Application, *by Professor Frieda N. Persons, which is designed for the student who is not a science major. Naturally, you think your book is far superior to that published by First-Rank Press. Descriptive material on the Persons book appears on the next page.*

NEW BOOK INFORMATION
erit publishing company

TITLE: CHEMISTRY FOR GENERAL APPLICATION

AUTHOR: Professor Frieda N. Persons
State University
Klamath, Oregon

SIZE: 7 1/4 x 10 1/4, 448 pp.

PUBLICATION DATE: March 19--   PRICE: $9.95

TEXT

The presentation of the field of chemistry to groups of college students
who have virtually no background in mathematics and who are not interested
in a career in science requires very special treatment. The author has
taught large nonscience major classes in chemistry and has recognized the
shortcomings of existing textbooks designed for these students.

Initially, basic concepts of structure, bonding, and writing of formulas
and equations are introduced to the student. The student is then guided
through a number of current and crucial topics of the day in which chemistry plays a significant role. These topics include air pollution, water
pollution, household chemicals, drugs, agriculture chemicals, radiochemistry,
nuclear energy, and polymers. While the student is examining these subjects,
additional principles are drawn in and expanded.

Questions and projects are included with each chapter, and a glossary of
scientific terms is in the back. In the appendix there are listed for
the instructor a number of excellent short films that can be worked into
the lecture material. In addition, there are suggestions for audiovisual
aids, laboratory work, and student atomic model kits. Although quantita-
tive reasoning is frequently called for, the text does not require the
use of formal mathematics. Removal of the mathematical barrier is of
extreme importance to nonscience students, who will gain from this book
not only a foundation in the important chemical theories and principles
but also an understanding of the relevance of chemistry to their day-to-
day living.

CONTENTS

General. Structure of the Atom. The Elements and Their Families. Chemical
Bonding. Research in Schools. Research in Industry. Drugs and Clinical
Chemistry. Agricultural Chemicals. Polymers I. Polymers II. Food
Additives. Water Pollution. Air Pollution. Household Chemical Products.
Radiochemistry and Nuclear Energy.

Situation 3

Arts and Science Department

College of Southern Arkansas
Texarkana, Arkansas 75501

October 2, 19--

Merit Publishing Company
1640 Stemmons Freeway
Dallas, Texas 75201

OCT 4 REC'D

Gentlemen:

I have adopted and am now using your text, <u>Principles of Anthropology, Second Edition</u>, by Coulsen.

On August 30, I requested an answer key for this book, and I was sent a key for another book by mistake, which I returned with a second request. Any effort that you could make to see that I receive the correct answer key for the above-mentioned text in the shortest possible time would be greatly appreciated.

Thank you.

Sincerely yours,

James A. Patterson

James A. Patterson
Professor

NOTES: *When professors adopt a textbook, they are supplied with an answer key without charge.*

Situation 4

Levitan-Todd College
McKenzie Memorial Library

Carsonville, Arizona 85703

October 1, 19--

OCT 4 REC'D

Dear Sirs:

Please mail and bill me for the following books:

    1 Louvrain: THE BEGINNING OF EDUCATION
                       IN AMERICA

    1 Morrissey: THE INFLUENCE OF HORACE
                      MANN ON PUBLIC EDUCATION

    1 Black: EDUCATION IN TRANSITION

I am aware that the first two items listed above
are no longer listed in your catalog and may be out
of print. If you cannot supply these items, will
you please tell me where I may be able to secure
these books.

Sincerely yours,

Abraham R. Kosy

Abraham R. Kosy

NOTES: *The first two books listed are Merit publications, but they are out of print, as Mr. Kosy suggested. You have tried on other occasions to locate copies by writing to the New York office, but they can't help. Such books are sometimes available at bookstores. You also know of two firms that specialize in finding hard-to-obtain books: Aardvarks Booksearchers, Box 668, San Diego, CA 92110, and International Bookfinders, Box 3003-S, Beverly Hills, CA 90213. The third book listed, Black's* Education in Transition, *has not yet been published; it is due off the press sometime next January.*

Situation 5

MONSERRAT UNIVERSITY
LaMar, New Mexico 87509

Graduate School

October 1, 19--

The President   OCT 4   RECD
Merit Publishing Company
Dallas, Texas 75201

Dear Sir:

    I have just had the opportunity to read a pamphlet called
History as Literature, by D. F. Acheson, which you have been
distributing to educators. It is a delightful essay, and I should
appreciate it if you would send me a copy for my use. If it is
not asking too much, could you spare me two dozen copies for distribution in class? In any case, I should like at least the one
for myself. Are there others in this pamphlet series?

    Thanking you for your cooperation and for your encouragement
of history and historians, I am

                    Very truly yours,

                    Alvin D. Rausche

                    Alvin D. Rausche
                    Graduate Adviser
                    Department of History

NOTES: *Merit published and distributed free to customers five pamphlets, each
by a different author, entitled* History as Literature. *You have 20 copies of the one
Mr. Rausche wants and will give them to him. The only copy left of each of the others
is in the company archives. Because there has been some demand for them, however, these were typed and mimeographed; single manuscripts, with permission to
reproduce them, are given those requesting them. The person to contact is Miss Isa-
belle Lancer, Company Communications, in New York.*

Situation 6

Canfield Oil and Refining Company
440 Scott Street, Little Rock, Arkansas 72201

Marketing Department

I didn't answer this since you at Merit have the copyright – so please handle.
JMG

October 1, 19--

Professor J. Morrison Gunther
Cherokee Nation Community College
Poteau, Oklahoma 74953

OCT 4   RECD

Dear Professor Gunther:

    We are preparing an operations manual for our service station dealers in the Southwest, and we would like to reproduce Chapter 11 ("Keeping Customers Coming Back") from your book, SERVICE STATION OPERATION AND MANAGEMENT. May we have your permission to do so?

    We expect to print about 2,500 copies, which will be supplied free to our dealers. The materials will not be sold and will not, of course, be in competition with your book (which we think is excellent, by the way).

    I would appreciate an early reply.

          Sincerely yours,

          William A. Perkinson

          William A. Perkinson
          Marketing Manager

WAP:mst

NOTES: *The above letter, addressed to the author, was forwarded to you with his handwritten comment. All requests for permission to reproduce copyrighted Merit books must be directed to Ms. Kathryn DuPree, manager of Permissions and Copyrights, in New York. No one else in the company is authorized to grant such permission.*

Situation 7

RAYBURN JUNIOR COLLEGE
ROPESVILLE, TEXAS 79358

Purchasing Department

October 2, 19--

OCT 5 RECD

Merit Publishers
Stemmons Freeway
Dallas, Texas 75201

Gentlemen:

Many thanks for sending me a replacement copy of
Symonds: PRINCIPLES OF GENETICS for my defective
copy. I appreciate your fast service.

Would you please send me the instructor's manual for
this book? Thank you.

Sincerely,

Carmen Diaz

Ms. Carmen Diaz
Purchasing Assistant

NOTES: *Merit has a strict policy about sending instructor's manuals and answer keys to unauthorized people because they may eventually find their way into the hands of students. The procedure is for the appropriate department head in the college or university to authorize the issuance of the manual—which could be as simple as an OK on the above letter, signed by the department head. The key will be billed to Ms. Diaz (the book has not been adopted by Rayburn Junior College) at the usual discount.*

Situation 8

CLOVIS TECHNICAL INSTITUTE
347 Commerce Street   Clovis, New Mexico 88101

October 2, 19--

OCT 5   REC'D

Manager, College Department
Merit Publishing Company
1640 Stemmons Freeway
Dallas, Texas 75201

Dear Sir:

    Would you please send me the instructor's
manual and key to a HISTORY OF ELECTRICITY, Third
Edition. Also, if there are tests to accompany this
book, I would like to see them. I assume these
materials are free.

    Thank you.

Sincerely,

Richard L. Loganberry

Richard L. Loganberry
Lecturer

NOTES: *As you know, Merit's policy is to provide instructor's keys without charge only when the book has been purchased for class use; otherwise, a charge is made (in this case, $2.40, including the discount). Your records show that Clovis Technical Institute has not adopted the book. However, there is a chance that it will be adopted (Mr. Loganberry only recently requested an examination copy). Separate tests have not been published for this book. However, the instructor's manual contains 12 tests that may be duplicated for use by the teacher.*

WESTERN ARKANSAS
STATE COLLEGE
PINE BLUFF, ARKANSAS 71601

October 2, 19--

Merit Book Co., Inc.
1640 Stemmons Freeway
Dallas, Texas 75201

Gentlemen:

Thank you for the fifty tests for MOLECULAR STRUCTURE
AND ATOMIC CONCEPTS, by Rich and Wasstone.

The enclosed invoice indicates that I have been charged
$41 for these tests. It was my understanding that
these tests were furnished free to instructors using
your textbook.

I have placed an order through the college bookstore
for several copies of this particular textbook for
use during the coming quarter, but if you are going
to charge me for this supplementary material I will
simply cancel the order and return your tests.

I shall appreciate your checking this matter as I
do not wish to pay this $41 invoice.

Very truly yours,

Gerald F. Fisk

Gerald F. Fisk

NOTES: *Although a few publishers furnish free tests when books are adopted,
most charge for them. If free tests were provided, the cost of producing them would
have to be included in the price of the textbook—and those schools that don't want
the tests might object. Too, establishing a modest price for the tests enables the publisher to invest more editorial and production excellence in them.*

*You don't want the customer to cancel his textbook order with the bookstore;
yet you would set a dangerous precedent by giving away the tests.*

Situation 10

Free Examination Invitation Card

PEDERSEN: HANDBOOK OF POLLUTION CONTROL

Merit Publishing Company
1640 Stemmons Freeway
Dallas, Texas 75201

OCT 5 REC'D

I accept your invitation. Please send me this handbook for ten days' examination on approval. Within 10 days of receipt I will send you (*check one*) ☑ the full purchase price of $12.00 or ☐ $4.00 down and $4.00 monthly until the price of the book is paid. (We pay delivery costs if you remit with this card. Same return privileges.)

Print Name Duane R. Stapleton, Ph.D.
Street College of Engineering, Room 440
City Maywood City *State* Arizona *ZIP* 86124
Company Crofton University
Position Professor of Engineering

NOTES: *The above postcard was included in an advertising circular for a new book,* Handbook of Pollution Control, *by Pedersen. Today you received 33 cards such as the one above, 11 of which were each enclosed in an envelope with a check for $12 and 3 of which were each accompanied by a $4 check. Professor Stapleton was one who sent $12.*

Unfortunately, an error was made in the printing of the card. The price of the handbook is $23.50, the amount to be paid down is $5.50, and the monthly payments are $6. The circular of which the card was a part listed the price correctly.

Merit can't honor orders at the $12 price; it wouldn't be economically feasible.

Situation 11

SANDSTONE
SSU
STATE
UNIVERSITY
SAYRE, OKLAHOMA 73662

DEPARTMENT OF CHEMISTRY
AND CHEMICAL ENGINEERING

October 2, 19--

Merit Publishers
1640 Stemmons Freeway
Dallas, Texas 75201

OCT 5 RECD

Ladies and Gentlemen:

    A recent flood in Western Oklahoma just about wiped out
our chemistry laboratory here at the university. Among some
valuable possessions lost were about 25 Merit textbooks,
reference books, and handbooks in chemistry and chemical
engineering. These were my personal property, and I valued
them highly. Incidentally, I feel that Merit books are ex-
cellently made.

    I wish to replace these volumes. Is there a special
discount you might give me in a situation of this kind? As
soon as I have your answer, I will try to put together a
list.

                     Sincerely yours,

                    F. P. Dekker

                    F. P. Dekker
                    Associate Professor

FPD:tn

NOTES: *You are pleased to give Professor Dekker a special discount of 25 percent
on the Merit books he wants replaced. Professor Dekker should place his order with
you directly so that you can make sure he gets the discount promised.*

Situation 12

Purvis-Addison Teachers College
Fort Lee, New Mexico 88037

Department of Educational
Psychology and Sociology

October 2, 19--

Chief Executive
Merit Publishing Company
1640 Stemmons Freeway   OCT 5 RECD
Dallas, Texas 75201

My dear Sir:

Recently I bought a copy of Popham's WRITINGS ON
MENTAL DEFICIENCY (for which I paid $18.50), and I
was shocked to discover a few days later that the
binding is falling apart.

I think $18.50 is a high price, and I do not under-
stand how a company of Merit's reputation could send
out such shoddy merchandise. I expect a high-quality
book. I am very distressed and annoyed.

Very truly yours,

J. Wilson Walton
Professor of Psychology

NOTES: *Now and then, but very rarely, a defective book is shipped to a customer.
Although each book is inspected by the manufacturer before it is shipped to Merit's
warehouses, and again by Merit's order fulfillment clerk, sometimes a defective one
slips through. You replace such books without charge, of course, taking the customer's word for it (but you ask the customer to return the defective book so that you
can show it to the manufacturer).*

$\mathscr{ST.anns}$

SCHOOL OF NURSING | HOSPITAL OF TULSA

Morningside Heights
Tulsa, Oklahoma 74114
Area Code 918/808-8080

October 4, 19--

OCT 6 REC'D

Merit Publishing Company
1640 Stemmons Freeway
Dallas, Texas 75201

Gentlemen:

We recently purchased thirty (30) copies of
Elements of Nutrition, Second Edition, by
Russell and Finkelstein, for use in our
classes. (Purchase Order A6369)

Do you have instructional aids to accompany
this book? If so, I would appreciate knowing
about them.

Sincerely yours,

Sarah L. Bacardi

Sarah L. Bacardi
Chairperson
Department of Nutrition

NOTES: *Dr. Bacardi, you find, did purchase the book and is entitled to the instructor's source book without charge. Also available are objective tests (48 pages, $1.20 list price), a laboratory manual (224 pages, $4.60 list), and a set of transparencies (a kit of 12 four-color transparencies that sells for $48 net). You are glad to send the instructor's source book, a set of objective tests, and a laboratory manual without charge. You enclose a flier on the transparencies.*

Red River Agricultural College
Fort Towson, Oklahoma 74735

October 4, 19--

Merit Publishing Company
Dallas, Texas 75201

OCT 6   REC'D

Attention Manager

Dear Sir:

On August 17, I sent you a check for $62.48 in payment
of my book order (Invoice 468-2) of July 12. Today I
received another bill. Of course, I will not pay it;
indeed, I don't understand how you could make such an
error because I have my canceled check to prove that I
paid you. This is not the first time this has happened
to me.

Yours truly,

Milton H. Grannitt

Milton H. Grannitt, Chairperson
Agronomy Department

NOTES: *Professor Grannitt is right; the second invoice was sent in error. After careful searching by the Customer Billing Department, it was discovered that Professor Grannitt's check was credited to M. O. Grannet, another customer. As chairperson of the Agronomy Department, Professor Grannitt is an important purchaser, and it is especially embarrassing that he should be the victim of such an error, not only once but on other occasions.*

texas gulf college
Center for Continuing Education
Beaumont, Texas 77708

October 4, 19--

OCT 6 RECD

Merit Publishing Corporation
1640 Stemmons Freeway
Dallas, Texas 75201

Ladies and Gentlemen:

Do you have a new text in world geography that might
be suitable for our continuing education classes (these
people use high school level books)? We are planning
to introduce this course in our Center for Continuing
Education next spring, and I am examining the various
books available.

Sincerely,

Sybil L. Mooter

Ms. Sybil L. Mooter
Director

NOTES: *Merit has just published* Our World Environment—Patterns and Cultures, *by Morris L. Jason and Michele T. DuBois, which you believe would be ideal for Ms. Mooter's classes (several colleges have adopted it for their adult education evening classes). You will send a complimentary copy of the book. It lists for $9. Assume, in writing to Ms. Mooter, that you will enclose a colorful brochure describing the book and its accompanying workbook, tapes, transparencies, tests, and facsimile key for the instructor.*

Situation 16

MOUNT TILFORD HIGH SCHOOL
Mount Tilford, New Mexico 88501   505/414-1001

Superintendent: Curtis J. Davis, Ph.D.   Principal: Miriam Alvarez, Ed.D.

October 4, 19--

OCT 6 REC'D

Merit Publishing Company
1640 Stemmons Freeway
Dallas, Texas 75201

Gentlemen:

Please send me a free examination copy of SWITCHING
CIRCUIT AND FINITE AUTOMATA, by Charles Bohrmann. I
would also like a copy of the instructor's handbook
and student's guidebook for this book.

Sincerely yours,

(Miss) Donna Bustamente

Donna Bustamente
Mathematics Teacher

NOTES: *The book referred to in Miss Bustamente's letter is designed for graduate school courses in colleges and universities; it is not suitable for high schools. It is possible that Miss Bustamente teaches in a local university and wants the book for a graduate class, but you think it is unlikely. She may purchase the book, of course. The list price is $17.50.*

Southern Arizona College of Fine Arts

Phoenix, Arizona 85012

October 2, 19--

General Manager
Merit Publishing Company
1640 Stemmons Freeway
Dallas, Texas 75201

OCT 6 Rec'd

Dear Sir:

The enclosed letter arrived from your attorney, and I find it so ridiculous that I thought I ought to share it with you.

I have been constantly harangued about a bill that I have already paid. It was paid in two installments, and I have the canceled checks to prove it. Due to inefficient bookkeeping, Merit Publishers (where did you get that name Merit?) has continued to pester me with bills. I have received no acknowledgments of my payments or my letters telling you that I had paid the bills--only more bills.

So, I say to your attorney, come and get me. I would welcome a suit which would cause you more unflattering publicity than we have already been able to spread. I am a professor here, and I have certainly let the faculty know of this incident and the very rude manner in which our letters have been ignored. Please instruct your college book sales representative not to bother contacting me here, as I want no part of such an organization.

Yours truly,

Claud Quillan

Claud Quillan, M.F.A.

CQ:nn
Enclosure

NOTES: *You made a very thorough investigation of this situation, and you find that Professor Quillan is right. Through a series of errors in the Customer Accounts Department, Professor Quillan did not receive credit for his payments, and his letters unaccountably got filed without being answered. Records show that Professor Quillan is a good customer (he uses several Merit art books in his classes) and has always paid his bills on time.*

Theodore R. Watkins

Counselor at Law

416 Brooker Building, One Fillmore Circle, New York, New York 10022

September 28, 19--

OCT 6 REC'D

Mr. Claud Quillan
304 Quigley Avenue
Phoenix, Arizona 85018

Dear Sir:

As attorney for Merit Publishing Company, I
have been requested to commence legal action
to enforce payment on your account.

Before doing so, however, I want to continue
my policy of attempting to settle collection
matters in a friendly way.

Therefore, rather than proceed immediately
with measures which will ultimately add a
considerable amount to what you now owe, I
suggest that you take advantage of this
opportunity to settle your account IMMEDIATELY.

Sincerely yours,

Theodore R. Watkins

Theodore R. Watkins

IRG

The only excuse you have to give Professor Quillan is that Merit's billing and collection system has been undergoing conversion to a computerized system, and correspondents and others have been tied up in learning new procedures brought about by the change in the system. (Several other people got similar letters who shouldn't have.) You think now that all the bugs are ironed out.

327 Dogwood Lane
Kirkwood, Missouri 63122
October 2, 19--

Merit Publishing Company   OCT 6 RECD
1640 Stemmons Freeway
Dallas, Texas 75201

Gentlemen:

    I would like to apply for a sales job with Merit
Publishing Company, and I am particularly interested in
selling college textbooks.

    I am a college graduate, with a major in political
science. Since I finished school two years ago, I have
been working in the research department of Krutchfield-
Samuelson Oil Company. I find this work too confining,
however, and I want a job that will give me a chance to
travel and meet interesting people. I believe a sales
job where I would travel to college campuses and meet
with professors would be ideal.

    I can come to Dallas at your convenience for an
interview. Please write me at the address above, or
if you would prefer to telephone me, my number is
314-632-4149.

                 Very truly yours,

               Sally T. Karsten

               Miss Sally T. Karsten

NOTES: *You have an opening in Arizona-New Mexico territory and another in
the Oklahoma-Arkansas territory for which you have been interviewing candidates.*

Situation 19

Pine Canyon, Texas 75968

                        October 4, 19--

General Manager, College Department   OCT 6 REC'D
Merit Publishing Company
1640 Stemmons Freeway
Dallas, Texas 75201

Dear Sir:

Well, you've done it again! I ordered items 3, 9, and 13 as
follows:

Item	Quantity	Title
3	312	Beers: Nursing Procedures, 3d Edition
9	50	Monk and Freed: Elements of Botany
13	210	Archer: Cost Accounting, 6th Edition

Instead of the above, I received the following:

312	Colfax: Internal Medicine, 4th Edition
53	Zabor: Plant Pathology
210	Mays-Gerber: Legal Secretary's Handbook

I have sent back the books I did not order and request <u>urgently</u>
that you ship me the right ones. Classes for the second semester
are already under way, and we're in a real bind. You can imagine
what kinds of names I'm being called.

                        Very truly yours,

                        Cynthia Hindemith

                        Mrs. Cynthia Hindemith

*NOTES: Investigation shows that Mrs. Hindemith's complaint is fully justified—
the wrong books were shipped. (The same thing happened in September to an order
from Argyle College Bookstore.) You're making arrangements to ship items 3 and 13
immediately by bus express. Unfortunately, Monk and Freed:* Elements of Botany
is out of stock, and you don't expect a new supply for about three weeks.

Situation 20

MONTEGO COMMUNITY COLLEGE
Montego, New Mexico 87734

OCT 7 RECD

October 5, 19--

Merit Publishing Company
1640 Stemmons Freeway
Dallas, Texas 75201

Dear Sir:

Please rush me 30 copies of Kunsthalle: ANTHOLOGY OF
EASTERN LITERATURE, and bill me at the regular discount.

Yours truly,

Martin Thomas

Martin Thomas
Instructor

NOTES: *The college owes Merit Publishing Company $647.80 for books purchased at various times during the year, and although many letters have been written by Merit, the bill has not been paid nor has any explanation been offered. You have been notified by the New York office not to ship Montego Community College any more books on credit; it will be a cash-only transaction. The books requested above amount to $402.60*

Situation 21

middleton
furniture company

814 Dallas Avenue
Houston, Texas 77002

                                        October 5, 19--

                                              OCT 7 REC'D

Merit Publishing Company
1640 Stemmons Freeway
Dallas, Texas 75201

Gentlemen:

    One of our customers, Professor Lucas R. Manger, is,
I understand, an author of yours. We have had a great
deal of difficulty collecting an amount he owes us and
have had to threaten suit.

    Would you please tell me what Professor Manger's
royalty income is from his book? This information will
help me to prove his capacity for paying his bills.

    Thank you.

                                Sincerely yours,

                                George S. Lemon

                                George S. Lemon

NOTES: Information about authors' royalties is maintained in the New York of-
fice, and you cannot grant Mr. Lemon's request. At the same time, you know that
such information is not released by the company.

LANCASTER CITY COLLEGE

Lancaster, Missouri 63548

October 5, 19--

Merit Publishing Company   OCT 7 RECD
1640 Stemmons Freeway
Dallas, Texas 75201

Gentlemen:

Please send me the following books and bill me at the
regular discount.

    40 Clampett: GEOLOGY FOR PETROLEUM ENGINEERS,
       2d Edition
    20 Gregory-Mischler: STRENGTH OF MATERIALS,
       8th Edition
    16 Levine: OIL WELL CEMENTING, 2d Edition
    36 Likert-Bast-Moore: PETROLEUM PHYSICS

I should like to have these books by October 16 when my
fall classes begin, so please rush shipment.

Very truly yours,

A. J. Rusmisel

A. J. Rusmisel, Chairperson
Petroleum Engineering Department

NOTES: *Your office does not serve the Missouri area, and you must refer the letter
to Merit's St. Louis office at 517 North Fourth Street, 63144.*

Situation 23

<table>
<tr><td colspan="2">

anniversary
reminder

</td><td colspan="2">
Personnel Relations Department

Merit publishing company
</td></tr>
<tr><td colspan="2"></td><td colspan="2">

To: (Your Name)

Date: October 1, 19--   OCT 7 REC'D
</td></tr>
</table>

Next month's anniversaries in your department are as follows:

Name		Anniversary Date	Year
Mrs. Deborah Bertrand	(10 years)	November 9	19--

NOTES: *The document above is sent by the Personnel Relations Department on first, fifth, tenth, fifteenth, twentieth, etc., anniversaries to the appropriate supervisors and is their signal to acknowledge the occasion appropriately.*

As indicated, Mrs. Bertrand has been an employee of Merit for ten years; for the past four years she has been a sales correspondent in the College Department. She is very personable and effective in her job. She is a skillful letter writer, who has made many friends among Merit's customers because of her personal attention to their problems—wrong books shipped, delayed shipments because books were out of stock, incorrect billings, and so on. In fact, she is a great asset to your department and you value her highly.

Merit publishing company

MEMORANDUM

TO: All Regional Sales Managers   FROM: Stanley G. Wright

SUBJECT: Expenses   DATE: October 5, 19--

OCT 7   RECD

Again I want to remind you that sales expenses for the year are far ahead of budget and nearly twice what they were last year. Of particular concern to me are expenses of your sales representatives in the following categories:

1. Entertainment. Although I am aware of the need for entertaining important customers, I am very doubtful that our people are being really selective about whom they entertain and realistic about the amounts being spent. For example, I have an expense account on my desk for a single dinner party of two customers that came to $97.40. Although this may be completely justifiable, I think it calls for an explanation.

2. Conventions. I think we must be more selective about the conventions at which we are represented and the number of people we send. For example, I note that we had four sales representatives at a recent regional speech convention which, according to figures, drew only 34 professors. I would question whether even one sales representative was needed at such a meeting, but certainly we didn't need four.

3. Automobile Expenses. Mileage expenses this year are shockingly out of line with previous years, which makes me wonder whether our sales representatives are properly planning their trips or are, in fact, running helter-skelter without any kind of itinerary.

4. Complimentary Copies. I am well aware that we can sell books only when professors have a chance to examine them, but I am seeing far too many requests from sales representatives to send complimentary (as opposed to examination) copies to professors. The sales representatives must make sure that when copies are sent on a complimentary basis the recipient is a very hot prospect. On my desk at the moment is a request from a sales representative to send a complimentary copy of Campbell's CANADIAN GEOGRAPHY to a professor of music!

Will each of you audit your sales representatives' expense and sales reports carefully and let them know immediately that you are doing so. I know that I will see a far different picture in October than I have seen in August and September. By the way, it is only fair that I tell you that I am continuing to spot-check expense reports of all sales personnel and that I will call to your attention situations that require an explanation.

SGW

NOTES: *Mr. Wright is vice president and general manager of the College Department of Merit Publishing Company in New York.*

Y'ALL COME!

SOUTHWEST MUSIC EDUCATORS NATIONAL CONFERENCE

Annual Meeting

December 27-30

Sam Houston Hotel

San Antonio, Texas

PROGRAM HIGHLIGHTS

Keynote Address: "Changing Moods of Modern Music," Dr. Edna Gaines, Midwood Music School

Banquet: 7 p.m., December 29--All-musical program!

Twelve Challenging Workshops (See attached list.)

ADDED ATTRACTIONS

Special "live music" demonstrations

Continuous film showings

Exhibits of the newest in equipment and publications

REGISTRATION

Fill in and return enclosed card.

Special rates offered at Sam Houston Hotel.

Register early for best accommodations.

NOTES: *The Southwest Music Educators National Conference has announced it is having its annual meeting December 27–30, in San Antonio. Merit Publishing Company has planned a special exhibit (other publishers, musical instrument manufacturers, and various other educational suppliers will also exhibit).*

At Merit's exhibit, all the latest textbook materials in music education will be on display. In addition, Merit has a large selection of records, cassette tapes, etc., which it sells to libraries, music educators, and others. A special feature of the exhibit is a soundproof booth in which teachers can play records and tapes. The College Department has also arranged to show its films continuously in a "Little Theater," which has been arranged for with the hotel.

You want to attract as many convention members as possible to the Merit exhibit booth and to the special movies scheduled. Prepare a promotion letter to those who are likely to attend the convention (you have a good, up-to-date mailing list of music educators in your district).

LAMONT
COMMUNITY COLLEGE
Lamont, New Mexico 88338

October 4, 19--

Merit Publishing Company
1640 Stemmons Freeway
Dallas, Texas 75201

OCT 7   RECD

Ladies and Gentlemen:

    I want to tell you how much I am enjoying using the Friedson-McKenna book, DYNAMIC RETAIL MERCHANDISING TECHNIQUES, in my classes. This is precisely the book I have been searching for, and the result I am obtaining in my classes is evidence that the students like it too. They especially like the cases that introduce each chapter and the Continuing Retailing Project that applies in a most practical way the principles they have learned.

    The laboratory manual is exceedingly helpful, as is the very excellent teacher's guide. Are you planning transparencies? I am anxious to obtain some--indeed, I have developed some of my own, though I'm afraid the art and the reproduction is somewhat crude. I have also prepared some tapes for use in the section on retail selling, and my students like them very much. Essentially, they consist of dialogues between customer and sales representative, showing the right and wrong ways to sell.

    In any event, I thought you would want to know that I'm an ardent fan of the Friedson-McKenna approach, and I'd like to see anything else your company publishes in the retail merchandising field.

Sincerely yours,

Frederick Marck

Frederick Marck, Professor
Distributive Education

NOTES: *There was some discussion about transparencies at the last sales meeting in New York, but as far as you are able to determine, there are no plans to publish them. You do think the editor in New York, Marcia Stebbins, would be interested in seeing Professor Marck's transparencies and also hearing the tapes he spoke about.*

WF
Wichita Falls Institute of Technology
Wichita Falls, Texas 76301

October 6, 19--

OCT 8 RECD

Merit Publishing Company
1640 Stemmons Freeway
Dallas, Texas 75201

Gentlemen:

Enclosed is our purchase order (3Y7621) for 300 copies
of INTEGRATED CIRCUITS--Theory and Applications, by
Stroll and Travis. I hope you will be able to get
these books to me early in December for use in a
special industrial training program which our institute
is conducting.

Sincerely yours,

O. L. Fairchild

O. L. Fairchild, Ed.D.

OLF:eh
Enclosure

NOTES: *This is the first order Dr. Fairchild has placed with Merit in two years. There was some difficulty between Dr. Fairchild and a Merit sales representative over two years ago (the sales representative is no longer employed by Merit). At that time Dr. Fairchild said he was "through with Merit and will in the future order every one of my textbooks from other publishers."*

Situation 28

MEMORANDUM

TO: (Your name)   FROM: Travis Funseth

SUBJECT: Professor Lucius Goldman   DATE: October 6, 19--

OCT 8 REC'D

Today Professor Lucius Goldman informed me that he
will become Dean of the School of Architecture at
Crockett University in July of next year. He has
wanted this position for a long time (he thinks the
department is much too conservative) and is very ex-
cited about it. Apparently the appointment is no
secret--the professors in the department know about
it.

TF

NOTES: *Professor Goldman is one of Merit's most distinguished authors, having written two very successful textbooks and collaborated on a "picture book" on architecture for trade sale. He is a somewhat flamboyant man, in his late 30s, and is a special friend of Merit's VIPs. You have met him on several occasions, but you cannot consider him a close, personal friend.*

Situation 29

Here's the form letter we send customers about books they return in unsalable condition.

D.W.

Dear Customer:

    Our Receiving Department has notified us that your return of Merit books contains books that are not salable. (Date)

    Specifically, the following books are (either/or): 1. Out of Print 2. Soiled or Shopworn 3. Beyond Cleaning 4. Price-Marked (which has proved too costly to remove) 5. Price-Marked (which cannot be removed) 6. Cover Damaged.

    (List quantity, author, title, and condition--taken from receiving ticket; e.g., 20 Bailey: RENAISSANCE POETS - Out of Print)

    You will agree, we are sure, that the present Merit Returns Policy is very liberal. Basically, our main concern is that books returned be in resalable condition. To this extent we feel justified in requesting that customers remove prices and, in general, be certain that books being returned are in salable condition.

    Since no credit can be issued, may we please have your decision relative to the disposition of these books. Please reply to my attention by noting at the bottom of this letter your decision.

               Sincerely,

               Returns Section

NOTES: *It has come to your attention that your customers who return books for credit have been receiving a form letter that is not altogether satisfactory in wording and general tone, and you asked to see a copy. In the interest of good customer relations, you decide to offer suggestions to the Returns Section on how the letter might be improved. (You do not supervise this department; Darlene Wilson does.)*

MEMORANDUM

TO: (Your name)   FROM: Stanley G. Wright

SUBJECT: Exhibit   DATE: October 6, 19--

OCT 8 RECD

Concerning your need for a new exhibit, which we discussed on

the telephone last week, I understand that Dramatic Visuals, in

Tulsa, has come out with a new portable exhibit that is very

good looking, reasonably priced, and easy to pack, transport,

and store. It's called, I understand, "Port-a-Visual." Why

not write these people for information? Their address is

3000 South Harvard, Tulsa 74114.

                                  SGW

NOTES: *With several end-of-year regional conventions in the offing, you have been looking for a compact, "foolproof" exhibit to use in displaying Merit books. You want one that is attractive but not too high-priced since you would like to order several so as to keep them moving around the convention circuit. Last week when you discussed this need with your boss, Stanley G. Wright, he promised to get details on one he had seen and liked. His memo is shown above.*

erit publishing company

MEMORANDUM

TO: (Your name)   FROM: Ed Lancaster

SUBJECT: American Marketing   DATE: October 6, 19--
          Association Meeting

OCT 8 RECD

Last night I attended a dinner meeting of the American
Marketing Association in **Phoenix** as a guest of Professor
John Fleming. The featured speaker was Clement K.
Richter, vice president for marketing of Ramsing Corporation in Kansas City (I understand Ramsing manufactures automotive parts). Mr. Richter talked on
professionalism. I know that sounds like a pretty dull
topic, but he made it really exciting. His theme was
that we are all managers no matter what our job title;
we manage ourselves and we manage the territories
assigned to us. He thinks selling is the highest
"calling" a person could aspire to and that a sales
representative today is actually the customer's buying
consultant. This may not sound like heady stuff, but
I must confess that he gave me a complete new perspec-
tive of my job. The guy speaks extremely well, uses
slides and tapes for dramatic effect, and relates
perfectly with an audience.

Perhaps you may wish to consider Richter as a possible
speaker at our March sales conference. Professor
Fleming tells me that Richter does a lot of speaking
throughout the country; apparently he enjoys it, and
his company thinks it's good PR.

                        EL

NOTES: *You are putting together now a program for the next sales conference in March, and you have been considering getting an outside speaker. The theme you have settled on for your conference is "Market Management," in which you plan to emphasize the need for better sales planning, territory coverage, product knowledge, and customer relations. The conference dates are March 12–14. You expect to use your field sales supervisors as discussion leaders. The outside speaker would kick off the conference at 10 a.m. on the first day and can have all the time he or she wants (but you think an hour would be about right). The conference site is the Lakeway Inn and Marina in Austin, Texas.*

2330 Northwest 16 Street
Oklahoma City, Oklahoma 73106
October 5, 19--

Merit Publishing Company
1640 Stemmons Freeway
Dallas, Texas 75201

OCT 8 *RECD*

Gentlemen:

The Maple Gardens Parents Association is holding a bazaar in
February for the purpose of raising money for the Maple Gardens
Elementary School. Several companies are contributing products
that will be auctioned off to the highest bidders. The proceeds
will go toward new playground equipment, a sound movie projector
(the one the school now owns is beyond repair), and a larger
freezer for the school cafeteria.

It was suggested that an ideal item for our bazaar is your
ENCYCLOPEDIA OF MODERN SCIENCE, which several people have seen
at the local library. Would you be willing to donate this set
of books for our bazaar? We would certainly appreciate it,
and you would be doing a marvelous thing for our community.

Yours sincerely,

Abigail Harrison

Mrs. Abigail Harrison

NOTES: *The* Encyclopedia of Modern Science, *to which Mrs. Harrison refers, is a
20-volume set that sells for $495 net, and Merit is not in a position to honor Mrs.
Harrison's request. Merit does, however, have a large inventory of a book called*
Faces and Places, *a picture book on world cultures, which has proved to be unsalable. It is priced at $17.95, and you can supply a copy of this book for the bazaar.*

**southern
california
paper
corporation**

500 Mission Valley Center West
San Diego, California 92914

Personnel Relations

October 5, 19--

Merit Publishing Company
1640 Stemmons Freeway
Dallas, Texas 75201

OCT 8 RECD

Attention College Department

Ladies and Gentlemen:

Mr. E. Walter Boudreau has applied to us for a
sales position. In his resume, Mr. Boudreau lists your
firm as an employer for the year 19--.

Can you make any comments concerning Mr. Boudreau's
qualifications, his character, and his performance? I
assure you that any information you give me will be kept
in strictest confidence.

Very truly yours,

Janice M. Nance

Ms. Janice M. Nance
Personnel Specialist

ene

NOTES: *Mr. Boudreau was a sales representative under your supervision for a
year. Although he showed considerable ability when he tried, you had difficulty getting him to be productive. He did not seem to like selling; although he was very good
at developing friendships, he made few sales, and you concluded that he was not
forceful enough to succeed in selling. You liked him (everybody did) and you did not
want to let him go, but after several talks with him the two of you decided that selling
college textbooks was not his forte, and he left the company.*

REFERENCE SECTION

FORMS OF ADDRESS

BUSINESS LETTER STYLES

ABBREVIATIONS OF STATES,
TERRITORIES, AND POSSESSIONS
OF THE UNITED STATES

PROOFREADER'S MARKS AND SYMBOLS

FORMS OF ADDRESS

Refer to the following list whenever you need the correct forms of address for government, military, religious, or education officials. In addition to forms of address, the list includes appropriate salutations, listed in order of decreasing formality.

The forms of address and salutations given include (for the sake of simplicity) only the masculine forms. Of course, change *Mr.* to *Miss, Mrs.,* or *Ms.,* and change *Sir* to *Madam,* as appropriate.

Government Officials

PRESIDENT OF THE UNITED STATES
The President
The White House
Washington, DC 20500

Mr. President:
Dear Mr. President:

VICE PRESIDENT OF THE UNITED STATES
The Vice President
United States Senate
Washington, DC 20510

Or: The Honorable . . . (*full name*)
Vice President of the United States
Washington, DC 20501

Sir:
Dear Mr. Vice President:

CHIEF JUSTICE OF THE UNITED STATES
The Chief Justice of the United States
Washington, DC 20543

Or: The Chief Justice
The Supreme Court
Washington, DC 20543

Sir:
Dear Mr. Chief Justice:

CABINET MEMBER
The Honorable . . . (*full name*)
Secretary of . . . (*department*)
Washington, DC   ZIP Code

Or: The Secretary of . . .
(*department*)
Washington, DC   ZIP Code

Sir:
Dear Mr. Secretary:

UNITED STATES SENATOR
The Honorable . . . (*full name*)
United States Senate
Washington, DC 20510

Or: The Honorable . . . (*full name*)
United States Senator
(*local address and ZIP Code*)

Sir:
Dear Senator . . . :

UNITED STATES REPRESENTATIVE
The Honorable . . . (*full name*)
House of Representatives
Washington, DC 20515

Or: The Honorable . . . (*full name*)
Representative in Congress
(*local address and ZIP Code*)

Sir:
Dear Mr. . . . :

GOVERNOR
In Massachusetts, New Hampshire, and by courtesy in some other states:

His Excellency the Governor of . . .
State Capital, State   ZIP Code

In other states:
The Honorable . . . (*full name*)
Governor of . . .
State Capital, State   ZIP Code

Sir:
Dear Governor . . . :

STATE SENATOR
The Honorable . . . (*full name*)
The State Senate
State Capital, State   ZIP Code

Sir:
Dear Senator . . . :

STATE REPRESENTATIVE OR ASSEMBLY MEMBER
The Honorable . . . (*full name*)
House of Representatives
   (**or** The State Assembly)
State Capital, State   ZIP Code

Sir:
Dear Mr. . . . :

MAYOR
The Honorable . . . (*full name*)
Mayor of . . . (*city*)
City, State   ZIP Code

Or: The Mayor of the City of . . .
City, State   ZIP Code

Sir:
Dear Mr. Mayor:
Dear Mayor . . . :

Members of the Armed Services

The addresses of both officers and enlisted men in the armed services should include title of rank, full name followed by a comma and the initials USA, USN, USAF, USMC, or USCG. Below are some specific examples together with the appropriate salutations.

ARMY, AIR FORCE, AND MARINE CORPS OFFICERS
Lieutenant General . . . (*full name*), USA
Address

Sir:
Dear General . . . :
(**not:** Dear Lieutenant General . . . :)

For first and second lieutenants, use:

Dear Lieutenant . . . :

NAVY AND COAST GUARD OFFICERS
Rear Admiral . . . (*full name*),
   USN
Address

Sir:
Dear Admiral . . . :

For officers below the rank of Commander, use:

Dear Mr. . . . :

ENLISTED MEN
Sergeant . . . (*full name*), USA
Address

Seaman . . . (*full name*) USN
Address

Dear Sergeant (**or** Seaman) . . . :

Roman Catholic Dignitaries

CARDINAL
His Eminence . . . (*given name*)
   Cardinal . . . (*surname*)
Archbishop of . . . (*place*)
Address

Your Eminence:
Dear Cardinal . . . :

ARCHBISHOP AND BISHOP
The Most Reverend . . . (*full name*)
Archbishop (**or** Bishop) of . . .
   (*place*)
Address

Your Excellency:
Dear Archbishop (**or** Bishop) . . .

MONSIGNOR

The Right Reverend Monsignor
... (*full name*)
Address

Right Reverend Monsignor:
Dear Monsignor ... :

PRIEST

The Reverend ... (*full name,
followed by comma and initials
of order*)
Address

Reverend Father:
Dear Father ... :

MOTHER SUPERIOR

The Reverend Mother Superior
Address

Or: Reverend Mother ... (*name,
followed by comma and initials
of order*)
Address

Reverend Mother:
Dear Reverend Mother:
Dear Mother ... :

SISTER

Sister ... (*name, followed by
comma and initials of order*)
Address

Dear Sister:
Dear Sister ... :

PROTESTANT EPISCOPAL DEAN

The Very Reverend ... (*full
name*)
Dean of ...
Address

Very Reverend Sir:
Dear Dean ... :

METHODIST BISHOP

The Reverend ... (*full name*)
Bishop of ...
Address

Reverend Sir:
Dear Bishop ... :

CLERGYMAN WITH DOCTOR'S DEGREE

The Reverend Dr. ... (*full name*)
Address

Or: The Reverend ... (*full name*),
D.D.
Address

Reverend Sir:
Dear Dr. ... :

CLERGYMAN WITHOUT DOCTOR'S DEGREE

The Reverend ... (*full name*)
Address

Reverend Sir:
Dear Mr. ... :

Protestant Dignitaries

PROTESTANT EPISCOPAL BISHOP

The Right Reverend ... (*full
name*)
Bishop of ... (*place*)
Address

Right Reverend Sir:
Dear Bishop ... :

Jewish Dignitaries

RABBI WITH DOCTOR'S DEGREE

Rabbi ... (*full name*), D.D.
Address

Or: Dr. ... (*full name*)
Address

Dear Rabbi (*or* Dr.) ... :

RABBI WITHOUT DOCTOR'S DEGREE

Rabbi . . . (*full name*)
Address

Dear Rabbi . . . :

Education Officials

PRESIDENT OF A COLLEGE OR UNIVERSITY

. . . (*full name, followed by comma and highest degree*)
President, . . . (*name of college*)
Address

Or: Dr. . . . . (*full name*)
President, . . . (*name of college*)
Address

Dear President . . . :
Dear Dr. . . . . :

PROFESSOR

Professor . . . (*full name*)
Department of . . .
. . . (*name of college*)
Address

Or: . . . (*full name, followed by comma and highest degree*)
Department of . . .
. . . (*name of college*)
Address

Or: Dr. . . . . (*full name*)
Professor of . . . (*subject*)
. . . (*name of college*)
Address

Dear Professor (*or* Dr.) . . . :
Dear Mr. . . . . :

SUPERINTENDENT OF SCHOOLS

Mr. (*or* Dr.) . . . (*full name*)
Superintendent of . . . Schools
Address

Dear Mr. (*or* Dr.) . . . :

MEMBER OF BOARD OF EDUCATION

Mr. . . . (*full name*)
Member, . . . (*name of city*)
 Board of Education
Address

Dear Mr. . . . . :

PRINCIPAL

Mr. (*or* Dr.) . . . (*full name*)
Principal, . . . (*name of school*)
Address

Dear Mr. (*or* Dr.) . . . :

TEACHER

Mr. (*or* Dr.) . . . (*full name*)
. . . (*name of school*)
Address

Dear Mr. (*or* Dr.) . . . :

Society for Scientific Management
Burdine Building
849 Peachtree, N.E.
Atlanta, Georgia 30308

August 14, 19--

Mr. Philip G. Oliver, President
Oliver Associates
201 Massachusetts Avenue, N.W.
Washington, DC 20001

Dear Mr. Oliver:

It was good to talk with you yesterday and to learn that you
can be with us at our October 15 meeting. The topic you suggested, "Motivation Through Employee Participation," seems just
right; it ties in beautifully with this year's theme of personnel
development.

Our meeting, which is held in the Green Room of the Ambassador
Plaza Hotel (98 Forsyth, N.W.), starts off with a social hour at
5:30. Dinner begins at 6:30, followed by your talk at 7:30. We
hope you will plan to speak for about 30 minutes and then to
answer questions for another half hour.

If you would like to be picked up at the airport, please tell
me when you expect to arrive and I'll be there. I have made a
reservation for you at the Ambassador Plaza.

Sincerely yours,

Kati Farnsworth

Miss Kati Farnsworth
Program Chairman

KF:eh

*THE BLOCKED LETTER STYLE. The blocked letter is very popular in business.
The date line, complimentary closing, and writer's identification are typed at the
center of the page. All the other letter parts are typed flush with the left-hand
margin.*

kennel-treat Inc.

2408 North Louise
Sioux Falls, South Dakota 57107

December 18, 19--

Mr. A. R. Allen, President
Allen Distributing Company
2525 West 26 Street
Sioux Falls, South Dakota 57105

Dear Al:

    As the year closes, I want to express my appreciation
for your support of Kennel-Treat products. You know how tough
it is for a new enterprise to get a foothold in a highly competitive market, and there were times during the year when even
our faith wavered a bit. Thank goodness, yours didn't. And
because of you and a few other loyal supporters, we are winding
up the year in good shape, and we're happy to say that the
future looks promising.

    I hope that we can show our appreciation to you by giving
you even better products, faster service, and "pencil-sharpened"
prices during the coming year. We're all dedicated to that goal.

Cordially yours,

Bob Barbot

Robert T. Barbot
President

RTB:cn

THE SEMIBLOCKED LETTER STYLE. *The semiblocked letter is typed exactly as the blocked letter except for the paragraph indentions. In the semiblocked letter, each paragraph is indented five spaces.*

Peninsula Engineering Company

2422 El Camino Real, Palo Alto, California 94306

March 16, 19--

Mr. Leon G. Monroe, Plant Manager
Nu-Way Electronics Inc.
3124 West Coast Highway
Newport Beach, California 92660

Dear Mr. Monroe:

I want to thank you sincerely for your patience with us during
the past couple of months. I realize that you had a lot of
complaints from your customers because we couldn't deliver the
parts you ordered, but I also know that you understand there
was very little we could do about it. We couldn't get them
either.

It looks as though the labor problems of our major supplier
have at last been straightened out. Although there may be a
few gaps until production catches up with the backlog, I'll
certainly try to see that you get the highest priority.

My guess is that you are having an excellent first quarter. I
certainly hope so, and that the second quarter will be even
better.

Yours very sincerely,

C. T. Austad

C. T. Austad, Manager
Customer Services

CTA/fl

THE FULL-BLOCKED LETTER STYLE. *In the full-blocked letter, every line is typed flush with the left-hand margin. Because full-blocked letters save typing time, many companies prefer this style.*

Placement Services Unlimited

Armitage Building • Bristol, Tennessee 37620

August 14, 19--

Dear Ms. O'Rourke:

It was a real pleasure to read in <u>Banking News</u> and in the
local papers that you have been elected president of the Women
in Banking Association at that organization's annual convention
in Washington.

You do honor not only to Bristol but also to the entire profession of banking, and I congratulate you on this recognition
of your ability.

We at Placement Services Unlimited are happy to be associated
with you and the other fine people at American National, and
we hope that we can continue to be of service to you.

Cordially yours,

Chuck

C. K. Milford

Ms. Patricia O'Rourke
First Vice President
American National Bank
Bristol, Tennessee 37620

THE SOCIAL-BUSINESS LETTER STYLE. *In the social-business letter, the inside address is usually typed at the bottom of the letter, starting at the left-hand
margin, five lines below the typewritten signature. Note that the typist's reference
initials are omitted. In social-business letters, a comma is frequently used after the
salutation, and the salutation is often informal, such as* Dear Mike *or* Dear Elaine.

PROOFREADER'S MARKS AND SYMBOLS

Mark	Meaning	Example
∧	Insert word	and∧it
—	Omit word	and ~~so~~ it
....	No, don't omit	and ~~so~~ it
\	Omit stroke	and sob it
/	Make letter small	And so it
⸗	Make a capital	if he is
≣	Make all capitals	I hope so
⊐	Move as indicated	and so⊐
⹀	Line up, even up	TO: John
‖	Line up, even up	‖ If he is
ss [	Use single spacing	and so it
∽	Turn around	mad it so
ds [	Use double spacing	and so it
⊸	Insert a hyphen	white-hot
5⹁	Indent — spaces	5 If he is

Mark	Meaning	Example
#	Insert a space	and#so it
⎰	Insert a space	and so it
⌒	Omit the space	10 a. m.
___	Underscore this	It may be
⌒	Move as shown	it is not
⌣	Join to word	the port
word	Change word	and if he
⊙	Make into period	to him.
⟨⟩	Don't abbreviate	Dr. Judd
◯	Spell it out	1 or 2 if
⊞	New paragraph	If he is
⌄	Raise above line	Hale says
⌐#	More space here	It may be
—#	Less space here	If she is
2#	2 line spaces here	It may be

ABBREVIATIONS OF STATES, TERRITORIES, AND POSSESSIONS OF THE UNITED STATES

AL	Alabama	Ala.	MO	Missouri	Mo.
AK	Alaska	...	MT	Montana	Mont.
AZ	Arizona	Ariz.	NE	Nebraska	Nebr.
AR	Arkansas	Ark.	NV	Nevada	Nev.
CA	California	Calif.	NH	New Hampshire	N.H.
CZ	Canal Zone	C.Z.	NJ	New Jersey	N.J.
CO	Colorado	Colo.	NM	New Mexico	N. Mex.
CT	Connecticut	Conn.	NY	New York	N.Y.
DE	Delaware	Del.	NC	North Carolina	N.C.
DC	District of Columbia	D.C.	ND	North Dakota	N. Dak.
			OH	Ohio	...
FL	Florida	Fla.	OK	Oklahoma	Okla.
GA	Georgia	Ga.	OR	Oregon	Oreg.
GU	Guam	...	PA	Pennsylvania	Pa.
HI	Hawaii	...	PR	Puerto Rico	P.R.
ID	Idaho	...	RI	Rhode Island	R.I.
IL	Illinois	Ill.	SC	South Carolina	S.C.
IN	Indiana	Ind.	SD	South Dakota	S. Dak.
IA	Iowa	...	TN	Tennessee	Tenn.
KS	Kansas	Kans.	TX	Texas	Tex.
KY	Kentucky	Ky.	UT	Utah	...
LA	Louisiana	La.	VT	Vermont	Vt.
ME	Maine	...	VI	Virgin Islands	V.I.
MD	Maryland	Md.	VA	Virginia	Va.
MA	Massachusetts	Mass.	WA	Washington	Wash.
MI	Michigan	Mich.	WV	West Virginia	W. Va.
MN	Minnesota	Minn.	WI	Wisconsin	Wis.
MS	Mississippi	Miss.	WY	Wyoming	Wyo.

Use the two-letter abbreviations on the left when abbreviating state names in addresses. In any other situation that calls for abbreviations of state names, use the abbreviations on the right.

INDEX